THE WORLD OF EARLY EGYPTIAN CHRISTIANITY

CUA STUDIES IN EARLY CHRISTIANITY

GENERAL EDITOR

Philip Rousseau, *Andrew W. Mellon Professor
of Early Christian Studies*

EDITORIAL BOARD

Katherine L. Jansen, *Department of History*
William E. Klingshirn, *Department of Greek and Latin*
David J. McGonagle, *The Catholic University of America Press*
Francis Moloney, S.D.B., *School of Theology and Religious Studies*
Timothy Noone, *School of Philosophy*
Michael O'Connor, *Department of Semitic and
Egyptian Languages and Literatures*

INTERNATIONAL EDITORIAL BOARD

Pauline Allen, *Australian Catholic University*
Lewis Ayres, *Emory University*
Daniel Boyarin, *University of California, Berkeley*
Gillian Clark, *University of Bristol*
Angelo di Berardino, O.S.A., *Istituto Patristico Augustinianum, Rome*
Hubertus R. Drobner, *Theologische Facultät, Paderborn*
David W. Johnson, S.J., *Jesuit School of Theology, Berkeley*
Judith Lieu, *King's College, London*
Robert A. Markus, *University of Nottingham*
Frederick W. Norris, *Emmanuel School of Religion*
Éric Rebillard, *Cornell University*
John Rist, *University of Toronto*
Linda Safran, *University of Toronto*
Susan T. Stevens, *Randolph-Macon Woman's College*
Rita Lizzi Testa, *Università degli Studi di Perugia*
Michael A. Williams, *University of Washington, Seattle*

THE WORLD OF EARLY EGYPTIAN CHRISTIANITY

LANGUAGE, LITERATURE, AND SOCIAL CONTEXT

Essays in Honor of David W. Johnson

EDITED BY

James E. Goehring and Janet A. Timbie

The Catholic University of America Press
Washington, D.C.

Copyright © 2007
The Catholic University of America Press
All rights reserved
Printed in the United States of America

Reprinted in paperback 2008

The paper used in this publication meets the minimum requirements of American National Standards for Information Science—Permanence of Paper for Printed Library Materials, ANSI Z39.48-1984.

∞

Library of Congress Cataloging-in-Publication Data
The world of early Egyptian Christianity : language, literature, and social context /
edited by James E. Goehring and Janet A. Timbie.
p. cm. — (CUA studies in early Christianity)
Includes bibliographical references and indexes.
ISBN-13: 978-0-8132-1480-1 (cloth : alk. paper)
ISBN-13: 978-0-8132-1579-2 (pbk) 1. Egypt—Church history—Early church, ca. 30–600. 2. Coptic Church—History. I. Goehring, James E., 1950– II. Timbie, Janet . III. Johnson, David W., 1938– IV. Title. V. Series.
BR190.W67 2007
281'.72—dc22
2006010007

To David W. Johnson, S.J.

*In gratitude for his contributions
as scholar, teacher, and friend*

CONTENTS

Introduction	ix
Abbreviations	xiii
David W. Johnson: Publications	xix

I. LANGUAGE AND LITERATURE

1. The Coptic Ecclesiastical History: A Survey — 3
   Tito Orlandi

2. Rhetorical Structure in Coptic Sermons — 25
   Mark Sheridan

3. *Sarabaitae* and *Remnuoth:* Coptic Considerations — 49
   Monica J. Blanchard

4. Reading and Rereading Shenoute's *I Am Amazed:* More Information on Nestorius and Others — 61
   Janet A. Timbie

5. Questions and Related Phenomena in Coptic and in General: Final Definitions Based on Boole's Laws — 72
   Leo Depuydt

II. SOCIAL CONTEXT

6. Earliest Christianity in Egypt: Further Observations — 97
   Birger A. Pearson

7. Philo, Origen, and the Rabbis on Divine Speech and Interpretation — 113
   Daniel Boyarin

8. Cannibalism and Other Family Woes in Letter 55　　130
of Evagrius of Pontus
Robin Darling Young

9. The Successors of Pachomius and the Nag Hammadi　　140
Codices: Exegetical Themes and Literary Structures
Philip Rousseau

10. Keeping the Monastery Clean: A Cleansing Episode　　158
from an Excerpt on Abraham of Farshut and Shenoute's
Discourse on Purity
James E. Goehring

11. Illuminating the Cult of Kothos: The *Panegyric on Macarius*　　176
and Local Religion in Fifth-Century Egypt
David Frankfurter

Bibliography　　189
Contributors　　211
General Index　　213
Index to Scripture　　225

INTRODUCTION

David W. Johnson, S.J., who is being honored by this collection of essays, has a remarkable range of interests. Those who know him can attest to the breadth of his reading: from science fiction to mathematics to the complete works of Barry Gifford. In languages, ancient and modern, his studies have included Russian and Japanese, as well as several languages of the Near East. His teaching and research interests encompass both Coptic and Syriac, and the history of the Christian Near East. But Egypt has been the focal point of his work, so when it was time to ask for written contributions and assemble a collection of essays, it was fitting to make the "language, literature, and social context" of Christianity in Egypt the organizing principle.

The essays that were produced in response to the invitation fall into two broad groups: first, language and literature; and second, social context. Within these groups, a wide range of methods and approaches are used. The tools of modern social science are sometimes in use, as is the application of literary theory to Coptic literature. The same insights in information theory that produced computer design elucidate the structure of the question in Coptic. Traditional methods of manuscript study and translation are also brought to bear on familiar texts to produce surprising new information. It is hoped that the diversity represented in this collection of essays reflects in some small way the tremendous intellectual curiosity and deep knowledge of, and respect for, the achievements of past scholarship on the Christian Near East evidenced in the life and works of the honoree.

Part One, "Language and Literature," includes essays that highlight the strengths of earlier research while providing crucial new information. Tito Orlandi analyzes the Coptic *History of the Church,* isolating the author's particular point of view through a careful study of the sources used and the method of their translation into Coptic. Monica Blanchard returns to the often-discussed question of the identity of the "sarabaites" in Cassian (and the related "remnuoth" in Jerome) with a careful examination of etymological problems that have been glossed over in earlier discussions. She also brings unpublished evidence into the discussion. Janet Timbie reexamines the manuscripts that preserve a discourse by Shenoute of Atripe (*I Am Amazed*) and corrects portions of the published edition. In the process, Shenoute's access to, and use of, written documents from the Council of Ephesus (431) is demonstrated. While the foregoing essays essentially rely on traditional methods of textual criticism, Mark Sheridan uses the tools of rhetorical criticism to analyze the structure of a group of Coptic sermons. After reviewing (and critiquing) the pioneering work of C. D. G. Müller, Sheridan goes on to show how four Coptic sermons share the rhetorical style of certain Greek works of the fourth and fifth centuries. Leo Depuydt begins his essay with a brief historical tour showing how George Boole's work on logic led Claude Shannon to insights that created the field of information theory. Depuydt then applies these theoretical insights to the structure of questions in Coptic. The rhetorical question—so prominent in the writings of Shenoute—is clarified by this deep structural analysis.

Part Two, "Social Context," includes essays that address some of the most strenuously debated points in Coptic studies and the history of Christianity in Egypt. Some contributors focus on a single text (Young, Frankfurter) or a small group of texts (Rousseau, Goehring) to shed light on their problem. Others (Pearson, Boyarin) address broader issues. Robin Young offers a new translation of letter 55 (advice to a monk) by Evagrius of Pontus and explicates the careful use of scripture in the letter. Evagrius is shown to rely on Clement and Origen for some concepts; yet, by his use of Proverbs, he demonstrates that he is completely at home in Kellia, his Egyptian monastic base. David Frankfurter begins with the *Panegyric on Macarius* (edited by David Johnson), identifies the god "Kothos" whose cult is attacked in *Panegyric* 5, and then brings comparative evidence to bear in order to understand the pagan/Christian transition in Upper Egypt.

Philip Rousseau analyzes the exegetical strategies at work in the catecheses of Theodore and Horsiesios, aided in part by Michael Williams's study of the structure of individual Nag Hammadi codices, *Rethinking Gnosticism*. James Goehring contrasts a White Monastery manuscript dealing with Abraham of Farshut (a sixth-century Pachomian abbot) with certain discourses of Shenoute to reveal the lasting influence of Shenoutean ideas about purity.

Finally, Birger Pearson and Daniel Boyarin comment on a variety of texts and authors in their analyses of the Jewish context and connections of Christianity in Egypt. Pearson is concerned with connecting the sparse evidence of first-century Christianity with the better-known evidence from the second century. Boyarin traces the development of allegorical interpretation from Philo of Alexandria to his Christian heirs, Clement and Origen, and then contrasts this stream with the slightly later rabbinic methods of interpretation. Both streams emerge from a Jewish context and grapple with the same texts—sometimes with the same verse (e.g., the kiss in Song of Songs 1.2)—using different methods that Boyarin carefully delineates.

In sum, we hope these essays represent a sampling of issues in the forefront of Coptic Studies, and Late Antique Studies generally. All are grounded in close reading of texts, which is certainly one of the strengths of the work of David Johnson. Ancient texts are cited in the original language when that is important and the source of all translations is indicated, as is the source of the text (whether published or unpublished). We hope that the accuracy and completeness of notes and bibliography make this volume even more useful, and a more adequate means of honoring our colleague David W. Johnson, S.J.

ABBREVIATIONS

AB Analecta Bollandiana
ABD Anchor Bible Dictionary
ACW Ancient Christian Writers
AJSL American Journal of Semitic Languages and Literature
AKGWG Abhandlungen der königliche Gesellschaft der Wissenschaften zu Göttingen, Philologisch-historische Klasse
ANRW Aufstieg und Niedergang der römischen Welt. Geschichte und Kultur Roms im Spiegel des neueren Forschung
APF Archiv für Papyrusforschung und verwandte Gebiete
ASAE Annales du Service des Antiquités de l'Égypte
ASPTLA Ashgate Studies in Philosophy and Theology in Late Antiquity
AttiLin Atti della Accademia Nazionale dei Lincei. Rendiconti, Classe di scienze morali, storiche e filologiche
BEHE Bibliothèque de l'École des Hautes Études: Recueil d'Études Égyptologiques
BH Biblioteca Herder
BHG Bibliotheca Hagiographica Graeca
BHL Bibliotheca Hagiographica Latina Antiquae et Mediae Aetatis
BHO Bibliotheca Hagiographica Orientalis
BIFAO Bulletin de l'Institut Français d'Archéologie Orientale
BiM Bibliothèque du Muséon
BRHE Bibliothèque de la Revue d'histoire ecclésiastique
BSAC Bulletin de la Société d'Archéologie Copte
BSEP Biblioteca degli studi di egittologia e papirologia

Budé	Collection des Université de France, publiée sous le patronage de l'Association Guillaume Budé
CBibCopte	Cahiers de la Bibliothèque copte
CGC	Catalogue général des antiquités égyptiennes du Musée du Caire
CH	*Church History*
CMCL	Corpus dei Manoscritti Copti Letterari
CMP	Cultural Memory in the Present
CPG	Clavis Patrum Graecorum
CPJ	*Corpus Papyrorum Judaicarum*
CRINT	Compedia rerum iudaicarum ad Novum Testamentum
CSCO	Corpus scriptorum christianorum orientalium
CSEL	Corpus scriptorum ecclesiasticorum latinorum
CSS	Cistercian Studies Series
CWS	Classics of Western Spirituality
EI²	Encyclopedia of Islam New Edition
Enchoria	*Enchoria. Zeitschrift für Demotistik und Koptologie*
EPRO	Études preliminaries aux religions orientales dans l'empire romain
EVO	*Egitto e Vicino Oriente*
FCNT	Fathers of the Church: A New Translation
Figurae	Figurae: Reading Medieval Culture
FZPhTh	*Freiburger Zeitschrift für Philosophie und Theologie*
GBS	*Göttinger Beiträge zur Sprachwissenschaft*
GGA	*Göttingische Gelehrte Anzeigen*
GLECS	*Groupe linguistique d'Études chamito-sémitiques*
GM	*Göttinger Miszellen*
GRBS	*Greek, Roman and Byzantine Studies*
HA	*Handbuch der Altertumswissenschaft*
HDR	*Harvard Dissertations in Religion*
HeyJ	*Heythrop Journal*
HKA	*Handbuch der Klassischen Altertumswissenschaft*
HPSMB	Hieratische Papyri aus den Staatlichen Museen zu Berlin, Preussischer Kulturbesitz
HTR	*Harvard Theological Review*

IEEE	*Institute of Electrical and Electronic Engineers, Transactions on Information Theory*
IFAO	Institut Français d'Archéologie Orientale
JA	*Journal asiatique*
JAC	*Jahrbuch für Antike und Christentum*
JBL	*Journal of Biblical Literature*
JCS	*Journal of Coptic Studies*
JEA	*Journal of Egyptian Archaeology*
JECS	*Journal of Early Christian Studies*
JEH	*Journal of Ecclesiastical History*
JHS	*Journal of Hellenic Studies*
JHSex	*Journal of the History of Sexuality*
JJP	*Journal of Juristic Papyrology*
JJS	*Journal of Jewish Studies*
JRAfr	*Journal of Religion in Africa*
JRS	*Journal of Roman Studies*
JSJ	*Journal for the Study of Judaism*
JSL	*Journal of Symbolic Logic*
JThS	*Journal of Theological Studies*
LCL	Loeb Classical Library
MASP	*Mémoires de l'Académie Impériale des Sciences de St.-Pétersbourg*
MCopte	*Le Monde copte. Revue de la culture copte*
MMAF	Mémoires publiés par les membres de la Mission archéologique française au Caire
Muséon	*Le Muséon. Revue d'études orientales*
Nclio	*La nouvelle Clio*
NHC	Nag Hammadi Codex
NHMS	Nag Hammadi and Manichaean Studies
OECS	Oxford Early Christian Studies
OLA	Orientalia Lovaniensia Analecta
OLZ	*Orientalistische Literaturzeitung*
OP	Occasional Papers
OrChr	*Oriens Christianus*

OTM	Oxford Theological Monographs
OTP	*The Old Testament Pseudepigrapha*, ed. James H. Charlesworth
PAAAS	*Proceedings of the American Academy of Arts and Sciences*
Par	*La Parola del Passato*
PDM	*Papyri Demoticae Magicae*
PG	*Patrologia graeca*, ed. J.-P. Migne
PGM	*Papyri Graecae Magicae* (I–LXXI), ed. K. Preisendanz
PO	Patrologia orientalis
P&P	*Past and Present*
PSBA	*Proceedings of the Society of Biblical Archeology*
PTS	Patristische Texte und Studien
RAC	*Reallexikon für Antike und Christentum*
RAM	*Revue d'ascétique et de mystique*
RB	Riggisberger Berichte
RdE	*Revue d'égyptologie*
RHR	*Revue de l'histoire de religions*
RivSO	*Rivista degli Studi Orientali*
RPap	*Recherches de papyrologie*
RSLR	*Rivista di Storia e Letteratura Religiosa*
SA	Studia Anselmiana
SAA	Société archéologique d'Alexandrie
SAC	Studies in Antiquity and Christianity
SBLSCS	Society of Biblical Literature Septuagint and Cognate Studies
SBLSP	Society of Biblical Literature Seminar Papers
SC	Sources chrétiennes
ScrHier	Scripta hierosolymitana
SDAW	Sitzungberichte der deutschen [until 1944: preussischen] Akademie der Wissenschaften zu Berlin. Klasse für Sprachen, Literatur und Kunst.
SEAug	Studia Ephemeridis Augustinianum
SHR	Studies in the History of Religions
StAns	Studia Anselmiana
StPal	Studien zur Paläographie und Papyrologie

StPatr	*Studia Patristica*
StTGL	Studien zur Theologie des geistlichen Lebens
StTh	*Studia Theologica*
SWGS	Schriften der Wissenshaftlichen Gesellschaft in Strassburg
TAIE	*Transactions of the American Institute of Engineers*
TAPA	*Transactions of the American Philological Association*
TCH	Transformation of the Classical Heritage
TDSA	Testi e Documenti per lo Studio dell'Antichità
Teubner	Bibliotheca Scriptorum Graecorum et Romanorum Teubneriana
TS	Texts and Studies
TTH	Translated Texts for Historians
TU	Texte und Untersuchungen zur Geschichte der altchristlichen Literatur
VC	*Vigiliae Christianae*
VCSupp	Vigiliae Christianae Supplement
VetChr	*Vetera Christianorum*
WS	World Spirituality: An Encyclopedic History of the Religious Quest
WUNT	Wissenschaftliche Untersuchungen zum Neuen Testament
ZÄS	*Zeitschrift für ägyptische Sprache und Altertumskunde*

DAVID W. JOHNSON

Publications

"Further Fragments of a Coptic History of the Church: Cambridge Or.1699R." *Enchoria* 6 (1976): 7–17, 3 plates.

"Further Remarks on the Arabic history of the patriarchs of Alexandria." *OrChr* 61 (1977): 103–16.

Ed. *A Panegyric on Macarius Bishop of Tkôw Attributed to Dioscorus of Alexandria.* CSCO 415 (text)–416 (translation), Scriptores coptici 41–42. Louvain: Secrétariat du CorpusSCO, 1980.

Dictionary of the Middle Ages. Ed. Joseph R. Strayer. 13 vols. New York: Scribner, 1982–89. Articles contributed: Adoptionism; Arian, Arius, Arianism; Docetism; Eutyches; Eutychius of Alexandria; Manichaeans; Monophysitism; Nestorianism; Nestorius; Nubian Christianity; Persia, Christian Church in.

"Anti-Chalcedonian Polemics in Coptic Texts, 451–641." In *The Roots of Egyptian Christianity*, ed. Birger Pearson and James Goehring, 216-34. Philadelphia: Fortress Press, 1986.

"Coptic Reactions to Gnosticism and Manichaeism." *Muséon* 100 (1987): 199–209.

"The Dossier of Apa Zenobius." *Orientalia* 58 (1989): 193–212.

"Coptic Versions." In *The New Jerome Biblical Commentary*, ed. R. E. Brown, J. A. Fitzmyer, and R. E. Murphy, 1102–3. Englewood Cliffs, N.J.: Prentice-Hall, 1990.

The Oxford Dictionary of Byzantium. Ed. Alexander P. Kazhdan. 2 vols. New York: Oxford University Press, 1991. Articles contributed: Africa, Continent of; Axum; Ceylon; China; Ethiopia; Ethiopian Literature; John of Nikiu; Nile; Nubia.

The Coptic Encyclopedia. Ed. Aziz S. Atiya. 8 vols. New York: Macmillan, 1991. Articles contributed: Macarius of Tkôw, Saint; Nestorius.

"Dating the *Kebra Nagast*: Another Look." In *War and Peace in Byzantium*, ed. T. S. Miller and J. Nesbitt, 197–208. Washington, D.C.: Catholic University of America Press, 1995.

"Pope Timothy II Aelurus: His Life and His Importance for the Development of Christianity in Egypt." *Coptica* 1 (2002): 77–89.

PART I LANGUAGE AND LITERATURE

Tito Orlandi

THE COPTIC ECCLESIASTICAL HISTORY

A Survey

Coptic studies are cultivated by a limited number of scholars, many of whom know each other personally through the activities of the International Association for Coptic Studies. Various members of the association inevitably choose a more restricted field of investigation, and I am privileged in this regard to share an interest in Coptic historiography with David Johnson, a prominent member of the association who organized its fifth international congress in Washington, D.C., in 1992, and to whom this volume is dedicated. In this connection, I believe that I can offer no better homage to him than a summary of my most recent ideas on the *Histories of the Church,* a text that he dealt with admirably in connection with its Copto-Arabic counterpart, the *History of the Patriarchs of Alexandria.*[1] I submit these ideas for his judgment, confident that he will appreciate at least my devotedness to the subject.

---

1. David W. Johnson, "Coptic Sources of the History of the Patriarchs of Alexandria" (Ph.D. diss., Catholic University of America, 1973); David W. Johnson, "Further Fragments of a Coptic History of the Church: Cambridge Or.1699R," *Enchoria* 6 (1976): 7–17; David W. Johnson, "Further Remarks on the Arabic *History of the Patriarchs of Alexandria,*" *OrChr* 61 (1977): 103–16.

The Historical Memories of the Church of Alexandria

Fabulous Alexandria, probably the most beautiful and prestigious city of the Roman world, did not boast a Christian bishop until relatively late, perhaps not before the beginning of the second century. When it finally constituted a bishopric, there is no doubt that the new institution contained the same features found in the other institutions of the city, whether the court, the temples, the gymnasia, and so on. Included among these would have been an office charged with recording and preserving the historical memories of the institution, both in the form of its official documents and in the production of a kind of chronicle.[2] Eusebius of Caesarea used such materials in his *Ecclesiastical History*, as did other later authors who dealt with the history of the Alexandrian patriarchate. While Sozomen is perhaps the best known and most important of these, other anonymous figures making use of the archive include the authors of the *Historia acephala*, the *Index* to the festal letters of Athanasius,[3] the *Passio Petri alexandrini*,[4] the *Passio Metrophanis et Alexandri*.[5]

In the tormented times of the Chalcedonian controversy, when various elements among the Egyptian clerics and people opposed one another, the patriarch Timothy Aelurus (457–77) commissioned a history of the Church based on the historical records preserved in the archive. It would serve to convey the official interpretation of the Alexandrian patriarchate to the Christian world, in the hope that it would provide the basis for the unity of the Church both inside and outside of Egypt. The work must have been written in Greek and quickly translated into Coptic. While the Greek text is unfortunately lost, two important witnesses to the Coptic translation survive, as well as the related Arabic *History of the Patriarchs*.[6]

With respect to the Coptic witnesses, the first is a long excerpt that de-

---

2. Tito Orlandi, "Ricerche su una storia ecclesiastica alessandrina del IV secolo," *VetChr* 11 (1974): 269–312.

3. Annick Martin and Micheline Albert, *Histoire "acephale" et index syriaque des "Lettres festales" d'Athanase d'Alexandrie*, SC 317 (Paris: Éditions du Cerf, 1985).

4. *BHG* 1502–3; *BHL* 6692–98; *BHO* 929–31; cf. *Clavis Patrum Copticorum* 0527. The *Clavis Patrum Copticorum* (hereafter *CPC*) listing can be found at http://rmcisadu.let.uniroma1.it/~cmcl (link: clavis).

5. *BHG* 1279–80. Cf. Friedhelm Winkelmann, "Die handschriftliche Überliefuerung der Vita Metrophanis et Alexandri," *StPatr* 7 = TU 92 (1966): 106–14; Friedhelm Winkelmann, *Untersuchungen zur Kirchengeschichte des Gelasios von Kaisareia*, SDAW, Klasse für Sprachen, Literatur und Kunst 1965, no. 3 (Berlin: Akademie-Verlag, 1966).

6. See note 9 below.

rives from the period of the Coptic Church history that dealt with the emperor Julian. The material found its way into a group of texts composed sometime around the seventh to eighth century that deal with the figure of the Decian martyr Mercurius.[7] A legend, deriving from a famous painting at Caesarea, attributed the killing of Julian in the Persian campaign to Mercurius's ghostly apparition. The story had apparently found its way into the Timothean history from which the relevant part was added first to the text of the *Passio*,[8] and then inserted together with a series of *miracula* into a seventh-century *Encomium in Mercurium* attributed to Acacius of Caesarea.[9]

The second Coptic witness occurs in a homily by the late sixth-century Coptic author Constantine of Sioüt. The passage in question uses a few sentences from the Timothean history word for word, though it places them in a very different context.[10] Two additional sixth- to seventh-century texts on the life of Athanasius[11] offer less literal witness to the Timothean history. Although they do not quote the history, they include episodes that are found only in the history.[12]

The Timothean Church history became a seminal work in both its Greek and Coptic forms for the anti-Chalcedonian Church in Egypt following the Chalcedonian division of Christianity. As such, it contributed to the birth of an Egyptian national Christian consciousness. While the Egyptian Church continued to consider itself part of the universal Church, its persecution by the Chalcedonian imperial forces led it to turn increasingly to its own history to underscore its special identity within the universal Church and the roots of its faithfulness to what it perceived to be the true doctrines and traditions of Christianity. In the process, by opposing the official doctrine of the empire, it set itself apart from many of the other churches within the empire.

In the tenth century, as Arabic was becoming the vernacular language of

---

7. Tito Orlandi, *Studi Copti: 1) Un encomio di Marco evangelista; 2) Le fonti copte della storia dei patriarchi di Alessandra; 3) La leggenda di S. Mercurio*, TDSA 22 (Milan: Cisalpino, 1968), 87–145; Tito Orlandi and Sara Di Giuseppe Camaioni, *Passione e miracoli di S. Mercurio*, TDSA 54 (Milan: Cisalpino-Goliardica, 1976).

8. *CPC* 0432.

9. *CPC* 0002.

10. Tito Orlandi, "Claudio Martire e Anatolio di Laodicea: Un problema letterario fra III e VI secolo," in *Divitiae Aegypti: Koptologische und verwandte Studien zu Ehren von Martin Krause*, ed. Cäcilia Fluck (Wiesbaden: L. Reichert, 1995), 237–45.

11. *CPC* 0108 and 0408.

12. Tito Orlandi, *Testi Copti: 1) Encomio di Atanasio; 2) Vita di Atanasio*, TDSA 21 (Milan: Cisalpino, 1968).

the Egyptian Church, the Timothean history served as the model and main source for the Arabic *History of the Patriarchs (of Alexandria)* (hereafter cited as *HPA*).[13] The *HPA* was used in turn by early European scholars as the basic source of information for the history of the Coptic Church. Johann Wansleben, who published a *Histoire de l'Église d'Alexandrie* in 1677,[14] appears to have had only indirect knowledge of it. Eusèbe Rénaudot, on the other hand, translated extensive parts of it into Latin in 1713 in his *Historia Patriarcharum Alexandrinorum Jacobitarum*,[15] and Étienne Quatremère used it at the beginning of the nineteenth century in his important studies of the Copts.[16]

The Greek version of the Timothean *History of the Church* was eventually lost. The Coptic version, however, has survived in a number of fragments of varying length. Georg Zoega published the first few fragments, some rather large, in 1808.[17] They derived from a codex in the Borgia collection[18] that originally belonged to the library of the Monastery of St. Shenoute at Atripe[19] (White Monastery codex FY; see below). While Zoega's efforts in his *Catalogus Codicum Copticorum Manuscriptorum* represented the first modern, scholarly contact with of the Coptic *History of the Church*, he offered in fact very few comments about the fragments. In 1888 Oscar von Lemm[20] paved the way for a modern study of the *History* by noting the parallels between the Bor-

---

13. B. Evetts, *History of the Patriarchs of the Coptic Church of Alexandria*, PO 1, 2, 4 (101–214, 381–518); 5, 1 (1–215); 10, 5 (357–551) (Paris: Firmin-Didot, 1904–15). For (better) editions of other codices and full information, see Johannes den Heijer, *Mawhub Ibn Mansur et l'historiographie copto-arabe. Étude sur la composition de l'Histoire des Patriarches d'Alexandrie*, CSCO 513, Subsidia 83 (Louvain: Peeters, 1989), xx, 238.

14. Johann Michael Wansleben, *Histoire de l'Église d'Alexandrie, fondée par S. Marc, que nous appelons celle des Jacobites-Coptes* (Paris: Chez la Veuve Clousier et Pierre Promé, 1677).

15. Eusèbe Rénaudot, *Historia Patriarcharum Alexandrinorum Jacobitarum a D. Marco usque ad finem saeculi XIII* (Paris: Franciscum Fournier, 1713).

16. Étienne Marc Quatremère, *Mémoires géographiques et historiques sur l'Égypte, et sur quelques voisines*, 2 vols. (Paris: F. Schoell, 1811); Étienne Marc Quatremère, *Recherches critiques et historiques sur la langue et la littérature de l'Égypte* (Paris: Imprimerie Impériale, 1808).

17. Georg Zoega, *Catalogus Codicum Copticorum Manuscriptorum qui in Museo Borgiano Velitris Adservantur* (Rome: Sacrae Congregationis de Propaganda Fide, 1810).

18. See Paola Buzi, *Titoli e autori nella letteratura copta. Studio storico e tipologico*, BSEP 2 (Pisa: Giardini, 2005).

19. Tito Orlandi, "The Library of the Monastery of St. Shenute at Atripe," in *Perspectives on Panopolis: An Egyptian Town from Alexander the Great to the Arab Conquest*, ed. A. Egberts et al. (Leiden: Brill, 2002), 211–31.

20. Oskar Eduardovich von Lemm, "Koptische Fragmente zur Patriarchengeschichte Alexandriens," *MASP, VIIe série* 36, 11 (1888): 1–45.

gia fragments and the text of the *HPA* translated by Rénaudot. Von Lemm's work addressed the problems of authorship, sources, and originality. In 1902 Walter E. Crum revisited the question.[21] He had identified additional fragments of the *History* that belonged to the same White Monastery codex FY as those previously published, as well as other fragments from a second White Monastery codex (HY; see below) that preserved portions of the first part of the *History*. The new evidence allowed him to evaluate the relationship between the two main manuscripts and conclude that, when complete, codices FY and HY contained the same text. In addition, he established their relationship with the *HPA*, noted their parallels with the Eusebius of Caesarea's *Ecclesiastical History*, and proposed Timothy Aelurus as the author and Greek as the original language.

In the first half of the twentieth century, additional fragments of codex FY were published by L. Saint-Paul Girard, Henri Munier, and Carl Wessely,[22] though they did not specifically identify their provenance from the same manuscript. In the second half of the century, attention was concentrated on the codicological analysis of the two codices and the reconstruction of the Coptic and Arabic texts. Following the publication of my edition of the *History* in 1968–70,[23] additional important contributions were made by Jean Gribomont (the relationship between the Coptic and Arabic texts), Heinzgerd Brakmann (the unity of the text), David Johnson (the relationship between the Coptic history and the Arabic *History of the Patriarchs*), Theofried Baumeister (the history of research), and Johannes den Heijer (again, and most extensively, on the relation between the Coptic history and the Arabic *History of the Patriarchs*).[24] Currently, the most complete edition of all of

21. Walter Ewing Crum, "Eusebius and Coptic Church Histories," *PSBA* 24 (1902): 68–84.
22. Louis Saint-Paul Girard, "Un fragment sahidique de la vie de Saint Arsene le grand precepteur des enfants de Théodose, anachorète a Scète et a Toura (vers 410)," *BIFAO* 30 (1931): 195–99; Henri Munier, *Manuscrits coptes*, CGC 74 (Cairo: IFAO, 1916); Carl Wessely, *Griechische und koptische Texte theologischen Inhalts*, 5 vols., StPal 9, 11 12, 15, 18 (Leipzig: E. Avenarius, 1909–17), no. 241.
23. Tito Orlandi, *Storia della Chiesa di Alessandria*, TDSA 17 and 31 (Milan: Cisalpino, 1968 and 1970). Cf. Tito Orlandi, "Nuovi frammenti della Historia Ecclesiastica copta," in *Studi in onore di Edda Bresciani*, ed. S. F. Bondì (Pisa: Giardini, 1985), 363–84.
24. Jean Gribomont, "L'historiographie du trone d'Alexandrie avec quelques remarques sur S. Mercure S. Basile et S. Eusèbe de Samosate," *RSLR* 7 (1971): 478–90; Heinzgerd Brakmann, "Eine oder zwei koptische Kirchengeschichte?" *Muséon* 87 (1974): 129–42; Johnson, *Coptic Sources* and "Further Fragments"; Theofried Baumeister, "Koptische Kirchengeschichte. Zum Stand der Forschung," in *Actes du IVe congrès Copte, Louvain-la-Neuve, 5–10 septembre 1988*, ed. M. Rassart-Debergh and J. Ries (Louvain-

the witnesses is located on the web page of the Corpus dei Manoscritti Copti Letterari.[25]

The Coptic *History of the Church*

The Coptic *History of the Church* (for the correct title, see below) is known today mainly from two fragmentary codices. Before proceeding further, it is necessary to indicate the precise meaning of the codicological terms employed in the following discussion. *Manuscript* is used as a general term, indicating an object with handwritten text without further precision as to its form. *Codex*, on the other hand, refers to a book composed of quires bound together and placed inside a cover. The term *sheet* indicates a single leaf of parchment or papyrus containing a page on its front (recto) and back (verso) sides. A double sheet represents the two connected sheets (four pages) that were folded to form part of a quire. The term *fragment* refers to a portion of continuous text formed either by a single sheet or contiguous sheets from the same codex, or reconstructed by scholars from different witnesses.

White Monastery codex HY survives in five fragments, representing a total of eleven sheets (twenty-two pages) in various states of preservation.[26] The original length of the codex remains unknown, since a very long lacuna follows the last numbered page (322). Sixteen additional pages, all of which have lost their page numbers, appear to come from somewhere after the lacuna. While there is in fact no objective evidence that the sheets before and after the long lacuna belong to the same codex, that conclusion, following Crum and all other scholars, seems warranted since they share the same Coptic hand and page layout. A colophon at the end of the work reports that the monk Pirothe (Philotheos) donated the codex to the monastery of Shenoute when Basil served as steward (*oikonomos*).[27] Unfortunately, since the date of Basil's stewardship is

---

la-Neuve: Université Catholique de Louvain, Institut Orientaliste, 1992), 2:115–24; den Heijer, *Mawhub Ibn Mansur* and "À propos de la traduction copte de l'histoire ecclésiastique d'Eusèbe de Césarée: Nouvelle remarques sur les parties perdues," in *Actes du IVe congrès Copte*, 2185–93.

25. *CPC* 0200.

26. The sigla HY derives from the list of reconstructed codices of the monastery of Shenoute at Atripe. Cf. Orlandi, "Library of the Monastery," 211–31.

27. Arnold van Lantschoot, *Recueil des colophons des manuscrits chretiens d'Egypte*, BiM 1 (Louvain: J.-B. Istas, 1929), no. LXXV.

unknown, so too is the date for the actual production of the manuscript. The codex may be assigned on palaeographic grounds to the ninth century, again following Crum and van Lantschoot. One should further note the existence of two subscriptions in the manuscript at the end of the fourth and twelfth sections of the work, each separated from the text by means of ornamentation. They read "End of the fourth [the other: twelfth] history of the holy Church. In the peace of God, amen."[28]

The second White Monastery codex, FY, survives in ten fragments, representing a total of thirty-two sheets (sixty-four pages), some of which have been damaged. Significantly, two titles and an index to the book appear on page 67. While the information offered in the titles is contradictory, the error can be explained. The first title appears at the beginning of the page and is set off by ornamentation above and below it. It is, in fact, the title of the index, "Contents of the eleventh history of the Church," which lists the content of the following section of the *History*. The index title is followed by a second title, again set off between lines of ornaments, that reads "Chapter 10" (ⲕⲉⲫⲁⲗⲁⲓⲟⲛ ⲓ̄). While the numbers in the two titles do not agree and the term *chapter* is confusing, the inscription to the corresponding Mercurian excerpt (see below) confirms the number eleven. More significantly, scholars now recognize that the Coptic *History of the Church* was divided into sections, each identified separately as a "history" and together as the "histories." The use of the term *chapter(s)* may also have occurred at some point in the text's history, though it was probably not original. It remains remotely possible that two overlapping subdivisions in history and chapter appeared together in the manuscript FY.

A single sheet (Vienna, Nationalbibliothek, Papyrussammlung, K9620) from the *History* survives from a third codex, but as it is the only surviving sheet, little can be said about the codex.

Turning to the reconstruction of the text itself, one must first note that any such reconstruction is limited by the nature of the surviving evidence. Beyond the surviving fragments of the Coptic text in the above codices, the reconstruction depends on parallels in and conjectural additions based on the Greek text of Eusebius's *Ecclesiastical History*, the Coptic dossier of the martyr Mercurius, the Arabic text of the *History of the Patriarchs*, and the index

28. Cf. ibid. for comments.

described above. Various other texts, whose content preserves parallels to the content of the Coptic history, may shed additional indirect light on the composition of the Timothean *History*. As their evidence is less direct, however, they will be treated later in the discussion of the sources behind the various fragments. In the end, while it is possible to formulate relatively good theories as to the overall structure of the Coptic *History*, the nature of the evidence precludes at many points a detailed reconstruction of the narrative. Many questions concerning the content of the *History* are destined to remain unanswered.

The text of the *History* appears to have been divided into two main parts. The first part, taken almost entirely from the first eight (or seven?) books of Eusebius's *Ecclesiastical History*, was extended to the great persecution of Diocletian. The second part most probably began with the Diocletian persecution and Peter's episcopacy, and concluded with the patriarchate of Timothy Aelurus. Codex HY either contained both parts, which would have required more than five hundred pages, or represents one volume of a two-volume set produced by the same scribe. Codex FY, on the other hand, contained only the second part or was the second volume of a two-volume set in which the pagination began anew in the second volume.

It is important to note that where parallel fragments survive from the two main codices (HY and FY), the texts are remarkably consistent. The degree of agreement is unusual in the Coptic manuscript tradition, where scribes often considered themselves redactors, changing words or expressions to meet immediate needs. The same may be said for the two other manuscripts (the Vienna fragment and the Excerpt). The practice suggests that the text of the *History* was considered authoritative, like that of the Bible and the works of Shenoute. In such cases, Coptic scribes adhered to the same faithfulness and accuracy that characterized the intention, if not always the actual practice, of their Western colleagues.

Turning to the title of the work, it is fair to say that it has not received the careful scrutiny it deserves.[29] As was noted above, a title appears in codex FY to an index to one of the books contained in the *History*. Similar titles undoubtedly existed for each of the other indices to the other books of the *Histo-*

---

29. But cf. Orlandi, "Nuovi frammenti," and Brakmann, "Eine oder zwei koptische Kirchengeschichte?"

ry, following the pattern of the indices attached to the books in Eusebius's *Ecclesiastical History*. The title preserved in codex FY reads ⲚⲀⲒ ⲚⲈ ⲚⲈⲦϢⲞⲞⲠ ⲀⲚ ⲦⲘⲈϨⲘⲈⲦⲞⲨⲈ ⲚϨⲒⲤⲦⲞⲢⲒⲀ ⲚⲦ(Ⲉ)Ⲕ(ⲔⲀⲎⲤⲒⲀ), which translates, "This is the content of the eleventh History of the holy Church." A similar phrase occurs in a colophon in codex HY. It reads ⲦⲘⲈϨⲘⲚ̄ⲦⲤⲚⲞⲞⲨⲤⲈ Ⲛ̄ϨⲒⲤⲦⲞⲢⲒⲀ ⲈⲦⲞⲨⲀⲀⲂ ⲀⲤϪⲰⲔ ⲈⲂⲞⲎ, or "End of the twelfth History of the Holy Church." So too the *inscriptio* of the *excerptum* in the *Encomium in Mercurium* (see above) found in one manuscript (New York, P. Morgan Library M588, p. 16) reads ⲤⲈⲤⲨⲎⲀⲚⲈ ⲚⲀⲚ ⲘⲠⲀⲒ ϨⲚ ⲦⲘⲈϨⲘⲎⲦⲈ ⲘⲚ ⲦⲘⲈϨⲘⲈⲦⲞⲨⲈ ⲚϨⲒⲤⲦⲞⲢⲒⲀ ⲚⲦⲈⲔⲔⲎⲀⲤⲒⲀ, which translates, "It is narrated in the tenth and eleventh History of the Church," and in a second manuscript (London, British Library Or. 6801, p. 28), ⲦⲈϢⲠⲎⲢⲈ ⲚⲈⲤⲤⲎϨ ϨⲚ̄ ⲦⲘⲈϨϮⲦⲈ Ⲛ̄ϨⲒⲤⲦⲞⲢⲒⲀ Ⲛ̄ⲦⲈⲔⲔⲎⲀⲤⲒⲀ, or "The miracle is written in the ninth History of the Church." From the evidence, it is apparent that each section of the work (what we call a book) was called a *History of the Church* and accompanied by its numerical identification as the *First, Second* (etc.) *History of the Church*. The general title of the work must therefore have been *The (Twelve) Histories of the Church*.

The precise relationship between the first part of the *Histories of the Church* (henceforth *HsC*) and the text of Eusebius's *Ecclesiastical History* is yet to be clarified.[30] One of the major problems in this regard is the surprising degree of semantic difference between the two texts. It has been extensively discussed and various explanations have been proposed. A second difficulty involves alterations in the content and structure of Eusebius's text as it appears in the *HsC*. This problem has received little attention. With respect to the semantic differences, Crum had observed that in most instances the meaning of the Coptic text differed completely from that of the Greek text. While the most obvious explanation for this would be the Coptic translator(s)' misunderstanding of the Greek, the solution is not entirely satisfactory. Coptic translations of patristic texts, of which there are many, are generally quite good.[31] While translation errors occasionally occur, the complete misunderstanding of large parts of a text is unusual.

---

30. Cf. den Heijer, *Mawhub Ibn Mansur*.
31. Among many possible examples, note the translation of the difficult text by Gregory of Nazianzus, *In Ecclesiastem* (*CPC* 0197). Cf. Tito Orlandi, "Gregorio di Nissa nella letteratura copta," *VetChr* 18 (1981): 333–39.

In fact, Crum already pointed out that the Coptic text was not simply a translation of the Greek but rather a reworking of it. The reworking does not, however, conform to any observable aim, as one would expect it to if it had been undertaken intentionally to conform the text to a particular ideological goal. While the Coptic translator(s) have altered the facts found in the Greek text, often making them incorrect, the changes follow no discernable pattern. A careful analysis of the texts, in fact, indicates that the problem lies not in the translation of the individual words but rather in the altering of their arrangement in the formation of the Coptic sentences. As a result, while the Coptic sentences are correct as Coptic sentences, they not only fail to convey the meaning of the Greek, they also often enough fail even to convey a satisfactory general meaning.

The only possible explanation for this[32] is the use of a special method of translation, which, while perhaps not common in antiquity, is attested in a number of cases.[33] Two stages were involved in the translation effort. First, the Greek text was written vertically, one word per line, with the corresponding Coptic terms added on the right side. In the second stage, the Coptic words were rearranged and where necessary inflected or conjugated so as to form proper Coptic sentences. One suspects that in the case of the *HsC* something went wrong between the two stages. While the person or persons who produced the Coptic text as we have it were provided with the right Coptic words, they were not able to arrange them so as to effectively capture the meaning of the Greek text.

It is impossible to know how much of the first part of the *HsC* was affected by this error, since, as Crum observed, the *HsC* uses only the first seven (or eight) books of Eusebius's *Ecclesiastical History*, i.e., the *Ecclesiastical History* as it probably existed in its first edition before Eusebius added materials covering the period between Decius and Diocletian, and then from the great persecution to Constantine. Crum noted in addition that significant discrepancies between the Coptic version and the Eusebian text, as it exists today, occur apart from those caused by the events discussed above. In the seventh book, for ex-

---

32. Tito Orlandi, "La traduzione copta di Eusebio di Cesarea, HE," *AttiLin,* 9th ser., 5 (1994): 399–456.

33. Cf. the trilingual text in Johannes Kramer, *Glossaria bilinguia in papyris et membranis reperta* (Bonn: R. Habelt, 1983), 97–108 (no. 15); and the medieval case in Walter Berschin, *Medioevo grecolatino: Da Gerolamo Niccolò Cusano* (Naples: Liguori, 1989), 151–52.

ample, the *HsC* inserts a long account of the life of Mani after the text that corresponds to Eusebius's *Ecclesiastical History* VII 31,2. The end of book 7 is also altered. The text that corresponds with *Ecclesiastical History* VII 30,22 appears in the *HsC* immediately after VII 32,3 and is followed by VII 32,5ff. These and other minor differences might represent a preliminary redaction of the *Ecclesiastical History* by Eusebius himself or they might depend on the work of later Alexandrian redactors.

In any event, the reason why the Alexandrian patriarchate should have chosen Eusebius as the preferred historian for the period to the end of the third century is far from obvious. After Nicaea, Eusebius assumed a position opposed to that of Athanasius. It is tempting to suppose that his history had in fact been included in the historical archives of Alexandria before the beginning of the Arian controversy, i.e., in the first years of the fourth century or even at the end of the third, possibly without the name of the author. It is notable that the subscription of the *Fourth History* in the White Monastery codex HY does not mention the name of Eusebius. Timothy Barnes has, in my opinion, reasonably proved that the first edition of the history was in fact published at the end of the third century.[34] This may explain why the *HsC* use, as far as we can tell, only the first seven (or eight) books of Eusebius. There was in fact good accord between Eusebius's doctrinal position and that of Alexandria at this point in time. In the history, Rome and Alexandria are treated as the two most important episcopal sees, a fact that led the text to acquire almost immediately the same authoritative position in Alexandria that it enjoyed everywhere else.

Another major issue in the study of the *HsC* is the relationship between it and the *History of the Patriarchs*. The issue has two aspects. The first is philological, namely, the extent of agreement between the Coptic and Arabic text in the places where they are parallel.[35] At such points, the Arabic text for the most part follows the Coptic text faithfully. This is evident from the fact that in those places where, as we have seen above, the meaning of the Coptic text is obscure, the Arabic translator is clearly in distress.[36] Some interesting differences also appear in the proper names, especially where the original

---

34. T. D. Barnes, "The Edition of Eusebius' Ecclesiastical History," *GRBS* 21 (1980): 191–201.
35. The portions where the *HPA* is translating the Coptic version of the *HsC*.
36. Cf. den Heijer, *Mawhub Ibn Mansur*, 166–71.

Greek form (from Latin) was easily subject to confusion. The names of Constans, Constantius, and Constantinus, for example, may have been confused by an inadvertent scribe or in the translation when they appeared in the same passage, an error facilitated by inconsistencies in the Arabic and especially Christian-Arabic medieval graphic systems. Unfortunately, in the commentary to my edition, my limited Arabic, which has not improved, meant that I had to rely on B. Evetts's translation of the *HPA,* which is based on a single bad manuscript. While the problem has been studied by Gribomont[37] and partially by den Heijer,[38] more needs to be done. A thorough knowledge of the Coptic and Arabic textual tradition would make possible the consideration of passages where the Arabic might indicate the use of a Coptic text different from the one we possess.

The second factor concerns the content of the *HPA* and the use of it to fill lacunae before and after a Coptic fragment of the *HsC.* In this regard, it is important to distinguish as far as possible the parts of *HPA* that depend on the *HsC* from the parts that depend on the other sources used by the first redactor, Severus of Ashmunein or Mawhub. It is important here to keep in mind the fundamental work of den Heijer, who, in connection with the question of the identity of the first author (Severus or Mawhub), reveals the complexity of the redactional efforts carried out on the *HPA.* The differences between the manuscripts can no longer be understood simply as variations of a single original text, but rather must be seen as constituting more or less independent versions.

With respect to the Coptic and Greek sources of the *HPA,* there is currently considerable consensus among myself, David Johnson, and Johannes den Heijer. The prefaces and the *Sacerdotium Christi* do not concern us here. The source(s) of chapter 1, on the life of Mark, are unknown, though Coptic or Greek texts of this kind were common enough. Chapter 2, the martyrdom of Mark, derives from the Metaphrastic version of the *Passio.* Chapter 3 contains very brief notices about Annianus, Avilius, Cerdo, Primus, Iustus, Eumenes, Mark, Celadios, Agrippinus, and Julian, which the author may have fabricated himself with *loci communes* on the basis of a simple *Chronology.* Chapter 4, on Demetrius, derives from the first part of a Coptic homily, the *Encomium in*

---

37. Gribomont, *L'historiographie* du trône d'Alexandrie.
38. Den Heijer, *Mawhub Ibn Mansur.* It is the most extensive analysis to date.

Demetrium et Petrum.[39] It is interesting to note that the two parts of the homily were originally independent. It was probably in this form that the author of the *HPA* had access to them, using the first part for his chapter on Demetrius and the second at a later point in his text. The second part of chapter 4 through the first part of chapter 6 (Heraclas, Dionysius, and Maximus) corresponds roughly to the relevant parts of books 6 and 7 of Eusebius's *Ecclesiastical History*, with of course many changes. Some of the changes are also found in the preserved fragments of the *HsC,* which suggests that the *HsC* was also used here as a source (so den Heijer). On the other hand, it is possible that the Arabic author made some of his own changes, following other Coptic or Greek texts that he had read. The latter part of chapter 6, which contains the life of Theonas, begins with a brief statement about his nomination, which may come from anywhere. Most of the account, however, corresponds with few changes to the Coptic *Encomium in Petrum ep. Alexandriae,*[40] and deals with the career of Peter before the episcopate rather than with the life of Theonas.

The part of the *HsC* translated from Eusebius comes to an end at this point, and the original part begins, of which unfortunately we have only one fragment from the life of Peter. The *HPA*, after one of its usual brief statements about the consecration of the bishop, incorporates the text of the *Passio Petri*, which we have in Greek, Latin, and Coptic (Bohairic and Sahidic).[41] This is followed by a hagiographic legend that corresponds to the second part of the *Encomium in Demetrium et Petrum* mentioned above. It is followed by a text that corresponds to a part of the *Passio Petri* that is preserved only in the Sahidic version. It is possible that this passage comes directly from a source called the "Fonte A,"[42] which we believe corresponds with the memories of the Alexandrian patriarchate mentioned at the beginning of this paper, as they were "published" by Athanasius.[43] This text also served as the source of part

---

39. *CPC* 0155; E.A.T.W. Budge, ed., *Coptic Martyrdoms etc. in the Dialect of Upper Egypt, Edited, with English Translations* (London: British Museum, 1914), 137–56.

40. *CPC* 0015; Henri Hyvernat, ed., *Les Actes des Martyrs de l'Egypte tires des manuscrits coptes de la Bibliotheque Vaticane et du Musee Borgia* (Paris, Leroux, 1886–87); Tito Orlandi, "La versione copta (saidica) dell'Encomio di Pietro Alessandrino," *RivSO* 45 (1970): 151–75.

41. Cf. note 36 above.

42. Cf. Orlandi, *Studi Copti;* accepted by den Heijer, *Mawhub Ibn Mansur*, 130–32n9.

43. A full discussion of this point lies beyond the scope of this paper.

of the *Passio Petri* found in the Latin version of Guarimpotus.[44] In any event, the lives of Achillas (end of chapter 6), Alexander (chapter 7), and Athanasius (chapter 8) depend both on the *HsC* and the "Fonte A," augmented occasionally with special documents like a *Life of Athanasius* otherwise unknown, and a catalogue of Athanasius's works different from that in the *HsC*.

Chapters 9 and 10 contain a brief mention of Peter II and Timothy. Chapter 11 on Theophilus depends for the first part on the *HsC*, but where the *HsC* report the peculiar episode concerning Philip of Anatolia, the *HPA* omits it. It uses abbreviated versions of two independent hagiographic sources, the *Relatio Theophili*, which survives in Coptic in the form of a homily attributed to Cyril,[45] and the *Historia Horsiesi*, which also survives in Coptic.[46] It is possible that the version of the *HsC* known to the redactor of the *HPA* did not contain the episode of Philip of Anatolia. At the end of chapter 11, the *HPA* inserts portions of a *Life of Cyril*, otherwise unknown. Chapter 12 on Cyril is almost totally dependent on the *HsC*. While the *HsC* continue into the period of Dioscorus and Timothy Aelurus, the *HPA* does not follow it at that point, making only brief statements about these two important bishops.

One can see that the portions of Arabic text thought to be translated from the *HsC*, and therefore representing the Coptic text even where it is not preserved, are rather well defined. Table 1-1 presents the current state of the textual evidence for the *HsC* and its relationship to the *HPA* and the *Ecclesiastical History* of Eusebius.

As may be assumed from the title (see above) and the last subscription in White Monastery codex HY, the text, in its final Timothean redaction, was conceived as a unit formed from twelve "histories" of the Church. The term history here may be considered akin to the other literary term, very popular in the fifth and sixth centuries, namely, "plerophory." While the modern scholar, on the basis of Eusebius, might prefer the term "book" for the individual subsections, it is better and more correct to retain the original terminology. Furthermore, it is important to note that the general subject was not the Church

---

44. *BHL* 6692–93.

45. *CPC* 0397; cf. Réné-Georges Coquin, "Discours attribué au Patriarche Cyrille, sur la dédicace de l'église de S. Raphaël, rapportant les propos de son oncle Théophile," *BSAC* 33 (1994): 25–56.

46. Walter Ewing Crum, ed., *Der Papyruscodex Saec. VI–VII der Phillipps-Bibliothek in Cheltenham: Koptische theologische Schriften* Strassburg, SWGS 18 (Strassburg: K. J. Trübner, 1915); cf. Tito Orlandi, "Due fogli papiracei da Medinet Madi (Fayum): L'historia Horsiesi," *EVO* 13 (1990): 109–26.

Table 1-1. Textual Evidence for the *Histories of the Church*

Frg.	Bishops	Episodes	monb.hy	monb.by	bL6801	HPA	Eusebius
1		Heresies: Menander, Basilides	s.n. = pn129.14.092				4.7.1–9
2		Writers: Tatian, Bardesanes	s.n. = pn129.14.144				4.29.4–30.3
3		Episcopal successions Imperial successions Anatolius	319–322 = pn129.14.096–7				7.31.1–[30.22–3]–32.9
4	Peter	Arius and Melitius		33–34 = wk.09605			
5	Alexander	Struggle for Arius		s.n. = vb160.01		409	
	Athanasius	Death of Arius		53–60 = vb160.02–05	27–34	410	
		Exiles of Athanasius		67–70 = vb160.06–07	35–38	411	
		Cyril of Jerus.		71–74 = vb160.08–09	39–40	412–415	
		Julian		75–76 = vb160.10		415–419	
		Jovian				420–421	
6	Theophilus	Serapeum and Canopus		83–86 = vb160.11–12		425–426	
		Philip of Anatolia		87–90 = vb160.13–14			
7	id.	Arsenius		111–112 = pn129.13.46 [113–114] = pn129.13.81 115–116 = wko9407			
8	id.	Arcadius, Honorius, Alarichus		121–122 = wko9408	s.n. = wko9620		
9	id.	John Chrysost.		127–128 = pn129.13.57 129–130 = pn1315.016			
10	id.	id.		s.n. = bl3581b.43			
11	id.	id.		s.n. = bl3581b.42			
12	Cyril	Contra Iulianum	s.n. = cc9242	163–170 = vb160.15–18		430	
		Nestorius	s.n. = nm664b.13+ cu.1699r.4	s.n. = su.024		431–432	
		Ephesus				433–435	
						436	
						437–440	
13	id.	Nestorius and Shenute	s.n. = cu1699r.1				
	Dioscorus	Chalcedone	s.n. = cu1699r.2	207–208 = pn129.14.72			
		Juvenal	s.n. = cu1699r.3	[209–210] = ob.d421			
	Timotheus	Proterius	s.n. = nm664b.14				
			s.n. = pn129.14.098	211–212 = pn129.14.73			

of Alexandria or Egypt (which were considered the same at that time), but the Church as a whole. This is proved by the use of Eusebius in the first part, where in fact Eusebius had little to say about the internal facts of the Egyptian Church, as well as from the frequent references to the international situation in the second part of the work that is not based on Eusebius.

While the continuous numeration of the "histories" in the *HsC* indicates that it was seen as a single work, its division into two parts raises some interesting questions. While they cannot at present be answered for lack of evidence, it is important to note them before proceeding to a list of the sources for the second part of the *HsC*. The clearest difference between the two parts of the *HsC* lies in the nature of their conception. The first is simply a revised version of an already existing text, the *Ecclesiastical History* of Eusebius. The second, on the other hand, is an originally conceived work that draws on many special sources. One is reminded of the earlier, analogous work of Rufinus of Aquileia, who likewise "added" two books to Eusebius's *Ecclesiastical History*. Is it possible that the second part of the Coptic *HsC* was similarly conceived as an independent continuation of an existing "Egyptian" edition of Eusebius? It is worth noting in this connection that the Coptic translation of the two parts is quite different in both quality and, as was noted above, method. While it is true that we do not possess a copy of the second part in Greek, which must have existed, and therefore cannot judge the accuracy of the translation, the Coptic is quite coherent and perfectly intelligible, unlike the Coptic at many places in the first part.

The situation is far from clear, and some peculiarities in the Coptic version of the second part remain problematic. We cannot know precisely how the redactor(s) managed the transition between the two parts of the *HsC*, because no fragment exists from the material after Eusebius, *Ecclesiastical History* VII.32 (in the episcopate of Dionysius) and before page 33 of White Monastery codex FY (the episcopate of Peter), which one assumes began with the second part. According to some calculations, the second part began with *History* 9, which would leave space for an eighth section from Eusebius at the end of the first part. This would, however, complicate the question of which edition of Eusebius's *Ecclesiastical History* the redactor(s) used (see above). We cannot in fact even be sure that the books from the version of Eusebius used by the redactor(s) in this part were coincident in number and extension with those in the surviving Greek manuscripts of the *Ecclesiastical History*.

The Sources

Keeping all of these issues in mind, we can now indicate, as far as possible, the sources used in the second part of *HsC*.[47] While it is impossible, given the nature of the evidence, to identify the sources themselves, one can extrapolate as to their nature from parallels found in various other historical texts. This will be the method followed here.

Fragments 1–3

These fragments belong to the first part of the *HsC*, the primary source of which was the *Ecclesiastical History* of Eusebius, augmented with limited additional material.

Fragment 4

The first fragment of the second part presents the relationships between the archbishop Peter, Melitius, and Arius. Interesting parallels exist in the report of Sozomen (*HE* I.15) and the *Passio Petri*. A common source (see below) probably lies behind all three texts.

Fragment 5

The next fragment begins with the episode of the death of Arius at Constantinople. Parallels to the account exist in some of the *Epistles* of Athanasius, the continuation of Eusebius's *History* by Rufinus, and the hagiographic *Vita Metrophanis et Alexandri*. Socrates, Sozomen, and Theodoret offer different versions of the same events. Here also one may suppose a common source, probably the same one that lies behind fragment 4. The source reveals interesting features, namely, a direct Athanasian influence and an inclination for hagiographic traditions like those inspiring the *Passio Petri* and *Vita Metrophanis*, which were political pamphlets also under the influence of Athanasius. I have argued elsewhere that they depended on some sort of official Athanasian chronicle of the bishopric of Alexandria,[48] and I propose here to identify this chronicle with the source in this part of the *HsC*. The same source prob-

---

47. For the following part, cf. Orlandi, *Storia della Chiesa* and *Studi Copti*, 53–86, with the bibliographical references.

48. Orlandi, *Ricerche su una storia ecclesiastica*. Part of this chronicle has been recently discovered in an Ethiopic manuscript, on which work is now in progress.

ably lies behind the following section, which records the exiles of Athanasius. It likewise agrees with certain hagiographic texts[49] against the major ecclesiastical historians.

What follows next is more peculiar. The allure remains more hagiographic than chronological, but the episodes do not correspond with the interests of the Alexandrian episcopate. They include the apparition of the cross of light in the sky over Jerusalem, a legend about Julian, the uncle of the Apostate, the relationship between Basil of Caesarea and Julian the Apostate, Julian and the temple of Jerusalem, and the slaying of Julian by the ghost of St. Mercurius. The coincidence with the hagiographic cycle of St. Mercurius,[50] and, to a lesser extent, that of Theodoret, suggests an Antiochene source, which probably became popular in Alexandria when the two churches struggled together against the decisions of the Council of Chalcedon.

The small section dealing with the relationship between Athanasius and the emperor Jovian seems again to derive from the Alexandrian chronicle, since it finds parallels in the *Collatio Ioviani et Luci ariani*. The catalogue of Athanasius's works, on the other hand, as well as that of Theophilus that appears later, suggests the literary interests of the redactor. It further aligns the second part of the *HsC* with the first, which, following the character of its source, the *Ecclesiastical History* of Eusebius, includes such a literary interest.

Fragment 6

The Alexandrian chronicle must likewise be the source for this fragment, which recounts Theophilus's actions against the temples of Sarapis and Canopus. The stories are paralleled in several Coptic hagiographic texts.[51] While these texts, which derive from a "cycle of Theophilus,"[52] are relatively late (c. seventh century), they were surely based on earlier traditions. The section of fragment 6 on Philip, "Bishop of Anatolia," has no parallel in any other Greek or Coptic text. A number of intriguing peculiarities, in fact, set it apart.

---

49. Vita e Encomio di Atanasio; cf. Orlandi, *Testi Copti*.

50. Cf. note 7 above.

51. Tito Orlandi, "Uno scritto di Teofilo alessandrino sulla distruzione del Serapeum?" *Par* 121 (1968): 295–304; Tito Orlandi, "Un frammento copto di Teofilo di Alessandria," *RivSO* 44 (1969): 23–26.

52. Tito Orlandi, "Cycles," in *The Coptic Encyclopedia*, ed. Aziz S. Atiya (New York: Macmillan, 1991), 3:666–68.

First, the figure of Philip appears to be a fabrication, given the fact that the position of bishop of Anatolia did not exist. Second, the emperors Valentinian and Valens are identified as "orthodox" in the episode, although we know that they were champions of Arianism. Finally, the episode is absent in the *HPA*. All of this suggests that the episode was a later addition, added perhaps to the Coptic version of the *HsC* by a later interpolator, who took it from an Arian source that he did not recognize as such.

Fragments 7–8

After a long lacuna that corresponds to about ten folios of White Monastery codex FY, *HsC* narrate the life of Arsenius, the monk. While Arsenius was a famous ascetic who practiced the solitary life in Egypt, the particulars of his career have in fact little or nothing to do with the history of the Church of Alexandria/Egypt. They connect rather with the history of the international Church, another clue to the fact that the scope of the *HsC* was conceived to be more general. The facts narrated by the *HsC* (Theodosius's summons of Arsenius, the great rhetor, to teach his two sons; the quarrel with Honorius; his retirement in Egypt; and his correspondence with Arcadius) find significant parallels in three Byzantine chronicles, those of George Hamartolos (the Monk), John Zonaras (*Epitome*), and Theophanes, as well as in the broader hagiographic tradition. They all appear to depend on a common tradition, and this, together with the case of John Chrysostom discussed under Fragments 9–11, indicates that the redactor of the *HsC* worked within the mainstream of Christian historiography.

Fragments 9–11

The next part of the *HsC*, which at the beginning is very incomplete in the surviving manuscripts, contained a catalogue of the literary works of Theophilus, probably derived, as in the case of the works of Athanasius, from a literary source akin to Jerome's *De viris illustribus*. It is certainly possible that the same source continued with a catalogue of the works of John Chrysostom, who was himself a victim of Theophilus, thereby giving the redactor the idea to include episodes from the final period of the Theophilus's life. It is noteworthy that the redactor's account of Theophilus's life begins with the catalogue, contrary to his normal practice of placing the catalogue at the end of the account of a person's life. Good parallels exist in Theophanes and Zonaras, pointing again to a common source that was international rather than Alexandrian in origin.

Fragments 12–13

The redactor returned to the Alexandrian chronicle for the last sections, dedicated to Cyril, Dioscorus, and Timothy Aelurus. After a lacuna in the manuscripts, the *HsC* report on the confutation written by Cyril against the *Adversus Galilaeos* of Julian, including details and observations not found in other Byzantine texts. It next treats the Council of Ephesus, apparently drawing on an Alexandrian-Egyptian version of the Acts. While we cannot go into detail here,[53] our examination of the Greek and Coptic evidence suggests that two Egyptian versions existed, one coming from the Shenoutean milieu and the other from the Pachomian milieu, distinguished from each other by the role given to their respective archimandrites, Shenoute and Victor. The *HsC*, on the other hand, seem to depend directly on the Alexandrian redaction of the Acts, mentioning neither Shenoute nor Victor. This is probably the reason why in the Coptic translation we find an addition on Shenoute and Nestorius that is absent in the *HPA*.

As indicated above, the redactor of the *HPA* does not seem to have known the parts of the *HsC* on Dioscorus and Timothy Aelurus. This may point to the fact that he used an incomplete copy of the *HsC*, or, less likely, that he used a first edition of the *HsC* that ended with Cyril and later enlarged it to include the lives of Dioscorus and Timothy. In any event, the Coptic literary tradition includes a number of texts with parallels to the *HsC*, most notably the *Encomium in Macarium*,[54] which is itself a collection of many texts following the custom of the *Plerophories,* thereby suggesting once again the use of the usual common source, the Alexandrian chronicle.

Historical Value

Given the evidence outlined above, it is worthwhile to discuss briefly the historical value of *HsC*. Because the topic is difficult and to a certain extent

---

53. Cf. the analysis in Orlandi, *Storia della Chiesa,* 113–16.
54. David W. Johnson, ed., *A Panegyric on Macarius Bishop of Tkôw Attributed to Dioscorus of Alexandria,* CSCO 415–16 (Louvain: Peeters, 1980).

unrewarding, nobody seems willing to make use of the text in this regard. As a result, the *HsC*, an important work, has been largely ignored in the reconstruction of the history of the Church. Given the philological difficulties inherent in the text, one can readily understand why it has not played a role in more general studies. It is, however, a pity that even in specialized histories of the Christian Orient, where one would expect to find the *HsC* treated along with the other usual sources, it is almost always neglected.

In terms of the stories preserved in the *HsC*, one cannot hope to establish otherwise unknown events from Church history on the basis of its evidence. When it reports facts or events that are not found in other texts or in the more authoritative historians, it is virtually impossible to know whether or not they are accurate. Like many other historical Coptic texts of the post-Chalcedonian period belonging to the category of the *plerophoriae*, the *HsC* supply valuable evidence for the Egyptian view of the facts in general, and for the official view of the Alexandrian patriarchate in particular.

It should be noted that the versions or interpretations given in the *HsC* are not banal or popular, in the restrictive sense of the words. The choice of arguments is not an obvious one, as can be seen from a few examples. In the case of the Arian crisis, various details appear that deserve discussion. The vicissitudes and exiles of Athanasius, for example, differ at points from the accounts found in the classic ecclesiastical historians. The section dealing with the reign of Julian shows affinity with the hagiographic school that created the group of texts inspired by the "Julian martyrs." It may, in fact, help illuminate the origin and scope of that literature. In a similar vein, the actions of Theophilus against the temples and his relationship with the Pachomian monks may derive in part from inside information. The section on the Council of Ephesus fits in with what we know from the international sources, especially the official acts of the council. At the same time, however, it shows evidence of an Egyptian controversy that opposed the soon declining Pachomians and the Shenouteans with respect to the role played by their respective archimandrites in Ephesus at Cyril's side. For the subsequent period of Dioscorus and Timothy Aelurus, it seems obvious that the *HsC* should be recognized as an important source.

The low opinion of the *HsC* and the little attention given to them by modern historians seems to be a result of its survival mainly in Coptic. One can perhaps understand this attitude if it arises from a lack of knowledge of the Coptic language or the recognition of the fragmentary nature of the text. If, on the other hand, it has been ignored simply as a result of a general mistrust of Coptic documents, it is time to correct this misperception and include the *HsC* in the reconstruction of Church history. If we continue to ignore them, our knowledge of various aspects of Christian history will remain less rich than it could be.

Mark Sheridan

RHETORICAL STRUCTURE IN COPTIC SERMONS

Although a significant number of Coptic sermons[1] have been published in the last fifty years, very little attention has been devoted to the literary and rhetorical analysis of this form of literature since the publications of C. D. G. Müller.[2] It may therefore be useful to begin by summarizing the state of the question as Müller left it.

After tracing the development of the Greek sermon (*Predigt*) from the

---

1. In modern English usage (as in other modern languages) no clear distinction is made between the terms "sermon" and "homily" (see the *Oxford English Dictionary*, s.v.). In Christian antiquity, however, the term "homily" usually referred to a specific text-based form of preaching, of which two types can be distinguished: the exegetical homily and the thematic homily. In the former type the preacher seeks to expound the meaning of the text, citing it and following it in order. In the second type, he takes the text as his point of departure but does not necessarily follow the order of the text in his exposition. See T. Steiger, "Homilie," *Historisches Wörterbuch der Rhetorik*, ed. Gert Ueding (Darmstadt: Wissenschaftliche Buchgesellschaft, 1996), 3:1510–21. In the present article the term "sermon" is used as a generic modern category for all forms of ancient preaching or fictive preaching and the term "homily" is reserved for text-based sermons. However, it must be admitted that even in antiquity, at least in Coptic, the distinction was not always so clear, as will be noted below. On the history of the "homily" see M. Sachot, "Homilie," *RAC* 16:148–75. See also Alexandre Olivar, *La predicación cristiana antigua*, BH 189 (Barcelona: Editorial Herder, 1991); Hughes Oliphant Old, *The Reading and Preaching of the Scriptures in the Worship of the Christian Church*, vol. 2, *The Patristic Age* (Grand Rapids: Eerdmans, 1998).

2. C. Detlef G. Müller, *Die alte koptische Predigt (Versuch eines Ueberblicks)* (Ph.D. diss., Heidelberg, 1953; Darmstadt, 1954); "Einige Bemerkungen zur 'ars praedicandi' der alten koptischen Kirche," *Muséon* 67 (1954): 231–70; "Koptische Redekunst und Griechische Rhetorik," *Muséon* 69 (1956): 53–72. See also C. Detlef G. Müller, "Koptische Homiletik," in *Kindlers Literatur Lexikon* (Zürich: Kindler Verlag, 1970), 6:5339–42, a shorter summary of earlier positions.

New Testament to the fifth century (Cyril of Alexandria, Theodoret of Cyrrus),[3] Müller investigated four groups of Coptic "sermons." The first group consists of homilies on biblical themes, the second of sermons on angels, the third of works devoted to the Virgin Mary, and the fourth of works devoted to the saints. The total number of sermons described or analyzed comes to about twenty-six. Many of these sermons, especially in the first category, are in the Bohairic dialect, which means that at least in their present form they are not earlier than the ninth century.[4] The earliest of those analyzed would be the ones attributed to Athanasius, if the attribution were correct and not pseudepigraphical. We would be dealing then with a period of almost five hundred years, a period in which significant internal and external events impinged on the life of the Egyptian Church.

In his general conclusions, Müller noted the importance of two "pillars" for the Coptic art of preaching, exhortations and stories (*Ermahnungen* and *Erzählungen*).[5] For the broad masses in Egypt exegesis and speculation were never a goal in themselves. Rather, raising the moral level of the congregation was the principal concern of the preacher. Consequently the Coptic preacher had no interest in rhetoric as such. His discourse is simple, without ornament, and avoids all play with words such as one finds in the rhetorical style of Greek preaching. Conversely, the stories introduced by the Coptic preacher are missing in Greek preaching. Müller observes that the homilies as we have them were edited and gathered together in volumes for liturgical use, for reading during the liturgical services in monasteries, and that we possess only a small portion of the Coptic literature that once existed. He notes as well the great length of some of these writings, which would have lasted up to two hours if actually preached, but insists that this was normal in antiquity.

In an article published two years later, Müller sketched the development

---

3. Müller, *Die alte koptische Predigt*, 4–21. The authors are not treated in chronological order. Thus Eusebius of Caesarea follows at the end after Cyril of Alexandria and Theodoret.

4. See Ariel Shisha-Halevy, "Bohairic," in *The Coptic Encyclopedia*, ed. Aziz S. Atiya (New York: Macmillan, 1991), 8:53–60, who notes that the old controversial question over the origins of Bohairic as a literary dialect remains unresolved. However, there are no literary manuscripts older than the tenth century other than biblical fragments. According to Lefort, the origins of Bohairic as a literary dialect are to be found in the reconstruction of the library of St. Macarius in the ninth century. See L.-Th. Lefort, "Littérature bohaïrique," *Muséon* 44 (1931): 115–35.

5. Müller, *Die alte koptische Predigt*, 343. The conclusions are summarized and repeated in Müller, "Einige Bemerkungen zur 'ars praedicandi.'"

of Greek rhetoric and, relying on the analysis of Norden, Volkmann, and others,[6] remarked that Greek prose rhetoric was essentially poetry transposed into prose. As later standardized, Greek (and Latin) rhetoric fell into three distinct categories: that intended for the assembly, that intended for the courts (forensic), and the epideictic.[7] Later were added the encomium and the panegyric. Precise canons for these were developed, which included the internal divisions and the use of a variety of ornaments, comparisons, tropes, and figures. Müller insisted that, although there were never manuals of rhetoric in Coptic, there was in fact an established canon of preaching that the young priest would learn. This would have included a proper introduction and conclusion and a few types of discourse, such as "argumentation," but as far as the influence of Greek rhetorical style goes, it was practically nil.[8] The Coptic preacher used long stories to illustrate the moral exhortation. The typical features of Greek rhetoric, such as irony, sarcasm, plays on words, etc., are absent from Coptic preaching and, if they are found, should be regarded as non-Egyptian. Although he admitted the difficulty of even sketching a history of Coptic rhetoric, Müller insisted also on distinguishing between monastic literature (intended for a monastic audience) and preaching for a more general public. Shenoute would be the principal representative of the former. As the Coptic Church became progressively a monastic church and the older form of discourse addressed only to monks became less frequent, the miracle story seems to have quickly conquered the field.[9]

From the perspective of fifty years later, Müller's pioneering investigations and conclusions pose some serious problems of methodology. First of all, the juxtaposition of works produced over the course of five hundred years without a serious effort to locate them in their historical setting makes it impossible to detect or speak of development. The whole group of Bohairic pieces needs to

---

6. Eduard Norden, *Die antike Kunstprosa vom VI. Jahrhundert v. Chr. bis in die Zeit der Renaissance*, 2 vols. (Leipzig: Teubner, 1923); R. Volkmann, *Rhetorik der Griechen und Römer*, HKA 2, 3, 3d ed., ed. Caspar Hammer (Munich: Beck, 1901). The latter work has since been replaced by Josef Martin, *Antike Rhetorik, Technik und Methode*, HA 2.3 (Munich: Beck, 1974).

7. These divisions go back in fact to Aristotle. For a useful discussion of Aristotle's rhetorical theory, see George A. Kennedy, *Classical Rhetoric and Its Christian and Secular Tradition from Ancient to Modern Times*, 2d ed. (Chapel Hill: University of North Carolina Press, 1999), 74–93; see also H. Lausberg, *Handbuch der literarischen Rhetorik*, 3d ed. (Stuttgart: Franz Steiner, 1990), §§59–65.

8. Müller, "Koptische Redekunst und Griechische Rhetorik," 58.

9. Ibid., 70–71.

be treated separately from the Sahidic literature. The former may indeed be a witness to earlier literature transposed from Sahidic into Bohairic, but without specific analysis, Bohairic cannot be used as a witness to the period before the Arab Conquest. The few cases where we have comparable pieces in Sahidic and Bohairic show such considerable reworking that it would be better to say that the Bohairic version was inspired by the Sahidic.[10]

Another problem is posed by the large amount of material that is pseudepigraphical, that is, falsely attributed either deliberately or through accident of transmission. Many of the homilies analyzed by Müller fall into these categories. However, it belongs to the very nature of such works (deliberate false attribution) that they were never intended to be delivered orally, at least not by the persons to whom they are attributed. In many cases the false attribution cannot be simply a case of mistaken attribution or errors of transmission, since the fictive authorship is built into the construction of the literary pieces. Such is the case with the compositions attributed to Evodius, discussed below. The whole question of the reasons for the existence of this large body of literature in Coptic has never been dealt with adequately.[11]

Given the fact that a significant portion of the "homiletic" literature falls into this category, one must pose the question also of literary genre. Müller did not attempt to define the category "Predigt" and perhaps with good reason. It may not be possible to do so in a satisfactory way.[12] Nevertheless, some effort must be made to distinguish the different literary genres and subgenres in this category. The material that Müller analyzed was designated by a number of labels in antiquity, including ⲗⲟⲅⲟⲥ, ϩⲟⲙⲓⲗⲓⲁ, ⲉⲝⲉⲅⲏⲥⲓⲥ, ⲉⲅⲕⲱⲙⲓⲟⲛ,

---

10. Such is the case with the two homilies (Sahidic and Bohairic) attributed to Evodius of Rome. On the relationship of these, see J. Mark Sheridan, "A Homily on the Death of the Virgin Mary Attributed to Evodius of Rome," in *Coptic Studies on the Threshold of a New Millennium: Proceedings of the Seventh International Congress of Coptic Studies, Leiden, 27 August–2 September 2000*, ed. Mat Immerzeel and Jacques Van der Vliet, OLA 132–33 (Louvain: Peeters, 2004), 132:393–405.

11. The most important study to appear in the past fifty years on this subject is Wolfgang Speyer, *Die literarische Fälschung im heidnischen und christlichen Altertum: Ein Versuch Ihrer Deutung* (Munich: C. H. Beck, 1971). See also Wolfgang Speyer, "Fälschung, pseudoepigraphische freie Erfindung und 'echte' religiöse Pseudepigraphie," in *Pseudepigrapha* I, ed. Kurt von Fritz (Vandoeuvres-Geneve: Fondation Hardt, 1972), 331–66. For a hypothesis regarding the reasons for the pseudepigraphical homilies by Evodius, see my article mentioned in note 10.

12. Sachot (see note 1) gives a working definition of "homily" (for his article) as "die Ansprache im Anschluß an die gottesdienstliche Verlesung biblischer Schriften" (p. 148). Such a definition would exclude many of the compositions analyzed by Müller.

ⲙⲁⲣⲧⲩⲣⲓⲁ, ⲃⲓⲟⲥ, ⲡⲟⲗⲩⲧⲓⲁ, ⲕⲁⲑⲏⲕⲏⲥⲓⲥ.[13] Whether all of these terms should be grouped together under the heading of "sermon" or "homily" (or *Predigt* in German) may be questioned. From the point of view of literary genre and rhetorical style, the one thing they may have in common is that they were all compositions intended somehow for liturgical use. But in terms of literary genre and the rhetorical style associated with diverse genres, they may be quite different. Müller himself was well aware that the material he had studied did not represent the actual text or form of sermons as they had been delivered.[14] However, he does not seem to have understood (or at least did not indicate clearly) that a great many of them were composed not for delivery but rather to provide material for public reading in a liturgical context.

Only a careful analysis of the language used in homilies can provide clues regarding the time frame in which they were composed and the purpose of the authors. Many of the Coptic authors were quite sensitive to correct theological language. For example, Rufus of Shotep (end of the sixth century– beginning of the seventh) warns his congregation: "He is a son, beloved, for whom your mind needs a terminological security lest robbers or thieves punch holes in the door of your faith and carry off the riches of your nobility."[15] Rufus also uses a number of other phrases that reflect at least a post-Chalcedonian terminology.[16] Similarly, the homilies attributed to Evodius of Rome exhibit concerns that are certainly post-Chalcedonian and, more probably, attributable to the time of Damian (578–604).[17]

Given the current state of research, the lengthy time period involved, and the lack of detailed analysis of the texts available, it is very hazardous to make generalizations about the nature of the Coptic "homily." Only detailed examination of the terminology, literary genre, and rhetorical style can aid in developing a more reliable overview of the development of this literature and its

13. Müller, *Die alte koptische Predigt*, 303–4. Müller himself used the term "Homilie" to indicate more than text-based preaching. In this he was following ancient usage. See pp. 34–35, 83, 284. In Coptic the most common designation of text-based homilies seems to have been ⲗⲟⲅⲟⲥ. The designation of the homilies on Matthew by Rufus of Shotep is ⲗⲟⲅⲟⲥ, but those on Luke are designated by ⲉⲝⲉⲅⲉⲥⲓⲥ. See J. Mark Sheridan, *Rufus of Shotep: Homilies on the Gospels of Matthew and Luke; Introduction, Text, Translation, Commentary*, Unione Accademica Nazionale, CMCL (Rome: C.I.M., 1998), Coptic index, s.v.
14. Müller, "Einige Bemerkungen zur 'ars praedicandi,'" 268.
15. Sheridan, *Rufus of Shotep*, 232.
16. Ibid., 53–57.
17. See Sheridan, "Homily on the Death of the Virgin Mary."

historical function. Müller himself noted that a more exact knowledge of Coptic methods of composition and rhetorical forms might help to solve many disputed questions of origin and help to piece together many fragments.[18] Since he made his contributions, however, very little has been added in the way of concrete analysis, and unfortunately, as he also observed, the way in which Coptic texts have been published often obscures rather than illuminates the rhetorical structure of the pieces.[19] Indeed the form in which the homilies are presented in the manuscripts may often be much more revealing about the compositional methods of the author and the way he conceived the form of the work. The rest of this essay will be devoted to some specific examples of rhetorical analysis that might serve to improve methodology in this field.

Two Sermons Attributed to Athanasius

Among the sermons examined by Müller is one attributed to Athanasius entitled "The Resurrection of Lazarus" by the editor,[20] and *De Lazaro e mortuis reuocato* in the Clavis[21] where it is classified under "dubia." It is a text-based homily in the strict sense.[22] There is in fact no known Greek text to which it corresponds, and the homily is contained in only one manuscript in the Morgan collection dated 855.[23] Müller described the content of the homily, but without noting its precise rhetorical characteristics, except to observe that it showed strong Greek influence and lacked what he considered typical Coptic elements, such as the moral exhortations and catalogues of vices.[24] There is no doubt that the homily makes use of typically Greek rhetorical devices, but whether one can clearly distinguish what is Greek and what is Coptic in Coptic sermons is a more difficult question. Even if there were no manuals of rhetoric available in Coptic, there were available translations of classical examples

---

18. Müller, "Koptische Redekunst und Griechische Rhetorik," 54, 57.
19. Ibid., 58.
20. J. B. Bernardin, "The Resurrection of Lazarus," *AJSL* 57 (1940): 262–90.
21. CPG 2185; Coptic clavis 0049.
22. See note 1 above.
23. L. Depuydt, *Catalogue of Coptic Manuscripts in the Pierpont Morgan Library*, Corpus of Illuminated Manuscripts 4–5 (Louvain: Peeters, 1993), no. 170, 8 (p. 348). The manuscript is M595, fols.108r–18r.
24. Müller, *Die alte koptische Predigt*, 90–97.

of rhetorical style such as the sermons of Basil, Gregory Nazianzen, Gregory of Nyssa, Pseudo-Epiphanius,[25] and Proclus of Constantinople.[26] The dating of these translations is of course difficult, but some were probably available by the late fourth or early fifth century.

The homily on Lazarus begins with an elaborate exordium (proemium), a stylistic feature that can be found in other Coptic homilies. The purpose of the exordium in general is to capture the attention of the listeners for the subject to be treated.[27] This exordium is composed of two anaphoras,[28] the first of which contains a description (*ecphrasis*) of the parts of Christ's body and of his actions:

ⲚⲂⲀⲖ ⲘⲠⲨⲞⲈⲒⲤ ϨⲈⲚⲀⲔⲦⲒⲚ ⲚⲞⲨⲞⲈⲒⲚ ⲚⲈ · ⲈⲨⲢⲞⲨⲞⲈⲒⲚ ⲈⲚⲈⲦϨⲘⲠⲔⲀⲔⲈ ⲘⲚⲐⲀⲒⲂⲈⲤ ⲘⲠⲘⲞⲨ ·

ⲠⲖⲀⲤ ⲘⲠⲬⲤ ⲈϤⲘⲈϨ ⲚⲰⲚϨ ⲚⲞⲨⲞⲚ ⲚⲒⲘ ⲚⲦⲀⲠⲘⲞⲨ ⲢⲬⲞⲈⲒⲤ ⲈϪⲰⲞⲨ ·

ⲚϬⲒϪ ⲘⲠⲈⲬⲤ ϨⲈⲚⲢⲈϤⲦⲀⲚϨⲞ ⲚⲈ · ⲈϢⲀϤϮⲦⲞⲞⲦⲞⲨ ⲚⲞⲨⲞⲚ ⲚⲒⲘ ⲚϤⲦⲀϨⲞⲞⲨ ⲈⲢⲀⲦⲞⲨ ·

ⲚϨⲞⲒⲦⲈ ⲘⲠⲈⲬⲤ ϨⲈⲚⲢⲈϤⲦⲀⲚϨⲞ ⲚⲈ · ⲈϢⲀⲨⲐⲈⲢⲀⲠⲈⲨⲈ ⲚⲚⲈϨⲒⲞ[ⲘⲈ] · [108v] ⲈⲢⲈⲠⲤⲚⲞϤ ϨⲀⲢⲞⲞⲨ ·

ⲚⲈⲞⲨⲈⲢⲎⲦⲈ ⲘⲠⲈⲬⲤ ϨⲈⲚⲢⲈϤⲔⲰⲦⲈ ⲚⲈ ⲚⲤⲀ ⲚⲈⲤⲞⲞⲨ ⲚⲦⲀⲨⲤⲰⲢⲘ ⲈϤⲔⲦⲞ ⲘⲘⲞⲞⲨ ⲈϨⲞⲨⲚ ⲈⲦⲀⲨⲖⲎ ⲈⲦⲚⲀⲚⲞⲨⲤ ·

ⲠⲞⲨⲈϨⲤⲀϨⲚⲈ ⲘⲠⲈⲬⲤ · ⲞⲨⲢⲈϤⲦⲀⲖϬⲞ ⲠⲈ · ⲈϢⲀϤⲦⲀⲖϬⲞ ⲚⲈⲦⲤⲞⲂϨ ⲚϤⲔⲀⲐⲀⲢⲒⲌⲈ ⲘⲘⲞⲞⲨ ·

ⲘⲠⲀϬⲤⲈ ⲈⲦⲚϨⲞⲨⲚ ⲈⲢⲰϤ ⲘⲠⲈⲬⲤ · ϨⲈⲚⲔⲞⲖⲖⲎⲢⲒⲞⲚ ⲘⲠⲀϨⲢⲈ ⲚⲈ ⲚⲢⲈϤϮⲞⲨⲞⲈⲒⲚ ⲈϢⲀϤϮⲞⲨⲞⲈⲒⲚ ⲈⲚⲂⲀⲖ ⲘⲠⲂⲖⲖⲈ ⲘⲘⲒⲤⲈ ·

ⲦϬⲒⲚϬⲰϢⲦ ⲘⲠⲈⲬⲤ ⲞⲨⲢⲈϤⲦⲰⲚϨ ⲦⲈ · ⲀϤϬⲰϢⲦ ⲈⲠϢⲎⲢⲈ ⲚⲦⲈⲬⲎⲢⲀ · ⲈⲨϤⲒ ⲘⲘⲞϤ ⲈⲂⲞⲖ ⲈϤⲘⲞⲞⲨⲦ ⲀϤⲦⲞⲨⲚⲞⲤϤ ⲚⲀϤ ·

ⲦϬⲒϪ ⲘⲠⲈⲬⲤ ⲞⲨⲢⲈϤⲦⲈϨⲘⲢⲰⲘⲈ ⲈⲠⲰⲚϨ ⲦⲈ .. ⲀϤⲈⲒ ⲈϤⲘⲞⲞϢⲈ ⲈϤⲦⲰϨⲘ ⲚⲚⲈϤⲀⲠⲞⲤⲦⲞⲖⲞⲤ ⲈϨⲞⲨⲚ ⲈⲦⲘⲚⲦⲈⲢⲞ ⲚⲘⲠⲎⲨⲈ..

---

25. Ibid., 193, 217–23. Müller included one of the Pseudo-Epiphanius sermons in his analysis, apparently not realizing that it was a translation from the Greek and noting that it was very Greek in style. For observations on the style of Pseudo-Epiphanius, see Hendrik Stander, "Stylistic Devices and Homiletic Techniques in Ps.-Epiphanius' Festal Sermons," in *Nova et Vetera. Patristic Studies in Honor of Thomas Patrick Halton*, ed. John Petruccione (Washington: Catholic University of America Press, 1998), 96–114.

26. In addition to the authentic sermons of these authors translated into Coptic, other compositions were attributed to them in Coptic. See the Coptic clavis of Tito Orlandi (http://rmcisadu.let.uniroma1.it/~cmcl/) for lists of both types and also Tito Orlandi, "Cycles," in Atiya, *Coptic Encyclopedia*, 3:666–68.

27. On the exordium in general and its varieties, see Lausberg, *Handbuch der literarischen Rhetorik*, §§263–88; K. Schöpsdau, "Exordium," in Ueding, *Historisches Wörterbuch der Rhetorik*, 3:136–40.

28. For the rhetorical device of anaphora, see C. Blasberg, "Anapher," in Ueding, *Historisches Wörterbuch der Rhetorik*, 1:542–45.

ⲧϭⲓⲛⲡⲁⲣⲁⲅⲉ ⲙ̄ⲡⲉⲭ̄ⲥ̄ ⲟⲩϩⲏⲩ ⲧⲉ ⲉϥⲡⲁⲣⲁⲅⲉ ⲇⲉ ⲁϥϯⲡⲟⲩⲟⲉⲓⲛ ⲉⲃⲁⲗⲉ ⲥⲛⲁⲩ ⲉⲩϩⲓⲧⲉϩⲓⲏ : ~

ⲙ̄ⲙⲛ̄ⲧⲱⲛϩⲧϥ̄ ⲙ̄ⲡⲉⲭ̄ⲥ̄ ϩⲉⲛⲁⲧϫⲓⲏⲡⲉ ⲙ̄ⲙⲟⲟⲩ ⲛⲉ · ⲁϥϣⲛ̄ϩⲧϥ̄ ⲅⲁⲣ ϩⲁϯⲟⲩ ⲛ̄ϣⲟ ⲛ̄ⲣⲱⲙⲉ ⲉⲩϩⲕⲁⲉⲓⲧ · ⲁⲩⲱϩⲉ ⲛ̄ⲧⲟⲩ ⲛ̄ⲟⲉⲓⲕ ⲛⲉⲓⲱⲧ · ⲁϥⲧⲣⲉⲩⲟⲩⲱⲙ ⲧⲏⲣⲟⲩ ⲁⲩⲥⲓ : ~

The eyes of the Lord are rays of light lighting up those who are in the "darkness and the shadow of death" [Luke 1:79].

The tongue of Christ is full of life for everyone over whom death has ruled.

The hands of Christ are life giving, with which he gives a hand to all and sets them on their feet.

The garments of Christ are life giving, healing the women with hemorrhages [cf. Matt. 9:20–22; Mark 5:25–34; Luke 8:43–48].

The feet of Christ are seekers after the strayed sheep, which he brings back to the good sheepfold [John 10:16; Luke 15:6].

The commandment of Christ is a healer, with which He heals those who are leprous and cleanses them [cf. Luke 5:12; 17:11–19].

The salivas that are in the mouth of Christ are healing, light-giving salves, with which He gives light to the eyes of the man born blind [John 9:6].

The gaze of Christ is life giving. He gazed at the son of the widow as he was being carried out dead and it gave life to him [Luke 7:11–17].

The hand of Christ is an inviter of man to life. He came walking and calling his apostles to the kingdom of the heavens [cf. Luke 7:12–14].

The passing by of Christ is beneficial. As he was passing by he gave sight to two blind men along the way [cf. Matt. 20:29–34].

The mercies of Christ are innumerable. For he had pity on five thousand men who were hungry. They needed five thousand barley loaves and he made them all eat and they were satisfied [cf. Matt. 14:15–21; 16:9; Mark 6:35–44; 8:19; Luke 9:12–17; John 6:5–13].[29]

Except for the first item in the list, which mentions the eyes of the Lord (ⲙ̄ⲡϫⲟⲉⲓⲥ), all of them contain the phrase ⲙ̄ⲡⲉⲭ̄ⲥ̄, thus emphasizing the repetitive characteristic of an anaphora. The second anaphora contains a catalogue of the miracles or "mighty works" that Jesus performed:

ⲉⲓⲛⲁϫⲉ ⲟⲩ · ⲡⲉⲩⲟⲉⲓϣ ⲅⲁⲣ <ⲛ̄>ⲛⲁⲕⲁⲁⲧ ⲉⲓϣⲁϫⲉ ⲉⲧⲃⲉ ⲛϭⲟⲙ ⲛ̄ⲧⲁⲡⲉⲭ̄ⲥ̄ ⲁⲁⲩ ϩⲙ̄ⲡ-
ⲕⲟⲥⲙⲟⲥ · ⲙⲛ̄ⲛⲉϥϣⲡⲏⲣⲉ ⲧⲏⲣⲟⲩ ⲉⲧⲉⲙ̄ⲡⲣⲙ̄ⲛ̄ⲥⲁⲣⲝ̄ ⲛⲁϣϫⲓⲏⲡⲉ ⲙ̄ⲙⲟⲟⲩ · ⲟⲩⲇⲉ
ⲙ̄ⲛ̄ⲅⲣⲁⲙⲙⲁⲧⲉⲩⲥ ⲛ̄ⲥⲡⲟⲩⲇⲉⲟⲥ ⲛⲁϣϫⲓⲏⲡⲉ ⲙ̄ⲙⲟⲟⲩ · ⲛ̄ϥ̄ⲥϩⲁⲓⲥⲟⲩ ⲉϫⲱⲱⲙⲉ ·
ⲙ̄ⲙⲟⲟⲩ ⲛ̄ⲧⲁⲩⲣ̄ⲣⲏⲣⲡ ·
ⲙ̄ⲡ̄ⲡⲉⲧⲥⲏϩ · ⲛ̄ⲧⲁϥϫⲓ ⲙ̄ⲡⲉϥϭⲁⲗⲟϭ [109ⲅⲓ] ⲁϥⲙⲟⲟϣⲉ

29. The arrangement of the text, the emphasis, and the translations from this homily are my own and do not correspond to the version published by Bernardin (see note 20 above). The text has been checked against the manuscript.

ⲙⲛ̄ⲛ̄ⲇⲁⲓⲙⲟⲛⲓⲟⲛ ⲛ̄ⲧⲁϥⲛⲟϫⲟⲩ ⲉⲃⲟⲗ ·
ⲙⲛ̄ⲛ̄ⲙ̄ⲡⲟ ⲛ̄ⲧⲁϥⲧⲣⲉⲩϣⲁϫⲉ ·
ⲙⲛ̄ⲛ̄ⲁⲗ ⲛ̄ⲧⲁϥⲧⲣⲉⲩⲥⲱⲧⲙ̄ ·
ⲙⲛ̄ϭⲓϫ ⲉⲧϣⲟⲩⲱⲟⲩ ⲛ̄ⲧⲁϥⲧⲁⲗϭⲟⲟⲩ ·
ⲙⲛ̄ⲑⲁⲗⲁⲥⲥⲁ ⲛ̄ⲧⲁϥⲙⲟⲟϣⲉ ⲉⲃⲟⲗ ϩⲓϫⲛ̄ⲛⲉⲥⲙⲟⲟⲩ ⲛ̄ⲑⲉ ⲛ̄ⲟⲩⲡⲉⲧⲣⲁ ⲛ̄ⲱⲛⲉ ·
ⲙⲛ̄ⲧⲃⲱⲛ̄ⲕⲛ̄ⲧⲉ ⲉⲧⲙ̄ⲡⲉϥϭⲛ̄ⲕⲁⲣⲡⲟⲥ ⲛ̄ⲧⲁϥⲧⲣⲉⲥϣⲟⲟⲩⲉ ·
ⲙⲛ̄ϩⲟⲉⲓⲙ ⲛ̄ⲑⲁⲗⲁⲥⲥⲁ ⲛ̄ⲧⲁⲩⲣ̄ϩⲟⲧⲉ ϩⲏⲧϥ̄ ⲙ̄ⲡⲉϥϣⲁϫⲉ ⲁⲩⲑ̄ⲃⲃⲓⲟⲟⲩ ⲉⲡⲉⲥⲏⲧ.
ⲙⲛ̄ⲧϣⲉⲉⲣⲉ ⲛ̄ⲡⲁⲣⲭⲓⲥⲩⲛⲁⲅⲱⲅⲟⲥ ⲛ̄ⲧⲁⲥⲃⲟϭⲥ̄ ⲁⲥⲁϩⲉⲣⲁⲧⲥ̄ ⲁⲥⲱⲛϩ̄ ⲛ̄ⲧⲉⲣⲉⲧϭⲓϫ
ⲙ̄ⲡⲉⲛⲧⲁϥⲧⲁⲙⲓⲟⲥ ⲁⲙⲁϩⲧⲉ ⲙ̄ⲙⲟⲥ :
ⲛⲁⲓ̈ ⲁⲛϫⲟⲟⲩ ⲉⲧⲃⲉ ⲛ̄ϭⲟⲙ ⲛ̄ⲧⲁⲡⲉⲭⲣⲓⲥⲧⲟⲥ ⲁⲁⲩ ⲉⲁⲛⲟⲩⲟⲛϩⲟⲩ ⲉⲃⲟⲗ :

What shall I say? For the time would not permit me to speak *concerning the mighty works that Christ* did in the world and all the wonders that no human being would be able to count. Nor is there a zealous scribe who would be able to number them and write them in a book [cf. John 21:25].

Water was made wine [John 2:2–11]

and *the lame man* who took up his bed [109r1] and walked [Matt. 9:1–8; Mark 2:1–12; Luke 5:17–26];

and *the demons* that he cast out; [cf., e.g., Mark 1:23–26; 5:1–13]

and *the dumb* that he caused to speak; [cf., e.g., Mark 7:32–35]

and *the deaf* that he caused to hear; [cf., e.g. Mark 7:32–35]

and *the withered hands* that he healed [Matt. 12:10; Mark 3:5];

and *the sea* upon whose waters He walked as upon a stony rock [Matt. 14:22–36; Mark 6:45–52; John 6:16–21];

and *the fig tree* on which he did not find fruit, which he caused to wither [Mark 11:13, 20];

and *the waves* of the sea, which were thoroughly frightened at His speech and calmed down [Matt. 8:23–27; Mark 4:25–41; Luke 8:22–25];

and *the daughter* of the ruler of the synagogue who leapt up, stood on her feet, and lived, when the hand of her Creator took hold of her [Matt. 9:18–26; Mark 5:22–43; Luke 8:41–56].

These things have we spoken and disclosed *concerning the mighty works that Christ did.*

This second anaphora is framed by an inclusion: ⲉⲧⲃⲉ ⲛ̄ϭⲟⲙ ⲛ̄ⲧⲁⲡⲉⲭⲣⲓⲥⲧⲟⲥ ⲁⲁⲩ, "concerning the mighty works that Christ did," and most of the items in the list are introduced by ⲙⲛ̄. Together the two anaphoras set the stage for the account of the great miracle of the raising of Lazarus. The first one, however, with the description of the parts of Christ's body, provides a contrast for the description of the parts of Lazarus's body that will follow later.

After a transitional passage that locates the homily in the context of the liturgy mentioning "The word that was read to us today in the Gospel according to John," the author poses the rhetorical question "What, indeed, is the word which was read to us?" and proceeds to quote John 11:1–3. He then asks the hearer/reader to note in particular the phrase "She who *anointed* the Lord with ointment" (John 11:2). There follows a set of antitheses in the form of an apostrophe addressed to this Mary, of which the first is:

ⲱ ⲧⲉⲓⲛⲟϭ ⲛϣⲡⲏⲣⲉ ⲉⲧⲟϣ ·
ⲛ̄ⲧⲟ ⲙⲉⲛ ⲁⲣⲧⲁϩⲥⲧ̄ ⲛ̄ⲟⲩⲥⲟϭⲛ̄ · ⲁⲛⲟⲕ ϩⲱ †ⲛⲁⲧⲁϩⲥⲉ ⲙ̄ⲡⲛⲉϩ ⲛ̄ⲧⲉⲥⲫⲣⲁⲅⲓⲥ ⲛ̄ⲁⲧⲃⲱⲗ ⲉⲃⲟⲗ ϩⲙ̄ⲡⲁⲣⲁⲛ ⲙⲛ̄ⲡⲣⲁⲛ ⲙ̄ⲡⲁⲉⲓⲱⲧ ⲙⲛ̄ⲡⲉⲡⲛⲉⲩⲙⲁ ⲛ̄ϩⲁⲅⲓⲟⲛ ·

O this great wonder which is read!
You, indeed, have anointed me with an ointment; I for my part shall anoint you with the oil of the unbreakable seal, in my name and the name of My Father and the Holy Spirit.

Each of the three antitheses is carefully balanced with the same verb repeated in the first person preceded by the phrase ⲁⲛⲟⲕ ϩⲱ. In the first and third antitheses, the same verb is repeated. Then John 11:3 is quoted again, followed by a brief exclamatory piece on the love Jesus had for the three: Martha, Mary, and Lazarus.

The structure of the rest of the homily follows the same pattern of quotations and comments. Most of the comments are in the form of anaphoras or sets of antitheses built upon a phrase of the verses quoted. A number of these are in the form of an apostrophe.[30] An example will suffice to illustrate the technique. After quoting John 11:14–16, which concludes with Didymus saying, "Let us go ourselves that we may die with him," the author introduces the following apostrophe addressed to Didymus/Thomas:

ⲱ ⲑⲱⲙⲁⲥ ⲡⲁϣ ⲛ̄ϩⲉ ⲉⲕⲣ̄ϩⲟⲧⲉ ⲙ̄ⲡⲙⲟⲩ ⲉⲣⲉⲡⲱⲛϩ ⲙⲟⲟϣⲉ ⲛⲙ̄ⲙⲁⲕ · ⲕ̄ⲛⲁⲥⲟⲩⲱⲛϥ̄ ⲧⲉⲛⲟⲩ ϫⲉ ⲛ̄ⲧⲟϥ ⲡⲉⲧⲟⲩⲛⲁⲙⲟⲟⲩⲧϥ̄ ϫⲓⲛ ⲙ̄ⲙⲟⲛ ⲛ̄ⲧⲟϥ ⲡⲉⲧϩⲁⲣⲡⲁϩⲉ ⲛ̄ⲕⲉⲟⲩⲁ ⲉⲃⲟⲗ ϩⲛ̄ ⲧϭⲓϫ ⲙ̄ⲡⲙⲟⲩ :

ⲟⲩⲁϩⲕ̄ ⲛ̄ⲥⲱⲓ ⲱ ⲑⲱⲙⲁⲥ ⲧⲁⲧⲥⲁⲃⲟⲕ ⲉⲡⲧⲩⲡⲟⲥ ⲛ̄ⲧⲁⲁⲛⲁⲥⲧⲁⲥⲓⲥ ⲉϯⲛⲁⲁⲁϥ ⲙ̄ⲡⲥⲱⲛⲧ̄ ⲧⲏⲣϥ̄ ·

ⲁⲙⲟⲩ ⲛⲙ̄ⲙⲁⲓ ⲧⲁⲧⲥⲁⲃⲟⲕ ⲉⲡⲥⲱⲙⲁ ⲛ̄ⲗⲁⲍⲁⲣⲟⲥ ⲛ̄ⲧⲁϥⲕⲛⲟⲥ ⲁϥϣⲉϣ ⲥ̄ϯⲃⲱⲱⲛ ⲉⲃⲟⲗ ⲙⲛ̄ⲡⲱ ⲉϯⲛⲁⲙⲟⲩⲧⲉ ⲉⲧⲉϥⲯⲩⲭⲏ ⲧⲁⲧⲣⲉⲥⲃⲱⲕ ⲉϩⲟⲩⲛ ⲉⲡⲉϥⲥⲱⲙⲁ ⲛ̄ⲕⲉⲥⲟⲡ ·

ⲟⲩⲁϩⲕ̄ ⲛ̄ⲥⲱⲓ ⲱ ⲇⲓⲇⲩⲙⲟⲥ ⲧⲁⲧⲣⲉⲕⲑⲉⲱⲣⲓ ⲛ̄ⲛ̄ϭⲓϫ ⲛ̄ⲗⲁⲍⲁⲣⲟⲥ ⲙⲛ̄ⲛⲉϥⲟⲩⲉⲣⲏⲧⲉ ⲛ̄ⲧⲁⲩⲙⲟⲣⲟⲩ ⲙⲛ̄ⲛ̄ϩⲁϭⲉ ⲛ̄ⲙ̄ⲙⲏⲣⲣⲉ[31] ⲙ̄ⲡⲙⲟⲩ: ⲉⲓ̈ⲛⲁϯ ⲡⲱⲛϩ ⲛⲁⲩ ⲛ̄ⲕⲉⲥⲟⲛ ⲛ̄ⲥⲉϩⲩⲡⲉⲣⲉⲧⲉⲓ ⲙ̄ⲙⲟⲓ̈ ·

ⲙⲟⲟϣⲉ ⲛⲙ̄ⲙⲁⲓ ⲱ ⲇⲓⲇⲩⲙⲟⲥ ⲧⲁⲧⲥⲁⲃⲟⲕ ⲉⲛ̄ⲃⲁⲗ ⲛ̄ⲗⲁⲍⲁⲣⲟⲥ ⲉⲁⲩϣⲧⲁⲙ ⲉⲛ̄ⲛⲟⲩⲟⲉⲓⲛ ⲛ̄ϩⲏⲧⲟⲩ · ⲉⲓ̈ⲛⲁⲟⲩⲱⲛ ⲙ̄ⲙⲟⲟⲩ ⲛ̄ⲕⲉⲥⲟⲡ ⲛ̄ⲧⲁϯ ⲡⲟⲩⲟⲉⲓⲛ ⲉⲣⲟⲟⲩ ·

---

30. See A. W. Halsall, "Apostrophe," in Ueding, *Historisches Wörterbuch der Rhetorik*, 1:830–36.
31. Ms reads: ⲛⲛⲛⲙ̄ⲙⲏⲣⲣⲉ.

ⲁⲙⲟⲩ ⲉⲡⲧⲁⲫⲟⲥ ⲛⲙⲙⲁⲓ ⲱ ⲑⲱⲙⲁⲥ ⲧⲁⲧⲥⲁⲃⲟⲕ ⲉⲧⲧⲁⲡⲣⲟ ⲉϥϣⲧⲁⲙ ⲁⲩⲱ ⲡⲉϥⲗⲁⲥ
ⲉϥⲗⲉϥⲗⲱϥ ⲉⲙⲡⲛⲓⲃⲉ ϩⲛⲛⲉϥϣⲃⲱⲁ · ⲉⲓⲛⲁⲟⲩⲱⲛ ⲛⲧⲉϥⲧⲁⲡⲣⲟ ⲛⲧⲁⲧⲣⲉⲡⲉϥⲗⲁⲥ ϣⲁϫⲉ
ⲁⲩⲱ ⲛⲧⲁϯ ⲡⲛⲉⲩⲙⲁ ⲉⲣⲟϥ ·
ⲁⲙⲏⲓⲧⲛ ⲛⲙⲙⲁⲓ ⲧⲏⲣⲧⲛ[32] ⲱ ⲛⲁⲙⲁⲑⲏⲧⲏⲥ ⲉⲧⲟⲩⲁⲁⲃ ⲛⲧⲉⲧⲛⲥⲱⲧⲙ ⲉⲣⲟⲓ ⲉⲓⲛⲁⲙⲟⲩⲧⲉ
ϩⲛⲧⲉⲥⲙⲏ ⲛⲧⲁⲙⲛⲧⲛⲟⲩⲧⲉ ⲛⲧⲉⲗⲁⲍⲁⲣⲟⲥ ⲥⲱⲧⲙ ⲉⲣⲟⲓ ⲛϥⲙⲟⲟϣⲉ ⲛϥⲉⲓ ϣⲁⲣⲟⲓ ⲉϥⲟⲛϩ:
ⲁⲩⲱ ⲛⲧⲉⲣⲉϥϫⲉ ⲛⲁⲓ ⲁϥⲙⲟⲟϣⲉ ⲙⲛⲛⲉϥⲙⲁⲑⲏⲧⲏⲥ ⲉⲧⲣⲉϥⲃⲱⲕ ϣⲁⲣⲟϥ:

O *Thomas*, how is it that you fear death, when life is walking with you? You will know Him now because the one whom they will put to death among us, is the one who seizes another from the hand of death.

Follow me, *Thomas*, and I will show you the model of my Resurrection, which I shall perform for every creature.

Come with me, that I may show you the body of Lazarus, which has decayed and spread abroad a foul smell; and the way in which I shall call to his soul so as to make it enter his body again.

Follow me, *Didymus*, so that I may cause you to see the hands of Lazarus and his feet, which were bound with cords and the bindings of death; to them I shall give life again that they may minister to me.

Walk with me, *Didymus*, that I may show you the eyes of Lazarus, which have closed, there being no light in them; these I shall open again and give light to them.

Come to the tomb with me, *Thomas*, so that I may show you the mouth closed and his tongue decayed, there being no breath in his nostrils; his mouth I shall open and I shall make his tongue speak and I shall give breath to him.

Come with me, all of you, my holy disciples, and listen to me as I shall call in the voice of my divinity and Lazarus will hear me and will walk and come to me alive. And when he had said these things, He walked with his disciples to go to him.

The description of the dead body of Lazarus, with emphasis on the different parts of the body that have decayed—eyes, mouth, tongue, etc.—corresponds to the description later on of the body of Lazarus brought back to life. In fact, the mention of the body parts, whether of Christ or of Lazarus, and their corresponding good odor or bad odor, forms a leitmotiv that helps to tie the whole together. For example, when Christ arrives at the tomb, after describing the condition of Lazarus in the tomb, the following anaphora is inserted:

ⲁϥⲉⲓ ⲇⲉ ⲉⲧⲙⲏⲧⲉ ⲛϭⲓ ⲓⲏⲥⲟⲩⲥ
ⲧⲁⲡⲱⲑⲏⲕⲏ ⲉⲧⲙⲉϩ ⲛⲱⲛϩ ·
ⲧⲧⲁⲡⲣⲟ ⲉⲧⲙⲉϩ ⲛⲥϯⲛⲟⲩϥⲉ ·
ⲡⲗⲁⲥ ⲉⲧϯϩⲟⲧⲉ ⲙⲡⲙⲟⲩ ·

32. Ms reads: ⲧⲏⲣⲧⲣ.

ⲡⲁⲩⲛⲁⲧⲟⲥ ϩⲛ̄ⲛⲉϥⲟⲩⲉϩⲥⲁϩⲛⲉ ·
ⲡⲣⲁϣⲉ ⲛ̄ⲛⲉⲧⲣ̄ⲏϩⲃⲉ ·
ⲡⲧⲱⲟⲩⲛ ⲛ̄ⲛⲉⲛⲧⲁⲩϩⲉ ·
ⲧⲁⲛⲁⲥⲧⲁⲥⲓⲥ ⲛ̄ⲛⲉⲧⲙⲟⲟⲩⲧ ·
ⲡⲥⲱⲟⲩϩ ⲉϩⲟⲩⲛ ⲛ̄ⲛⲉⲧϫⲟⲟⲣⲉ ⲉⲃⲟⲗ ·
ⲑⲉⲗⲡⲓⲥ ⲛ̄ⲛⲉⲧⲉⲙⲛ̄ⲧⲟⲩϩⲉⲗⲡⲓⲥ:

But into the midst came Jesus,
the storehouse full of life,
the mouth that is full of sweet odor,
the tongue that frightens death,
the Mighty One in His commands,
the Joy of those who are sorrowful,
the Rising of those who have fallen,
the Resurrection of the dead,
the Assembly of the those dispersed,
the Hope of the hopeless.

Although the homily in general seems to follow the text of John 11, there are a number of chiastic elements built into the structure as a whole. The center of the homily is devoted to the scene of Lazarus's resurrection. After a number of apostrophes addressed to Lazarus and to Christ, the author concludes the description of his return to life with an anaphora describing each part of his body:

<u>ⲛ̄ⲃⲁⲗ</u> ⲛ̄ⲧⲁⲩϣⲧⲁⲙ ⲉⲧⲛ̄ⲟⲩⲱⲛ ϣⲁⲉⲛⲉϩ ⲁⲩⲟⲩⲱⲛ <u>ⲛ̄ⲕⲉⲥⲟⲡ</u> ⲁⲩⲙⲟⲩϩ ⲛ̄ⲟⲩⲟⲉⲓⲛ ⲁⲩⲛⲁⲩ ⲉⲣⲱⲙⲉ ⲛⲓⲙ ·

<u>ⲛ̄ⲧⲁⲡⲉ</u> ⲛ̄ⲧⲁⲩⲙⲟⲣⲥ̄ ⲛ̄ⲡⲥⲟⲩⲇⲁⲣⲓⲟⲛ ⲁⲥⲃⲱⲗ ⲉⲃⲟⲗ ⲁⲥⲧⲁⲭⲣⲟ <u>ⲛ̄ⲕⲉⲥⲟⲡ</u> ⲁⲥⲡⲣⲟⲥⲕⲩⲛⲉⲓ ⲙ̄ⲡⲉⲭⲣⲓⲥⲧⲟⲥ ·

<u>ⲛ̄ⲙⲁⲁϫⲉ</u> ⲛ̄ⲧⲁⲩⲧⲱⲙ[33] ϩⲓⲧⲛ̄ⲧⲉϥϣⲉ ⲙ̄ⲡⲙⲟⲩ ⲁⲩⲟⲩⲱⲛ <u>ⲛ̄ⲕⲉⲥⲟⲡ</u> ⲁⲩⲥⲱⲧⲙ̄ ⲉⲡⲉⲭⲣⲓⲥⲧⲟⲥ ⲉϥⲙⲟⲩⲧⲉ ⲉϩⲟⲩⲛ ⲉⲡⲧⲁⲫⲟⲥ ϩⲛ̄ⲧⲉϥⲥⲙⲏ ⲛ̄ⲛⲟⲩⲧⲉ ·

<u>ⲡϣⲁⲛⲧϥ̄</u> ⲛ̄ⲧⲁϥϣ̄ⲱⲙⲟ ⲉⲡⲛⲓⲃⲉ ⲛ̄ⲱⲛϩ̄ ⲁϥⲉⲛⲉⲣⲅⲓ <u>ⲛ̄ⲕⲉⲥⲟⲡ</u> ⲁϥϣⲱⲗⲙ̄ ⲉⲡⲉⲥϯⲛⲟⲩϥⲉ ⲙ̄ⲡⲉⲭⲣⲓⲥⲧⲟⲥ ·

<u>ⲡⲗⲁⲥ</u> ⲛ̄ⲧⲁϥⲕⲁⲧⲟⲟⲧϥ̄ ⲉⲃⲟⲗ ⲉⲧⲛ̄ϣⲁϫⲉ ⲛ̄ⲟⲩⲱϩⲙ̄ ⲁϥⲕⲓⲙ <u>ⲛ̄ⲕⲉⲥⲟⲡ</u> ⲁϥⲥⲟⲟⲩⲧⲛ̄ ⲁϥⲥⲙⲟⲩ ⲉⲡⲛⲟⲩⲧⲉ ·

<u>ⲛⲉⲥⲡⲟⲧⲟⲩ</u> ⲛ̄ⲧⲁⲩϣⲧⲁⲙ ⲛ̄ⲙⲟⲟⲩ ϫⲉ ⲛ̄ⲛⲉⲩϣⲁϫⲉ <u>ⲛ̄ⲕⲉⲥⲟⲡ</u> ⲁⲩⲟⲩⲱⲛ ⲛ̄ⲕⲉⲥⲟⲡ ⲁⲩϣⲁϫⲉ ⲙ̄ⲡ̄ϣⲏⲣⲉ ⲙ̄ⲡⲛⲟⲩⲧⲉ ·

<u>ⲡϩⲏⲧ</u> ⲛ̄ⲧⲁϥⲃⲱⲗ ⲉⲃⲟⲗ ⲉⲧⲛ̄ϣⲁϫⲉ ⲉⲧⲛ̄ⲙⲉⲉⲩⲉ[34] ⲉϣ̄ⲧⲙ̄ⲛⲁⲩ ⲉⲣⲱⲙⲉ ⲉⲥⲟⲩⲱⲛϥ̄ ⲟⲩⲇⲉ ⲛ̄ⲛⲉϥⲉϣⲁⲓⲥⲑⲁⲛⲉ ⲉⲧⲃⲉ ⲗⲁⲁⲩ ⲁϥⲧⲁⲭⲣⲟ <u>ⲛ̄ⲕⲉⲥⲟⲡ</u> ⲁϥⲥⲟⲩⲛ̄ ⲡⲉⲛⲧⲁϥⲧⲁⲙⲓⲟϥ ·

33. Ms reads: ⲛ̄ⲧⲁⲩⲧⲱⲟⲩⲛ.
34. Ms reads: ⲉⲓⲉⲉⲙⲏⲉⲩⲉ.

ⲙ̄ⲙⲉⲗⲟⲥ ⲧⲏⲣⲟⲩ ⲛ̄ⲧⲁⲩⲗⲟϥⲗⲉϥ ⲁⲩⲃⲱⲗ ⲉⲃⲟⲗ ϩⲛ̄ϩⲧⲏϥ ⲙ̄ⲡⲕⲁϩ ⲁⲩⲱⲛϩ̄ ⲛ̄ⲕⲉⲥⲟⲡ ⲁⲩϩⲩⲡⲉⲣⲏⲧⲉⲓ ⲙ̄ⲡⲥⲱⲙⲁ ·
ⲛⲉⲟⲩⲉⲣⲏⲧⲉ ⲛ̄ⲧⲁⲩⲥⲟⲛϩⲟⲩ ⲉⲧⲙ̄ⲧⲣⲉⲩⲙⲟⲟϣⲉ ⲉⲛⲉϩ ⲁⲩⲃⲱⲗ ⲉⲃⲟⲗ ⲛ̄ⲕⲉⲥⲟⲡ ⲁⲩⲱ ⲁⲩⲥⲟⲟⲩⲧⲛ̄ ⲁⲩⲇⲓⲁⲕⲟⲛⲉⲓ ⲉⲡⲉⲭⲣⲓⲥⲧⲟⲥ ⲓⲏⲥⲟⲩⲥ ⲡϣⲏⲣⲉ ⲙ̄ⲡⲛⲟⲩⲧⲉ ϩⲛ̄ⲟⲩϩⲩⲡⲟⲙⲟⲛⲏ:

The eyes, which had closed so as never to open, opened *again* filled with light and saw everyone.

The head, which had been bound with a napkin, loosed itself and became strong *again* and bowed to Christ.

The ears, which had been closed by the stroke of death, opened *again* and heard Christ calling in the tomb in His divine voice.

His nose, which had been a stranger to the breath of life, functioned *again* and smelled the sweet odor of Christ.

The tongue, which had ceased speaking any more, moved *again*, stretched, and praised God.

The lips, which had closed so as not to speak *again*, opened *again* and spoke with the Son of God.

The mind, which had dissolved so as not to speak or to think or to be able to see a man to know him or to be able to perceive anything, became strong *again* and knew the one who had created it.

All the members, which had decayed and dissolved in the earth, became alive *again* and ministered to the body.

The feet, which had been bound so as never to walk, were loosed *again* and stretched and ministered patiently to Christ Jesus, the Son of God.

Other rhetorical features of this homily that deserve mention include a carefully crafted polemical section (a *psogos*)[35] against the Pharisees or high priests (who appear to be confused with one another), taking John 11:46–50 as its point of departure and a number of exclamatory "O" anaphoras. The concluding peroration of the homily contains a list of miracles that corresponds to the list in the exordium. It is doubtful that this homily could have been delivered extemporaneously even by an experienced preacher. The rhetorical construction is far too complicated and suggests very careful composition. It is filled with biblical citations and allusions, as may be observed from some of the passages quoted. Of course the homily could have been composed and then memorized for delivery.

Another homily attributed to Athanasius, "on the sufferings of Christ Jesus and on the fear of the judgment place," contains similar rhetorical fea-

---

35. On this rhetorical figure, see Lausberg, *Handbuch der literarischen Rhetorik*, §§61 and 1129.

tures.[36] The homily itself is shorter and somewhat less ornate, but begins with an elaborate exordium in two parts in the form of an invitation to the "marriage feast." After an initial exhortation not to be like the foolish virgins and to "prepare yourselves inwardly and outwardly to go into the marriage feast," a lengthy anaphora of ten antitheses is introduced, of which I quote only the first three [fol. 100v2]:

ΝΡΜΜΑΟ ΜΜΑΤΕ ΑΝ ΝΕΤΝΚΑΛΕΙ ΜΜΟΟΥ · ΑΛΛΑ ΤΝΚΑΛΕΙ ΟΝ ΝΝ2ΗΚΕ
Ν2ΟΟΥΤ ΜΜΑΤΕ ΑΝ ΝΕΤΝΚΑΛΕΙ ΜΜΟΟΥ ΑΛΛΑ ΤΝΚΑΛΕΙ ΟΝ ΝΝΚΕ2ΙΟΜΕ ·
Ν2ΕΝ6ΙΝΟΥΩΜ ΑΝ ΕΥΧΑ2Μ ΝΕΤΟΥΝΑΚΑΑΥ 2ΑΡΩΤΝ · ΑΛΛΑ
2ΝΤΡΟΦΗ ΜΠΝΙΚΟΝ ΝΕΤΟΥΝΑΚΑΑΥ 2ΑΡΩΤΝ ΕΤΡΕΤΕΤΝΧΙ ΕΒΟΛ Ν2ΗΤΟΥ

Not only the rich do we invite, but we also invite the poor.
Not only men do we invite, but we also invite women.
No defiled food will be offered you, but spiritual food will be offered you to partake of.

The second section of the exordium consists of a series of exhortations also based on the theme of the marriage feast—not to come with dirty clothing, not to lust after the wives of others, not to slander the other guests, etc. The exordium ends with an exhortation to beseech God to send his Spirit "to supply us with speech and to open the heart of each one of us that we may keep the commandments of God and of His only begotten Son, Jesus Christ our Lord."

The rest of the homily is divided into three sections, loosely text-based and each with the theme of one of the three times that "the Father grieved." The first section is based on a series of quotations from Genesis beginning with the creation of man (Gen. 1:26) and mentioning the creation of woman, the killing of Abel, and the flood, and concluding with the Father grieving over Adam when his body was buried. The second, longer section is dedicated to the grief of the Father when his Son was crucified by the Jews on the cross. It is based on the account in John's Gospel and contains polemic against the "lawless Jews." This second section concludes with a lengthy anaphora on the grief of the Father, which begins as follows:

ΑΝΑΥ 6Ε ΕΠΕΙΩΤ ΕΨΘΕΩΡΕΙ ΜΠΕΨΩΗΡΕ ΕΥΤΕΙΒΤ ΝΑΨ Ε2ΟΥΝ ΕΠΩΕ
ΜΠΕΣΤΑΥΡΟΣ

---

36. J. B. Bernadin, "A Coptic Sermon attributed to St. Athanasius," *JTS* 38 (1937): 113–29. Depuydt, *Catalogue of Coptic Manuscripts*, no. 170, 7 (p. 348). The manuscript is M595, fols. 100v–108r. CPG 2184: In passionem.

ⲁⲛⲁⲩ ⲉⲡⲉⲙ̄ⲕⲁϩ ⲛ̄ϩⲏⲧ [fol.104v2] ⲙ̄ⲡⲉⲓⲱⲧ ⲉⲣⲉⲛⲉϥϣⲏⲣⲉ ⲁⲓⲧⲉⲓ ⲛ̄ⲟⲩⲕⲟⲩⲓ̈ⲙ̄ⲙⲟⲟⲩ ϩⲓⲡⲉⲥⲧⲁⲩⲣⲟⲥ ⲉⲩϯ ⲛⲁϥ ⲛ̄ⲟⲩϩⲙ̄ϫ ⲙ̄ⲡⲟⲩⲥⲓϣⲉ ·
ⲁⲛⲁⲩ ⲉⲡⲉⲓⲱⲧ ⲉⲣⲉⲙ̄ⲙⲁⲧⲟⲓ̈ ⲡⲱϣ ⲛ̄ⲛ̄ϩⲟⲓ̈ⲧⲉ ⲙ̄ⲡⲉϥϣⲏⲣⲉ ⲉϫⲱⲟⲩ ⲉⲩⲛⲉϫ ⲕⲗⲏⲣⲟⲥ ⲉϫⲛ̄ⲧⲉϥϩⲃ̄ⲥⲱ ·

Behold, indeed, the Father as He looked upon his Son as they nailed him to the wood of the cross.

Behold the deep sorrow of the Father as his Son asked for a little water on the cross and they gave him vinegar and gall.

Behold the Father as the soldiers divided the garments of his Son among them and cast lots for his clothing.

After a brief transitional passage summarizing the sorrows of the Father, the homily passes to the third section, on the final judgment. This contains an intricate passage in which the heathen are questioned about their worship of the sun, the moon, the stars, the idols, and sticks and stones. Each of these objects of worship then comes before the judgment seat to testify against the heathen. The homily concludes with a final peroration on the great division to take place on the last day and the grief of the Son and the Father and the angels over the destruction of sinners.

Although these two homilies belong to two different forms of the text-based homily, they contain a sufficient number of rhetorical elements in common, including the elaborate exordium, the frequent use of anaphora, and the polemic against the Jews, that a common authorship could be imagined. The comparison of the Lord weeping over Lazarus with the grief of the Father over Adam at the end of the first section of the second homily suggests another contact between the two pieces: "For as our Saviour in His goodness wept over Lazarus in Bethany [John 11:35], so on the other hand again did the Father grieve over Adam when his body was buried under the earth."

Two Sermons Attributed to Evodius of Rome

It may be instructive to compare the rhetorical elements in these two pseudepigraphical works with two other pseudepigraphical compositions attributed to Evodius of Rome, a sermon (ⲗⲟⲅⲟⲥ) on the death of the Virgin Mary and a sermon (ⲗⲟⲅⲟⲥ) on the Passion and Resurrection.[37] Evodius of Rome,

---

37. The latter has been published with translation by P. Chapman in *Homiletica from the Pierpont Morgan Library: Seven Coptic Homilies Attributed to Basil the Great, John Chrysostom, and Euodius of*

unlike the well-known historical figure of Athanasius, is a nonexistent or fictive person created by the author or authors of these homilies. However, the intent was probably pseudepigraphical, that is, to attribute the contents of the writings to an authoritative figure, in this case a person who supposedly belonged to the group of the "seventy disciples" mentioned in Luke's Gospel.[38] The first of these sermons begins with a statement of the theme, praise of the Virgin Mary:

ΟΥΠΡΕΠΩΝ ΠΕ ΑΥΩ ΟΥΔΙΚΑΙΟΝ ΠΕ · ΝΙΜ · 2Ι ϹΜΟΥ ΝΙΜ ΝΤΝΧΟΕΙϹ ΤΗΡΝ ΤΕΘΕΩ-
ΔΟΚΟϹ ΕΤ ΕΤΡΕΝ†ΤΑΙΟ ΟΥΑΑΒ ΜΑΡΙΑ · ΤΝΠΡΕϹΒΕΥΤΗϹΤΕ ΤΠΡΕϹΒΕΥΕ 2ΑΡΟΝ
ΝΟΥΟΕΙϢ ΝΙΜ ΝΝΑ2ΡΗ ΠΝΟΥΤΕ · ΤΡΡΩ ΜΠΓΕΝΟϹ ΤΗΡϤ ΝΝΕ2ΙΟΜΕ · ΑΥΩ ΤΜΑΑΥ ΜΠΡ-
ΡΟ ΝΝΡΡΩΟΥ · ΠΝΧΟΕΙϹ Ι͞Ϲ ΠΕΧ͞Ϲ :~

It is fitting and right for us to give all praise and all blessing to our Lady of us all, the holy Theotokos Mary. She is our intercessor, interceding for us at all times in the presence of God, the Queen of the whole race of women and the Mother of the king of kings, our Lord Jesus the Christ.

There follows an intricate exordium comparing the wedding feast prepared by an earthly king for his son with that prepared in the heavens for this feast. After a lengthy description of the earthly marriage feast, the author turns to a description of the heavenly one with the transitional comment:

ΑΥΩ ΝΑΙ ΤΗΡΟΥ ϢΑΥϢΩΠΕ ΕΤΒΕ ΟΥϢΕΛΕΕΤ ΝΤΕ ΠΕΙΚΟϹΜΟϹ : ~
ΚΑΙ ΓΑΡ ϢΑΡΕΠΕΥΡΑϢΕ ΚΟΤϤ ΕΥ2ΗΒΕ · ΜΝΝϹΑ ΟΥΚΟΥΪ 2ΙΤΜ ΠΜΟΥ :~
ΕΙΕ ΟΥΑϢ ΝϬΟΤ ΠΕ ΠΡΑϢΕ ΕΤΠΟΡϢ ΝΑΝ ΕΒΟΛ ΜΠΟΟΥ 2Ν ΤΜΗΤΕ ΝΝΤΑΓΜΑ ΤΗΡΟΥ
ΝΜΠΗΥΕ: ·
ΝΑΓΓΕΛΟϹ ΜΝ ΝΑΡΧΑΓΓΕΛΟϹ · ΝΕΧΕΡΟΥΒΙΝ · · ΜΝ ΝΕΖΕΡΑΦΙΝ · · ΝΕΘΡΟΝΟϹ · · ΜΝ
[Ν]Μ̄ΜΝΤ̄Ϭ̄Ϲ · ΝΑΡΧΗ · ΜΝ ΝΕΕΞΟΥϹΙΑ · ΕΥΡΑϢΕ ΕΥϹΤΟΛΙΖΕ · ΕΥΧΩΡΕΥΕ 2Ν
ΤϢΕΛΕΕΤ Μ̄ΠϢΗΡΕ ΜΠΡΡΟ · ·

And all these things happen on account of a bride of this world.
For indeed their rejoicing will turn to mourning after a little while because of death.
Then what sort of rejoicing is spread out for us today in the midst of the whole hierarchy of
    the heavens?

Rome, ed. Leo Depuydt et al., CSCO 524–25 (Louvain: Peeters, 1991), 524:79–106 (text); 525:83–114 (translation). The former has been published by Stephen J. Shoemaker, "The Sahidic Coptic Homily on the Dormition of the Virgin Attributed to Evodius of Rome: An Edition from Morgan MSS 596 & 598 with Translation," *AB* 14 (1999): 241–83. The translations of the "homily on the Dormition" quoted in this essay, however, are my own.

38. That is already evident in the unusually long inscriptions at the beginning of the two homilies, which include fictive elements (the dedication of a church to the Theotokos, Evodius as successor of Peter at Rome).

The angels, the archangels, the cherubim, the seraphim, the thrones, the dominations, the principalities and the powers [Col. 1:16], are rejoicing, are dressing up, and are setting forth[39] for the marriage of the king's son.

The exordium continues then with praise of the Virgin and an invitation to the kings (David and Solomon) and prophets (Isaiah, Ezekiel) to come to the feast. These are addressed explicitly because in each case a text attributed to them is invoked to describe a quality of the Virgin. The exordium concludes with the universal statement: "Blessed are you, O Mary, among the whole creation of women that God has created," which forms an inclusion with the opening of the sermon. This exclamation is also the beginning of an apostrophe addressed to the Virgin in which Evodius stresses his personal knowledge of the adult Jesus but also the wish that he could have seen him as a child with Mary: "I saw them with my eyes, I Evodius, the least,[40] who is speaking now in this sermon [ⲉⲝⲏⲅⲏⲥⲓⲥ], I and my fathers, the apostles, and the seventy-two disciples" (cf. Luke 10:1). There follow a series of three anaphoras. The first expresses these wishes:

ⲁⲗⲗⲁ ϩⲛⲛⲁⲓ̈ ⲧⲏⲣⲟⲩ ⲛⲉⲓⲟⲩⲱϣ ⲡⲉ · ⲉⲁⲓⲣⲡⲉⲙⲡϣⲁ ⲛⲛⲁⲩ ⲉⲣⲟϥ · ⲙⲡⲛⲁⲩ ⲉϥⲧⲁⲗⲏⲩ ⲉϫⲛ ⲛⲟⲩⲡⲁⲧ ⲉϥϭⲱϣⲧ ⲉϩⲟⲩⲛ ϩⲙ ⲡⲟⲩϩⲟ · ⲉϥⲥⲱⲃⲉ ⲉϩⲟⲩⲛ ⲉϩⲣⲁ ϩⲙ ⲡⲥⲱⲃⲉ · ⲛⲧⲉϥⲙⲛⲧⲛⲟⲩⲧⲉ ··

ⲉⲓⲟⲩⲱϣ ⲉⲛⲁⲩ ⲉⲣⲟ ⲱ ⲧⲉϩⲓⲁⲓⲃⲉ ⲛⲁⲧⲧⲱⲗⲙ · · ⲉⲣⲁⲙⲁϩⲧⲉ ⲛⲧϭⲓϫ ⲛⲙⲙⲁⲛⲟⲩⲏⲗ ⲡⲟⲩϣⲏⲣⲉ ⲉⲣϣⲁϫⲉ ⲛⲙⲙⲁϥ ⲉⲣϫⲱ ⲙ [f. 21r, col. 2] ⲙⲟⲥ ϫⲉ ⲙⲟⲟϣⲉ ⲙⲟⲟϣⲉ ⲡⲁϣⲏⲣⲉ ⲛⲑⲉ ⲛⲛϣⲏⲣⲉ ϣⲏⲙ ⲧⲏⲣⲟⲩ ⲉⲧⲟⲩⲧⲥⲁⲃⲟ ⲙⲙⲟⲟⲩ ⲉⲙⲟⲟϣⲉ · ⲛⲧⲟϥ ϩⲱⲱϥ ⲓ̅ⲥ̅ ⲡⲁϫⲟⲉⲓⲥ ⲡ̅ⲛⲉϥϭⲉⲓⲟⲩⲱϩ ⲟⲩⲱϩ · ϩⲛ ⲛⲉϥⲕⲟⲩⲓ ⲛϭⲟⲡ ⲉϥⲙⲟⲟϣⲉ ⲉϥϫⲓⲧⲁϭⲥⲉ · ⲛⲑⲉ ⲛⲛϣⲏⲣⲉ ⲕⲟⲩⲓ̈ ⲧⲏⲣⲟⲩ

ⲉⲓⲟⲩⲱϣ ⲉⲛⲁⲩ ⲉⲣⲟ ⲱ ⲡⲁϩⲟ ⲉⲧⲛⲉⲥⲱϥ ⲙⲡⲛⲁⲩ ⲉⲧϥϭⲱϣⲧ ⲉϩⲣⲁⲓ ϩⲁ ⲡⲟⲩϩⲟ ϩⲱⲥ ⲉϥϫⲱ ⲙⲙⲟⲥ ⲛⲉ ϫⲉ ⲧⲁⲗⲟⲓ ⲉϫⲱ · ⲱ ⲧⲁⲙⲁⲁⲩ ϫⲉ ⲁⲓϩⲓⲥⲉ ⲉⲓⲙⲟⲟϣⲉ :.

ⲉⲓⲟⲩⲱϣ ⲉⲛⲁⲩ ⲉⲣⲟ ⲱ ⲧⲉϭⲣⲟⲟⲙⲡⲉ ⲉⲧⲛⲉⲥⲟⲥ ⲉϥⲥⲟⲟⲩⲧⲛ ⲛⲧⲉϥϭⲓϫ ⲉⲃⲟⲗ ⲉϥⲁⲙⲁϩⲧⲉ ⲛⲧⲟⲩⲉⲕⲉⲓⲃⲉ ⲛⲁⲧⲧⲱⲗⲙ · ⲉϥϯ ⲙⲙⲟⲥ ⲉϩⲟⲩⲛ ⲉⲧⲉϥⲧⲁⲡⲣⲟ ⲛⲛⲟⲩⲧⲉ :.

But in all these things *I was wishing* that I had been worthy to see him raised on your knees, looking into your face, laughing in your face with the laughter of his divinity.

It is you that I wish to see, O spotless lamb, grasping the hand of Emanuel, your son, talking with him, saying [f. 21r, col. 2], "walk, walk, my son," like all little boys are taught to walk.

---

39. The Coptic form (ⲉⲅⲭⲱⲣⲉⲩⲉ) could be interpreted as "set forth" (χωρέω) or "dance" (χορεύω).

40. An allusion to 1 Cor. 15:9; Eph. 3:8. The term used by Paul of himself is being applied to Evodius.

He also, Jesus my Lord, will not walk steadily with his little feet, walking, following like all little boys.[41]

It is you that I wish to see, O beautiful treasure, when he looks up into your face as he says to you, "pick me up to you, O my mother, because I have become tired of walking."

It is you that I wish to see, O beautiful dove, as he stretches forth his hand and takes hold of your spotless breast, putting it into his divine mouth.

The second anaphora is a set of comparisons in which the Virgin is exalted above the sun, the moon, the angels, etc. The third is a long set of titles with a scriptural reference of which I quote only a few:

ⲱ ⲧⲉⲕⲗⲟⲟⲗⲉ ⲉⲧⲁⲥⲱⲟⲩ ⲉⲧⲉⲣⲉⲡⲛⲟⲩⲧⲉ ⲧⲁⲗⲏⲩ ⲉϫⲱⲥ ·
ⲱ ⲡϭⲉⲗⲙⲁϭⲓⲛ ⲛ̄ⲛⲟⲩⲃ ⲉⲧⲉⲣⲉⲡⲙⲁⲛⲛⲁ ϩⲏⲡ ⲛ̄ϩⲏⲧϥ̄ ·
ⲱ ⲧⲉϩⲉⲇⲣⲓⲁ ⲛⲃⲣⲣⲉ · ⲛ̄ⲧⲁⲡⲉϩⲙⲟⲩ ⲉⲧⲉⲛϩⲏⲧⲥ ϫⲱⲕⲣ ⲛ̄ⲛⲉⲛⲯⲩⲭⲏ ⲛ̄ⲧⲁⲩⲃⲁⲃⲉ ϩⲓⲧⲙ ⲡⲛⲟⲃⲉ ·
ⲱ ⲧⲕⲓⲃⲱⲧⲟⲥ ⲉⲧⲟⲩⲁⲁⲃ ⲉⲧⲉⲣⲉⲛⲉⲡⲗⲁⲝ ⲛ̄ⲧⲇⲓⲁⲑⲏⲕⲏ ϩⲓϩⲟⲩⲛ ⲙ̄ⲙⲟⲥ :-

O swift cloud [Isa. 19:1] upon which God is raised.
O golden vase in which the manna is hidden [Heb. 9:4].
O new water jug, in which the salt within it seasons our souls that have become insipid [cf. Matt. 5:13] through sin.
O holy ark in which are the tables of the covenant [Heb. 9:4].

At the end of this litany of titles there begins a lengthy apostrophe addressed to or denouncing the "impious Jew":

ⲉⲕⲧⲱⲛ ⲧⲉⲛⲟⲩ ⲱ ⲡⲉⲓⲟⲩⲇⲁⲓ̈ ⲛⲁⲅⲛⲱⲙⲱⲛ ⲡⲣⲉϥϩⲱⲧⲃ̄ ⲙ̄ⲡⲉϥϫⲟⲉⲓⲥ · · ⲡⲉⲓⲣⲉϥⲣⲡⲡⲉⲑⲟⲟⲩ ⲛ̄ⲛⲉⲧⲉⲣⲡⲉⲧⲛⲁⲛⲟⲩϥ ⲛⲁϥ . : .
ⲙⲁⲣⲉϥⲉⲓ ⲉⲡⲉⲓⲙⲁ ⲛ̄ⲡⲟⲟⲩ ⲛ̄ϥ̄ϫⲓϣⲓⲡⲉ ⲛⲁϥ [f. 21v, col. 2] ⲉϥⲥⲱⲧⲙ ⲉⲛⲉⲓⲙⲛ̄ⲧⲙⲛ̄ⲧⲣⲉ ⲧⲏⲣⲟⲩ :- ⲛ̄ⲧⲁⲛⲏ ⲉⲃⲟⲗ ϩⲙ ⲡⲉϥⲅⲉⲛⲟⲥ ϣⲣⲡⲡⲣⲟⲫⲉⲧⲉⲩⲉ ⲙ̄ⲙⲟⲟⲩ ϩⲁ ⲧⲉⲓⲡⲁⲣⲑⲉⲛⲟⲥ · ⲙⲛ ⲡⲉⲥϫⲡⲟ ⲉⲧⲥⲙⲁⲙⲁⲁⲧ · · · -

Where are you now, O impious Jew, slayer of his Lord [cf. Acts 2:23, 36; 3:15; 4:10; 5:30; 10:39], this doer of evil to those who do good to him [cf. Luke 6:9, 11]?

---

41. Shoemaker, "Sahidic Coptic Homily," translates the phrase: "He ... would not take step on step with his little feet." (261). Apart from the question of understanding the verb (ⲛ̄ⲛⲉϥϥⲉⲓⲟⲩⲱϩ) as 3rd future vs. imperfect (for which there is no obvious justification), which he discusses in note 5 (pp. 280–81), there is the question of what the phrase really means. Here the context must be taken into account. There is a theological point involved, namely, the question of the full humanity of Jesus. If the phrase were translated to mean that Jesus did not have difficulty learning to walk like all little children, then it would be contrary to the idea expressed in #38 (using the phrase from Luke 2:52) that he did grow like all men. The sections 40–42 are spelling out this idea. Therefore I have suggested the translation: "He ... will not walk steadily with his little feet."

Let him come to this place today and be ashamed listening to all the testimonies that those from his nation prophesied ahead of time concerning this virgin and her blessed giving-birth.

This section, a diatribe in the modern but not ancient sense of the word, occupies the entire middle part of the sermon and is organized in the form of scriptural testimonies that the Jews have supposedly ignored or texts that bear witness against and condemn them. Much of it is directed to the Jews in the form of questions, as if it was delivered in a courtroom. At the end of this lengthy indictment, which contains its own rhetorical subdivisions, the "preacher" turns to the theme of the death of the Virgin, which occupies the last third of the sermon.

ⲡⲗⲏⲛ ⲙⲁⲣⲉⲛⲕⲱⲛⲥⲱⲛ ⲛⲛⲁⲓ ⲛⲧⲉⲓⲙⲓⲛⲉ ·· ⲛⲧⲉⲛⲕⲧⲟⲛ ⲉϩⲣⲁⲓ ⲉϫⲙ ⲡⲙⲉⲅⲉⲑⲟⲥ [f. 23v.] ⲛⲧⲉⲓⲡⲁⲣⲑⲉⲛⲟⲥ ⲛⲣⲉϥϫⲡⲉⲡⲛⲟⲩⲧⲉ ⲛ̄ⲧⲛ̄ⲧⲁⲙⲟⲧⲛ ⲉⲡⲉϩⲟⲟⲩ ⲙ̄ⲡⲉⲥϫⲱⲕ ⲉⲃⲟⲗ ⲉⲧⲧⲁⲉⲓⲏⲩ:. ϫⲉⲕⲁⲥ ⲉⲣⲉⲛⲡⲓⲥⲧⲟⲥ ⲛⲁⲥⲱⲧⲙ ⲛⲥⲉϯⲉⲟⲟⲩ ⲙ̄ⲡⲛⲟⲩⲧⲉ :. -

ⲁⲩⲱ ⲛⲉϯⲛⲁϫⲟⲟⲩ ⲧⲏⲣⲟⲩ ⲛ̄ⲕⲉⲟⲩⲁ ⲁⲛ ⲡⲛⲧⲁϥⲛⲁⲩ ⲉⲣⲟⲟⲩ ⲁϥϫⲟⲟⲩ ⲉⲣⲟⲓ · ⲁⲗⲗⲁ ⲁⲛⲟⲕ ⲡⲛⲧⲁⲓ̈ⲛⲁⲩ ⲉⲣⲟⲟⲩ ϩⲛ ⲛⲁⲃⲁⲗ · ⲁⲩⲱ ⲁⲓϭⲙϭⲱⲙⲟⲩ ϩⲛ ⲛⲁϭⲓϫ · ϫⲉ ϣⲁⲩⲧⲁⲛϩⲉⲧⲡⲛⲁⲩ ⲛϩⲛ̄ⲃⲁⲗ ⲉϩⲟⲩⲉ ⲉⲡⲥⲱⲧⲙ ⲛ̄ϩⲛⲙⲁⲁϫⲉ:. -

But let us leave behind things of this sort and return to the greatness of this Virgin, Godbearer, and tell you about the day of her noble end, in order that the believers may hear and give glory to God.

And all the things that I will recount are not from another who saw them and told them to me, but it is I who saw them with my own eyes and I touched them with my own hands, because the sight of eyes is more trusted than the hearing of ears.

In fact what follows is a retelling of what is by this time traditional material regarding the death of the Virgin.[42] This includes another appearance of Jesus to his apostles and disciples just before they are to disperse to preach the gospel to the whole world, and at this time he announces the death of his mother to take place the following day. However, even in the retelling, the author adds rhetorical flourishes of his own, as in the following set of contrasts inserted just before Jesus invites his mother to prepare herself for death:

ⲱ ⲧⲁⲙⲁⲁⲩ [f. 24r, col. 2] ⲕⲁⲛ ⲉϣϫⲉ ⲁⲣⲉⲣⲡϯⲥ ⲛⲉⲃⲟⲧ ⲉⲣⲧⲱⲟⲩⲛ ϩⲁⲣⲟ ϩⲛ ⲧⲟⲩⲕⲁⲗⲁϩⲏ ⲉⲧⲟⲩⲁⲁⲃ ··

ⲁⲛⲟⲕ ϩⲱ ϯⲛⲁⲧⲱⲟⲩⲛ ϩⲁⲣⲟⲓ̈ ϩⲛ ⲛⲉⲥⲡⲗⲁⲭⲛⲟⲛ ⲛ̄ⲧⲁⲙⲛⲧϣⲛϩⲧⲏϥ

---

42. For the most recent treatment of this tradition, see Stephen J. Shoemaker, *Ancient Traditions of the Virgin Mary's Dormition and Assumption*, OECS (Oxford: Oxford University Press, 2002).

ⲁⲩⲱ ⲉϣϫⲉ ⲁⲣϩⲗⲟⲟⲗⲉ ⲙⲙⲟⲓ̈ ϩⲓϫⲛ̄ <ⲛ>ⲟⲩⲡⲁⲧ ⲙⲛ <ⲛ>ⲟⲩϭⲃⲟⲓ̈ ·· -

ⲁⲛⲟⲕ ϩⲱ ϯⲛⲁⲧⲁⲗⲟ ϩⲓϫⲛ ⲟⲩⲑⲣⲟⲛⲟⲥ ⲉϥϩⲁⲉⲟⲟⲩ ⲉϥϩⲓⲟⲩⲛⲁⲙ ⲙⲙⲟⲓ̈ ⲙⲛ ⲡⲁⲉⲓⲱⲧ ⲛ̄ⲛⲁⲅⲁⲑⲟⲥ ·

ⲉϣϫⲉ ⲁⲣⲥⲟⲩⲗⲱⲧ ⲛ̄ϩⲛ̄ⲧⲟⲉⲓⲥ ⲙ̄ⲡⲉϩⲟⲟⲩ ⲛ̄ⲧⲁⲣϫⲡⲟⲓ̈ ⲛ̄ϩⲏⲧϥ̄ · ⲁⲣⲕⲱ ⲙ̄ⲙⲟⲓ̈ ϩⲛ<ⲟⲩ>ⲟⲩⲟⲙϥ̄ ⲁⲩⲉϩⲉ · ⲙⲛ ⲟⲩⲉⲓⲱ ⲣ̄ϩⲁⲓⲃⲉⲥ ⲉⲣⲟⲓ̈

ⲁⲛⲟⲕ ϩⲱ ϯⲛⲁⲥⲕⲉⲡⲁⲍⲉ ⲙⲙⲟ ϩⲓϫⲉⲛ ⲛⲉⲧⲛϩ ⲛ̄ⲛⲉⲍⲉⲣⲁⲫⲛ : -

ⲁⲩⲱ ⲉϣϫⲉ ⲁⲣⲁⲥⲡⲁⲍⲉ ⲙⲙⲟⲓ̈ ϩⲛ ⲧⲟⲩⲧⲁⲡⲣⲟ ⲁ<ⲣ>ⲥⲁⲛⲟⲩϣⲧ ϩⲛ ⲧⲟⲩⲉⲣⲱⲧⲉ ⲙ̄ⲡⲁⲣⲑⲉⲛⲓⲕⲱⲛ ··

ⲁⲛⲟⲕ ϩⲱ ϯⲛⲁⲁⲥⲡⲁⲍⲉ ⲙⲙⲟ ⲙⲡⲙ̄ⲧⲟ ⲉⲃⲟⲗ ⲙ̄ⲡⲁⲉⲓⲱⲧ ⲉⲧϩⲛ̄ⲙ̄ⲡⲏⲩⲉ · ⲁⲩⲱ ⲡⲁⲉⲓⲱⲧ ⲛⲁⲧⲙⲟ ⲉⲃⲟⲗ ϩⲛ ⲡⲟⲉⲓⲕ ⲙⲙⲉ ·

O my mother, even if you did indeed spend nine months bearing me in your holy womb,
   I for my part will bear you in the bowels of my mercy
and if you nursed me on your knees and with your arms,
   I for my part will set you on a glorious throne at the right hand of me and my good Father.
If you wrapped me in swaddling clothes on the day when you gave birth to me and laid me in a manger [Luke 2:7] and an ox and an ass overshadowed me [Isa. 1:3],
   I for my part will shelter you with the wings of the Seraphim.
And if you kissed me with your mouth and nursed me with your virgin milk,
   I for my part will embrace you in the presence of my Father who is in the heavens and my Father will nourish you with the true bread [John 6:32].

The sermon concludes with the account of the Virgin's death, the preparation of her body for burial, her reappearance (or that of her soul) on a chariot of light, the procession with her body to the tomb, during which angels come and bear her body away, and a final appearance of Jesus to reassure his disciples with the command to celebrate the feast of her death on the twenty-first of the month of Tobe. It is obvious that the sermon was composed to be read on that date.

The other sermon attributed to Evodius of Rome has many features in common with this one, but, from a rhetorical point of view, shows notable differences.[43] As in the case of the sermon on the Virgin, this one also has an unusually long inscription with fictive elements. Evodius is named the second "patriarch and archbishop of Rome" after Peter, and the sermon is said to have been delivered on the feast of the Resurrection on the day when he baptized "Didymus the Jew and high priest" during the consulate of Claudius the

---

43. See my article "A Homily on the Death of the Virgin Mary" (note 10 above) for a summary of the linguistic similarities.

emperor. Didymus had supposedly been spared expulsion when Claudius expelled all the other Jews. This notable error of chronology suggests that the author was not acquainted with the Eusebian traditions about the deaths of Peter and Paul during the reign of Nero or was confused about the chronology of the emperors.[44] As in the previous sermon, Evodius presents himself in the sermon as an eyewitness of the events he relates: "Rather, I too was there when this was about to happen" (#4).[45]

One of the striking features of this composition is the amount of legal language employed in it. The opening line states that "it is the custom of the Romans to establish justice at all times because they are lovers of mankind," and the author seems to suggest that the Romans have made use of the scriptures as well. The phrase "the laws of the Romans" (ⲚⲚⲞⲘⲞⲤ ⲚⲚⲈϨⲢⲰⲘⲀⲒⲞⲤ) occurs numerous times (#1,4,46,51), and the phrase "the entire law code of the Romans" (ⲦⲚⲞⲘⲞⲐⲨⲤⲒⲀ ⲦⲎⲢⲤ ⲚⲚⲈϨⲢⲰⲘⲀⲒⲞⲤ), once. Roman legal practice is portrayed favorably: "the Romans strive for all justice to stand" (#23); "the laws are carried out in that city" (#25). When Pilate announces that he will wash his hands, he is made to say, "For it is Solon and Dracon who have established the laws of my people. They command my people as follows: when the accusers stand up to prove someone's guilt, let not the judge pronounce a sentence because he will be worthy of responsibility and the person's blood will come on the head of the witnesses." Evodius continues: "The latter statement the Romans found in the teaching of the wise man Moses" (#46).

Much of the sermon reads like a legal review of the trial of Jesus in which the author argues against the charges of the Jews and portrays them as the lawless ones for bringing false charges. When Evodius arrives at the scene of Jesus before Pilate, he states, "he [Pilate] ordered that the prosecutors [ⲔⲀⲦⲎⲄⲞⲢⲞⲤ] speak first in accordance with the law of the Romans. Indeed, I recall that I said at the beginning of the homily [ⲦⲀⲢⲬⲎ ⲚⲞⲨⲠⲞⲐⲈⲤⲒⲤ] that the Romans strive for all justice to stand. For the prosecutors were numerous, but a true crime was not found." Here the translator has rendered the phrase as ⲦⲀⲢⲬⲎ ⲚⲞⲨⲠⲞⲐⲈⲤⲒⲤ, "the beginning of the homily." However, the word

---

44. See Eusebius *HE* 2.22 (SC 31:83–85). The History of the Patriarchs of Alexandria does not relate the death of Peter and Paul. Peter sends Mark to Alexandria in the fifteenth year after the Ascension. See B. Evetts, *History of the Patriarchs of the Coptic Church of Alexandria*, PO 1, 2, Arabic text edited, translated, and annotated by B. Evetts (Paris: Firmin-Didot, 1910), part I, chap. 1, p. 140.

45. The numbers are those of Depuydt's edition (see note 37 above).

ὑπόθεσι has a technical legal meaning translated in Latin as "causa."[46] Thus it refers to a legal process, which strengthens the impression that the author understands himself to be relating a legal process and thinking in terms of legal (forensic) rhetoric. This is further underlined by Evodius's answer to his own rhetorical question in an apostrophe to the Jews: "Why are you condemning Christ, O Jews? Tell me the crime. It is I who speak to you in his defense" (#17). In fact, the sermon is at the same time a defense of Jesus and a case for the prosecution of the Jews.

The Use of Scripture and the Technique of Composition

About halfway through the sermon (#40), the author introduces a hypothetical objection: "someone who is among the brothers will tell me, 'You have added to the words of the holy gospel.'" There follows a lengthy and elaborate explanation and justification of the author's method of composition:

> The wool provided for the purple cloth of the king, before its mixtures, with which it is dyed, are applied to it, can be made useful by being fabricated into clothing and being worn as one pleases. Yet when it is worked upon and dyed in colorful mixtures, it becomes exceedingly brilliant and becomes radiant clothing, so that the king wears it. Thus the holy gospels, when he who will be ordained a shepherd acts according to their words and reveals them, become illuminated exceedingly. And they are very brilliant in the heart of those who listen. Indeed the king will not find fault if beautifully crafted plaits are added to his garments, but he will commend those who have added them exceedingly, so that everyone might praise the garment because of the plaits which are on it. Thus, the Lord Jesus will not find fault with us if we add a few embellishments to the holy gospels, but he will commend us all the more and bless those who bear fruit through them.

The justification continues with the observation that there are many matters not treated in the Gospels, which the customs of the church have established, citing also John 21:25 that there are many things Jesus did that are not contained in the Gospels.

In fact the compositional technique of this writer is to embroider on the

---

46. See Lausberg, *Handbuch der literarischen Rhetorik*, section 73. The distinction of thesis and hypothesis apparently goes back to Hermagoras. See Kennedy, *Classical Rhetoric and Its Christian and Secular Tradition*, 99.

words of the gospel. An example will serve to illustrate his method. After citing Pilate's question to Christ, "Where are you from?" (John 19:9), "Evodius" continues:

When the judge saw that he did not reply on his own behalf, he spoke according to the authority of the world threateningly, "Why do you not speak to me? Do you not know that I am a governor and that you have been delivered to me so that I might act toward you according to my authority? If I wish to release you, there is no one who will be able to contradict me. And if I wish to crucify you, there is no one who will be able to oppose me" [cf. John 19:10]. "As for me, I am without sin, O governor, and I want to die for the sins of the entire world until I purify it. I want to draw the burden upon myself in order that that which I have formed walks swiftly into the kingdom while there is no one restraining them. My father has given you this authority, O governor, and I will not disobey you, O governor. I am an obedient God and I have humbled myself because of his will" [cf. John 19:11].

This technique of embroidery or expansion is repeated throughout the homily.

Summary and Conclusion

In the four homilies or sermons discussed above, we have noted four different ways of relating to the scriptures. The first homily attributed to Athanasius follows the classical pattern established by Origen of citing the text in short pericopes and then offering commentary.[47] In this case most of John 11 is quoted. The second homily, also attributed to Athanasius, is text-based in the sense that texts of Genesis and John are used as the points of departure for commentary. The third composition, the first of the Evodius pieces, is not text-based in the same sense, although it contains numerous citations of and allusions to scriptural texts. Its point of departure is rather praise of the Virgin centering on her death, an event narrated in the apocryphal tradition rather than in scripture. It belongs to the genre of encomium rather than that of text-based homily. The fourth sermon, also of Evodius, uses the passion narrative as a basis for its own narrative of the trial of Jesus, but embroiders and expands on it rather than commenting or interpreting it. This last sermon shows extensive affinity with the forensic rhetorical tradition. In all four of these sermons extensive use is made of traditional rhetorical figures and devices such

---

47. See Sheridan, *Rufus of Shotep*, 37–38. The homilies by Rufus are the only ones known in Coptic that follow Origen's practice of preaching on the basis of *lectio continua* of a biblical book.

as the elaborate exordium, apostrophe, anaphora, and antithesis. These compositions, apparently original in Coptic, show a certain acquaintance with the high rhetorical style of Greek works of the late fourth and early fifth centuries and are a witness to the Coptic literary culture of the fifth and sixth centuries.

Only a detailed analysis of all the literary compositions that fall into the broad category of homily or sermon in terms of their literary genre and their use of rhetorical devices, tropes, etc., will make it possible eventually to write a history of this material, which extends over a period of more than five hundred years. This could be facilitated if editors and translators were to take into account the ancient rhetorical forms and keep in mind that ancient writers did not think in terms of neatly organized paragraphs developing a theme in the manner of modern writers, but rather in terms of exordium, apostrophe, anaphora, and all the other traditional rhetorical devices that could be inserted into the composition.[48] In fact, almost everything remains to be done in this field. The purpose of this article has been to offer a few hints regarding the complex nature of the task.

---

48. In this regard it may be useful to underline the importance of the study of the *progymnasmata* or preliminary exercises in composition in later Greek rhetorical education. Varying lists of these exercises are given by ancient authors. See Kennedy, *Classical Rhetoric and Its Christian and Secular Tradition*, 52–73. Kennedy observes: "Much of later Greek literature can be analyzed in terms of structural units such as the narrative, the *thesis*, the *synkrisis*, and the *ecphrasis*, which are used as building blocks for larger works" (53). That this should hold true for the Coptic homilies analyzed here is hardly surprising, since the models were Greek. See now also George A. Kennedy, trans. with introduction and notes, *Progymnasmata. Greek Textbooks of Prose Composition and Rhetoric* (Atlanta: Society of Biblical Literature, 2003).

Monica J. Blanchard

SARABAITAE AND REMNUOTH

Coptic Considerations

Jerome (*Epist.* 22.34)[1] and Cassian (*Conlat.* 18.4,7)[2] independently list three different classes of Egyptian monks. Each list includes two classes, which are noted with approval. Jerome names first the cenobites (*coenobium*), who, he says, are called *sauhes* in Coptic.[3] The anchorites (*anachoretae*) are Jerome's

---

1. Jerome, *Epist.* 22.34 (CSEL 54:196–97).
2. Cassian, *Conlat.* 18.4 (CSEL 13:509, 513). Reprinted in SC 64:14.
3. For *sauhes*, see the entry "ⲤⲞⲞⲨϨⲤ, -ⲀϨⲤ," in Walter Ewing Crum, *A Coptic Dictionary* (Oxford: Clarendon Press, 1939), 373b–74a; also "ⲤⲞⲞⲨϨⲤ; ⲤⲞⲞⲨⲀϨⲤ," in Werner Vycichl, *Dictionnaire étymologique de la langue copte* (Leuven: Peeters, 1983), 202. ⲤⲞⲞⲨϨⲤ, "congregation, collection," translates variously the Greek ἐκκλησία (1 Cor. 16:19) and συναγωγή (Obad. 13). It includes among its meanings the sense of a monastic congregation. Crum cites its appearance in the Sahidic *Life of Apa Onophrios* in E. A. W. Budge, *Coptic Martyrdoms etc. in the Dialect of Upper Egypt, Edited, with English Translations* (London: British Museum, 1914), 210 (Coptic): ⲈⲒϢⲞⲠ ⲆⲈ ⲚϨ ⲞⲨⲤⲞⲞⲨϨⲤ ⲚⲘⲞⲚⲀⲬⲞⲤ ϨⲘⲠⲦⲞⲞⲨ ⲚϢⲘⲞⲨⲚ ⲚⲦⲈ ⲐⲎⲂⲀⲒⲤ ⲠⲢⲀⲚ ⲆⲈ ⲚⲐⲈⲚⲈⲈⲦⲈ ⲈⲦⲘⲘⲀⲨ ⲠⲈ ⲈⲢⲎⲦⲈ, and 460 (English): "I lived at one time in a habitation of monks, in the mountain of Shmûn of the Thebaïd. And the name of that monastery was Erête." Crum points out that in the Bohairic version of this *Life*, edited and translated by Émile Amélineau, "Voyage d'un moine égyptien dans le désert," *Recueil des travaux relatifs à la philologie et à l'archéologie égyptiennes et assyriennes* 6 (1885): 175, ⲤⲞⲞⲨϨⲤ is replaced by the word ⲀⲂⲎⲦ: ⲚⲀⲒϢⲞⲠ ⲠⲈ ϦⲈⲚ ⲞⲨⲀⲂⲎⲦ ⲘⲘⲞⲚⲀⲬⲞⲤ ϦⲈⲚ ⲠϬⲰϢ ϢⲘⲞⲨⲚ ϦⲈⲚ ⲪⲚⲀⲢⲎⲤ ⲤⲀⲂⲞⲖ ⲚⲈϨⲢⲒⲦ (175 top), and: "J'étais (auparavant) dans une laure de moines dans le nôme de Schmaun, dans le Sahid, en dehors de Ehrit." The Sahidic *Life* comes from B.M. Oriental no. 7027, which bears a date of A.M. 721, AH 395 [that is, AD 1004]. See Bentley Layton, *Catalogue of Coptic Literary Manuscripts in the British Library Acquired since the Year 1906* (London: British Library, 1987), 192–93. The Bohairic *Life* appears in Vatican Coptic 65, fols. 99–120ᵛ, dated A.M. 695 [that is, AD 979] according to Adolphe Hebbelynck and Arnold van Lantschoot, *Codices Coptici Vaticani, Barberiniani, Borgiani, Rossiani* (Vatican City: Bibliotheca Vaticana, 1937), 1:472.

second class of monks. Cassian's list also includes cenobites (*coenobitae*) and anchorites (*anachoretae*) as the first two of the three classes. Both Cassian and Jerome describe a third, somewhat disreputable group of monks, called *remnuoth* by Jerome and *sarabaitae* by Cassian. Jerome and Cassian present the terms as Coptic words. Both terms have occasioned much interest and speculation; neither one appears in extant Coptic monastic texts.[4]

In 1994 I presented a fuller version of this essay at the twentieth annual meeting of the Byzantine Studies Conference in Ann Arbor, Michigan. I reviewed various linguistically unsatisfactory Coptic etymologies proposed for *remnuoth* and *sarabaitae*. Most of them involved the Coptic word ⲀⲨⲎⲦ, ⲀⲂⲎⲦ with a meaning of "monastic congregation, monastery." I also drew attention to the more persuasive solutions first suggested by Paul Ernst Jablonski[5] for *remnuoth* and by Walter Ewing Crum for *sarabaitae*.[6] Since 1994 many scholars have examined the question. In this essay I connect my earlier conclusions with recent work in the hope that others may benefit from a review of the evidence, including unpublished material from the collection of the Institute of Christian Oriental Research at Catholic University.

Jablonski identified *remnuoth* as a compound of the Coptic ⲢⲰⲘⲈ man, Ⲛ̅- genitive marker, and ⲞⲨⲰⲦ single or one; thus ⲢⲘⲚⲞⲨⲰⲦ = Greek μονάζων.[7] His work was published in 1804, some fifty years after his death in 1757. Jablonski's thesis has received incidental support from the Coptic *Gospel of Thomas*, which contains *logia* or sayings in which the phrase ⲞⲨⲀ ⲞⲨⲰⲦ, i.e.,

---

4. Explicitly so by Cassian in *Conlat.* 18.7: "... a nonnullorum contemplatione paulatim longa incuria et temporis oblitteratione subtracto emersit istud Sarabaitarum genus, qui ab eo, quod semet ipsos a coenobiorum congregationibus sequestrarent ac singillatim suas curarent necessitates, Aegyptiae linguae proprietate Sarabaitae nuncupati sunt..." (CSEL 13.2.7). See note 16 below.

5. Paul Ernst Jablonski, *Pauli Ernesti Iablonskii Opuscula*, ed. Iona Guilielmus te Water (Lugduni Batavorum: Luchtmans, 1804–13), 1:229. For a modern appreciation of Jablonski as a Coptologist, see J. Helderman, "Jablonski en Te Water. Twee Koptologen uit de tijd van de 'Verlichting,'" *Phoenix* 30 (1984): 54–62. In 1912 Spiegelberg's student Adolf Jacoby published a brief article, "Der Name der Sarabaiten," in *Recueil de travaux relatifs à la philologie et à l'archéologie égyptiennes et assyriennes* 34 [i.e., n.s. 2] (1912): 15–16. In note 5 Jacoby describes Spiegelberg's acceptance of Jablonski's proposed etymology. Spiegelberg's *Koptisches Handwörterbuch* (Heidelberg: Carl Winters Universitätsbuchhandlung, 1921) does not include the spelling ⲖⲞⲨⲞⲦ. See pp. 2, 11.

6. See note 11 below.

7. Jacoby's 1912 note concerning Jablonski's proposed etymology of *remnuoth* seems to have attracted little if any attention. The credit for a clear and concise examination and presentation of Jablonski's etymology belongs to Werner Vycichl. See Vycichl, *Dictionnaire étymologique de la langue copte*, 173–74.

"single one,"⁸ appears in tandem with the Greek word μοναχός.⁹ These *logia* have been studied with a view to sorting out the various shades of meaning of μοναχός, μονάζων in the Greek-speaking tradition and of *iḥidayâ* in the Syriac-speaking tradition.¹⁰

Walter Crum understood *sarabaitae* as a corruption of an authentic Coptic word: ⲥⲁⲣⲁⲕⲱⲧⲉ, ⲥⲁⲣⲁⲕⲟⲧⲉ.¹¹ This word has been found in Coptic texts dating from the mid-fourth century to the last quarter of the fourteenth century. Latin *gyrovagus* and Greek κυκλευτής are within its range of meanings.¹²

8. On the Coptic words ⲟⲩⲁ ⲟⲩⲱⲧ, see Crum, *Coptic Dictionary*, 494a.

9. Cf., e.g., *Log.* 16 and 23 in Antoine Guillaumont, Henri-Charles Puech, Gilles Quispel, Walter Till, and Yassah 'Abd Al Masîh, *The Gospel According to Thomas: Coptic Text Established and Translated* (Leiden: Brill, and New York: Harper & Row, 1959), 11–13 (*Log.* 16), 18–19 (*Log.* 23). The translators underline a connection between the Greek and Coptic words in a note at the bottom of p. 19: "single one"; same sense as μοναχός in p. 84, 4.

10. Paul-Hubert Poirier has made the correlation between the Coptic ⲟⲩⲁ ⲟⲩⲱⲧ and the Syriac *iḥidayâ* in Aphrahat's *Demonstration* XVIII. See his "L'Évangile selon Thomas (*log.* 16 et 23) et Aphraate (*Dém.* XVIII, 10–11)," in *Mélanges Antoine Guillaumont: Contributions à l'étude des christianismes orientaux*, Cahiers d'Orientalisme 20 (Geneva: Patrick Cramer, 1988), 15–8. See also A. F. J. Klijn, "The 'Single One' in the Gospel of Thomas," *JBL* 81 (1962): 271–78. For more on the *iḥidayâ*, see Sidney H. Griffith, "'Singles' in God's Service: Thoughts on the Ihidaye from the Works of Aphrahat and Ephraem the Syrian," *The Harp* 4 (1991): 145–59; Sidney H. Griffith, "Monks, 'Singles', and the 'Sons of the Covenant': Reflections on Syriac Ascetic Terminology," in *Eulogēma: Studies in Honor of Robert Taft, S.J.*, ed. E. Carr, S. Parenti, A. A. Thiermeyer, and E. Velkovska, SA 110 (Rome: [Centro Studi S.Anselmo,] 1993), 141–60; Sidney H. Griffith, "Asceticism in the Church of Syria: The Hermeneutics of Early Syrian Monasticism," in *Asceticism*, ed. Vincent L. Wimbush and Richard Valantasis (New York: Oxford University Press, 1995), 220–45. On the Greek μοναχός, see Françoise E. Morard, "Monachos, moine. Histoire du terme grec jusqu'au 4e siècle: Influences bibliques et gnostiques," *FZPhTh* 20 (1973): 332–411; Françoise E. Morard, "Encore quelques réflexions sur monachos," *VC* 34 (1980): 395–401.

11. Crum, *Coptic Dictionary*, 354–55. Hugh G. Evelyn-White also made this connection around the same time. See his *The Monasteries of the Wadi 'n Natrûn* (New York: Metropolitan Museum of Art, 1926–33), 2:15n1: "Cassian's third class of monks, the Sarabaitae—Jerome's Remoboth—had no discipline or organization, and were of low repute; probably they were the unworthy successors of the earlier ascetics who dwelt outside towns and villages. As to the names given to these monks by Cassian and Jerome, the former surely equals the Coptic ⲥⲁⲣⲁⲕⲱⲧⲉ, 'man of Alexandria,' i.e., 'rogue,' the 'b' being a corruption of k." It would be possible to mishear/miswrite Coptic ⲥⲁⲣⲁⲕⲱⲧⲉ as *sarabaitae* in Latin. See Francis Thomas Gignac, *A Grammar of the Greek Papyri of the Roman and Byzantine Periods* (Milan: Istituto Editoriale Cisalpino–La Goliardica, 1976, 1981), 1:68, 76–86, on the interchange between Coptic K and Latin B.

12. Two etymologies have been suggested for ⲥⲁⲣⲁⲕⲱⲧⲉ. Crum, Werner Vycichl, Wolfhart Westendorf, and Peter Nagel list it as a compound form built up from ⲥⲁ + ⲉⲓⲣⲉ "to do" + ⲕⲱⲧⲉ, a verb meaning "to turn, to wander, to go astray"; J. Černý suggests instead the *participium coniunctum* form of ⲥⲱⲣⲉ, "to scatter, spread, distribute." See Crum, *Coptic Dictionary*, 316 (ⲥⲁ) and 354–55 (ⲥⲁⲣⲁⲕⲱⲧⲉ); Vycichl, *Dictionnaire étymologique de la langue copte*, 196; W. Westendorf, *Koptisches Handwörterbuch* (Heidelberg: Carl Winter Universitätsverlag, 1965, 1977), 194; J. Černý, *Coptic Etymological Dictionary*

New perceptions of early Egyptian monasticism have emerged from careful studies of nonliterary sources.[13] The categories of Jerome and Cassian have been reviewed as more attention has been paid to local Egyptian documentary materials. Efforts have been made to specify the geographical, historical, and theological contexts in which early monastic terminology is found in order to highlight ranges and shifts in meaning of the terms.[14] There has been considerable interest in monastic terminology in Coptic Egypt in the past ten years. The contributions of Jürgen Horn (1994), Antoine Guillaumont (1995), Ugo Zanetti (1997), Christian Cannuyer (2001), and Malcolm Choat (2004) are very important for an understanding of *sarabaitae* and *remnuoth*.[15] I refer the reader to Horn, Guillaumont, and Choat for their discussions of *remnuoth*.[16]

(Cambridge: Cambridge University Press, 1976), 161: "lit. 'he who spreads going round', cf. gyrovagus, κυκλευτής."

13. See, e.g., E. A. Judge, "The Earliest Use of Monachos for 'Monk' (P. Coll. Youtie 77) and the Origins of Monasticism," *JAC* 20 (1977): 72–89 ; E. A. Judge and S. R. Pickering, "Papyrus Documentation of Church and Community in Egypt," *JAC* 20 (1977): 47–71; and the following five articles by Ewa Wipszycka: "Fonctionnement de l'Église égyptienne aux IVe–VIIIe siècles (sur quelques aspects)," in *Itinéraires d'Egypte: Mélanges offerts au père Maurice Martin s.j.*, ed. Christian Décobert, Bibliothèque d'étude 107 (Cairo: IFAO, 1992), 115–45; "Les ordres mineurs dans l'eglise d'Égypte du IVe au VIIIe siècle," *JJP* 23 (1993): 181–215; "Le monachisme égyptien et les villes," *Travaux et mémoires* 12 (1994): 1–44; "Les communautés monastiques dans l'Égypte Byzantine," in *Valeur et distance: Identities et sociétés en Égypte*, ed. Christian Décobert (Paris: Maisonneuve et Larose, 2000),71–82; "Ἀναχωρητής, ἐρημίτης, ἔκλειστος, ἀποτακτικος." Sur la terminologie monastique en Égypte," *JJP* 31 (2001): 147–68.

14. James E. Goehring has contributed a series of important articles: "Through a Glass Darkly: Diverse Images of the Ἀποτακτικοί(αί) in Early Egyptian Monasticism," in *Discursive Formations, Ascetic Piety and the Interpretation of Early Christian Literature*, ed. Vincent L. Wimbush, (Atlanta: Scholars Press, 1992), 2:25–45; "The Encroaching Desert: Literary Production and Ascetic Space in Early Christian Egypt," *JECS* 1 (1993): 281–96; "Melitian Monastic Organization: A Challenge to Pachomian Originality," *StPatr* 25 (1993): 388–95. These are now conveniently collected in his *Ascetics, Society, and the Desert: Studies in Early Egyptian Monasticism*, SAC (Harrisburg, Pa.: Trinity Press International, 1999).

15. Jürgen Horn, "Tria sunt in Aegypto genera monachorum: Die ägyptischen Bezeichnungen für die 'dritte Art' des Mönchtums bei Hieronymus und Johannes Cassianus," in *Quaerentes Scientiam: Festgabe für Wolfhart Westendorf zu seinem 70. Geburtstag*, ed. Heike Behlmer (Göttingen: Seminar für Ägyptologie und Koptologie, 1994), 63–76; Antoine Guillaumont, "Les 'Remnuoth' de saint Jérôme," in *Christianisme d'Égypte: Hommages à René-Georges Coquin*, CBibCopte 9 (Paris: Peeters, 1995), 87–92; Ugo Zanetti, "Arabe serākūdā = copte sarakote = 'gyrovagues' dans la vie de s. Jean de Scété," *AB* 115 (1997): 280; Christian Cannuyer, "L'identité des sarabaïtes, ces moines d'Égypte que méprisait Jean Cassien," *Mélanges de science religieuse* 58 (April–June 2001): 7–19; Malcolm Choat, "Philological and Historical Approaches to the Search for the 'Third Type' of Egyptian Monk," in *Coptic Studies on the Threshold of a New Millennium: Proceedings of the Seventh International Congress of Coptic Studies*, ed. Mat Immerzeel and Jacques Van der Vliet, OLA 132–33 (Louvain: Peeters, 2004), 133:857–65.

16. Horn, "Tria sunt in Aegypto genera monachorum," 67–71; Guillaumont, "Les 'Remnuoth' de saint Jérôme," 87–92; Choat, "Philological and Historical Approaches," 858. Choat lists ⲡⲣ̄ⲛ̄ⲟⲩⲧ in the Manichaean *Homilies* (Hom. 92.2 reading ⲡⲣ̄ⲛ̄ⲟⲩⲧ ⲉ- for ⲡⲣ̄ⲛ̄ⲟⲩⲧⲉ) and *Kephalaia I* (98.20). See

The word *sarabaitae* is more problematic. No word has been found in Coptic texts that matches this transcription, even though Cassian explicitly states that it is an Egyptian word. Examples of unsuccessful connections with Coptic ⲁⲩⲏⲧ, ⲁⲃⲏⲧ can be found in Horn's article.[17] Horn supported an etymology for *sarabaitae* advanced in 1987 by Anthony Alcock.[18]

> It is without doubt a word of Egyptian origin, and I suggest the following etymology: ⲥⲁ "man (of)" and ⲣⲁⲩⲏ "community, neighbourhood." It is possible that the resulting form *ⲥⲁⲣⲁⲩⲏ may have become *σαραβήτης a form that would yield the plural ending -αι. It is generally thought that the *sarabaitae* were the equivalent of the *remnuoth* mentioned by Jerome (*Epistula* 32 [sic]).[19]

Alcock is referring to a compound formed with the derived Coptic noun ⲥⲁ + the genitive marker ⲛ- + the Coptic noun ⲣⲁⲩⲏ.[20] The first meaning listed by Crum for ⲥⲁ is "man of"; but one should read the second and third meanings listed, "maker of" and "dealer in," as well in order to understand the significance of the Coptic word. It has an emphatically mercantile sense. Crum lists more than thirty-nine modifying nouns that appear in combination with ⲥⲁ. All are materials that are made or sold or dealt in, e.g., glass, meat, cucumbers, garlic, salt, fish, pigs, copper, awls, sacks, tar, pitch. In other words, to take an example, if one translated the compound ⲥⲁⲛⲧⲃⲧ as "man of fish," it is with the understanding that "fish man" means in fact "fishmonger."[21] ⲥⲁ also appears in compounds denoting moral qualities, again with the sense of "dealing in," "being a distributor of." The Coptic word ⲣⲱⲙⲉ, "man," has the form ⲡⲙ-ⲛ-, ⲣⲉⲙ- "man of" with the sense of "belonging to." This seems to be how Alcock translates ⲥⲁ, "man of." However, ⲥⲁ should be compared with

---

also Iain Gardner, *The Kephalaia of the Teacher: The Edited Coptic Manichaean Texts in Translation with Commentary* (Leiden: Brill, 1995), 102.

17. Horn, "Tria sunt in Aegypto genera monachorum," 72–75.

18. Anthony Alcock, "Two Notes on Egyptian Monasticism," *Aegyptus* 67 (1987): 189–90. More recently Alcock's etymology has been cited in Ewa Wipszycka's 1994 study, "Le monachisme égyptien et les villes," 5.

19. Alcock, "Two Notes on Egyptian Monasticism," 189.

20. Lexical entries on ⲥⲁ include Crum, *Coptic Dictionary*, 316a; Vycichl, *Dictionnaire étymologique de la langue copte*, 181; Černý, *Coptic Etymological Dictionary*, 144; Westendorf, *Koptisches Handwörterbuch*, 173. See too Bentley Layton, *A Coptic Grammar with Chrestomathy and Glossary: Sahidic Dialect*, 2d ed., Porta linguarum orientalium n.s, vol. 20 (Wiesbaden: Harrassowitz Verlag, 2004), 88: "'maker of, dealer in.' Combines with some names of artisanal products (mostly in non-literary texts) and of vices."

21. See too the long list of such compounds listed under the entry ⲥⲁ in Vycichl, *Dictionnaire étymologique de la langue copte*, 181.

a different form of ⲣⲱⲙⲉ, namely, ⲣⲉϥ - (agent of verb). For example, ⲥⲁⲛ-ⲝⲓⲟⲩⲉ and ⲣⲉϥϫⲓⲟⲩⲉ (John 10:10) = κλέπτης = thief. ⲡⲥⲁⲛϫⲓⲟⲩⲉ ⲙⲁ-ϥⲉⲓ ⲉⲧⲃⲉ ⲗⲁⲩⲉ;[22] ⲡⲣⲉϥϫⲓⲟⲩⲉ ⲙⲉϥⲉⲓ ⲉⲧⲃⲉ ⲗⲁⲁⲩ.[23]

The form ⲣⲙ- makes a very common compound with the modifying noun that Alcock presents here, ⲣⲁⲩⲏ, namely, ⲣⲙⲣⲁⲩⲏ.[24] The primary sense of the Coptic word ⲣⲁⲩⲏ is "a quarter of town," or a neighborhood. The compound word that Alcock proposes as "a man (of) the community" appears in Coptic, but with the meaning "neighbor."[25] The English word "community" is freighted with monastic implications; and ⲣⲁⲩⲏ does appear in Coptic texts in a monastic context.[26] Yet even if ⲣⲁⲩⲏ has the appropriate monastic sense, ⲣⲙ-ⲣⲁⲩⲏ, not ⲥⲁⲣⲁⲩⲏ, would translate as "one belonging to the monastery/community."

The earliest known instance of ⲥⲁⲣⲁⲕⲱⲧⲉ, ⲥⲁⲣⲁⲕⲟⲧⲉ is found in a Coptic Manichaean psalm-book. It occurs in the title of one group of psalms, ⲯⲁⲗⲙⲟⲓ ⲥⲁⲣⲁⲕⲱⲧⲱⲛ. They were edited and translated by C. R. C. Allberry in 1938.[27] Allberry noted that the form ⲥⲁⲣⲁⲕⲱⲧⲱⲛ resembled a Greek genitive plural, for which one might expect in Greek σαρακωτοί or σαρακῶται; but he found no evidence of such a word in Greek. He found ⲥⲁⲣⲁⲕⲱⲧⲉ in Crum's Coptic dictionary, along with the translation "wanderer" or "vagrant"; but troubled by this sense of the word and still looking for a Greek form he remarked, "But this can hardly make such a form, and gives no very satisfactory

---

22. Herbert Thompson, *The Gospel of St. John According to the Earliest Coptic Manuscript: Edited with a Translation* (London: British School of Archaeology in Egypt, 1923), 20.

23. Hans Quecke, *Das Johannesevangelium Saïdisch: Text der Handschrift PPalau Rib. Inv.-Nr. 183 mit den Varianten der Handschriften 813 und 814 der Chester Beatty Library und der Handschrift M 569* (Rome: Papyrologica Castroctaviana, 1984), 145.

24. Crum, *Coptic Dictionary*, 306. It appears in Luke 1:58 as "neighbors" = οἱ περίοικοι.

25. See, e.g., Luke 1:58: ⲁⲩⲥⲱⲧⲙ ⲇⲉ ⲛϭⲓ ⲛⲉⲥⲣⲙⲣⲁⲩⲏ ⲛⲙ ⲛⲉⲥⲣⲙⲣⲁⲓⲧⲉ, in Hans Quecke, *Das Lukasevangelium Saïdisch: Text der Handschrift PPalau Rib. Inv.-Nr. 181 mit den Varianten der Handschrift M 569* (Barcelona: Papyrologica Castroctaviana, 1977), 103. And see too ⲟⲩⲟϩ ⲁⲩⲥⲱⲧⲉⲙ ⲛ̄ϫⲉⲛⲏ ⲉⲧⲉⲙⲡⲕⲱϯ ⲙⲡⲉⲥⲏⲓ ⲛⲉⲙ ⲛⲉⲥⲥⲩⲅⲅⲉⲛⲏⲥ [ⲛⲏ ⲉⲧϩⲉⲛⲡⲕⲱϯ in F; ⲛⲏ ⲉⲧⲕⲱϯ in H; ⲛⲉⲥⲥⲩⲅⲅⲉⲛⲏⲥ in Gr. L om. αὐτῆς] in George William Horner, *The Coptic Version of the New Testament in the Northern Dialect Otherwise Called Memphitic and Bohairic with Introduction, Critical Apparatus, and Literal English Translation. Vol. II. The Gospels of S. Luke and S. John Edited from MS. Huntington 17 in the Bodleian Library* (Oxford: Clarendon Press, 1898), 14–16.

26. See Horn, "Tria sunt in Aegypto genera monachorum," 79–81. See also Cannuyer, "L'identité des sarabaïtes," 15–16.

27. C. R. C. Allberry, ed. and trans., *A Manichaean Psalm-Book Part II* (Stuttgart: W. Kohlhammer, 1938).

sense."[28] In 1967 Peter Nagel reexamined the title. Nagel agreed with Allberry that ⲥⲁⲣⲁⲕⲱⲧⲱⲛ resembled a Greek genitive plural, but he also pointed to mixed Greek/Coptic phrases in the titles of other groups of psalms in the psalm-book. ⳨ⲁⲗⲙⲟⲓ ⲥⲁⲣⲁⲕⲱⲧⲱⲛ, while morphologically a Greek construction, lexically was a Greek-Coptic combination employing the Coptic word ⲥⲁⲣⲁⲕⲱⲧⲉ. And here in a liturgical context it could best be translated as "pilgrims." The title should be read as "Psalms of the Pilgrims."[29]

Paris B.N. Coptic ms 44, dated 1105 year of the Martyrs, i.e., 1389 CE, also has the word ⲥⲁⲣⲁⲕⲱⲧⲉ. The codex includes a Copto-Arabic ecclesiastical scala, i.e., a glossary or vocabulary list of Coptic and Greek words in church books with Arabic translation. It includes as well a grammatical preface written by Yûhannâ as-Sammanûdî, followed by an anonymous Sahidic Coptic, Greek, and Arabic vocabulary.[30] The plural ⲛⲥⲁⲣⲁⲕⲱⲧⲉ appears four times, always with the Arabic word *ar-raḫḫâlin* (wanderer), in connection with the words ⲙⲡⲁⲣⲁⲥⲓⲧⲟⲥ (fol. 64r, 77v, 99r) ⲛⲁⲭⲗⲟⲏ (ἀχλύο-εις), gloomy, dark) (fol. 90r), and ⲛⲉⲭⲗⲱⲛ (ἐνόχλησις, annoyance) (77v).[31] An earlier copy of the anonymous vocabulary appears in Paris B.N. Coptic ms. 43, which bears two dates: 1012 of Martyrs, i.e., 1296 CE, and 1026, i.e., 1310 CE[32] Crum cites the appearance of this word spelled as ⲥⲁⲣⲁⲕⲟⲧⲧⲉ in fol. 73. Crum also finds ⲙⲡⲁⲣⲁⲥⲓⲧⲟⲥ ⲛⲥⲁⲣⲁⲕⲟⲥⲧⲉ together in fol. 189 of Paris B.N. Coptic ms. 45, a manuscript of the fourteenth century. This is a different vocabulary, and here the Arabic gloss seems to be *abaʿin?*. Crum suggests Arabic *arbaʿin*, fortieth, as if σαρακοστή for τεσσαρακοστή.[33]

ⲥⲁⲣⲁⲕⲟⲧⲉ, spelled with ⲟ not ⲱ, appears in a Sahidic Coptic rhymed

---

28. Allberry, *Manichaean Psalm-Book*, xxii and n. 7.
29. Ibid., xix–xxiii, 133; P. Nagel, "Die Psalmoi Sarakoton des manichäischen psalmbuches," *OLZ* 62 (1967): 123–30. See also Nils Arne Pedersen, *Studies in the Sermon on the Great War: Investigations of a Manichaean-Coptic Text from the Fourth Century* (Aarhus: Aarhus University Press, 1996), 372–74.
30. Henri Munier, *La Scala copte 44 de la Bibliothèque Nationale de Paris. Tome Premier: Transcription*, Bibliothèque d'études coptes 2 (Cairo: Institut Français d'Archéologie Orientale, 1930).
31. See Crum's suggestion, *Coptic Dictionary*, 354: ⲛⲉⲭⲗⲱⲛ (l.? ⲕⲉⲕⲗⲱⲛ κυκλῶιν).
32. Ibid. See description of Paris B.N. Coptic mss. 43, 44, 45 in André Mallon, "Catalogue des Scalae coptes de la Bibliothèque Nationale de Paris," *Mélanges de l'Université Saint Joseph, Beyrouth* 4 (1910): 57–90.
33. Crum, *Coptic Dictionary*, 354. A comparison of the folios and texts of mss. 43 and 44 can be found in Henri Hyvernat's unpublished notebook "B. Na. Copte 43, 44," in the research collections of the Institute of Christian Oriental Research (ICOR) at CUA. I have not seen Paris B.N. Coptic Mss. 43 and 45.

poem of the early fourteenth century known as the *Triadon*. Four hundred twenty-eight of the original 732 numbered stanzas survive in one manuscript, now in Naples.[34] Composed at a time when Arabic was the language of Coptic Christians, the poem celebrates the Coptic language and the Coptic Christian tradition. It is accompanied by an Arabic translation. Based on internal evidence within the poem, the *Triadon* has been dated to 1322. Internal evidence also indicates that the work may have been composed by a Coptic monk.[35] Stanza 471 contains an interesting play on the meaning and sound of ⲥⲁⲣⲁⲕⲱⲧⲉ/ⲥⲁⲣⲁⲕⲟⲧⲉ. One can hear the wordplay in Coptic: "Every one who sees me says, 'This is a ⲣⲙⲣⲁⲕⲟⲧⲉ' [i.e., a man of Rakote, the Coptic name for Alexandria].[36] How did I become like some ⲥⲁⲣⲁⲕⲟⲧⲉ? I set aside all my ⲙⲉⲉⲩⲉ [thoughts/notions/principles] ⲉⲧⲣⲁ- [that I might, i.e., for me to] ⲕⲱⲧⲉ [go around/wander] from city to city according to the word of the Gospel."[37]

The Arabic word that translates ⲥⲁⲣⲁⲕⲱⲧⲉ in the *Triadon* is *rahhâlin*, the same word as in the *scalae* manuscripts, Paris B.N. Coptic 44 and 43. This

---

34. The *Triadon* remains a relatively little studied Coptic [and Arabic] text. Some of the strophes were published by Georg Zoega in his *Catalogus Codicum Copticorum Manuscriptorum qui in Museo Borgiano Velitris Adservantur* (Rome: Sacrae Congregationis de Propaganda Fide, 1810), 642. The entire extant Coptic text and Arabic translation was published by Oscar von Lemm, *Das Triadon: Ein sahidisches Gedicht mit arabischer Übersetzung* (St. Petersburg: Académie Impériale des Sciences, 1903). See also Marius Chaine, "Le Triadon: Son auteur, la date de sa composition," *Bulletin de l'Association des Amis de l'Art Copte* 2 (1936): 9–24. Peter Nagel translated the Coptic text into German in 1983: *Das Triadon: Ein sahidisches Lehrgedicht des 14. Jahrhunderts*, Wissenschaftliche Beiträge / Martin-Luther-Universität Halle-Wittenberg, 1983/23 (K7) (Halle [Saale]: Abt. Wissenschaftspublizistik der Martin-Luther-Universität Halle-Wittenberg, 1983).

35. Stanza 687 refers to a monk Barsûm as a contemporary of the poet. St. Barsûm or Barsûma the Naked, as he is known, served as secretary to the widow of the sultan al-Malik al-Sâlih in Cairo in 1250. He became a hermit, was arrested and released by Muslim authorities, and spent the last seventeen years of his life in the monastery of Dayr Shahrân, south of Cairo. He died in AM 1033/AD 1317, according to the Arabic Jacobite Synaxary. See René-Georges Coquin, "Barsum the Naked, Saint," in *The Coptic Encyclopedia*, ed. Aziz S. Atiya (New York: Macmillan, 1991), 2:348–49. Stanza 532 gives a date for the celebration of Easter that fits six years from 1322 to 1489. Using the known dates for Barsûm as a benchmark, the best choice of date is 1322, five years after Barsûm's death. See Chaine, "Le Triadon," 11–5.

36. Cf. Evelyn-White's description "rogue" in note 11 above.

37. Neither the Chaine's French translation nor Nagel's German one catches this play: "Tous ceux qui me voient disent: c'est un Alexandrin. Et comment suis-je devenu semblable à ces marchands ambulants? Ai-je mis toutes mes préoccupations à errer de ville en ville selon la parole de l'Évangile?" (Chaine, 17). "Ein jeder, der mich sieht, sagt: Das ist einer aus Alexandria! Wie bin ich denn 'Vagabunden' gleichgeworden? Ich habe in allen meinen Gedanken beschlossen, umherzuziehen von Stadt zu Stadt gemäss dem Wort des Evangeliums" (Nagel, 77).

is a term that takes on a number of meanings in the Arabic-speaking world. It can be translated "wanderer, traveler." In Islamic circles it comes to be used to describe scholars and devout and well-intentioned persons who travel throughout the Islamic lands looking for *hadith* and authorities for their transmission. It also becomes part of the technical vocabulary for pilgrimage in Islam.[38]

The word ⲥⲁⲣⲁⲕⲱⲧⲉ appears in a fragmentary Coptic papyrus sheet from the beginning of the seventh century, now in the Pierpont Morgan Library M662B (12). It contains an oath for the ordination of a priest. The relevant passage is ⲟⲩⲧⲉ ⲉⲛⲓⲡⲟⲣⲛⲉⲩⲉ ⲟⲩⲧⲉ ⲉⲛⲓⲕⲟⲓⲛⲱⲛⲉⲓ ⲙⲛ̄ ⲙⲟⲛⲁⲭⲟⲥ ⲛ̄ⲥⲁⲣⲁⲕⲱⲧⲉ ⲟⲩⲧⲉ ⲉϯ ⲑⲉ ⲛⲁⲩ ϩⲟⲗⲱⲥ ⲉϩⲱⲛ ⲉϩⲟⲩⲛ ⲉⲡⲁⲑⲩⲥⲓⲁⲥⲧⲏⲣⲓⲟⲛ ⲉⲧⲁⲗⲉ ⲑⲩⲥⲓⲁ ⲉϩⲣⲁⲓ ϩⲓ ⲭⲱϥ. "Nor [will I] fornicate with [practice idolatry?] nor associate with Sarakote monks nor (will I) make it possible for them [Sarakote monks] to approach my altar to offer sacrifice on it."[39]

ⲥⲁⲣⲁⲕⲱⲧⲉ appears in the Pierpont Morgan Library Coptic manuscript of the ninth–tenth century from the Monastery of St. Michael the Archangel in the Egyptian Fayyum. The manuscript M634 contains stories about the early life of the Virgin Mary. In a passage (fol. 14b) ⲥⲁⲣⲁⲕⲱⲧⲉ are identified as Melitian monks.[40] The Coptic text and English translation of Leo Depuydt are repeated here:

---

38. I. R. Netton, "Riḥla," *EI²* VIII, fasc. 139–40 (1994), 528; Jonathan Berkey, *The Transmission of Knowledge in Medieval Cairo: A Social History of Islamic Education,* Princeton Studies on the Near East (Princeton: Princeton University Press, 1992), 178.

39. See Theodore C. Petersen, Unpublished notebook, Coptic Documentary Papyri in the Pierpont Morgan Collection, document 12 (Washington, D.C.: Catholic University of America, Institute of Christian Oriental Research, n.d.); Leslie S. B. MacCoull, "A Coptic Marriage Contract in the Pierpont Morgan Library," in *Actes du XVe congrès international de papyrologie,* ed. Jean Bingen and Georges Nachtergaell (Brussels: Fondation Égyptologique Reine Élisabeth, 1978–79), 2:116–23; Florence D. Friedman, *Beyond the Pharaohs: Egypt and the Copts in the 2nd to 7th Centuries A.D.* ([Providence:]: Rhode Island School of Design, Museum of Art, 1989), 224; Martin Krause, "Ein Vorschlagsschreiben für einen Priester," in *Lingua Restituta Orientalis: Festgabe für Julius Assfalg,* ed. Regine Schulz and Manfred Görg, Ägypten und Altes Testament 20 (Wiesbaden: Otto Harrassowitz, 1990), 195–202; Martin Krause,, "Report on Research in Coptic Papyrology and Epigraphy," in *Acts of the Fifth International Congress of Coptic Studies, Washington, 12–15 August 1992,* ed. Tito Orlandi and David Johnson (Rome: C.I.M., 1993), 1:77–95, see esp. 85–86; Leo Depuydt, *Catalogue of Coptic Manuscripts in the Pierpont Morgan Library,* Corpus of Illuminated Manuscripts v.4–5, Oriental Series 1–2 (Louvain: Peeters, 1993), 1:542–43 and 2:443. Coptic text from Petersen and Depuydt; English translation by Petersen and, beginning from "nor (will I) make it possible ...," by Depuydt.

40. Bärbel Kramer and John C. Shelton tentatively linked Jerome's *remnuoth* with members of early Egyptian Melitian monastic communities. See Bärbel Kramer and John C. Shelton, *Das Archiv des Nepheros und verwandte Texte,* Aegyptiaca Treverensia 4 (Mainz am Rhein: Philipp von Zabern, 1987), 18–20.

ⲧⲉⲛⲟⲩ ⲛϭⲓ ⲙⲙⲉⲗⲓⲧⲁⲛⲟⲥ ⲉⲧϩⲩⲡⲟⲧⲝⲉ ϩⲁ ⲙⲉⲗⲓⲧⲟⲥ ⲡⲡⲁⲣⲁⲃⲁⲧⲏⲥ ⲛⲁⲓ ⲉⲧⲉⲣⲉ ⲛⲉⲣⲙⲛⲕⲏⲙⲉ ⲙⲟⲩⲧⲉ ⲉⲣⲟⲟⲩ ϫⲛⲥⲁⲣⲁⲕⲱⲧⲉ ⲛⲁⲓ ⲉⲧⲥⲧⲏⲩ ⲉⲃⲟⲗ ⲁⲩⲱ ⲛⲉⲧⲥⲟⲟⲩϩ ⲛⲙ- ⲙⲁⲩ ⲉⲛⲉⲩⲙⲁ ⲛϣⲓⲛⲉ ⲉⲧⲥⲟⲟϥ ⲉⲧⲉ ⲛⲉⲩⲙⲁ ⲛϣⲱⲡⲉ ⲛⲉ ⲙⲛ ⲟⲩⲟⲛ ⲛⲓⲙ ⲉⲧⲕⲟⲓⲛⲱⲛⲉⲓ ⲛⲙⲙⲁⲩ

The Melitians who serve under [?] Melitius the transgressor, those whom the Egyptians call "the Sarakote," those rejected people and those who gather with them in their defiled oracle places, which are their abodes, and every one who participates with them.[41]

ⲥⲁⲣⲁⲕⲱϯ appears as a Bohairic Coptic gloss in the Macarius text of the Arabic version of the *Canons of Athanasius of Alexandria*. It is linked to Meletians: "The singers shall not sing the writings of Meletius and of the ignorant ⲥⲁⲣⲁⲕⲱⲧⲓ, that sing without wisdom, not as David and in the Holy Spirit, but like the songs of the heathen, whose mouths ought to be stopped."[42]

Ugo Zanetti has identified Arabic *serākūdā* that represents the Coptic

---

41. Leo Depuydt, *Catalogue of Coptic Manuscripts in the Pierpont Morgan Library*, 1:208–11 (M634 = no. 108). Henri Hyvernat describes this passage in his unpublished "Catalogue of the Coptic Manuscripts in the Pierpont Morgan Library—New York City" (bound typescript, 1933, in Catholic University of America, Institute of Christian Oriental Research), 1:143–44: "Fol. 14r. col.2-16v.: The orator inveighs against 'the Meletians whom the Egyptians call *Sarakote* and all who meet with them in their impure *manshine*, i.e. their dwellings and share their heresies.' He reproaches them with *defiling* the Holy Trinity, the Father and the Son and the Holy Ghost, for which sin the 'pit of the abyss will swallow them' and God in His wrath will destroy them; also with practicing some abominable rites (the nature of which is not always clear owing to the bad condition of the ms.). He mentions in particular their libations (*spondai*) of which some (not of the sect?) partake thinking there is no sin in doing so. He mentions also on the faith of ocular witnesses, the small loaves in shape of *krypheion* which they use in their places of worship in connection with their detestable sacrifices. For Meletius gave them impure books (to that effect) which they keep in their abodes and read much to their detriment and that of all those who listen to them. 'One (of the books?) says that the Virgin Mary was a *Dynamis* (power) issued from the Father. One, that the Son of Mary was a creature,' (in a lacuna, 'still another that . . .') and 'that at the end of it . . . all the Virgin was taken up in a supernatural (?) way.' For saying such things they have been separated (excommunicated) they and all who believe them 'because they separate (from one another) the Father and the Son and the Holy Ghost, and it is not we who placed them under the ban, but the Catholic Church to whom they were disobedient and they separated themselves from her and adopted a foreign doctrine which their impious father Meletius taught them. Know ye I do not say this to you of the Melitians alone but of anybody who will detract from this Virgin.'"

42. Wilhelm Riedel and Walter E. Crum, *The Canons of Athanasius of Alexandria: The Arabic and Coptic Versions Edited and Translated with Introductions, Notes, and Appendices* (London: Williams and Norgate, 1904), 18 (Arabic), 24 (English). The English translation above is from this work. For the Macarian text, represented by Vatican Arabic Cod. 149 and 150 (1372 CE), and Paris B.N. 251 (AM 1069, i.e., 1353 CE), see ibid., x, xxviii–ix; also Wilhelm Riedel, *Die Kirchenrechtsquellen des Patriarchats Alexandrien. Zusammengestellt und zum Teil übersetzt* (Leipzig: A. Deichert'sche Verlagsbuchhandlung„ 1900), 122.

ⲥⲁⲣⲁⲕⲱⲧⲉ. It appears twice in the Arabic version of the *Life of St. John*, hegoumen of Scetis, in the seventh century.[43]

Une autre fois, un frère lui dit: "J'ai habité quelque temps en Haute Égypte, et j'y ai vu des gens que l'on appelle les 'Serākūdā' qui, après avoir fini de manger et de boire, quand c'est l'heure de la sainte oblation communient aux mystères alors qu'ils sont ivres." L'ancien lui dit: "Cette manière de faire est mauvaise et impure en presence de Dieu...."[44]

À present donc, qu'ils entendent, qu'ils craignent et qu'ils prennent garde désormais, ces 'Serākūdā' et ceux qui pratiquent l'hypocrisie, qu'ils (se gardent) d'entrer dans le sanctuaire en état d'ivresse.[45]

To summarize: the word ⲥⲁⲣⲁⲕⲱⲧⲉ has been found variously spelled in some eight Coptic documents ranging from the fourth to the fourteenth centuries; it also appears in Arabic transcription in a manuscript copy in the sixteenth century. Almost all of the attestations of the word are Sahidic. The earliest text is Manichaean; the rest are Christian. In five of the seven Christian texts ⲥⲁⲣⲁⲕⲱⲧⲉ appears in a monastic or ecclesiastical context; and two of these texts link the term ⲥⲁⲣⲁⲕⲱⲧⲉ to Melitian monks. The three Copto-Arabic *scalae* identify ⲥⲁⲣⲁⲕⲱⲧⲉ with παράσιτος (parasite, freeloader).[46] Two of the three *scalae* identify ⲥⲁⲣⲁⲕⲱⲧⲉ with the Arabic *rahhâlin* (wanderer, traveler); so does the *Triadon*. Only the Manichaean reference to ⲥⲁⲣⲁⲕⲱⲧⲉ is unambiguously positive.

There is yet another connection with Melitians and ⲥⲁⲣⲁⲕⲱⲧⲉ in a fragment of a Sahidic Coptic *Life of Pamin*. The connection here is the Greek κυκλευτής: "One of them was an orthodox of the holy Catholic Church, and as for the other he was a ΚΕΚΛΕΥΓΗΣ [*sic*] schismatic of the heresy of the Meletians."[47] Malcolm Choat has identified this term in a description of the

---

43. Zanetti, "Arabe serākūdā," 280; Ugo Zanetti, "La vie de saint Jean higoumène de Scété au VIIe siècle," *AB* 114 (1996): 273–405. The manuscript is from the Monastery of St. Macarius. It is designated hom. 35 and is dated 1265 AM, i.e. 1549 CE. See pp. 290–91.

44. Zanetti, "La vie de saint Jean," 306–7.

45. Ibid., 308–9.

46. Agapio Bsciai, "Novum Auctarium Lexici Sahidico-Coptici. II (n, o, p, q)," *ZÄS* 25 (1887): 58–73; see 70. Bsciai put it rather succinctly concerning the ⲥⲁⲣⲁⲕⲱⲧⲉ: "Sunt illi qui pervagantur, gyrovagi, et tres voces, scilicet coptica, graeca et arabica, hunc sensum optime indicant. A voce ⲥⲁⲣⲁ in compos. pro ⲥⲱⲣ et ⲕⲱⲧⲉ, ut ⲥⲁⲣⲁⲑⲟⲩ ⲁ ⲥⲱⲣ etc. Item cod. Paris. 44. 89 v. habet Νοχλοη."

47. Émile Amélineau, *Monuments pour servir à l'histoire de l'Égypte chrétienne aux IVe, Ve, VIe, et VIIe siècles. Texte copte publié et traduit*, MMAF 4, fasc. 2 (Paris: Ernest Leroux, 1895), 740. See too H. Winlock, *The Monastery of Epiphanius at Thebes* (New York: [Metropolitan Museum of Art,] 1926),

apostle Thomas in a Coptic list of the apostles on British Museum Ostracon 50235.⁴⁸ Thomas is a κυκλευτής, a wanderer. According to Choat, in this context κυκλευτής may have a positive or at least neutral meaning.⁴⁹

Choat suggests that Jerome's *remnuoth* and Cassian's *sarabaitae* were "terms of abuse *within* the wider Christian tradition" rather than specific names for a "'third type' of monasticism":⁵⁰

> To see the labels in derisive terms best explains why they are not used in the historical record with the meanings Jerome and Cassian attached to them. Rather than assisting in narrowing the terminology, they contribute to our knowledge of the diversity present in the vocabulary in both form and sense, and behind it the diversity of ascetic lifestyles within the broader Judeo-Christian tradition of the period.⁵¹

I suggest that the textual and documentary evidence also allows for a different interpretation: a progression from names associated with some recognized type of monasticism to terms of abuse.

1:125–26, also listed in Crum, *Coptic Dictionary*, 354. W. E. Crum was in charge of the literary material. See n. 12 above on κυκλευτής, *gyrovagus,* and cαρακωτε.

48. Malcolm Choat, "Thomas the 'Wanderer' in a Coptic List of the Apostles," *Orientalia* 74 (2005): 83–85. The provenance of B.M. Ost. 50235 is the monastery of Phoibammon, *floruit* 590–late eighth century CE. I thank Janet Timbie for this reference.

49. Choat, "Thomas the 'Wanderer,'" 85.

50. Choat, "Philological and Historical Approaches," 863.

51. Ibid., 865. For a historical overview of the wandering monk, see Daniel Caner, *Wandering, Begging Monks: Spiritual Authority and the Promotion of Monasticism in Late Antiquity*, TCH 33 (Berkeley and Los Angeles: University of California Press, 2002).

Janet A. Timbie

READING AND REREADING SHENOUTE'S *I AM AMAZED*

More Information on Nestorius and Others

The text of a discourse by Shenoute of Atripe first came to scholarly notice in the 1980s, through the work of Tito Orlandi. His 1982 article "A Catechesis Against Apocryphal Texts by Shenute and the Gnostic Texts of Nag Hammadi"[1] called attention to a little-known text and emphasized the Gnostic references, an understandable approach at that time. In 1985 his edition and translation *Shenute contra Origenistas* emphasized different content.[2] The text is important, in part, because it was written in Coptic by a fifth-century monastic leader and deals openly with some of the theological controversies that disturbed Egypt in the fourth and fifth centuries: Gnosticism, Origenism, Nestorian Christology, Manichaeism, etc. Following the 1985 publication of the text and translation, studies of fourth- and fifth-century theology began to make significant use of *I Am Amazed*. Grillmeier, in *Christ in Christian Tradition*, and Clark, in *The Origenist Controversy*, included lengthy excerpts from the discourse in support of their arguments, and others have cited the discourse.[3]

---

1. Tito Orlandi, "A Catechesis against Apocryphal Texts by Shenute and the Gnostic Texts of Nag Hammadi," *HTR* 75 (1982): 85–95.

2. Tito Orlandi, ed. and trans., *Shenute contra Origenistas: Testo con introduzione e traduzione* (Rome: Centro Italiano Microfiches, 1985).

3. Aloys Grillmeier, *Christ in Christian Tradition*, trans. O. C. Dean (London: Mowbray, 1995),

However, some scholarly use of *I Am Amazed* was compromised by dependence on the 1985 edition and translation. In 1993 Stephen Emmel studied the manuscript tradition of Shenoute and made a better reconstruction of *I Am Amazed* possible (and also assigned the correct title from the incipit list of Shenoute's works).[4] Problems with published editions have been uncovered through Emmel's codicological work: (1) material from another discourse was inserted into the text of *I Am Amazed*, (2) portions of *I Am Amazed* (Codex HB 67/68, 77/78) had been published by Amélineau, and placement of this material partially filled a gap in the 1985 edition, and (3) the festal letter of Theophilus of Alexandria for 401 was cited at length within the text of *I Am Amazed*.[5] A less obvious problem consists of gaps and incorrect readings in the transcription of the manuscripts. Critical editions of the works of Shenoute are in the early stages. However, because the Institute of Christian Oriental Research at Catholic University has a collection of photographs of many important Coptic manuscripts, I have been able to compare the Amélineau and Orlandi publications with the photographs, fill in gaps, and make some corrections in advance of the critical edition.

I Am Amazed is partially preserved in six manuscripts and in its entirety covered about 150 manuscript pages.[6] This total includes approximately forty-six pages devoted to a Coptic translation of most of the festal letter of 401 by Theophilus of Alexandria.[7] The beginning of the discourse is lost; thus the identification with Shenoute relies on Emmel's codicological reconstruction, the position of this work in a list of known Shenoute texts, and stylistic similarities.

2:167–228; Elizabeth Clark, *The Origenist Controversy* (Princeton: Princeton University Press, 1992), 151–58; James Goehring, "Monastic Diversity and Ideological Boundaries in Fourth-Century Christian Egypt," in Goehring, *Ascetics, Society, and the Desert* (Harrisburg, Pa.: Trinity Press International, 1999), 196–218; Alberto Camplani, "Un Episodio della recezione de ΠΕΡΙ ΕΥΧΗΣ in Egitto," SEAug 57 (1997): 159–72.

4. Stephen L. Emmel, *Shenoute's Literary Corpus*, CSCO 600 (Louvain: Peeters, 2004), 646–48.

5. Concerning (1), Orlandi pars. 200–262, pp. 16–20, belong to an acephalous work in Codex XY; see ibid., 599, 338–40. Concerning (2), see Émile Amélineau, *Oeuvres de Schenoudi: Texte copte et tranduction française* (Paris: Ernest Leroux, 1907), 1:332–35, for Coptic text and French translation of HB 67–68, 77–78. Concerning (3), the extent of the festal letter excerpt is demonstrated by Stephen L. Emmel, "Theophilus's Festal Letter of 401 as Quoted by Shenute," in *Divitiae Aegypti*, ed. Cäcilia Fluck et al. (Wiesbaden: Reichert, 1995), 93–98.

6. Emmel, *Shenoute's Literary Corpus*, CSCO 600, 794–99.

7. Emmel, "Theophilus's Festal Letter."

The discourse was written after the Council of Ephesus in 431, which Shenoute attended, but probably before the death of Nestorius in exile in Upper Egypt around 451.[8] In this discourse, Shenoute attacks a wide variety of ideas and practices: belief in multiple worlds based on the reading of apocryphal books, Arian-like Christology, belief in the preexistence of souls, treating the Eucharist as a mere symbol, doubts about the resurrection of the flesh, the exegesis of Origen, the errors of Nestorius, and the evil faith of Mani.[9] The attacks on Origen and on ideas attributed to him, whether rightly or wrongly, and the insertion of the festal letter of 401 suggest that the discourse could be read in the context of a letter from Dioscorus to Shenoute asking him to curb the activities of an Origenist priest. Dioscorus writes, "He [the priest] should not be found... either in the city of Shmin [Panopolis] or in any other city of the Eparchy of the Thebais, or in the monasteries or in the caves in the desert."[10] Therefore, the discourse may have been written during the episcopate of Dioscorus (444–54).[11] Orlandi places it slightly earlier, about 440, and thus does not find a cause-and-effect relationship between the letter of Dioscorus and the discourse.[12] Yet it is clear that Shenoute relied on an archive of documents to address various heterodox positions in the 440s. Theophilus's festal letter may have been pulled from the file and inserted. An interesting question, as yet unanswered, is whether Shenoute used an existing Coptic translation of the letter or had to produce his own translation for insertion into the discourse.

Two minor corrections to the published editions of *I Am Amazed* will be presented first. Though they do not change the direction of the argument,

---

8. For Nestorius's chronology, see Michael Gaddis, "Nestorius," in *Late Antiquity: A Guide to the Postclassical World*, ed. G. W. Bowersock, Peter Brown, and Oleg Grabar (Cambridge: Belknap Press, 1999), 603–4. The chronology of Shenoute and its difficulties are reviewed by Heike Behlmer in her edition of *De iudicio: Schenute von Atripe: De iudicio (Torino, Museo Egizio, Cat. 63000, Cod. IV)*, Catalogo del Museo Egizio di Torino, Serie Prima—Monumenti e Testi 8 (Turin: Ministero per i Beni Culturale e Ambientali, 1996), LV–LX; she concludes that likely dates for Shenoute are ca. 361/62–465.

9. Mani appears in the fragment of the text published in Amélineau, *Oeuvres de Schenoudi*, 1:333.

10. Herbert Thompson, "Dioscorus and Shenoute," in *Recueil d'études égyptologiques dédiées à la mémoire de Jean-François Champollion à l'occasion du centenaire de la lettre à M. Dacier relative à l'alphabet des hiéroglyphes phonétiques lue à l'Académie des inscriptions et belles-lettres le 27 septembre 1822*, BEHE 234 (Paris: Librairie Ancienne Honoré Champion, Édouard Champion, 1922), 373.

11. Dioscorus's death is fixed at 458 in Coptic sources; see Martiniano P. Roncaglia, "Dioscorus I," in *The Coptic Encyclopedia*, ed. Aziz S. Atiya (New York: Macmillan, 1991), 3:912–15.

12. Orlandi, *Shenute contra Origenistas*, 12. The contact between Dioscorus and Shenoute is also discussed by Clark, *Origenist Controversy*, 151–52.

these corrections strengthen Shenoute's rhetorical effect. The brackets mark where I differ with the published text, and I underline my translation where it reflects my corrected text. Orlandi's reading of the text is given in the footnote.

311 (HB 20A = Orlandi: 22) ϫⲉ ⲉⲛⲛⲁ[ϭⲱϣⲧ] ⲉⲃⲟⲗ ϩⲏⲧⲟⲩ ⲛϩⲉⲛⲁⲡⲟⲕⲣⲩⲫⲟⲛ "So will we <u>look for</u> apocrypha?"[13]

321 (HB 22B = Orlandi: 24) ⲉϣⲁϥϭⲱⲣϭ ⲇⲉ ϩⲛ ⲛⲓⲙ. [ⲏ ⲉϣⲁϥ ⲛⲓⲙ ⲛϭⲟⲣϭⲥ] ⲉⲟⲩⲙⲏⲏϣⲉ "Through whom does he entrap? <u>Or what sort of trap</u> does he make for a multitude?"[14] The entire paragraph (321) supports this correction. It includes two questions and two answers. "Through whom does he [the devil] entrap? Or what sort of trap does he make for a multitude? It is through those who say, 'We are teachers,' that he entraps. It is an entrapping text that he makes them trust until many are ensnared."

More significant corrections can be made in sections having to do with Nestorius. First, a summary of everything Shenoute has to say about Nestorius will put the corrections in context. After a defense of the Son's preexistence (paragraphs 461–63),[15] Shenoute attacks Nestorius by name as "the one whom the ruler of darkness bound in his thoughts," the one who could not persuade "the synod that took place at Ephesus." According to Shenoute, Nestorius said of Christ, "He is a man in whom God dwells" (464).[16] He then attributes to Nestorius a series of arguments from scripture, all making the same point: "He [Nestorius] spoke thus, 'If you explore the whole of Scripture, old and new, you will not find them calling the one who was crucified God'" (465). And also, "Jesus said to his disciples, 'Touch me and see that a spirit does not have bones and flesh as you see me having.' If he is a god—he said—he would say, 'Touch me and see that I am a spirit and a god'" (465).[17] Thus, according to Shenoute, Nestorius used Luke 24:39 to make his point and, for the same pur-

---

13. Orlandi (*Shenute contra Origenistas*, 22) reads ⲡⲱⲧ for the bracketed text. I cite the text according to the Orlandi paragraph and the codex citation system described by Bentley Layton in "Social Structure and Food Consumption in an Early Christian Monastery: The Evidence of Shenoute's *Canons* and the White Monastery Federation A.D. 385–465," *Muséon* 115 (2002): 54–55. I adapt his system to the needs of Shenoute's discourses, so codex reference is followed by published edition.

14. Orlandi, *Shenute contra Origenistas*, 24, reads ⲛⲉϣⲁϥⲣ ⲛⲓⲙ ⲛϭⲟⲣϭⲥ ⲉⲟⲩⲙⲏⲏϣⲉ in the bracketed text.

15. Ibid., 50. 16. Ibid.

17. Ibid., 50–52.

pose, cited Matthew 27:46 ("My God, my God, why have you forsaken me?") [470]).[18]

The central issue of the Virgin Mary is addressed as well: "But he [Nestorius] also said, 'Because of this it is not fitting to say that the Virgin gave birth to a god.' And, 'I will not say that the one who passed three months [cf. Luke 1:56] in the womb is a god. And he took the breast, he grew little by little.' And he said, 'It is written, "Take the little child and go down to Egypt"' [Matt. 2:13]. He did not say, 'Take the god'" (480).[19] To this Shenoute replies, "The blasphemies of that one are many!" (483).[20]

In response, Shenoute answers the arguments of Nestorius with his own scriptural citations. He returns to Luke 24:39: "He did not say, 'See the hands and the feet of a man,' merely. But he said, 'my feet—mine—and my hands,' not separating the body from the divinity" (466).[21] Shenoute also cites 1 John 1:1–10 (467) and John 19:37 (468) to prove that "the divinity was not separated from the body at all."[22] He answers Nestorius's use of Matthew 27:46 ("My God, my God") with a paraphrase of 1 Cor. 2:8: "But the words of the apostle reprove his ignorance, 'The one whom they crucified is the Lord of glory.' ... He did not say, 'He is a man joined with a god'" (471).[23] Matthew 2:13 ("take the little child") is answered with Matthew 1:23: "As it is written, 'Behold the virgin will conceive and give birth to a son and his name will be called Emmanuel, which means God is with us.' Therefore, the one to whom the Virgin gave birth is a god. And therefore it is necessary to confess that Mary is the one who gave birth to God, as our fathers said" (481–82).[24] The implied point in the answers of Shenoute is that Nestorius's use of scripture is too selective; the full range of passages is ignored in favor of a strained interpretation of a single passage.[25]

Corrections to several paragraphs in the Nestorian sections of *I Am Amazed* are based on my reading of manuscript photographs. Some parts of the text are

---

18. Ibid., 52.   19. Ibid., 56.
20. Ibid.
21. Ibid., 52. The possessed determinator pronoun ⲚⲞⲨⲒ is added by Shenoute to the scriptural citation to make the point.
22. Ibid.
23. Ibid. Shenoute also cites Acts 3.15 and Phil. 2.6 in paragraph 471.
24. Ibid., 56.
25. See paragraph 472, discussed below, for an appeal to ordinary speech as the context for interpreting scripture.

very difficult to read because ink from one page has bled through onto the reverse of that page.

469 (DQ 61=Orlandi: 52) ⲁⲩⲱ ϫⲉ ⲧⲙⲛⲧⲛⲟⲩⲧⲉ ⲃⲱⲕ ⲉⲡϫⲓⲥⲉ [ⲁⲥⲕⲁⲧⲥⲁⲣⲝ ϩⲓⲡϣⲉ].[26] With the correction, Shenoute states that Nestorius taught, "It is the flesh that cries out to the divinity, 'Why did you forsake me?' [Matt. 27:46]. The divinity went to the height. It left the flesh on the wood." The divinity, or divine nature, did not undergo the suffering of the flesh.

470 ((DQ 61=Orlandi: 52) ⲁϥϫⲟⲟⲥ ⲅⲁⲣ ϩⲛⲛⲉϥⲥϩⲁⲓ ϫⲉ ⲡⲁⲓ ⲉⲧⲱϣ ⲉⲃⲟⲗ ϫⲉ ⲡⲁⲛⲟⲩⲧⲉ ⲡⲁⲛⲟⲩⲧⲉ ⲉⲧⲃⲉ ⲟⲩ ⲁⲕⲕⲁⲁⲧ ⲛⲥⲱⲕ ϯⲟⲩⲱϣⲧ ⲛⲁϥ ϩⲱⲱϥ ⲙⲛ ⲧⲙⲛⲧⲛⲟⲩⲧⲉ ⲉⲃⲟⲗ ϫⲉ ⲁϥϩⲱⲧⲣ [ⲛⲙⲙⲁⲥ].[27] The corrected pronoun, the object of a preposition, simply clears up confusion. According to Shenoute, "He [Nestorius] said in his writings, 'This one who cries out, "My God, my God, why have you forsaken me?" [Matt. 27:46], I worship him with the divinity since he joined with it.'" The feminine pronoun in ⲛⲙⲙⲁⲥ makes it clear that Jesus joined with divinity, ⲧⲙⲛⲧⲛⲟⲩⲧⲉ, a feminine noun.

These corrections to paragraphs 469 and 470 clarify a confusing Coptic passage, but do not change the meaning to any great degree.

472–73 (DQ 61–62, DS 129=Orlandi: 52) ⲉⲃⲟⲗ ⲁⲛ ϫⲉ ⲁⲧⲉⲫⲩⲥⲓⲥ ⲛⲧⲙⲛⲧⲛⲟⲩⲧⲉ ⲙⲟⲩ. ⲁⲗⲗⲁ ⲛⲧⲁϥⲙⲟⲩ ϩⲛⲧⲥⲁⲣⲝ ⲛⲑⲉ ⲉⲧⲥⲏϩ ϫⲉ ⲡⲉⲭ̅ⲥ̅ ⲁϥϣⲡϩⲓⲥⲉ ϩⲛⲧⲥⲁⲣⲝ. ⲕⲁⲓⲅⲁⲣ ⲉⲣⲉⲧⲙⲛⲧⲛⲟⲩⲧⲉ ⲡⲟⲣϫ ⲁⲛ ⲉⲡⲥⲱⲙⲁ [ⲉϥϩⲓⲡϣⲉ. ⲛⲑⲉ ⲙⲡⲁⲓ ϩⲛⲟⲩⲡⲁⲣⲁⲇⲉⲓⲅⲙⲁ ⲉⲃⲟⲗ ⲛϩⲏⲧⲛ] ⲙⲏ ⲉⲩϣⲁⲛⲙⲟⲩⲟⲩⲧ ⲛⲟⲩⲣⲱⲙⲉ ⲉϣⲁⲩϫⲟⲟⲥ ϫⲉ ⲁⲩⲙⲉⲩⲧⲟⲩⲣⲱⲙⲉ. ⲙⲏ ⲉϣⲁⲩϫⲟⲟⲥ ⲁⲛ ϫⲉ [ⲁⲩⲙⲉⲩⲧⲡⲣⲱⲙⲉ] ⲧⲏⲣϥ ⲕⲁⲓⲧⲟⲓ ⲛⲧⲉϯⲯⲩⲭⲏ ⲙⲟⲩ ⲁⲛ. ⲁⲗⲗⲁ ⲡⲥⲱⲙⲁ ⲙⲁⲩⲁⲁϥ ⲡⲉⲧⲙⲟⲩ.[28] "Not that the nature of the divinity died, but it was in the flesh that he died, as it is written, Christ 'suffered in the flesh' [1 Pet. 4:1]. For surely the divinity is not divided from the body while it is on the wood. Similarly, in an example from us, if a man is killed, is it said that a body was killed? Isn't it said that the whole man was killed, even though the soul does not die? But it is the body alone that dies."

---

26. Orlandi, *Shenute contra Origenistas*, 52: ⲙⲡⲁⲧⲉϥⲙⲉϩ ⲛϣⲉ is read in the bracketed portion of the text that is cited here.

27. Ibid.: ⲛⲙⲙⲁϥ.

28. Ibid. At the first bracketed phrase, Orlandi has ⲉϥϩⲙ ⲡϣⲉ ϩⲁⲑⲏ ⲙⲡⲁⲓ ϩⲛⲟⲩⲡⲁⲣⲁⲇⲉⲓⲅⲙⲁ ⲉⲃⲟⲗ ⲛϩⲏⲧϥ. At the second, ⲁⲛⲙⲉⲩⲧⲡⲣⲱⲙⲉ ⲧⲏⲣϥ.

This correction provides a clear example of Shenoute's style of argument. In opposing Nestorius, he cites scripture (1 Pet. 4:1) and adduces a parallel from human existence with ⲉⲃⲟⲗ ⲛ̄ϩⲏⲧⲛ̄, "from us." Typical of Shenoute is the argument through sarcastic rhetorical question, here expecting a negative answer: "If a man is killed, is it said that a body was killed?"

474 (DS 129, DQ 62 = Orlandi: 52) ⲧⲁⲓ ⲧⲉ ⲑⲉ ⲙ̄ⲡϫⲟⲉⲓⲥ ⲁϥⲙⲟⲩ ϩⲛ̄ⲧ-ⲥⲁⲣⲝ̄ [ⲉϥⲟ ⲇⲉ ⲛⲁⲧⲙⲟⲩ ϩⲛ̄ⲧⲉϥⲙⲛ̄ⲧⲛⲟⲩⲧⲉ]. ⲛ̄ⲧⲉⲓϩⲉ ⲅⲁⲣ ⲛⲧⲁϥϫⲟⲟⲥ ϫⲉ ⲁϥⲕⲟⲓⲛⲱⲛⲉⲓ ⲉⲥⲛⲟϥ ϩⲓ ⲥⲁⲣⲝ̄ ⲕⲁⲧⲁ ⲑⲉ [ⲛ̄ⲧⲁⲛϫⲟⲟⲥ ⲛ̄ϩⲁϩ ⲛ̄ⲥⲟⲡ ϫⲉ ⲁⲡⲗⲟⲅⲟⲥ ⲣ̄ⲥⲁⲣⲝ̄ ⲛ̄ⲧⲁϥⲣ̄ⲥⲁⲣⲝ̄ ⲇⲉ ⲧⲱ̄ ⲉⲓⲙⲏⲧⲓ ϩⲛ̄ⲧⲡⲁⲣⲑⲉⲛⲟⲥ. ⲙⲏ ⲛ̄ⲧⲁϥⲣ̄ⲣⲱⲙⲉ ⲁⲛ ϩⲛ̄ϩⲧⲥ ⲛ̄ⲑⲉ ⲉⲧϥⲟⲩⲁϣⲥ ϩⲛ̄ⲧϭⲟⲙ ⲛ̄ⲧⲉϥⲙⲛ̄ⲧⲛⲟⲩⲧⲉ. ⲙⲏ ⲛ̄ⲧⲁⲩϫⲟⲟⲥ ⲁⲛ ϫⲉ ⲁⲩϭⲛ̄ⲧⲥ̄ ⲉⲥⲉⲉⲧ ⲉⲃⲟⲗ ϩⲛ̄ⲟⲩⲡ̄ⲛ̄ⲁ̄ ⲉϥⲟⲩⲁⲁⲃ. ⲁⲩⲱ ϫⲉ ⲟⲩⲡ̄ⲛ̄ⲁ̄ ⲉϥⲟⲩⲁⲁⲃ ⲡⲉⲧⲛⲏⲩ ⲉϩⲣⲁⲓ ⲉϫⲱ].[29] "So it is with the Lord; He died in the flesh <u>but in His divinity He is immortal.</u> For so he said: he 'shared blood and flesh' [Heb. 2:14]. <u>As we said many times, 'The Word became flesh' [cf. John 1:14].</u>[30] <u>Where did He become flesh except in the Virgin? Didn't He become man</u>[31] <u>in her womb just as He willed in the power of His divinity? Isn't it said, 'She was found with child through a holy spirit' [Matt. 1:18]? And 'It is a holy spirit that is going to come down upon you' [Luke 1:35]?</u>"

The example "from us" in paragraph 473 is meant to offer a common-sense alternative to the strained interpretations of Nestorius. If we understand how it is with us, we know that "so it is with the Lord" in paragraph 474. This paragraph is particularly unclear in the manuscripts; the above contains suggested readings that further study may modify. The phrase "in His divinity He is immortal," replacing "immortal in the entire soul" in Orlandi, makes it clear that Shenoute did not maintain that Christ's soul avoided the feelings associated

---

29. Ibid. Orlandi's reading is very different from mine and leaves gaps in the places that are most difficult to read. ⲧⲁⲓ ⲧⲉ ⲑⲉ ⲙ̄ⲡϫⲟⲉⲓⲥ ⲁϥⲙⲟⲩ ϩⲛ̄ⲧⲥⲁⲣⲝ̄ ⲉϥⲟ ⲇⲉ ⲛⲁⲧⲙⲟⲩ ϩⲛ̄ⲧⲉϥⲯⲩⲭⲏ ⲧ(ⲏⲣⲥ). ⲛ̄ⲧⲉⲓϩⲉ ⲅⲁⲣ ⲛ̄ⲧⲁϥϫⲟⲟⲥ ϫⲉ ⲁϥⲕⲟⲓⲛⲱⲛⲉⲓ ⲉⲥⲛⲟϥ ϩⲓ ⲥⲁⲣⲝ̄ ⲕⲁⲧⲁ ⲑⲉ ⲉⲛⲧⲁϥϫⲟⲟⲥ ⲛ̄ϩⲁϩ ⲛ̄ⲥⲟⲡ ϫⲉ (......) ⲧⲥⲁⲣⲝ̄. ⲛ̄ⲧⲁϥⲣ̄ⲥⲁⲣⲝ̄ ⲉⲧⲱ(ⲛ) ⲉⲓⲙⲏⲧⲉⲓ ϩⲛ̄ⲧⲡⲁⲣⲑⲉⲛⲟⲥ. ⲙⲏ ⲛ̄ⲧⲁϥ(.......)ϩ ⲛ̄ϩⲧⲥ (......)ⲉ ⲁⲛ. (......) ⲛ̄ⲑⲉ (......)ⲱⲥ ϩⲛ̄ⲧ(....) ⲛ̄ⲧⲉϥⲙⲛ̄ⲧⲛⲟⲩⲧⲉ ⲙ(ⲙⲉ. ⲛ̄ⲧⲁⲩ)ϫⲟⲟⲥ ⲁⲛ ϫⲉ (......) (......) ⲉⲃⲟⲗ ϩⲛ̄ ⲟⲩⲡⲛ(ⲉⲩⲙ)ⲁ ⲉϥⲟⲩⲁⲁⲃ ⲡⲉⲧⲛⲏⲩ ⲉϩⲣⲁⲓ.

30. Perhaps the statement also shows familiarity with an explicit statement of Athanasius, as in *Tomus ad Antiochenos* 7 (*PG* 26:804): ὁ λόγος σὰρξ ἐγένετο. A similar statement is found in the Coptic texts relating to the Council of Nicaea; see Eugène Revillout, "Le Concile de Nicée," *JA* 7 (1875): 252.

31. Georg Zoega, *Catalogus Codicum Copticorum Manuscriptorum qui in Museo Borgiano Velitris Adservantur* (Rome: Sacrae Congregationis de Propaganda Fide, 1810), 242. The phrase "become man" (ⲣⲣⲱⲙⲉ) is found in the Coptic version of documents from the Council of Nicaea.

with death. In Shenoute, soul (ϮⲮⲨⲬⲎ) is often the interior capacity to think and feel (though it is sometimes used interchangeably with spirit/ⲠⲚⲈⲨⲘⲀ), so Christ shares a soul with humans just as he shares blood and flesh.³² Shenoute is not an Apollinarian.³³ Having established that Christ became flesh while remaining divine, Shenoute turns to the role of the Virgin Mary, answers Nestorius, and states his own argument in another sarcastic rhetorical question: "But where did He become flesh except in the Virgin?" The next sentence is very unclear, but I believe there is another rhetorical question beginning with ⲘⲎ and expecting an affirmative answer: "Didn't He become man in her womb just as He willed in the power of His divinity?" Two gospel citations (Matt. 1:18 and Luke 1:35) support the argument. Mary is the *theotokos* because a holy spirit came down upon her.

475 (DQ 62, DS 129=Orlandi: 54) [ⲈⲦⲂⲈ ⲠⲀⲒ ϬⲈ] ⲈⲂⲞⲖ ⲬⲈ ⲠϢⲎⲢⲈ ϢⲞⲂⲈ ⲀⲚ ⲈⲠⲒⲰⲦ. [ⲞⲨⲠⲚⲀ ⲠⲈ ⲠⲒⲰⲦ]. ⲞⲨⲠⲚⲀ ⲞⲚ ⲠⲈ ⲠϢⲎⲢⲈ. ⲀⲨⲰ ⲠⲚⲞⲨⲦⲈ ⲠⲈ ⲈⲂⲞⲖ ϨⲘⲠⲚⲞⲨⲦⲈ. ⲀⲨⲰ ⲠϢⲎⲢⲈ ⲠⲈ ⲈⲂⲞⲖ ϨⲘⲠⲒⲰⲦ ⲚⲦⲀϤϪⲠⲞϤ.³⁴ "Because of this, therefore, since the Son is not different from the Father, the Father is a spirit, the Son also is a spirit. And He is God from God. And He is Son from the Father who begot Him."

With this correction, the connection between paragraphs 474 and 475 becomes clear. Because a "holy spirit" came down upon Mary (474), and because the Father and the Son are not different (475), both the Father and the Son are "spirit." Shenoute relies on Nicene language instead of a biblical citation. The Son is "God from God" and Son because the Father "begot him."³⁵ Later, in paragraph 482, Shenoute affirms Mary's status against Nestorius's criticism: "Therefore, the one whom the Virgin gave birth to is a god. And because of this, it is necessary to confess that Mary is the one who gave birth to God, just as our fathers said."³⁶

---

32. This usage is amply illustrated in the Behlmer edition of Shenoute's *De Iudicio*. See the Greek index entries (Behlmer, *Schenute von Atripe*, 313–14) for ϮⲮⲨⲬⲎ (thirty-four occurrences) and ⲠⲚⲈⲨⲘⲀ (sixteen occurrences) to track Shenoute's usage.

33. Apollinaris of Laodicea (c. 310–90), a supporter of Nicene doctrine and ally of Athanasius, also taught that Christ did not possess a human mind or soul.

34. Orlandi (*Shenute contra Origenistas*, 54) at the first bracketed section has ⲈⲦⲂⲈ ⲞⲨ. At the second, ⲞⲨⲆⲈ ⲘⲠⲈⲠⲒⲰⲦ.

35. Felix Haase, in *Die koptischen Quellen zum Konzil um Nicäa* (Paderborn: Ferdinand Schöningh, 1920), discusses the various witnesses to the documents of Nicaea in Coptic.

36. Orlandi, *Shenute contra Origenistas*, 54.

Following paragraph 483, the Orlandi edition of *I Am Amazed* has a gap of twelve manuscript pages. Amélineau published part of the text that belongs in this gap, a total of four manuscript pages.[37] In the following excerpt, Shenoute quotes Nestorius.

HB 67=Amél.1: 332 ϯⲛⲁⲩ ⲉⲣⲱⲧⲛ ⲉⲩⲛⲧⲏⲧⲛ ⲙⲙⲁⲩ ⲛⲟⲩⲙⲛⲧⲣⲉϥⲣϩⲟⲧⲉ ⲉϩⲟⲩⲛ ⲉⲡⲛⲟⲩⲧⲉ ⲁⲗⲗⲁ ⲧⲉⲧⲛⲥⲟⲣⲙ ϩⲛⲧⲡⲓⲥⲧⲓⲥ ⲡⲉⲅⲕⲗⲏⲙⲁ [ⲡⲁⲛⲗⲁⲟⲥ] ⲁⲛ ⲡⲉ ⲁⲗⲗⲁ ⲡⲁⲛⲣⲉϥⲧⲥⲃⲱ (ⲡⲉ) ϫⲉⲕⲁⲥ (....) [ⲛⲛⲉⲓⲥⲉϣϥⲛϩⲱⲃ] ⲉⲡⲉϩⲟⲩⲟ ⲏ [ⲛⲧⲁⲓⲧϭⲁⲉⲓⲟϥ. ⲡⲁⲓ ⲇⲉ ⲟⲛ ⲡⲁⲛⲣⲉϥϯ(ⲥⲃ)ⲱ ⲡⲉ ⲉⲧϩ(.....)ⲏ ϫⲉ ⲙⲡ(ⲟⲩ)ϭⲛⲡⲉⲟⲩⲟⲉⲓϣ ⲏ ⲙⲡⲟⲩⲛⲟⲉⲓ] ⲉⲧⲥⲁⲃⲉ ⲑⲏⲩⲧⲛ ⲉⲛⲇⲟⲅⲙⲁ ⲉⲧⲟⲩⲟϫ.[38] "I [Nestorius] see you are God-fearing, but you err in the faith. The charge does not <u>concern the people</u>, but the teachers ... <u>not that I scorn</u> the matter greatly or <u>trivialize it. But this concerns the teachers who are ..... since they did not find time or know how</u> to teach you sound doctrine."

This passage concludes the Nestorian citations in *I Am Amazed*. As Shenoute says, "These, then, are the impieties of that one," ⲛⲁⲓ ⲙⲉⲛ ⲛⲉ ⲙⲙⲛⲧⲁⲥⲉⲃⲏⲥ ⲙⲡⲉⲧⲙⲙⲁⲩ.[39]

Based on these corrections to the text of *I Am Amazed*, two points can be made. First, Grillmeier's assessment of the Christology of Shenoute, which has been influential, is flawed because it is based on a flawed text. Grillmeier quotes paragraphs 473 and 474 in the Orlandi edition and adds his own commentary:

"If one for instance kills a person, does one then say: 'A body was killed'? Does one not say that the whole person was killed, even if the soul does not die but only the body?" (Then follows the application to Christ. One would now expect:) "Thus if Christ was killed only in regard to the body, then 'God' was killed, because Christ is inseparably God and human being." Yet Shenoute stays with the strict application of the anthropological comparison to Christ and thereby misses what he wanted to say vis-à-vis Nestorius, even if in so doing he brings to expression something different, namely, his teaching of the soul of Christ.[40]

37. Amélineau, *Oeuvres de Schenoudi*, 1:332–35.
38. Ibid., 1:332. In the text cited, the material within brackets marks passages where my reading of the manuscript differs from or expands on Amélineau's. The material in parentheses is a suggested reading of uncertain text. Amélineau has ϯⲛⲁⲩ ⲉⲣⲱⲧⲛ ⲉⲩⲛⲧⲏⲩⲧⲛ ⲙⲙⲁⲩ ⲛⲟⲩⲙⲛⲧⲣⲉϥ ϩⲟⲧⲉ ⲉϩⲟⲩⲛ ⲉⲡⲛⲟⲩⲧⲉ ⲁⲗⲗⲁ ⲧⲉⲧⲛⲥⲟⲣⲙ ϩⲛ ⲧⲡⲓⲥⲧⲓⲥ. ⲡⲉⲅⲕⲗⲏⲙⲁ ⲡⲁ ⲡⲗⲁⲟⲥ ⲁⲛ ⲡⲉ ⲁⲗⲗⲁ ⲡⲁ ⲛⲣⲉϥϯ ⲥⲃ.. ϫⲉⲕⲁⲥ....... ⲛⲛⲉⲓⲥⲉϣ...ⲡϩⲱⲃ ⲉⲡⲉϩⲟⲩⲟ ⲏ ⲛⲧⲁϥϭⲁⲉⲓⲟϥ ⲡⲁⲓ ⲇⲓⲟⲛ ⲡⲁ ⲛⲣⲉϥϯ.... ⲡⲉ ⲉⲧϩ.... ϩⲏ ϫⲉ ⲙ...... ⲏ ⲡⲉⲟⲩⲟⲉⲓϣ ⲏ ⲙⲡⲟⲩϫⲛⲟⲉⲓ ⲉⲧⲥⲁⲃⲉ ⲑⲏⲩⲧⲛ ⲉⲡⲇⲟⲅⲙⲁ ⲉⲧⲟⲩⲟϫ.
39. HB 67 = Amélineau, *Oeuvres de Schenoudi*, 1:332.
40. Grillmeier, *Christ in Christian Tradition*, 211.

Another quotation from 474 follows in Grillmeier, again with commentary:

"Thus the Lord also died in the flesh, whereas he was immortal in his entire soul. So said [the apostle]: 'He participated in body and soul'" (where what is meant is probably Heb. 2:14 . . .).[41]

But this passage (paragraphs 473–74) actually has little to say about the soul of Christ, as the corrected reading above shows. It has more to do with Shenoute's objections to the style of argument used by Nestorius, and with the counterarguments Shenoute makes based on the conventions of ordinary speech. "It is said" that a man died, even though his soul is immortal; similarly, we say that Christ died, even though his divinity does not die. Thus Shenoute says nothing here that is not in agreement with the tradition of the Coptic Church that Christ had a human soul.[42]

Second, it is likely that Shenoute consulted written sources for his citations of Nestorius. Shenoute attended the Council of Ephesus,[43] but when he produced this discourse some ten to fifteen years later, he seems to have relied on a file of Nestorian material (just as he relied on the festal letter of 401 to organize his anti-Origenist remarks).[44] Several of the scripture-based arguments that Shenoute attributes to Nestorius can be found in the writings of Nestorius that are excerpted in the acts of the Council of Ephesus.[45] Both the "my God, my God" argument that Shenoute attributes to Nestorius (470) and the "take the child" argument (480) can be found in the council documents, specifically in the *Book of Nestorius* excerpted in the acts.[46] The Amélineau material corrected above included the statement in which Shenoute quotes Nestorius: "I see you are God-fearing, but you err in the faith. This charge does not concern the people, but the teachers . . . since they did not find time or know how to teach you sound doctrine."[47] This is very close to the text of an ex-

---

41. Ibid.
42. Ibid., 211 n. 112.
43. Emmel, *Shenoute's Literary Corpus*, CSCO 599, 8–9, presents ample evidence for this from Shenoute's own writings.
44. Grillmeier, *Christ in Christian Tradition*, 209–10, addresses this question to some extent.
45. A. J. Festugière, trans., *Ephèse et Chalcédoine: Actes des Conciles* (Paris: Beauchesne, 1982), 237–44.
46. Ibid., 241, for par. 470, and 237–38 for par. 480.
47. HB 67 = Amélineau, *Oeuvres de Schenoudi*, 1:332.

cerpt from the *Book of Nestorius:* "I see, he said, that our faithful people have great piety and burning fervor, but have gone astray through ignorance of the knowledge of God in that which concerns doctrine. The error is not that of the faithful, but—how can I put it humbly—that of the teachers who have not had the opportunity to teach you doctrine more correctly."[48] The parallel supports the conclusion that Shenoute relied on written records of the Council of Ephesus when he criticized Nestorius in *I Am Amazed*. Did Shenoute himself translate these excerpts into Coptic in order to insert them in this discourse? Or did he use a Coptic version prepared and circulated by the patriarch in Alexandria? The corrected text of *I Am Amazed* may provide enough material for a comparison at some future point between the Greek acts of the council, contemporary Coptic translations from other sources, and known works of Shenoute. Study of the Greek, Latin, and Coptic versions of Theophilus's festal letter of 401 may provide useful parallels as well.[49]

These corrections to the Nestorian material in *I Am Amazed* make it necessary to modify the conclusions of Grillmeier and begin again in the study of the Christology of Shenoute, which is a crucial witness to the development of popular Egyptian anti-Chalcedonianism. As more of the discourses of Shenoute appear in critical editions, such analysis will become possible.

    48. Festugière, *Ephèse et Chalcédoine,* 244, my translation. Friedrich Loofs (*Nestoriana* [Halle: Max Niemeyer, 1905], 283) has the Greek text: καὶ προσέχω τοῖς ἡμετέροις δήμοις εὐλάβειαν μὲν πολλὴν κεκτημένοις καὶ θερμοτάτην εὐσέβειαν, ἀπὸ δὲ τῆς περὶ τὸ δόγμα θεογνωσίας ἀγνοίᾳ ὀλισθαίνουσι. τοῦτο δὲ οὐκ ἔγκλημα τῶν λαῶν. ἀλλά--πῶς ἂν εὐπρεπῶς εἴποιμι;--τὸ μὴ ἔχειν τοὺς διδασκάλους καιρὸν κάι τι τῶν ἀκριβεστέρων ὑμῖν παραθέσθαι δογμάτων.
    49. Fragments of the festal letter of 401 are preserved in Greek by Franz Diekamp, *Doctrina patrum de incarnatione verbi* (Münster: Aschendorff, 1907), 180–83. Jerome translated the entire letter; see Jerome, *ep.* 96 (CSEL 55:159–81).

Leo Depuydt

QUESTIONS AND RELATED PHENOMENA IN COPTIC AND IN GENERAL

Final Definitions Based on Boole's Laws

> Nothwendigerweise steht das präs(ens) II für das präsens eines f r a g e s a t z e s, dessen interrogativ dem verbum folgt, z. b. . . . ⲉϥⲃⲏⲕ ⲧⲱⲛ (wohin geht er?)
>
> —Ludwig Stern, *Koptische Grammatik*
> (Leipzig: Weigel, 1880), 213 (cf. 216 and 220)

This essay is an attempt to apply George Boole's ideas on the nature of thought to grammar in general and to Coptic and Egyptian grammar in specific. In presenting a line of argument, utmost parsimony is envisioned, in an effort to emulate that "character of steady growth which belongs to science" (Boole, *Investigation* [see note 1], 2). Parsimony involves refraining from extending concepts to areas where one cannot confidently do so. Specific phenomena are for the first time defined fully in line with the laws of thought as described by Boole. These phenomena include the question, the distinction between two kinds of questions, and the rhetorical question.

The present efforts supplement attempts made elsewhere by this writer to define contrastive emphasis and the distinction between condition and premise, also in Boolean fashion. The study of condition and premise was itself inspired by the fact that Egyptian exhibits verb forms that strictly depend on conditions and never result from premises. An example is Middle Egyptian (For transliteration purposes, I will use the codes used by the Glyph transliteration font as they appear before being converted into that font.) The difference between condition and premise thus leaves a deep and incisive mark on the Egyptian verbal system.

One observation is fundamental to the following argument. It is the fact that contrastive emphasis and the question, two components of the basic grammar of any language, are intimately connected. The epigraph from Ludwig Stern's Coptic grammar is meant to evoke this pivotal link. It follows that anyone firmly convinced that contrastive emphasis cannot be defined in any other way than in Boolean terms can find no rest until a final definition along the same terms has been attempted for related grammatical phenomena such as the question. What is meant by "final" is clarified below. The answers presented below may be in part provisional. But I believe that the direction has been firmly indicated in which any answers need to be sought. Further reflection in this direction is hereby encouraged. In fact, since completing this essay I have finished a book-length manuscript on different but closely related subject matter entitled *The Other Mathematics: Language and Logic in Egyptian and in General.*

This essay has four main parts. Part one briefly sketches the place of Boole's ideas in the history of thought. Part two is a short *apologia pro* the inclusion of this essay in the present volume. Part three is about defining the zone of intellectual activity to which the phenomena studied in this essay belong. This area remains for the time being the exclusive domain of the human intellect. "Incipient thought" or "formation of propositions" is suggested as a provisional designation for this area. Finally, part four does what this essay's title announces.

Boole's Laws of Thought, Information Theory, and the Study of Language

In 1854, in a work bearing the grandiose title *Investigation of the Laws of Thought,* George Boole (1815–64) made logic permanently into a part of mathematics, divorcing it once and for all from philosophy.[1] Bertrand Russell (1872–1970) once wrote that pure mathematics was the greatest discovery of the nineteenth century and Boole its discoverer. The field of mathematics most closely associated with Boole's laws is the theory of probability, which was pioneered by Blaise Pascal (1623–62), when he was "not yet withdrawn from the interests of science by the more distracting contemplation of the 'greatness and misery of man.'"[2] Indeed, the laws of the mind describe how we always think in spite of ourselves. In thinking, we are obviously often very much concerned with how likely it is that certain events will happen or have happened, given what else we now know. Probability is measured by numbers. These numbers are ratios of cases favorable to the sum of cases favorable and unfavorable, all cases being equally possible. Thus, in rolling the dice, the chance of obtaining a given number is 1 in 6. The probability is measured by the fraction ⅙, which is the ratio of cases favorable (1) to the sum of cases favorable and unfavorable (1 + 5).

Boole's insights rendered Aristotelian and scholastic logic obsolete, even if not unworthy of continued study. In Boole's words,

[Scholastic logic] is not a science, but a collection of scientific truths, too incomplete to form a system of themselves, and not sufficiently fundamental to serve as the foundation upon which a perfect system may rest. It does not, however, follow that because the logic of the schools has been invested with attributes to which it has no just claim, it is therefore undeserving of regard. A system which has been associated with the very growth of language, which has left its stamp upon the greatest questions and the most famous demonstrations of philosophy, cannot be altogether unworthy of attention.[3]

---

1. The full title of the work is *An Investigation of the Laws of Thought, on Which Are Founded the Mathematical Theories of Logic and Probabilities* (London: Walton and Maberly, 1854; reprint, New York: Dover, 1951 and 1958). The methods of this work are "more general, and its range of applications far wider" (see the preface) than the earlier *The Mathematical Analysis of Logic, Being an Essay towards a Calculus of Deductive Reasoning* (Cambridge: Philosophical Library, 1847; reprint, Oxford: Oxford University Press, 1948). The *Investigation* of 1854 holds "the results, matured by some years of study and reflection, of a principle of investigation relating to the intellectual operations" first presented in the *Mathematical Analysis* of 1847, "which was written within a few weeks after its idea had been conceived." Both works are also republished in *George Boole's Collected Logical Works* (Chicago: Open Court, 1916).

Three other names emerge with some prominence in the history of symbolic logic: Augustus De Morgan (1806–71), Charles Sanders Peirce (1839–1914), and Friedrich Wilhelm Karl Ernst Schröder (1841–1902). De Morgan's work precedes Boole's and Boole acknowledges it. But Boole's is a new beginning and the basis of everything that followed. Curiously, symbolic logic is said to be "largely an invention of the twentieth century" in the college textbook by Virginia Klenk, *Understanding Symbolic Logic* (Englewood Cliffs, N.J.: Prentice-Hall, 1983), 13.

2. Boole, *Investigation of the Laws of Thought*, 243.
3. Ibid., 241–42.

For several decades, Boole's theory of the nature of thought led a kind of shadow existence. It was like a voice crying in the desert. Some years after the *Investigation* appeared, Charles Sanders Peirce (1839–1914) reported on Boole's ideas to the American Academy of Arts and Sciences in Cambridge, Massachusetts.[4] Peirce also developed Boole's ideas. In part owing to Peirce, Boole's logic was at least taught at American universities. One captivated undergraduate student was Claude E. Shannon (1916–2001).

In 1936, freshly graduated from the University of Michigan and equipped with a knowledge of Boolean algebra, Shannon arrived as a graduate student at the Massachusetts Institute of Technology. In Cambridge, he tended to Vannevar Bush's (1890–1974) "differential analyzer," a mechanical behemoth built to solve differential equations. The desire, however, was for replacing the movements of shafts and gears and disks by electronic circuitry. Shannon saw the potential of Boolean algebra and ran with it. The result was an essay entitled "A Symbolic Analysis of Relay and Switching Circuits," hailed as "one the most important master's theses ever written" (H. H. Goldstine in his *The Computer from Pascal to Von Neumann*).[5] In 1940 Shannon earned both a master's degree in electrical engineering and a Ph.D. in mathematics from MIT. Shannon also collaborated with Alan M. Turing in the 1930s. The computer age had begun. The disciplines of information theory and communication theory were born.[6] The new universal unit was the binary digit, "bit" for short,

---

4. Charles Sanders Peirce, "On an Improvement in Boole's Calculus of Logic (Presented 12 March 1867)," *PAAAS* 7 (1865–68): 250–61.

5. Claude E. Shannon, "A Symbolic Analysis of Relay and Switching Circuits," *TAIE* 57 (1938): 713–23; reprinted in *Claude Elwood Shannon: Collected Papers*, ed. N. J. A. Sloane and Aaron D. Wyner (New York: Institute of Electrical and Electronics Engineers, 1993), 471–95. The crucial work was done in the summer of 1937. The following quotation from an interview with Shannon is revealing: "I knew about symbolic logic at the time from a course at Michigan, and I realized that Boolean algebra was just the thing to take care of relay circuits and switching circuits. I went to the library and got all the books I could on symbolic logic and Boolean algebra [cf. Alonzo Church, "A Bibliography of Symbolic Logic," *JSL* 1, no. 4 (1936): 121–218, which is cited at the end of Shannon's M.A. thesis; Boole is listed with four items in no. 19 of the bibliography's 547 numbers], started interplaying the two, and wrote my Master's thesis on it." About the connection between a relay circuit and Boolean algebra, he said, "Trivial, actually, once you make it. The connection was not the main thing. The more important, harder part was working out the details, how to interleave the topology of the switching circuits, the way the contacts are connected up and so on, with the Boolean algebra expressions. Working that out was a lot of fun. I think I had more fun doing that than anything else in my life, creatively speaking. It worked out so well." Shannon, *Collected Papers*, xxv–vi (reprinted from *Omni* magazine).

6. The classic manifesto of communication theory is Claude E. Shannon's *The Mathematical Theory of Communication*, which first appeared in the *Bell System Technical Journal* (July 1948): 379–423, and (October 1948): 623–56; reprinted with minor corrections and additions in C. E. Shannon and Warren

a term first suggested by John W. Tukey. It should be noted that Boolean algebra and Shannon's application of such algebra to the organization of electronic switches either in series or in parallel in countless combinations are not completely identical. An investigation of the differences might produce interesting observations on what differentiates the computer from the brain. But such an investigation exceeds the scope of this essay.

Neither Boole nor Shannon was interested in grammar per se. Their intention was never to do linguistic research. The mathematician dominated in Boole. The electrical engineer dominated in Shannon. Then again, in reading Boole's *Investigation,* one throughout encounters a delicate approach to the structure of language. An example is Boole's definition of the sign. The posthumous publication, in 1916, of Ferdinand de Saussure's (1857–1913) *Cours de linguistique générale,* the Magna Charta of modern linguistics, elevated the *signe linguistique* to the status of fundamental unit of language.[7] It is frustrating to see what little role the sign plays in more recent linguistics, as if it is somehow no longer hip. Mathematical theorems, once discovered, are forever young. Then why does the sign seem at times to be regarded as a mere fad?

One of the sign's striking properties is the characteristic combination of

---

Weaver, *The Mathematical Theory of Communication* (Urbana: University of Illinois Press, 1963); also in Shannon, *Collected Papers,* 5–83. Weaver writes, "Dr. Shannon has himself emphasized that communication theory owes a great debt to Professor Norbert Wiener [the pioneer of cybernetics (1894–1964)] for much of its basic philosophy. Professor Wiener, on the other hand, points out that Shannon's early work on switching and mathematical logic antedated his own interest in this field" (3n1). For more detail on the pioneering 1930s and 1940s along with further bibliography, see the last chapter in Dirk J. Struik, *A Concise History of Mathematics,* 4th rev. ed. (New York: Dover Publications, 1987), 214–17.

7. The standard critical edition is Ferdinand de Saussure, *Cours de linguistique générale,* critical edition by Tullio de Mauro based on the posthumous edition of 1916 by Charles Bally and Albert Sechehaye, with the collaboration of Albert Riedlinger (Paris: Payot, 1972), with de Mauro's introduction and notes of 1967 translated from the Italian by Louis-Jean Calvet. Arbitrariness is called "(l')arbitraire" (100) and fixedness is called "immutabilité." According to de Mauro (ix), "Saussure voit dans l'arbitraire du signe le principe fondamental de toute la réalité linguistique." De Mauro mentions Boole in connection with the arbitrariness of the sign, but also suggests that the works of William Dwight Whitney (1827–94) were a more direct source of inspiration for de Saussure on this point (442n137).

On how the study of language in modern times led up to Saussure's *Cours,* see Hans Aarsleff's invaluable *From Locke to Saussure: Essays on the Study of Language and Intellectual History* (Minneapolis: University of Minnesota Press, 1982). The great merit of this work is the rehabilitation of Condillac and John Locke as veritable pioneers of modern linguistic thought. Neither Boole nor the place of the sign in symbolic logic is mentioned.

The importance of the sign as the fundamental unit of language is also advocated in relation to the analysis of scripts in my "Champollion's Ideogram and Saussure's *signe linguistique,*" *Orientalia* 64 (1995): 1–11.

arbitrariness and fixedness. The sign is *arbitrary* because French speakers attach the sound pattern *chien* and English speakers the sound pattern *dog* to the general notion that they share of a certain animal. The sign is *fixed* because, once *chien* is arbitrarily chosen, one must link that sound pattern to the mental image of the animal in question in order to be understood by speakers of French. Significantly, the linguistic sign is neither the sound pattern *chien* nor the mental image of the animal. It is the *link* between the two, that is, the tacit agreement to always use that sound pattern in order to trigger the picture of that animal in one's own mind and in the minds of others. Boole describes this quintessential balance of arbitrariness and fixedness as follows.

In the first place, a sign is an *arbitrary* mark. It is clearly indifferent what particular word or token we associate with a given idea, provided that the association once made is permanent. The Romans expressed by the word "civitas" what we designate by the word "state." But both they and we might equally well have employed any other word to represent the same conception.

In the second place, it is necessary that each sign should possess, within the limits of the same discourse or process of reasoning, a fixed interpretation.[8]

But in spite of his insights into the structure of language, Boole was ultimately interested in language only as the instrument of thought. In Boole's interpretations of sentences, the search is not for phonetic, phonological, semantic, or syntactic structure, but for the *intended logical purport*. Thus he states,

Before attempting to translate our data into the rigorous language of symbols, it is above all things necessary to ascertain the *intended* purport of the words we are using. But this necessity cannot be regarded as an evil by those who value correctness of thought, and regard the right employment of language as both its instrument and its safeguard.[9]

An example of this search for the intended purport of sentences is as follows.

Consider next the case of universal negative propositions, e.g. "No men are perfect beings." Now it is manifest that in this case we do not speak of a class termed "no men," and assert of this class that all its members are "perfect beings." But we virtually make an assertion about "*all men*" to the effect that they are "*not perfect beings*." Thus the true meaning of the proposition is this: "All men (subject) are (copula) not perfect (predicate)."[10]

 8. Boole, *Investigation of the Laws of Thought*, 26.
 9. Ibid., 60–61.
 10. Ibid., 62. Subject and predicate are loaded terms these days. A massive amount has been written about them. There are as many theories about them, it seems, as there are students of them. I regard

Likewise, Shannon and his collaborators were not interested in writing grammar books but in building thinking-machines. Sure, English graduate students have written papers trying to apply information theory to literature. In this respect, Shannon complained of a "bandwagon effect." "Information theory has perhaps ballooned to an importance beyond its actual accomplishments," he lamented.[11] This lament should serve as a warning to anyone seeking to expand Boole's ideas into fields for which they were in origin not designed, such as grammar. The danger is that a theoretical scheme is plastered as a veneer of sophistication onto the treatment of a problem without penetrating the problem's essence.

Can Boole's theory provide firm answers to problems of basic grammar, problems of the everyday analysis of language? This writer has recently tried to expand Boole's ideas to explain two undeniable empirical phenomena: (1) emphasis (or contrast, or focus, or whatever one may wish to call it);[12] (2) the distinction between condition (ϥϣⲁⲛ- in Coptic) and premise (ⲉϣⲱⲡⲉ), including the fact that a condition can be subordinated to a premise (as in ⲉϣⲱⲡⲉ ⲉϥϣⲁⲛ-... "if it is the case that when[ever] he..."), but a premise cannot be subordinated to a condition.[13]

---

subject and predicate as ghost concepts, mere holdovers from scholastic logic, which is now obsolete. Likewise, to Boole, subject and predicate mean nothing more than the following:

> Suppose that we extend the meaning of the terms *subject* and *predicate* in the following manner. By *subject* let us mean the first term of any affirmative proposition, i.e. the one which precedes the copula *is* or *are*; and by *predicate* let us agree to mean the second term, i.e. the one which follows the copula. (Ibid., 59)

Evidently, these definitions say nothing about the nature of the term that precedes and the term that follows the verb "be."

11. See George Johnson's obituary of Claude E. Shannon in the *New York Times*, 27 February 2001, B7. The source is a one-page article by Shannon: "The Bandwagon," *Institute of Radio Engineers: Transactions on Information Theory* (became *IEEE*) 2 (1956): 3; reprinted in Shannon, *Collected Papers*, 462 (cf. also ibid., xxvii–viii).

12. See Leo Depuydt, "Contrast in Egyptian and in General and the Laws of Thought in Boolean Algebra," *GBS* 2 (1999): 37–60. This article states in error (p. 42) that Boole's wife, Mary, née Everest, with whom he had five daughters, was Sir George Everest's daughter. She was his niece. Boole taught at Queen's College in Cork, on Ireland's south central coast (Struik, *Concise History of Mathematics*, 176, erroneously places Queen's College in Dublin).

13. See Leo Depuydt, "Condition and Premise in Egyptian and Elsewhere and the Laws of Thought in Expanded Boolean Algebra," *ZÄS* 126 (1999): 97–111. Errata: (p. 102, line 5 from bottom) for "then" read "than"; (p. 110, line 4) for "1" read "0" (twice).

My first efforts at comprehending the difference between condition and premise concerned a proposal to interpret three instances of *xr=f sDm=f* in the Heqanakhte Letters as *xr=f* "so he says" plus prospective *sDm=f*, and not as the verb form *xr=f sDm=f*. One of the three examples (II, 35–36) contains

An effort was made, first, to set forth these two expansions in a fully self-sufficient manner by presenting all the elements needed to afford readers optimal circumstances for criticism; second, to define as sharply as possible that which needs to be proved, commonly referred to as the point of the argument; and third, to direct the line of argument by discretely recognizable and tightly interlocked steps toward a proof of the point.

The resulting definitions of contrastive emphasis and of the distinction between condition and premise were deemed to be final. The term "final," which also appears in the title of this essay, does not imply that criticism is not welcome or that the solutions proposed might not perhaps be found to be in error, even if these solutions are proffered in challenge to the reader as correct. "Final" involves the undeniable fact that the laws of thought define the absolute limitations of our mental faculties. There is no thinking beyond them. A definition that is reduced to this level has met an absolute limit and is in that sense final. About higher modes of thought, Boole muses that "it is impossible for us, with our existing faculties, adequately to conceive [their real nature], but... we might still investigate [their laws] as an object of intellectual speculation."[14] Thinking about spaces with more than three dimensions is similar to some extent. Then again, the mathematics of n-dimensional spaces has produced practical results.

Do Boole's ideas hold more potential for basic grammar? The aim of what follows is to suggest that they do. But first it is necessary to address a possible misconception.

In popular opinion, Boolean algebra is readily associated with 1 and 0, or ON and OFF, or AND/OR/NOT. These associations are not false. But they do not capture the essence of what Boole's theory tells us about the nature of

---

the sequence *jr ... xr=f sDm=f. xr=f* would then mark the contents of the preceding initial clause introduced by *jr* as a quote. In support of this interpretation, the following recently published passage contains an unambiguous instance of exactly such a use of the defective verb *xr* "say": *jr hAb=k Hr=s xrw=fy sw hAb=k ...* "when you write about it, as he says (you will), then you should write..." (Papyrus Illahun 10063, line 4; edited by Ulrich Luft, *Das Archiv von Illahun: Briefe 1*, HPSMB 1 [Berlin: Akademie-Verlag, 1992]).

14. Boole, *Investigation of the Laws of Thought*, 51. By the same token, we are unable to understand why we think the way we do and not in some other way. "It may, perhaps, be permitted to the mind," writes Boole, "to attain a knowledge of the laws to which it is itself subject, without its [*sic*] being also given to it to understand their ground and origin, or even, except in a very limited degree, to comprehend their fitness for their end, as compared with other and conceivable systems of law" (ibid., 11).

thought. Boole above all showed that the mind simply cannot conceive of, or reason about, anything without in the background also considering its supplementary class. Thus, we are unable to think about, say, sheep (s) without also implicitly operating with all-but-sheep, $1 - s$ in Boole's notation, that is, the universe of thought (1), or everything we could possibly think about, minus ($-$) sheep (s).

The implicit presence of supplementary classes constitutes the fundamental fiber of thought. Nothing better lays bare this fundamental fiber of mental operations than contrast, or focalization, or contrastive emphasis, or whatever it has been called. An example of contrast is "*sheep!* (of all things, as opposed to certain other animals, or the like)." The mind focalizes when it conceives of the supplementary class of the supplementary class, that is $1 - (1 - s)$ "not-not-sheep." Now, the supplement of the supplement of a class is obviously the original class itself. In Boolean notation: $1 - (1 - s) = 1 - 1 + s = 0 + s = s$. Therefore, "*sheep!*" ("not not-sheep") refers to the same reality. But in "*sheep!*" the class of sheep is explicitly set apart from anything else we could possibly think about by presenting that class *as the supplement of its supplement*. That is the total meaning of focalization or contrastive emphasis, which is marked in Coptic and Egyptian by so many Second tenses and cleft sentences.

What guarantee is there that the said definition of contrastive emphasis is correct? How can it be checked? It needs to be admitted that the level where final confirmation is to be found remains inaccessible. It is the level of empirical observation. This is the biological level, or the level of brain chemistry. This level remains terra incognita. But the decades ahead should bring change. Enormous advances in brain science are reasonably to be expected.

Meanwhile, we are compelled to do what Boole did: that is, to extract the intended logical purport from a statement. In that respect, it is somehow easy to understand the exclamation "*sheep!*" as the equivalent of "sheep, and not something else." Obviously, "something else" is the equivalent of "everything else but sheep," or $1 - s$, the universe of thought (1) minus ($-$) sheep (s). "*Not* something else" is then the negation of $1 - s$, namely $1 - (1 - s)$. It takes no great feat of the intellect to realize that "not-not-sheep" is the same as "sheep."

Perhaps the strongest argument in favor of the final definition of emphasis proposed above is that it can be fully incorporated in a universally accepted theory of the nature of thought, namely, the one first articulated by Boole.

The most striking characteristic of this theory is the omnipresence of supplementary classes in our thinking. Contrastive emphasis brings the supplementary classes out of hiding, as it were.

Everything in science is rooted in experience. But there is a difference between the laws of nature and the laws of thought. The laws of nature are inductive. They derive from many empirical observations. By contrast, no large number of observations is needed to establish the laws of thought. "[T]he knowledge of the laws of the mind," writes Boole, "does not require as its basis any extensive collection of observations. The general truth is seen in the particular instance, and it is not confirmed by the repetition of instances."[15] Also, "the general truths of Logic are of such a nature that when presented to the mind they at once command assent, wherein consists the difficulty of constructing the Science of Logic."[16] The same applies to the aforementioned definition of emphasis, which develops Boole's ideas. Insight in the definition is not increased by contemplating, in addition to "*sheep*!" many, or even any, other specific instances of contrastive emphasis applied to other words or phrases.

The omnipresence of supplementary classes that lurk just below the surface of all our thoughts is also evident from Boole's theorem of development:[17]

$$f(x) = f(1)x + f(0)(1 - x)$$

Any function of, or statement about, x can be developed with this formula. Note the presence of both x and its supplement, $1 - x$. An analysis of this absolutely fundamental theorem exceeds the scope of this essay. Boole shows that this theorem is just a variant of Taylor's theorem, one of the most productive theorems of calculus. The variation is that the theorem is applied to an algebra whose only two quantities are 1 and 0. In an article on Boole for the *Dictionary of Scientific Biography*, T. A. A. Broadbent reports that Boole dropped the association with "MacLaurin's theorem" in his *Investigation* of 1854 after having introduced it in his *Analysis* of 1847 (for full titles, see note 1).[18] To the

---

15. Ibid., 4.   16. Ibid.
17. Ibid., 72.
18. T. A. A. Broadbent, "Boole, George," in *Dictionary of Scientific Biography*, ed. Charles Coulston Gillispie (New York: Charles Scribner's Sons, 1970), 297.

contrary, Boole retains the crucial link in 1854, and even explicitly presents a proof of their identity.[19] Only he calls the theorem more appropriately "Taylor's theorem." As regards the theory's name, Struik writes,

> In his *Treatise of Fluxions* (1742), [Colin] Maclaurin [1698–1746]... deals with the famous "series of Maclaurin." This series, however, was no new discovery, since it had appeared in the *Methodus Incrementorum* (1715), written by Brook Taylor [1685–1731], for a while secretary of the Royal Society. Maclaurin fully acknowledged his debt to Taylor.... Taylor explicitly mentions the series for $x = 0$, which many college texts insist on naming "Maclaurin's series."... The full importance of Taylor's series was not recognized until [Leonhard] Euler [1707–83] applied it in his differential calculus (1755). [Joseph-Louis] Lagrange [1736–1813] supplied it with the remainder and used it as the foundation of his theory of functions.[20]

It was Boole who showed that the theorem dominates the operations of the mind.

Apologia

It is customary that, in a volume dedicated to a scholar, one establishes general or specific connections with the scholar's person and his work. In general, the term "Coptic" in the title of this essay would seem to justify inclusion of this essay in a volume celebrating the career of someone whose main area of expertise is Coptic language and literature. In specific, I first met Professor David Johnson in the fall of 1985 on the Yale campus in the apartment of H. J. Polotsky, then visiting at Yale. The general problems addressed in this essay were at the time very active in my mind and have occupied me time and again since then. Later, Father Johnson served as a reader of my Ph.D. dissertation for Yale, a catalogue of the Pierpont Morgan Library's Coptic manuscripts, and much improved the quality of this work.

I can only hope that I have strayed from philology narrowly speaking only as far as is needed to find answers to problems of basic grammar for which philology itself does not provide any. The purpose of what follows is not to indulge in theoretical speculation but to provide firm answers. May others judge whether that aim has been reached. I hope that the dedicatee enjoys this attempt at a Boolean escapade as a token of my esteem.

19. Boole, *Investigation of the Laws of Thought*, footnote to 72–73.
20. Struik, *Concise History of Mathematics*, 130, 133.

Incipient Thought or the Formation of Propositions:
A Zone of Intellectual Activity, Not Part of Logic Yet Describable Partly in Boolean Terms, Not Involving the Process of Thought but Rather the Formation of Thought as Resulting from Outside Impulses

Why are contrastive emphasis, the distinction between condition and premise, and questions not treated in Boole's *Investigation?* The short answer to this question is that computers cannot (yet), on their own, ask questions. A machine might be programmed with sound card and sensors to ask at dawn, "Is it time to get up?" But this statement is not the result of a spontaneous intellectual act of curiosity. The statement only mimics questions without really being a question. Questions require reactions to certain impulses from outside the mind. The mode of asking questions is still mostly the prerogative of human beings.

Boole was concerned with the logical operations of the mind. These operations proceed by invariable laws that are independent of the human will—a "truth," Boole would say, that is "not a private or arbitrary thing, not dependent, as to its essence, upon any human opinion."[21] It will be useful to impress upon the reader the absolute invariability of these processes by means of a few examples. One statement used by Boole for development is the Jewish law, "Clean beasts (x) are those which both divide the hoof (y) and chew the cud (z)."[22] This proposition may be represented by the equation $x = yz$. Many derivations are possible. All are invariably true. The supplementary classes $1 - x$ ("unclean beasts"), $1 - y$ ("beasts not dividing the hoof"), and $1 - z$ ("beasts not chewing the cud") are omnipresent. Examples of derivations are as follows: $xy(1 - z) = 0$ "clean beasts (x) dividing the hoof (y) but not chewing the cud ($1 - z$) do not exist ($= 0$)"; $z = xy + v(1 - x)(1 - y)$ "chewers of the cud (z) are ($=$) either clean beasts (x) dividing the hoof (y), or belong to an indefinite remainder (v) of objects that are neither clean beasts ($1 - x$) nor dividers of the hoof ($1 - y$)"; $x(1 - y) = 0$ "clean beasts (x) not dividing the hoof ($1 - y$) do not exist ($= 0$)"; $1 - y = (1 - x)z + v(1 - x)(1 - z)$ "those that do not divide the hoof ($1 - y$) are ($=$) either unclean beasts ($1 - x$) that chew the cud (z), or belong to an indefinite remainder (v) of objects that are neither clean beasts

---

21. From the preface to his *Investigation of the Laws of Thought.*
22. Ibid., 84.

$(1 - x)$ nor chewers of the cud $(1 - z)$." These derivations from the original equation are inescapable. That is what captivated Boole.

Boole studied the structure of thought only in as far as logical operations run their course *inside the mind*. Boole was interested in how the mind takes a proposition such as "clean beasts are those which both divide the hoof and chew the cud" and derives all kinds of other propositions from that initial proposition in invariable ways, without considering reality outside itself at all, and yet ends up with derivations that are fully in accordance with reality as we know it. This is deductive thinking, common in mathematics. Long operations are performed independently from reality. Yet the end result matches reality.

But another domain is also of interest. Boole barely touched it. Let us attempt to define it. One characteristic of this domain is contact between the mind and the world outside the mind. That contact consists of impulses that reach the mind from outside. It is obvious that the mind reacts to outside impulses. Now, the fact is that some of these reactions can be described strictly in line with the nature of thought as described by Boole. What part of the mind's reactions to what is outside itself can be described in this way is not clear at present. All one can do is to sparingly identify specific instances that one feels one can put forward for consideration as being absolutely certain.

It will be useful to further clarify the relation between the domain here under investigation and the domain of Boole's laws. Boole's laws describe how thinking *proceeds inside* the mind about what is already in the mind. The laws define the absolute limitations of thought. The term "logic" may be reserved for these processes. However, what is in the mind needs to get there in the first place. To derive propositions from an initial proposition, there first needs to be a proposition. When an outside impulse enters the mind, it is received by a certain structure that is firmly in place. That structure has its limitations. These limitations are implied to some extent in Boole's laws. An outstanding characteristic of this invariable structure is the omnipresence of the supplementary classes.

In sum, Boole's laws pertain to how a chain of thought proceeds in light of a certain invariable structure of the mind, a structure that is limited. By contrast, the area of intellectual activity investigated in this paper pertains to how that same invariable structure receives and absorbs impulses from outside and inevitably leads them into fixed channels. That absorption finds expression in language. To that extent, the matter becomes relevant to basic grammar. Two phenomena defined elsewhere, namely, contrastive emphasis and the distinction between condition and premise,[23] may now be interpreted along these lines.

Consider contrastive emphasis, or the difference between "sheep" and "*sheep*!" How can this difference be interpreted as impulses made on the mind and processed by the mind in accordance with Boole's laws? The observation of the class of sheep provides an impulse to the mind. On a certain level, there are two modes of referring to this class, and two only, namely, as sheep and not-not-sheep. The limitation to the two choices comes with the mind's invariable structure.[24] As one can see, contrastive emphasis is not part of logic strictly speaking. The laws of logic run their course inside the mind without impulses from outside. By contrast, emphasis involves the input of the human will. There is a choice. Then again, the choice is absolutely limited to two options. The question arises: What makes anyone choose one option over the other? That is difficult to answer at this time. It is like asking why we say certain things at certain times and not other things. Such chains of causality are the object of chaos theory. Chaos theory is becoming more comfortable in predicting the weather, but not yet the stock market, and certainly not human emotions.

Consider the difference between condition and premise. "When it rains," in "when it rains I stay at home," is a condition. "If it is raining," in "if it is raining, I am staying at home," is a premise. A simple test exposes the difference. From "when it rains I stay at home," it is not possible to derive the two independent statements "it rains" and "I stay at home." But from "if it is raining, I am staying at home," one *can* derive the two independent statements (1) "it is raining" and (2) "I am staying at home." How can this difference be interpreted as impulses made on the mind and processed by the mind in accordance with Boole's laws?

Let us assume that the mind has adopted the policy "when it rains I stay

23. See notes 12 and 13.
24. There seems to be no regular use of not-not-not-sheep. But it would be equivalent to not-not-sheep. Thus one might imagine someone reacting to someone else's stating "Did he say 'sheep'?" by saying, "No, *not sheep* (is what he said)" (implying "and not something else than not-sheep"; or in effect "not-not-not-sheep").

inside."²⁵ In respect to this policy, exactly four impulses from outside, no more and no less, can make an impression on the mind at the present moment in time. They are (1) "it is raining," (2) "it is not raining," (3) "I am staying inside," and (4) "I am not staying inside." These four impulses are premises. They are assumptions that a statement is or is not true, regardless of whether the statement is indeed true or one assumes so just for the sake of the argument. Each impulse has its own reaction, which is invariably the same. Two premises, (2) and (3), allow no conclusion. The two other premises, (1) and (4), both have their own fixed conclusion.

As for (2), if it is not true that it is raining, then I may be staying inside or I may not be. There is no way to know. As for (3), if it is true that I am staying inside, then it may be raining or it may not be. There is no way to know. The two other cases, however, invariably lead to a fixed conclusion. As for (1), if it is true that it is raining, then I am definitely now staying inside. As for (4), if it is not true that I am staying inside, then it is definitely now not raining. All these derivations could be presented rigorously in Boolean algebra. But such detail exceeds the scope of this essay.²⁶ The point is to show that impulses are received by the mind and classified immediately in certain invariable ways. There is choice. The human will plays a role. But choice is strictly limited and the options are fully definable.

In sum, a zone of intellectual activity has been cordoned off that is not quite logic. And because that area of thought finds expression in language, it becomes relevant to the study of language and even to the explanation of certain characteristics of the basic grammar of any language. Logic is strictly speaking about how one thinks. But the domain at hand is about how one *begins* to think or embarks upon thought.²⁷ Logic is about the progression of

---

25. In Boolean algebra, this statement might be rendered as $r = vi$ "the time during which it is true that it rains (r) is all, some, or none (v or the indefinite class) of the time during which I stay inside (i)" (so during the time when it does not rain, I may or I may not stay inside). All kinds of derivations are possible according to invariable developments, including: $r(1 - i) = 0$ "the time during which it rains and I do not stay inside is nothing (0)"; $1 = ri + (1 - r)i + (1 - r)(1 - i)$ "the totality of time (1) consists of the time when it rains and I stay inside plus the time when it does not rain and I stay inside plus the time when it does not rain and I do not stay inside."

26. For a fuller account, see section 3.2 of the article cited in note 13 above.

27. Boole does not say much about the onset of thought. The following quotation is relevant:

[W]ith reference to any particular ideas or conceptions presented to it, the mind possesses certain powers or faculties by which the mental regard may be fixed upon some ideas, to the exclusion

thought. The present concern is with certain circumstances in which thought is triggered or initiated. The mind apprehends reality. But it does so under certain strictly definable limitations. This paper concerns some of those limitations.

Certain Phenomena of Basic Grammar Located in the Zone of Incipient Thought

So far, a specific area of intellectual activity has been delineated. It may be called incipient thought. Incipient thought is about how the mind instantly classifies incoming signals. As impulses enter the mind, they are processed in certain invariable ways owing to the structure of thought itself. Two phenomena have so far been assigned to this area, namely, contrastive emphasis and condition and premise. The purpose of what follows is to assign more phenomena to this zone of intellectual activity.

First Step: Emphasis and Question. This line of argument needs a point of departure as its first step. Step one is an observation. It is the observation that *questions* and *contrastive emphasis* are linked somehow. As early as 1880 Ludwig Stern noted that *questions* and *"Second"* tenses are linked.[28] One of three passages in which he does is cited in the epigraph to this essay. In the summer of 1936, a year before Shannon's first applications of Boolean algebra to relays and switches (see note 5), H. J. Polotsky (1905–91) linked *Second tenses* and *contrastive emphasis*. As a result, *questions* now came to be linked to *contrastive emphasis*. But the nature of this link was not subjected to further investigation.

Interlude: The Link between Questions and Second Tenses. The empirical observation of this link played an indirect role, that of a catalyst, in the massive overhaul of Coptic and Egyptian grammar in the second half of the twentieth century. In view of the historical significance of this development, the

---

of others, or by which the given conceptions or ideas may, in various ways, be combined together. To those faculties or powers different names, as Attention, Simple Apprehension, Conception or Imagination, Abstraction, &c., have been given,—names which have not only furnished the titles of distinct divisions of the philosophy of the human mind, but passed into the common language of men. (*Investigation of the Laws of Thought,* 41)

28. Ludwig Stern, *Koptische Grammatik* (Leipzig: T. O. Weigel, 1880; reprint, Osnabrück: Biblio Verlag, 1971), 213, 216, and 220.

following detail regarding the history of research will be useful. Before defining the function of Coptic Second tenses and their ancestors in the summer of 1936,[29] Polotsky made three brief statements on the uses of Second tenses, as follows.[30]

1931
(1) Dagegen wäre das Perf[ekt] I im Fragesatz im Faij[umischen] möglich.

1934
(2) [Die] ... faij[umische] Negierung des Perf[ekts] I durch ɴ- — ⲉⲛ ... wird, wie im Sah[idischen] und Boh[airischen] das durch (ɴ-) — ⲁⲛ negierte Perf[ekt] II ..., im Unterschied von ⲙⲡⲉϥⲥⲱⲧⲉⲙ dann angewandt, wenn nicht das Faktum selbst sondern eine modale oder adverbiale Bestimmung oder d[er]gl[eiche] in Abrede gestellt wird.

(3) Im Fragesatz mit Interrogativpronomen oder -adverb sind [die zweiten Tempora] *obligatorisch*, wenn das Fragewort nach dem Verbum steht.

Quotations (1) and (3) report the affinity of Second tenses and questions (*Fragesatz*) as an undeniable descriptive fact. In (1), the fact is implied, namely, by stating that the affinity is *not* found in Faiyumic. Yet it is. Polotsky would later, in 1937, be the first to observe that the Faiyumic First and Second tenses of the past are often both written ⲁϥⲥⲱⲧⲉⲙ,[31] obscuring the fact that Faiyumic Second tenses are also typical in questions. As regards quotation (2), then, "adverbiale Bestimmung oder d[er]gl[eiche] in Abrede gestellt" prefigures the breakthrough of 1936. "Modale" does not.

Second Step: Boolean Definition of the Question. Step two is a logical conclusion from step one. Emphasis was defined above in Boolean terms. Step one indicates that emphasis and question are connected. The inevitable consequence of such a view is that the question, as a feature of grammar, must be defined in Boolean fashion as well.

Third Step: Two Types of Question. Emphasis and questions are connected.

---

29. For details, see my "Sentence Pattern and Verb Form: Egyptian Grammar since Polotsky," *Muséon* 108 (1995): 39–48. A full account appeared in 1944 (reprinted in Polotsky, *Collected Papers* [Jerusalem: Magnes Press, 1971], 125–202), preceded by two short preliminary reports in 1937 and 1940 (H. J. Polotsky, "Deux verbes auxiliaries méconnus du copte," *GLECS* 3 [1937]: 1–3, reprinted in Polotsky, *Collected Papers*, 99–101; and Polotsky, "Une règle concernant l'emploi des formes verbales dans la phrase interrogative en néo-égyptien," *ASAE* 40 [1940]: 241–45, reprinted in Polotsky, *Collected Papers*, 33–37).

30. Polotsky, *Collected Papers* (see there for full bibliographical detail), 354 (first appeared in *OLZ* 34 [1931]: col. 841) and 365 and 368–69 (*GGA* 196 [1934]: 60 and 63–64). The three quotations are part of two reviews of works by Walter Till.

31. Polotsky, *Collected Papers*, 99.

But it is a fact that there are two main types of questions. They may be called questions for corroboration (yes or no questions), as in "Did he come?" and questions for specification, as in "*Who* came?" or "*When* did he come?" Emphasis is typically connected with one of the two types only, namely, questions for specification, as in ⲉⲕⲃⲏⲕ ⲧⲱⲛ "where are you going?" This restriction too therefore requires a definition that accords with the laws of thought and is "unembarrassed by exception or failure."[32]

Fourth Step: Six Phenomena. It follows inevitably from the preceding steps that the laws of thought are the place where definitions for the following concepts must be found. But there is a level to which such definitions cannot (yet) penetrate. It is the biochemical level.

(1) The question.

(2) The two types of propositions, primary and secondary, and the two types of questions, for specification and for corroboration.

(3) The association of contrastive emphasis with questions for specification.

(4) Contrastive emphasis in primary propositions and in secondary propositions.

(5) The rhetorical question.

(6) Derivation of Coptic interrogatives ⲁⲱ and ⲟⲩ from indefinite *jx(t)* "thing" and *wa* "one."

(1) *The Question.* In the order of things, it is impossible to begin by defining *the* question as such. Something else must come first. That something else is the fact that thought progresses by means of *two* kinds of propositions.

(2) *The Two Types of Propositions, Primary and Secondary, and the Two Types of Questions.* "Logic is conversant with two kinds of relations," writes Boole, "—relations among things, and relations among facts."[33] Relations among things are expressed by primary propositions. Relations among facts are expressed by secondary propositions. These are the "two great divisions of the science of Logic."[34] Furthermore, "[s]econdary Propositions are those

---

32. Boole, *Investigation of the Laws of Thought*, 92.

33. Ibid., 9.

34. Ibid., 150. I have elsewhere proposed the existence of a tertiary proposition (see note 11). Tertiary propositions can be derived from secondary propositions. Thus, a tertiary proposition containing a

which concern or relate to Propositions considered as true or false. The relations of things we express by primary propositions. But we are able to make Propositions themselves also the subject of thought, and to express our judgments concerning them."[35] Boole goes into great detail showing that primary propositions and secondary propositions are subject to the same laws, which are mathematical in nature. But the details exceed the scope of the present essay.

Consider the proposition already mentioned above, "Clean beasts are those which both divide the hoof and chew the cud." It is a fundamental characteristic of thought that reasoning can be performed on two distinct and separate levels regarding this statement.

First, the statement can be taken as a primary proposition. On this primary level, various propositions can be derived without fail from the original proposition, for example, "Clean beasts not dividing the hoof do not exist." Such derivations reshuffle, as it were, relations between things in various ways. Other examples of such derivations have been mentioned above.

Second, the statement can be taken as a secondary proposition. "[W]e are able," writes Boole, "to make Propositions themselves also the subject of thought, and to express our judgments concerning them."[36] On this secondary level, the aforementioned statement is said to be either true or false. The derivations on this level concern the relations between facts. For example, the statement "it is true that clean beasts are those which both divide the hoof and chew the cud" can be combined with other statements, for example, "it is true that cows are (some of the) clean beasts." The following statement unfailingly follows from this combination: "Cows are some of those that chew the cud and divide the hoof."

The transition from ignorance to knowledge can be achieved in different ways. One way is observing. Another way is asking, that is, appealing to the knowledge of others. The constitution of the intellect is such that, in asking, a fundamental choice instantly imposes itself between asking on the primary level and asking on the secondary level. As a result, there are two types of questions. Consider the proposition, "Clean beasts are those which both divide the

---

premise can be derived from a secondary proposition containing a condition by certain fixed procedures. Details regarding such derivations have been presented above.

35. Ibid., 160.
36. Ibid.

hoof and chew the cud." On the primary level, one might ask: "Which beasts divide the hoof and chew the cud?" or "What do clean beasts do?" These are called questions for specification. They ask about things. On the secondary level, one might ask: "Do clean beasts divide the hoof and chew the cud?" or more explicitly, "Is it true (or not true) that clean beasts divide the hoof and chew the cud?" These are questions for corroboration. They ask about facts.

It appears, then, that the area of intellectual activity where a true and final definition of the two types of questions can be found has been identified. Further refinement will be possible when the biochemical nature of this area has been described.

(3) *The Association of Contrastive Emphasis with Questions for Specification.* Contrastive emphasis is more or less mandatory in certain questions for specification. But first of all, why are Second tenses or cleft sentences *not* mandatory with questions for corroboration? An example of such a question is "Did he arrive?" or also "He arrived?" The intended purport of "He arrived?" seems to be to submit a primary proposition to hearers or readers and to invite them to elevate that primary proposition to a secondary proposition by making a commitment as to whether the proposition is true or false. Two things seem obvious about "He arrived?" First, it is not a secondary proposition, because there is clearly no commitment as to whether "he arrived" is true or not. To find out whether it is true or not is precisely why the question is asked in the first place. But second, there is also an invitation to *produce* a secondary proposition and make such a commitment. Rising intonation alone in "He arrived?" and rising intonation plus inversion of word order in "Did he arrive?" somehow signal the invitation or the appeal to the interlocutor. One is reminded of how a sharply *falling* intonation strongly avers a commitment to truth or falsehood, as in "He arrived. Period." It comes perhaps as no surprise, then, that a *rising* intonation denotes the absence of such a commitment, along with an invitation to fill that absence.

Again, why is contrastive emphasis not associated with questions for corroboration? To begin, it will be useful to observe carefully what *does* happen when contrastive emphasis appears in a question for corroboration. Consider the question "*Did* he come?" or also "He *did* come?" In this case, the primary proposition "he *did* come" is submitted to the interlocutor for a commitment as to whether it is true or false. The primary proposition exhibits contrastive emphasis (*did*), which invokes the supplementary class, namely not-coming. The intended purport of the proposition is: "he did come, and not rather *not* come." Contrastive emphasis is then transferred from "He *did* come" to the question "*Did* he come?" As Boole states, "we are able to make Propositions themselves also the subject of thought."[37] If propositions can be made into the subject of thought, then it seems obvious that contrastive emphasis can be applied to that subject of thought.

What matters here is that the shift from "He *did* come," an affirmative proposition, to "*Did* he come?" a question for corroboration, does not trigger the addition of contrastive emphasis. Both propositions exhibit it. By contrast, the shift from "he came yesterday," an affirmative proposition, to "who came?" and "when did he come?"—both questions for specification—does produce contrastive emphasis. The proof is that, in Coptic, a cleft sentence is the norm in the first question and a second tense in the second question. Why is this? First of all, interrogative pronouns refer to things, in the present instances a certain person or a certain time. These things are unknown. They may therefore be represented by x. But what is more, the intended purport of interrogative words is to identify these things by singling them out from all other possible things, that is, by contrasting them with $1 - x$ "something else (but x)," or the universe (1) minus (−) x. It is easy to see, therefore, that interrogative words refer to $x\,[1 - (1 - x)]$ "x, and not something else." Contrastive emphasis is somehow natural. On the other hand, in questions for corroboration, the choice is between true and false. The choice is open. It is easy to see that there is no focus on either option, and therefore no contrastive emphasis.

That would be the answer submitted here to explain the phenomenon described in the epigraph to this essay. Further refinement remains possible.

(4) *Contrastive Emphasis in Primary Propositions and in Secondary Propositions.* Contrastive emphasis of course also appears outside questions. It seems possible to apply emphasis to anything that the mind can conceive of as a single subject of thought. Thus contrastive emphasis may apply to things. In Coptic, cleft sentences and Second tenses are then used. Contrastive emphasis may also apply to a proposition as a whole, as in "he *is* dead." That would appear to be the function of ⲡⲱ in Coptic, as in ϥⲙⲟⲟⲩⲧ ⲡⲱ "he *is* dead."[38] The Ger-

---

37. Ibid.
38. See my "The Meaning of the Coptic Particle ⲡⲱ and Related Constructions in Semitic and Other Languages," *JCS* 3 (2001): 113–28.

man enclitic particle *ja* appears similar in function. Compare *Das ist ja schön* with *Das ist schön. Ja* in origin means "yes." *Das ist ja schön,* "it *is* beautiful," therefore implies the suggestion that it is *not* beautiful. If the proposition "he is dead" is represented by V, then "he *is* dead" may be represented in Boolean fashion as $V[1 - (1 - V)]$ "V, and not $(1 -)$ something else but $V(1 - V)$." The secondary proposition "It is true that he *is* dead" would then correspond to $V[1 - (1 - V)] = 1$. And even this secondary proposition can presumably form a single subject of thought and be subjected in its own right to contrastive emphasis. Indeed, it is undeniably possible to state: "It *is* true that he *is* dead." Then there is the difference between "It *is* true that he is dead" and "It is true that he *is* dead." The difference seems subtle. Yet, it is undeniably possible to make both statements. Both are therefore deserving of an analysis in line with the laws of thought.

(5) *The Rhetorical Question.* A rhetorical question is not in effect a question. The answer is taken for granted. Thus the rhetorical question is about doubly affirming a proposition by questioning its negation. For example, "Is this not beautiful?" is more or less the same as stating, "It *is* beautiful." In Coptic, the Greek negation ⲙⲏ is used. An example is ⲙⲏ ⲛ̄ⲧⲟⲕ ϩⲱⲱⲕ ⲟⲛ ⲛ̄ⲧⲕ̄ ⲟⲩⲉⲃⲟⲗ ϩⲛ̄ ⲛⲉϥⲙⲁⲑⲏⲧⲏⲥ "You're not also one of his disciples, are you?" (John 18:25, after the NAB translation).

Any analysis of the mechanics of the rhetorical question should try to locate the right relays and switches in the mind. What follows is a provisional suggestion. It is clear that anyone asking the rhetorical question "Is it not beautiful?" is firmly convinced of the proposition "It *is* beautiful." If V is "it is beautiful" and $V = 1$ is "it is true $(= 1)$ that it is beautiful (V)," then the rhetorical question "Is it not beautiful?" is a primary proposition denoted by $1 - V$? It is not secondary because there is no commitment as to truth or falsehood. Strictly speaking, such a question for corroboration ought to be an invitation to choose between $1 - V = 1$ "(it is true that) it is not beautiful" and $1 - V = 0$ "it is not true that it is not beautiful." Since $1 - V$ is given by the asker at the outset and must be dealt with, the answer to which one is somehow steered by the device of the rhetorical question is $1 - (1 - V) = 1$ "it *is* beautiful" (literally: "it is true that it is not not beautiful").

(6) *Derivation of Coptic Interrogatives* ⲁϣ *and* ⲟⲩ *from Indefinite* jx(t) *"Thing" and* wa *"One."* Questions for specification such as "Who came?" presuppose that *someone* came. The purpose of "Who came?" is to reveal the iden-

tity of that someone. That explains why interrogative pronouns can be derived from indefinite pronouns *by the addition of contrastive emphasis*. Contrastive emphasis is marked in many languages by a rise in intonation. Compare the two instances of German *welche* in *Es gibt welche. Welche?* "There are some? Which?" or the two instances of *was* in *Ist was los? Also was?* "Is something wrong? So what?" In Greek, indefinite τι "something" bears no accent. But interrogative τί "what?" does. A difference in intonation may also be assumed for Latin *quis* "someone" and *quis* "who?" It is therefore altogether natural to assume that the Coptic interrogatives ⲁϣ and ⲟⲩ derive from indefinite *jx(t)* "thing" and *wa* "one" respectively.[39] ⲟⲩ "a" relates to ⲟⲩ "what?" as x does to x [$1 - (1 - x)$]. In a similar relationship in French, *oui* "yes" relates to *si* "yes" as x does to $1 - (1 - x)$. *Oui* in effect means "it is so" and *si* "it is not not so." In German, *ja* and *doch* relate to each other similarly.

In conclusion, this writer strongly feels that more explanatory gain is to be derived from Boolean ideas for the study of basic grammar. It is not clear how much. The need is for proceeding stepwise, phenomenon by phenomenon. Some of what has been said above may be subject to refinement. But this writer has every confidence that the solutions proposed generally point in the right direction. May others verify what is said above and, if possible, expand it.

39. It appears that Kurt Sethe has already proposed this etymology, but without specifying that contrastive emphasis is the distinguishing characteristic; see his "Untersuchungen über die ägyptischen Zahlwörter," *ZÄS* 47 (1910): 4.

PART II SOCIAL CONTEXT

Birger A. Pearson

EARLIEST CHRISTIANITY IN EGYPT

Further Observations

In September 1983 a conference was held in Claremont (with a day trip to Santa Barbara) devoted to the theme, "The Roots of Egyptian Christianity," with an international array of scholars participating. That conference, organized by James E. Goehring and myself and sponsored by the National Endowment for the Humanities, inaugurated a research project based at the Institute for Antiquity and Christianity in Claremont and directed by me. This project is devoted to the study of Christianity in Egypt from its origins in Alexandria to the time of the Arab Conquest in 641. The conference proceedings were published in 1986 as the first volume of a new series associated with the institute, "Studies in Antiquity and Christianity."[1] Several volumes of the "Roots of Egyptian Christianity" project have been published in that series since then.[2]

One of the participants in the conference and a contributor to the pro-

---

1. Birger A. Pearson and James E. Goehring, eds., *The Roots of Egyptian Christianity* (Minneapolis: Fortress Press, 1986).
2. Tim Vivian, *Saint Peter of Alexandria: Bishop and Martyr* (Minneapolis: Fortress Press, 1988); Birger Pearson, *Gnosticism, Judaism, and Egyptian Christianity* (Minneapolis: Fortress Press, 1990); David Frankfurter, *Elijah in Upper Egypt: The Apocalypse of Elijah and Early Egyptian Christianity* (Minneapolis: Fortress Press, 1993); Samuel Rubenson, *The Letters of St. Antony: Monasticism and the Making of a Saint* (Minneapolis: Fortress Press, 1995); James Goehring, *Ascetics, Society, and the Desert: Studies in Early Egyptian Monasticism* (Harrisburg: Trinity Press International, 1999); Birger A. Pearson, *Gnosticism and Christianity in Roman and Coptic Egypt* (New York: T. & T. Clark International, 2004).

ceedings was our jubilarian, David W. Johnson, S.J. He presented a very fine paper on "Anti-Chalcedonian Polemics in Coptic Texts, 451–641."[3] I have profited greatly from my contacts with David Johnson before and since, and I take great pleasure in contributing to this well-deserved Festschrift in his honor.

My own contribution to the 1983 conference and the conference volume was entitled "Earliest Christianity in Egypt: Some Observations."[4] The present essay is intended to follow up on that earlier one, with reference to studies that have appeared since. This discussion comprises three main parts: (1) the Jewish origins of Egyptian Christianity; (2) varieties of early Egyptian Christianity; and (3) Alexandrian precursors of Egyptian monasticism. A brief appendix on the *Epistula Apostolorum* is also included.

The Jewish Origins of Egyptian Christianity

I began my earlier article with a discussion of Colin Roberts's extremely important work, *Manuscript, Society, and Belief in Early Christian Egypt*.[5] His theory of the Jerusalem origins and Jewish context of earliest Christianity in Egypt is more convincing than Walter Bauer's theory of a "heretical," specifically "gnostic," type of Christianity in the Church's beginning stages in Egypt.[6] I then took up for discussion the Mark legend, as found in the fourth-century *Acts of Mark*, and pointed out that the places in Alexandria mentioned in the *Acts* are places that, in the first century, were parts of the main Jewish areas of Alexandria.[7] I concluded that the earliest Christian communities in Egypt were

---

3. In Pearson and Goehring, *Roots of Egyptian Christianity*, 216–34. It is my hope that a monograph by Johnson on Coptic Christianity post-Chalcedon will soon be published in the SAC series.

4. Ibid., 132–59.

5. Roberts's work constituted the Schweich Lectures of the British Academy for 1977 (London: Oxford University Press, 1979).

6. Walter Bauer, *Orthodoxy and Heresy in Earliest Christianity*, trans. and ed. Robert A. Kraft et al. (Philadelphia: Fortress Press, 1971), 44–53. See my discussion in "Christianity in Egypt," *ABD* 1:954–60.

7. That discussion was expanded in an article published in a memorial volume for a well-known Alexandrian archeologist: Birger A. Pearson, "The *Acts of Mark* and the Topography of Ancient Alexandria," in *Alexandrian Studies in Memoriam Daoud Abdu Daoud*, ed. Nabil Swelim, SAA 45 (1993) (Alexandria: Archeological Society of Alexandria, 1994), 239–46; reprinted in SBLSP 1997 (Atlanta: Scholars Press, 1997), 273–84. An updated version appears as chapter 3 in Pearson, *Gnosticism and Christianity*.

part of the large and variegated Jewish *politeuma* in first-century Alexandria up until the Jewish revolt against Trajan (115–17 CE). I might add here that even to speak of "Christians" in first-century Alexandria is an anachronism, since the term is not attested in Alexandrian sources until the second century.[8]

More recent studies have borne out the Jewish context of Christian origins in Egypt, with the result that one can speak of a growing scholarly consensus on that issue.[9] Nevertheless, "the obscurity that veils the early history of the Church in Egypt"[10] still remains. Also yet to be explained is the process whereby the various Christian groups that no doubt existed by the turn of the second century became separated from the Jewish community to which they originally belonged.

These issues are addressed by Joseph Modrzejewski in the epilogue to his important work on the Jews of Egypt. He notes that Bauer's thesis of the Gnostic origins of Alexandrian Christianity cannot explain the "silence" surrounding primitive Christianity, for "we have no better knowledge concerning Gnostics from this period than we have of 'orthodox' Christians." He proposes what he considers to be a more convincing explanation: "if primitive Christianity had not left any marks on Egyptian soil until the end of the second century, it was because it had been annihilated along with the entire body in which it was immersed—the Jewish community of Egypt." In this view there is a distinct discontinuity between primitive Christianity in Egypt and what follows after the revolt of 115–17: The "Judeo-Christianity in Alexandria" was destroyed and "replaced by a Greek and Egyptian pagano-Christianity."

---

8. The earliest attestation would appear to be in the *Kerygma Petri*, where "Christians" are referred to as a "third race." See frg. 2d (Clement of Alexandria, *Strom.* 6.5.41) in Wilhelm Schneemelcher, ed., *New Testament Apocrypha*, rev. ed., trans. Robert McLachlan Wilson (Cambridge: James Clarke, and Louisville, Ky.: Westminster/John Knox Press, 1991, 1992), 2:39. On the *Kerygma Petri*, see below.

9. See especially Adolf M. Ritter, "De Polycarp à Clément: Aux origines d'Alexandrie chrétienne," in *ΑΛΕΞΑΝΔΡΙΝΑ: Hellénisme, judaïsme et christianisme à Alexandrie, Mélanges offerts au P. Claude Mondésert* (Paris: Éditions du Cerf, 1987), 151–72; Joseph M. Modrzejewski, *The Jews of Egypt from Rameses II to Emperor Hadrian*, trans. Robert Cornman (Princeton: Princeton University Press, 1997), epilogue, 227–31; Gilles Dorival, "Les débuts du christianisme à Alexandrie," in *Alexandrie: Une mégapole cosmopolite: Actes du 9ème colloque de la Villa Kérylos à Beaulieu-sur-Mer les 2 & 3 octobre 1998*, ed. Jean Leclant (Paris: Académie des Inscriptions et Belles-Lettres, 1999), 157–74; and Attila Jakab, *Ecclesia alexandrina: Evolution sociale et institutionnelle du christianisme alexandrin (IIe et IIIe siècles)* (Bern: Peter Lang, 2001), 49–61. I should also mention here A. F. J. Klijn's article "Jewish Christianity in Egypt," in Pearson and Goehring, *Roots of Egyptian Christianity*, 161–75.

10. Colin H. Roberts, *Manuscript, Society, and Belief in Early Christian Egypt* (London: Oxford University Press, 1979), 1.

The first Christians in Egypt were Alexandrian Jews who had heeded the "Good News" emanating from Jerusalem. Together with the entire Jewish colony, of which they were a part, they were carried along into the midst of the fatal storm that was to break out some half-century later. Those who managed to survive were absorbed by the new community, recruited among Greek and Egyptian pagans.[11]

I do not find convincing Modrzejewski's theory of a complete rupture between primitive Egyptian Christianity and what comes after the Jewish revolt, for existing second-century evidence points to continuities between Alexandrian Judaism and post-117 Alexandrian Christianity. The most obvious signs of continuity are the retention and use by Alexandrian Christians of the Alexandrian Jewish Septuagint, and the collection and dissemination of the writings of Philo Judaeus.[12] Additional continuities come to light by extrapolating backward into the first-century hints from second-century sources,[13] and by taking into account first-century sources for Alexandrian Judaism.

I have explored such continuities in a recently published study, with special attention to the works of Philo Judaeus and two Alexandrian Christian texts, the *Epistle of Barnabas* and the *Teachings of Silvanus* (NHC VII, 4).[14] There I discuss Philo's delineation of various groups of Jews in first-century Alexandria, including a type of Jewish messianism that can be seen reflected in Philo's treatise *On Rewards and Punishments* (*De praemiis et poenis* 85–168). Philo himself reinterprets that tradition with reference to his doctrine of the Logos and typically interiorizes the messianic vision in terms of the growth of virtue in the human soul. For the two Christian texts the figure of Jesus Christ makes all the difference, even when first-century Jewish traditions are preserved and reinterpreted. Specifically Christian versions of first-century Alexandrian Jewish messianism are found in *Barnabas*, where one also finds a highly charged eschatology and a consciousness of living in the last times

---

11. Modrzejewski, *Jews of Egypt*, 228.

12. The writings of Philo were undoubtedly used by Alexandrian Christians years or decades before the war of 115–17; so Dorival, "Débuts du christianisme," 165.

13. That is what Bauer did when he extrapolated a primitive Christian Gnosticism from what we know of second-century Gnostic teachers such as Basilides, Carpocrates, and Valentinus. See my remarks in "Earliest Christianity," 149.

14. "Cracking a Conundrum: Christian Origins in Egypt," *StTh* 57 (2003): 1–15. Cf. also "Christians and Jews in First-Century Alexandria," chapter 2 in Pearson, *Gnosticism and Christianity*, an expanded version of an essay published earlier in a special issue of the *HTR*, a Festschrift for Krister Stendahl (*HTR* 79 [1984, publ. 1986]: 106–16).

(*Barnabas* 2.1; 4.1,5,9, etc.). Philo's Platonist-oriented wisdom theology receives a Christian dress in *Silvanus*. *Barnabas* clearly reflects a postrevolt situation and a marked alienation from the Jewish people, "the former people" (*Barnabas* 5.7; 7.5; 13.1–6, etc.). *Silvanus* represents a later stage of development, for no notice is taken of Jews or Judaism in that text.[15] Even so, as school texts both contain Alexandrian Jewish traditions from the first century.

But are we restricted to second-century Christian texts for information on first-century Jewish Christianity in Alexandria? I do not think so, for there is reason to think that the apostle Paul, already in the early 50s, encountered a variety of Alexandrian Christian teaching in Corinth and probably in Ephesus. I have commented elsewhere on the relationships among *Silvanus*, Philo, and 1 Corinthians 1–4, and have suggested that *Silvanus* retains, as part of its Alexandrian Christian tradition, a good deal of the "speculative wisdom" that so impressed members of his Corinthian church.[16] This wisdom was probably mediated by the Alexandrian Jewish teacher Apollos, "an eloquent man, well versed in the scriptures" (Acts 18:24; cf. 1 Cor. 1:12; 3:4–22; 4:6; 16:12; Acts 19:1). One can extrapolate from Paul's arguments in 1 Corinthians 1–4 a variety of Christian "wisdom" that reflects traditions at home in Philo's Alexandria, and I would go so far as to suggest that Apollos had been a pupil of Philo's before his departure from Alexandria.[17] It is not for nothing that later Alexandrian teachers such as Clement and Origen would regard Philo as one of their own predecessors.[18]

Varieties of Early Egyptian Christianity

As noted above, the *Epistle of Barnabas* reflects a type of Christianity that gives Christian expression to a Jewish messianism espoused by some Alexan-

---

15. The only opponents identifiable in *Silvanus* are Gnostics (94, 29–33; 116, 5–9).
16. "Philo, Gnosis, and the New Testament," chapter 11 in Pearson, *Gnosticism, Judaism, and Egyptian Christianity*, 165–82, esp. 177–81.
17. This has been suggested before by G. H. R. Horsley in his *New Documents Illustrating Early Christianity: A Review of the Greek Inscriptions and Papyri Published in 1976* (North Ride, N.S.W.: Macquarie University, Ancient History Documentary Research Centre, 1981), no. 50: "Apollos," p. 88.
18. Annewies van den Hoek, *Clement of Alexandria and His Use of Philo in the Stromateis: An Early Christian Reshaping of a Jewish Model*, VCSupp 3 (Leiden: Brill, 1988); David T. Runia, *Philo in Early Christian Literature: A Survey*, CRINT 3,3 (Assen: Van Gorcum, and Minneapolis: Fortress Press, 1993).

drian Jews and that, in fact, led to the disaster of 115–17.[19] The eschatology in *Barnabas* reflects a kind of "chiliasm" (in chap. 15) that persisted in Egypt for a long time, first presumably among literal-minded "simpliciores" who disapproved of philosophical speculation[20] and eventually among some Egyptian monks in the monasteries.[21] *Barnabas* also appears to reflect the existence in Alexandria of other Christian groups with which its author expresses his disagreement: Gnostics, Jewish Christians, and ascetically oriented Christians.

There is an implicit anti-Gnostic stance in *Barnabas,* with its repeated reference to halakic and exegetical *gnosis.*[22] Barnabas's *gnosis* can be seen as a precursor of the *gnosis* espoused by Clement of Alexandria, who distinguished the "true" gnosis from the "knowledge falsely so-called" (1 Tim. 6:20) espoused by heretics.[23] As is well known, the earliest Christian teachers in Alexandria known to us by name were Gnostic "heretics," Basilides, Valentinus, and Carpocrates, and one can easily posit the existence in Alexandria of a pre-Christian Jewish Gnosticism such as is reflected in *Eugnostos the Blessed* (NHC III,3 and V,1).[24] Christians of a more Jewish stamp may be referred to at Barnabas 4.6, where

19. The messianist roots of the Jewish revolt against Trajan is convincingly argued by Martin Hengel, "Messianische Hoffnung und politischer 'Radikalismus' in der jüdisch-hellenistischen Diaspora," in *Apocalypticism in the Mediterranean World and the Near East: Proceedings of the International Colloquium on Apocalypticism, Uppsala, August 12–17, 1979,* ed. David Hellholm (Tübingen: Mohr Siebeck, 1983), 655–86.

20. Rouel van den Broek, "Juden und Christen in Alexandrien im 2. und 3. Jahrhundert," in *Studies in Gnosticism and Alexandrian Christianity,* ed. Rouel van den Broek, NHMS 39 (Leiden: Brill, 1996), 181–96, esp. 188; Dorival, "Débuts du christianisme," 170–71. Bishop Dionysius paid a visit to Arsinoe to combat the chiliasm espoused by the bishop there, Nepos (Eusebius, *HE* 7.24–25). The *Apocalypse of Elijah* reflects a chiliastic eschatology at home in third-century Upper Egypt. See Frankfurter, *Elijah in Upper Egypt.*

21. For a fifth- or sixth-century Coptic apocalypse that contains references to the millennium, see Birger A. Pearson, "The Pierpont Morgan Fragments of a Coptic Enoch Apocryphon," in *Studies on the Testament of Abraham,* ed. G. W. E. Nickelsburg, SBLSCS 6 (Missoula: Scholars Press, 1976), 227–83. An updated version of that article is chapter 6 in Pearson, *Gnosticism and Christianity.*

22. On *gnosis* in Barnabas, see Robert A. Kraft, *Barnabas and Didache,* vol. 3 of *The Apostolic Fathers: A New Translation and Commentary,* ed. Robert M. Grant (New York: Thomas Nelson and Sons, 1965), 22–27; James C. Paget, *The Epistle of Barnabas: Outlook and Background,* WUNT 64 (Tübingen: Mohr Siebeck, 1994), 46–49, 244–45.

23. André Méhat, "'Vraie' et 'fausse' gnose d'après Clément d'Alexandrie," in *The Rediscovery of Gnosticism: Proceedings of the Conference at Yale March 1978,* ed. Bentley Layton, SHR 41 (Leiden: Brill, 1980), vol. 1: *The School of Valentinus,* 426–33.

24. Rouel van den Broek, "Jewish and Platonic Speculations in Early Alexandrian Theology: Eugnostus, Philo, Valentinus, and Origen," in Pearson and Goehring, *Roots of Egyptian Christianity,* 190–203. Cf. also my article, "Pre-Valentinian Gnosticism in Alexandria," in *The Future of Early Christianity: Essays in Honor of Helmut Koester,* ed. Birger A. Pearson (Minneapolis: Fortress Press, 1991),

there is a warning against "some" who say "that the covenant is both theirs and ours."²⁵ The author goes on to argue in verses 7–8 that the Jews lost the Mosaic covenant irrevocably when they turned to idols (the golden calf episode; cf. 14:1–6). The implication is that Christians are a new people, separate from Jews and presumably exempt from Jewish observances. It is probably among Jewish Christians that the *Gospel of the Hebrews* was read.²⁶ Christians of an ascetic orientation are probably in mind when "Barnabas" exhorts his readers not "by retiring [to] live alone as if you were already made righteous" (4:10). (We shall return to this passage in the following section.) It is among ascetically oriented Christians that the *Gospel of the Egyptians* probably circulated,²⁷ and its title implies use by Greek-speaking native Egyptians, perhaps those resident in the native Egyptian district of Rakotis in Alexandria.

Apocalyptically oriented Christianity is reflected not only in the *Epistle of Barnabas* but also in Alexandrian Sibylline writings in Christian dress.²⁸ Van den Broek calls attention to a prophecy in the *Sibylline Oracles* (2.161–64), part of a depiction of the end-time woes: "very wretched dread evildoers of the last generation, infantile, who do not understand that when the species of fe-

---

455–66; Pearson, "Gnosticism in Early Egyptian Christianity," chapter 13 in Pearson, *Gnosticism, Judaism, and Egyptian Christianity*, 194–213. On Basilides, see esp. Winfred Löhr, *Basilides und seine Schule: Eine Studie zur Theologie- und Kirchengeschichte des zweitzen Jahrhunderts*, WUNT 83 (Tübingen: Mohr Siebeck, 1996), and my article, "Basilides the Gnostic," in *A Companion to Second-Century Christian "Heretics,"* ed. Antti Marjanen and Petri Luomanen, VC Supp. 76 (Leiden: Brill, 2005), 1–31. On Valentinus, see esp. Christoph Markschies, *Valentinus Gnosticus? Untersuchungen zur valentinianischen Gnosis mit einem Kommentar zu den Fragmenten Valentins*, WUNT 65 (Tübingen: Mohr Siebeck, 1992), but his attempt to distance Valentinus from the Valentinian Gnosis of his followers is not convincing. On Carpocrates and Carpocratians, see esp. Morton Smith, *Clement of Alexandria and a Secret Gospel of Mark* (Cambridge: Harvard University Press, 1973), 295–350 (texts), 266–78 (discussion). Other varieties of Gnosticism are represented by second- or third-century texts composed or redacted in Egypt and extant in Coptic in the Nag Hammadi "Library." For translations, see James M. Robinson, ed., *The Nag Hammadi Library in English*, 3d ed. (San Francisco: Harper and Row, 1988).

25. Translation from Kirsopp Lake, ed., *The Apostolic Fathers*, 2 vols., LCL (Cambridge: Harvard University Press, 1912), 1:351.

26. For the fragments of the *Gospel of the Hebrews*, see Schneemelcher, *New Testament Apocrypha*, 1:172–78; cf. also Helmut Koester, *Introduction to the New Testament*, vol. 2, *History and Literature of Early Christianity*, 2d ed. (New York: Walter de Gruyter, 2000), 229–30. It should be noted that frg. 1 is certainly not part of the original *Gospel of the Hebrews*; see Rouel van den Broek, "Der Bericht des koptischen Kyrillos von Jerusalem über das Hebräerevangelium," in van den Broek, *Studies in Gnosticism and Alexandrian Christianity*, 142–56.

27. For the fragments of the *Gospel of the Egyptians*, see Schneemelcher, *New Testament Apocrypha*, 1:209–15; cf. Koester, *Introduction to the New Testament*, 2:235–36.

28. See John Collins's translation, with introductions, in *OTP* 1:317–472. For the Christian Sibyllines, see also Schneemelcher, *New Testament Apocrypha*, 2:652–85.

males does not give birth, the harvest of articulate men has come."[29] A similar prophecy of end-time woes is attributed to Jesus in the *Gospel of the Egyptians*, but there it is completely transformed into an encratic expression of "realized eschatology":[30] "When Salome asked, 'how long will death have power?' the Lord answered, 'So long as ye women bear children'" (frg. a).[31]

As we have seen, the *Teachings of Silvanus* represents yet another stream of early Alexandrian Christianity, with its wisdom orientation and its use of Alexandrian Jewish traditions of a Platonist stamp. That stream is somewhat similar to the Christianity reflected in the early second-century *Kerygma Petri*, of which some fragments remain thanks to Clement of Alexandria.[32] Attila Jakab rightly underscores the importance of this work for our knowledge of early second-century Alexandrian Christianity.[33] Despite its lamentable state of preservation, one can get a reasonable impression of its content by studying the remaining fragments. Its attribution to Peter and its reference to "the Twelve" situates the text in the tradition of the apostles, originally based in Jerusalem (frg. 3). It certainly reflects a "Logos Christology" (frg. 1). At the same time it maintains a credo centered upon one God, who created the world and can bring an end to it, a credo that can also be expressed in a "negative theology" (frg. 1). It finds in the biblical writings prophecies of the coming, death, and resurrection of Christ (frg. 4). It is the first Alexandrian writing, so far as we know, to use the adjective "Christian," defining Christians as a "third race" (frg. 2). It is clear that the *Kerygma Petri* represents a variety of Christianity that lies on a trajectory leading to the "mainline" Christianity of Clement, who quotes it.

A highly sophisticated Christian Platonism is reflected in one of the non-Gnostic tractates in the Nag Hammadi "Library," *Authoritative Teaching* (*Authentikos Logos,* NHC VI,3), composed in Alexandria toward the end of the second century. Showing some doctrinal similarities to the *Teachings of Silvanus* and to another Alexandrian Christian text, the *Sentences of Sextus*,[34] Au-

---

29. Collin's translation in *OTP* 1:349.
30. Van den Broek, "Juden und Christen," 187.
31. Schneemelcher, *New Testament Apocrypha,* 1:209.
32. Ibid., 2:34–41.
33. Jakab, *Ecclesia alexandrina,* 54–55. Walter Bauer ignored this work, which would have undermined his theory.
34. Henry Chadwick, *The Sentences of Sextus: A Contribution to the History of Early Christian Ethics,* TS, n.s. 5 (Cambridge: Cambridge University Press, 1959). Coptic fragments: NHC XII,1.

thoritative Teaching features an elaborate doctrine of the human soul. Rouel van den Broek has analyzed its Platonic and Christian elements and has demonstrated its importance for our understanding of Christian Platonism in Alexandria in the period before Clement.[35]

In this survey of the varieties of second-century Christianity in Alexandria we can see reflected the existence of several: apocalyptically oriented Christianity, Jewish Christianity, encratite Christianity, several types of Christian Gnosticism, proto-orthodox Christianity, and Christian Platonism. It should be noted that some of these groups represent continuities with varieties of Alexandrian Judaism. We might also add to this mix Marcionites, who probably arrived in Alexandria by midcentury.[36] Christian Gnosticism, of various stripes, would appear to be the dominant form of Christianity in Alexandria until the last quarter of the second century.

When we inquire into how these various Christian groups were organized, we find another continuity between Alexandrian Christianity and Alexandrian Judaism, namely, the presbyterate. It is likely that each Christian congregation had its own presbyter, and St. Jerome informs us (*Ep.* 146.1.6) that it was from these presbyters that early Alexandrian bishops would be chosen, at least until the end of the third century. The model for that type of organization was, of course, the institution of the synagogue.[37] To be sure, the most visible leaders (to us) are the prominent Christian teachers in Alexandria, many of whom we know by name. Thus a congregation would be organized under the direction of a presbyter but could include in its membership a prominent lay teacher. It is possible that in some groups teachers functioned as presbyters. That is probably true even in the case of some Gnostic "schools," for which worship services can be posited.[38] Valentinian and Basilidian groups, at least, had an active worship life.

---

35. Rouel van den Broek, "The Authentikos Logos: A New Document of Christian Platonism," in van den Broek, *Studies in Gnosticism and Alexandrian Christianity*, 206-34.

36. Dorival, "Débuts du christianisme," 171.

37. Van den Broek, "Juden und Christen," 188-91; Ritter, "De Polycarpe à Clément," 164. Ritter cites Acts 11:30 for a comparable organization among the churches of Judaea. The earliest attested use of the word πρεσβύτερος for a Jewish leader in the papyri is P. Monac. III 49, from second-century BC Heracleopolis in Egypt. See S. R. Llewelyn's discussion in his *New Documents Illustrating Early Christianity*, vol. 9, *A Review of the Greek Inscriptions and Papyri Published in 1986-87* (Grand Rapids: Eerdmans, 2002), no. 24, pp. 69-72.

38. On the alleged laxity of "heretical" worship services, see Tertullian, *De Praescriptione haereticorum* 41.

The role played by presbyters and teachers in Egyptian Christian communities is reflected later in the churches of the *chora,* as can be see in Dionysius's refutation of the chiliast teachings of Bishop Nepos of Arsinoe.[39] We are told that, on his visit to Arsinoe, Dionysius called together "the presbyters and teachers of the brethren in the villages" (Eusebius *HE* 7.24.6).

What about bishops? Unfortunately, we know little or nothing of the episcopacy in Egyptian Christianity until the time of Demetrius (189–232), for the successors of Mark named by Eusebius in his list of Alexandrian bishops seem to be nothing more than "a mere echo and a puff of smoke."[40] Indeed, in Eusebius's list, only Cerdo (d. 109) is referred to as a "bishop" (ἐπίσκοπος, 4.1); Demetrius's predecessor, Julian, is said to have been appointed to the "oversight" (ἐπισκοπή) of the churches in Alexandria. Whatever "oversight" these "bishops" exercised is completely obscure. We are informed by a later historian that, until the time of Demetrius, he was the only bishop in all of Egypt. Demetrius appointed three bishops and Heraclas, his successor, an additional twenty.[41]

It is clear that Demetrius played a crucial role in the development of the Egyptian Christian hierarchy; so it is no wonder that he has been referred to as "Second Founder of the church of Alexandria," and "Founder of the church of Egypt" in his role in the evangelization of areas outside of Alexandria.[42] To be sure, it took some time for Demetrius to consolidate his episcopal authority. The writings of Clement and Origen attest to this process of evolution "from the Christian community to an institutional church."[43] Demetrius's role in consolidating his authority also clearly included a concern for establishing "orthodoxy" and combating "heresy," and it is likely that the writ-

---

39. Cf. note 20, above.

40. Bauer, *Orthodox and Heresy,* 45. Eusebius's list has the following: Annianus (*HE* 2.24), Abilius (3.14), Cerdo (3.21), Primus (4.1), Justus (4.4), Eumenes (4.5.5), Markus (4.11.6), Celadion (4.11.6), Agrippinus (4.20), Julian (5.22), and Demetrius (5.22). This list may have been constructed artificially by Julius Africanus in his (lost) *Chronographies,* one of Eusebius's sources. So Robert Grant, *Eusebius as Church Historian* (Oxford: Clarendon Press, 1980), 51–52. Annianus, Abilius, Cerdo, and probably Primus ("Sabinus") were among Mark's first converts, whom Mark appointed for leadership in the church according to *Acts of Mark* 5. See my discussion in "Earliest Christianity," 141.

41. Eutychius, *Annales, PG* 111:982; cf. Eric W. Kemp, "Bishops and Presbyters at Alexandria," *JEH* 6 (1955): 125–42, esp. 137–38.

42. W. Telfer, "Episcopal Succession in Egypt," *JEH* 3 (1952): 1–13, esp. 2.

43. "De la communauté chrétienne à une église institiutionnelle," chapter 8 in Jakab, *Ecclesia alexandrina,* 175–214. On the testimony of Clement, see 179–88, on Origen, 188–214.

ings of Irenaeus of Lyon provided good ammunition for Demetrius in these efforts.[44]

Alexandrian Precursors of Egyptian Monasticism

Among the beautiful thirteenth-century wall paintings in the Old Church in the Monastery of St. Antony near the Red Sea, recently restored, are two paintings occupying prominent places in the nave of the church, one of St. Antony himself and another of St. Pachomius.[45] Accompanying each of the two monks is a Coptic inscription identifying these two great heroes of Egyptian monasticism: "Abba Antony, father of the monks," and "Abba Pachomius, father of the Koinonia."[46] Thus, at his monastery in the eastern desert, St. Antony is identified as the "father," i.e., founder, of Christian monasticism, and St. Pachomius as "father" or founder of its coenobitic variety, i.e., monks living in organized communities. These identifications are, of course, traditional. Antony went out into the desert as an "anchorite," that is to say, he "withdrew" into the desert and became a hermit. Others followed him into the desert, with the result that "the desert has been made a city," inhabited by monks who have "registered themselves for citizenship in the heavens."[47]

Recent research, especially that of James Goehring, has shown how wrong this picture is.[48] There were certainly ascetic hermits before St. Antony, as we

---

44. A second-century fragment of Irenaeus's treatise *Against Heresies* turned up at Oxyrynchus (P. Oxy. 405), on which see Roberts, *Manuscript, Society, and Belief*, 14, 23, 53. On Clement's use of Irenaeus, see Annewies van den Hoek, "How Alexandrian Was Clement of Alexandria? Reflections on Clement and His Alexandrian Background," *HeyJ* 31 (1990): 179–94, esp. 186, 190.

45. Elizabeth S. Bolman, ed., *Monastic Visions: Wall Paintings in the Monastery of St. Antony at the Red Sea* (New Haven: Yale University Press, 2002), xiii and 48.

46. Birger A. Pearson, "The Coptic Inscriptions in the Church of St. Antony," in Bolman, *Monastic Visions*, 217–39, 267–70 (notes), 293–96 (indexes), esp. 221, 223.

47. Athanasius, *Vita Antonii* 14 (PG 16.865), cited by James E. Goehring, "The Encroaching Desert: Literary Production and Ascetic Space in Early Christian Egypt," *JECS* 1 (1993): 282, reprinted in Goehring, *Ascetics, Society, and the Desert*, 74. Cf. Derwas J. Chitty, *The Desert a City: An Introduction to the Study of Egyptian and Palestinian Monasticism under the Christian Empire* (Oxford: Basil Blackwell, 1966).

48. Goehring, *Ascetics, Society, and the Desert*. See especially chapter 1, "The Origins of Monasticism," 13–35 (first published in *Eusebius, Christianity, and Judaism*, ed. Harold W. Attridge and Gohei Hata [Detroit: Wayne State University Press, 1992], 235–55); chapter 2, "The World Engaged: The Social and Economic World of Early Egyptian Monasticism," 39–52; chapter 3, "Through a Glass Darkly: Diverse Images of the Ἀποτακτικοί(αί) in Early Egyptian Monasticism," 53–72; and chapter 5, "With-

already knew from St. Jerome's *Life of Paul of Thebes*.[49] Indeed, there is a painting of Paul right next to that of Antony in St. Antony's monastery.[50] And there were monastic communities before the ones founded by Pachomius. Moreover, monastic communities, for the most part, were not located in the desert.[51]

Especially important in the new picture of Egyptian monasticism that we are getting is a third category alongside the "anchorite" and "coenobitic" varieties, village ascetics living in houses of their own. Especially important in this regard is the work of E. A. Judge, based on his study of a papyrus document from Karanis, dated 324 CE.[52] The document in question is a petition addressed by one Isidorus to the local *praepositus*, asking for justice in redressing wrongs committed by two persons named Pamonis and Harpalus. Isidorus had been viciously attacked by them and would probably have died had it not been for two people who came to his aid, "the deacon Antoninus and the monk Isaac" ('Αντωνίνου διάκονος καὶ' Ἰσὰκ μοναχοῦ).[53]

The "monk" Isaac in the document is clearly not a desert ascetic, nor is he a member of a monastic community. Rather, he lives in the village and participates actively in civil and church affairs. Isaac's situation is illuminated with reference to a denunciation by Jerome (*Ep.* 22.34) of a third class of monks in Egypt, in addition to the *coenobium* and the anchorites; these are called *remnuoth*. They are monks ("solitaries") living in small household communities, who exercise too much independence of clerical authority in Jerome's view. The *remnuoth* (obviously a Coptic word, ⲣⲙⲛⲟⲩⲱⲧ, "solitary") denounced by Jerome belong to the same class of ascetics as the *apotaktikai* ("renouncers," cf. Luke 14:33) referred to in other sources.[54] And it is this class of monks

---

drawing from the Desert: Pachomius and the Development of Village Monasticism in Upper Egypt," 89–109.

49. A convenient translation of the *Life of Paul* has recently been published by Caroline White, *Early Christian Lives* (London: Penguin Books, 1998), 71–84. On Paul of Thebes, see De Lacy O'Leary, *The Saints of Egypt* (London: SPCK, and New York: Macmillan, 1939), 222–23.

50. Bolman, *Monastic Visions*, xiii. Above the two figures is portrayed an event in their famous meeting: a raven bringing a loaf of bread to the two monks (*Life of Paul*, chapter 10).

51. Extensive discussions of these issues are found in Goehring, *Ascetics, Society, and the Desert*.

52. E. A. Judge, "The Earliest Use of Monachos for 'Monk' (P. Coll. Youtie 77) and the Origins of Monasticism," *JAC* 20 (1977): 72–89. Cf. Goehring, "Origins of Monasticism," and "Through a Glass Darkly."

53. Text and translation of the document in Judge, "Earliest Use of Monachos," 73.

54. Ibid., 79. This class of ascetics is referred to as "sarabaites" by John Cassian (*Conlationes* 18.4–7).

(μοναχοί, "solitaries") to which Isaac of Karanis belongs. When Isidorus (who may or may not have been a Christian) refers in his petition to a "deacon" and a "monk" he is referring to categories of local church members already well established by that time (324 CE).

Judge concludes from his consideration of the evidence that the apotactic movement, as later attested, began before the eremitic monasticism of Antony or the coenobitic monasticism of Pachomius. This movement "represents the point at which the men at last followed the pattern long set for virgins and widows, and set up houses of their own in town, in which the life of personal renunciation and service in the church would be practised."[55] Judge dates this new development in the third or early fourth century and suggests that a new name, *monachos*, was applied to such people by the general public. "P. Coll. Youtie 77 demonstrates that by 324 *monachos* was a recognized public style for the original apotactic type of ascetic, ranking alongside the ministers of the church."[56]

Could we by any chance push the development of apotactic monasticism further back in time? For one thing, Ewa Wipszycka refers to the type of asceticism represented by the *sarabaitae* or *remnuoth* as "un type archaïque d'ascétisme" antedating the types represented by Antony and Pachomius.[57] Based on her observations, Gilles Dorival has ventured to suggest that one or more groups of "sarabaites" could already have existed in second-century Alexandria.[58] Unfortunately, our evidence is incomplete. But the use of the term *monachos* to refer to Christian "solitaries" may very well go back to a period earlier than that posited by Judge.

The word μοναχός ("solitary") occurs in the Coptic text of the *Gospel of Thomas* in sayings 16, 49, and 75, sayings that represent an ascetic stance toward the world. These sayings are not represented in the Oxyrhynchus frag-

---

See the important discussion of Egyptian urban monasticism by Ewa Wipszycka, *Études sur le christianisme dans l'Égypte de l'antiquité tardive*, SEAug 52 (Rome: Institutum Patristicum Augustinianum, 1996), 281–336, esp. 285.

55. Ibid., 85. On early Christian groups of women ascetics in Alexandria, see Stephan J. Davis, *The Cult of Saint Thecla: A Tradition of Women's Piety in Late Antiquity* (Oxford: Oxford University Press, 2001), 87–89. On female asceticism in Egypt in late antiquity, see esp. Susanna Elm, *"Virgins of God": The Making of Asceticism in Late Antiquity* (Oxford: Clarendon Press, 1994), 227–372.

56. Ibid., 88. Cf. Goehring, "Through a Glass Darkly."

57. Wipszycka, *Études sur le christianisme*, 288.

58. Dorival, "Débuts du christianisme," 174.

ments of *Thomas*; so we do not know if the word μοναχός occurred in the Greek version on which the Coptic translation is based. I would guess that it did, and if that is the case the "solitaries" referred to in *Thomas* could conceivably be so called on the basis of the existence in late second-century Alexandria of a distinct class of Christian "solitaries." A Greek version of the *Gospel of Thomas* was undoubtedly circulating in Alexandria at that time.[59]

These *monachoi* may have created some suspicion in the minds of other Christians in Alexandria, which I suggest is reflected in the exhortation in the *Epistle of Barnabas* 4.10: "Do not by retiring apart live alone [μὴ καθ' ἑαυτοὺς ἐνδύνοντες μονάζετε] as if you were already made righteous, but come together and seek out the common good."[60] This passage calls to mind, too, Philo's description of the ascetic Jewish Therapeutae, who lived in a community near Lake Mareotis, west of Alexandria. Philo reports of them that they live a life of study and contemplation by themselves "in solitude" (μονούμενοι) in their own "cells" (μοναστήρια), meeting together only on the Sabbath (*De vita contemplativa* 30). There is no reason to doubt the essential veracity of Philo's description of the Therapeutae, as come scholars do.[61]

Thus it would appear that we can find early precursors in second-century Alexandria of the more well-known types of Egyptian monasticism represented later by Antony and Pachomius. It may also be the case that this early variety of Egyptian monasticism has Jewish roots.

Conclusions

In the preceding discussion I have tried with my "further observations" to shed some additional light on the origins of Christianity in Egypt by stressing

---

59. Koester, *Introduction to the New Testament*, 2:228, 230. The original version of the *Gospel of Thomas* is usually assigned to Syria. Indeed, Nicholas Perrin has recently made a good case for a Syriac original, though I find his arguments for a dependence of *Thomas* upon Tatian's *Diatessaron* far less convincing. See Perrin, *Thomas and Tatian: The Relationship between the Gospel of Thomas and the Diatessaron*, Academia Biblica 5 (Atlanta: Society of Biblical Literature, 2002). In any case, there can hardly be any doubt that a Greek version circulated in second-century Alexandria, and may even have been translated there from a putative Syriac original.

60. Translation from Lake, *Apostolic Fathers*, 1:353; cf. discussion above.

61. E.g., Troels Engberg-Pedersen, "Philo's *De Vita Contemplativa* as a Philosopher's Dream," *JSJ* 30 (1999): 40-64. On the Therapeutae and the group's relationship to the Alexandrian Jewish community, see now esp. Joan E. Taylor, *Jewish Women Philosophers of First-Century Alexandria: Philo's 'Therapeutae' Reconsidered* (Oxford: Oxford University Press, 2003).

the continuities between the varieties of second-century Christianity and the varieties of Alexandrian Judaism reflected in our first-century sources. Several varieties of early second-century Christianity are reflected in the sources available to us, and it would appear that Christian Gnosticism, in various manifestations, was the dominant form of Christianity in Alexandria until the last quarter of the second century, particularly during the last decade; when Bishop Demetrius was beginning to exert his episcopal authority. In a somewhat more speculative vein, I tried to show that there were Christian "monks" (*monachoi*) in Alexandria already in the second century. Perhaps my observations here will lead to "further observations" on earliest Christianity in Egypt by other scholars.

Finally, to my friend and colleague David Johnson I say: May you have a long and productive retirement in your new/old setting in Berkeley.

Appendix: The *Epistula Apostolorum*

The author of the *Epistula Apostolorum* uses a literary genre widely used by Gnostic Christians, a revelation dialogue featuring Jesus and his disciples in a post-Easter setting, to give expression to an anti-Gnostic "proto-orthodox" theology. Originally written in Greek, it is partially extant in a Coptic version discovered in 1895 and published in 1919.[62] It is completely extant in an Ethiopic version, first published in 1913.[63] Carl Schmidt, in his edition of the Coptic text, argued for an Asian provenance for the original Greek version, largely on the basis of the coupling of the Asian heretic Cerinthus with Simon Magus (chap. 1), its heavy reliance on the Gospel of John, the special place it assigns to the apostle John (chap. 2), and the Quartodeciman Easter praxis reflected in it (chap. 15). More recently, however, there has been a growing tendency to assign the text to Egypt.[64] A. F. J. Klijn uses the *Epistula Apostolorum* as one of

---

62. Carl Schmidt, Pierre Lacau, and Isaak Wajnberg, *Gespräche Jesu mit seinen Jüngern nach der Auferstehung: Ein katholisch-apostolisches Sendschreiben des 2. Jahrhunderts*, TU 43 (Leipzig: J. C. Hinrichs, 1919).

63. Louis Guerrier, with Sylvain Grébaut, *Le Testament en Galilée de Notre Seigneur Jésus Christ*, PO 9.3 (Paris: Firmin-Didot, 1913). English translations of the Coptic and Ethiopic versions by Hugo Duensing and C. D. G. Müller are found in Schneemelcher, *New Testament Apocrypha*, 1:249–84; cf. also Ron Cameron, *The Other Gospels: Non-Canonical Gospel Texts* (Philadelphia: Westminster Press, 1982), 131–62.

64. See esp. Manfred Hornschuh, *Studien zur Epistula Apostolorum*, PTS 5 (Berlin: Walter de

the texts on which he bases his discussion of Jewish Christianity in Egypt.⁶⁵ And Helmut Koester uses it in his discussion of the beginnings of Catholicism in Egypt.⁶⁶

In my earlier article I referred in a footnote to Hornschuh's stance favoring an Egyptian provenance for the *Epistula Apostolorum* and expressed the view that it was composed in Asia Minor, not Egypt. I pointed out that its attestation in Upper Egypt (in the Coptic version) and Ethiopia (Ethiopic version) is no argument in favor of a composition in Egypt. Asian Christian literature, including, e.g., Melito of Sardis's *Paschal Homily*, was early favored in Upper Egypt.⁶⁷ And now the tide has turned. Charles Hill has presented what I consider to be definitive arguments in favor of an Asian provenance for the *Epistula Apostolorum*, and for a date sometime in the period 117–48.⁶⁸

Therefore it will now be clear to the reader why I made no mention of *Epistula Apostolorum* in part 2, above.⁶⁹

Gruyter, 1965); C. D. G. Müller, "Epistula Apostolorum," in Schneemelcher, *New Testament Apocrypha*, 1:251. A Syrian provenance has also been proposed, e.g., by J. J. Gunther, "Syrian Christian Dualism," *VC* 25 (1971): 81–93, esp. 91. Julian Hills leaves the issue open, citing as the most likely places Asia Minor, Egypt, or Syria; see Hills, *Tradition and Composition in the Epistula Apostolorum*, HDR 24 (Minneapolis: Fortress Press, 1990), 9.

65. Klijn, "Jewish Christianity in Egypt."

66. Koester, *Introduction to the New Testament*, 2:243–45.

67. Pearson, "Earliest Christianity," 149 n. 93. On the circulation of Asian Christian writings in Upper Egypt and their translation into Coptic, see Tito Orlandi, "Coptic Literature," in Pearson and Goehring, *Roots of Egyptian Christianity*, 51–81, esp. 59.

68. Charles E. Hill, "The Epistula Apostolorum: An Asian Tract from the Time of Polycarp," *JECS* 7 (1999): 1–53. Cf. also Alistair Stewart-Sykes, "The Asian Context for the New Prophecy and of *Epistula Apostolorum*," *VC* 51 (1997): 416–38; Alistair Stewart-Sykes, *The Lamb's High Feast: Melito, Peri Pascha, and the Quartodeciman Paschal Liturgy of Sardis*, VCSupp 42 (Leiden: Brill, 1998), 25.

69. In *Gnosticism and Christianity* I survey the literary evidence for Christianity in Egypt through the third century. I include discussions of texts of disputed provenance, such as *Epistula Apostolorum* and others, and offer judgments on which of them can plausibly be assigned to Egypt.

Daniel Boyarin

PHILO, ORIGEN, AND THE RABBIS ON DIVINE SPEECH AND INTERPRETATION

In honor of a scholar and a mentsh [Yiddish!], David Johnson, S.J.

One of the most important of hermeneutical consequents of Logos theology was a proclivity for allegory as a mode of interpretation.[1] The concept of a Logos as both the site of absolute creativity as well as the revealer of absolute Truth, of Sophia, will promote allegory as a legitimate and choice mode of interpretation. Logos theology, which, as we shall see, is predicated on the notion of an Author, a speaker behind the written text, as well as a dual existence for language as signifier and signified, conduces to interpretation as a hermeneutic of depth. The ontology of human language itself consists in its privileged pairing of its signifiers with the transcendental signified of the Logos. The move toward allegorical interpretation within Christian writing is thus both epistemologically and ontologically (theologically) grounded.

Origen himself finds a hermeneutics ungrounded in the Logos to be the source of disagreement within "Judaism," and the context is interestingly not polemical in nature: "Any teaching which has had a serious origin, and is ben-

---

1. The question of allegory itself deserves a renewed consideration in this context, but this is beyond the scope of the present text—if not beyond the scope of the present inquiry. Mark J. Edwards, *Origen against Plato*, ASPTLA (Burlington, Vt.: Ashgate, 2002), 123–25, makes a gesture in that direction.

eficial to life, has caused different sects. For since medicine is beneficial and essential to mankind, and there are many problems in it as to the method of curing bodies, on this account several sects in medicine are admittedly found among the Greeks, and, I believe, also among the barbarians such as profess to practice medicine. And again, since philosophy which professes to possess the truth and knowledge of realities instructs us how we ought to live and tries to teach what is beneficial to our race, and since the problems discussed allow of considerable diversity of opinion, on this account very many sects indeed have come into existence, some of which are well known, while others are not. Moreover, there was in Judaism a factor which caused sects to come into being, which was the variety of the interpretations of the writings of Moses and the sayings of the prophets."[2] For Origen, obviously, the written word alone gives rise to multiple interpretation and thus to multiple religious opinions and even sects, all in good faith, similar to the good-faith disagreement and sectarianism of physicians and philosophers.

Origen's Jewish Alexandrian predecessor Philo had understood the problem and also proposed a solution to it. Philo explicitly expressed a theory of the "magic language"[3] of the Logos and its possible recovery. For Philo, only prelapsarian Adam among men had had direct access to the Logos. He had "been able to see the nature of each thing" (*Ebr.* 167), and had, therefore, been able to name everything with its perfect name, the name that corresponds perfectly to the language of *nous* or Logos. David Dawson explains that for all that human language is, however, inadequate for describing reality, one human, Moses, had the capacity for accurate knowledge of what he wished to say:

---

2. Origen, *Contra Celsum* 3.12 (GCS 2:211). Translation from *Origen: Contra Celsum,* trans. and ed. Henry Chadwick (Cambridge: Cambridge University Press, 1965), 135.

3. The term is Samuel Wheeler's (*Deconstruction as Analytic Philosophy,* CMP [Stanford: Stanford University Press, 2000], 117–20). Where, for Edwards (*Origen against Plato,* 22) one is called "Platonist" only if Platonism is understood as antonym to Christianity, my argument is that a certain rough or refined Platonism, insofar as a dual structure of material and spiritual was predicated to the universe, was essential to Christian thinking. In a sense, it only becomes significant then when we see the Rabbis articulating themselves as the antonym of such Platonism. I shall have much more to say about this in my ongoing project. D. V. Edwards himself is the tree upon which I can hang my point, for he writes, "There was some contention in Clement's time as to whether Christ assumed the 'psychic' flesh that all men receive from Adam or the spiritual flesh of the resurrection; even those who held the first position on the grounds that only a 'psychic' Christ would be truly human, would not have taught that the measure of humanity is the despotism of the alimentary canal" (Edwards, *Origen against Plato,* 23), but this, I stipulate—having defended the point elsewhere—is precisely what the Rabbis would have taught, and did.

"But Moses is not like 'most men,' because his perceptions are superior to the language at his disposal. His name-giving flows from an accurate 'knowledge that has to do with things'; consequently, he 'is in the habit of using names that are perfectly apt and expressive' (*Agr.* 1–2). Even so, Moses is forced to use ordinary language to express his extraordinary insights. As a result, his message is always clear and determinate once it is perceived, but it lies hidden in the very indirect linguistic expressions marked by various forms of semantic indeterminacy."[4] The role of the interpreter—necessarily, then, an allegorist—is to perceive and then describe this clear and determinate message. The allegorist reaches this level of interpretation through a process of contemplation, as described in Philo's *On the Contemplative Life*.[5] Thus too for Origen: "Even while we remain on earth the Christian life is grounded in a faithful and assiduous perusal of the scriptures, the depths of which cannot be mined unless we make use of the spiritual as well as carnal senses."[6]

Philo was an important model for Origen, but a problematic one.[7] As Mark Edwards has written, "From Paul to Clement allegory had been an indispensable tool for Christian expositors, all of whom, including Origen, were bound to hold that Philo's canon was incomplete and that no interpretation of the Prophets could be authoritative unless it yielded testimony to Christ."[8]

---

4. David Dawson, *Allegorical Readers and Cultural Revision in Ancient Alexandria* (Berkeley and Los Angeles: University of California Press, 1992), 92.

5. *Philo of Alexandria: The Contemplative Life, the Giants, and Selections*, ed. and trans. David Winston, CWS (New York: Paulist Press, 1981); David Winston, "Philo and the Contemplative Life," in *Jewish Spirituality from the Bible through the Middle Ages*, ed. Arthur Green, WS 13 (New York: Crossroad, 1988), 198–231.

6. Edwards, *Origen against Plato*, 111.

7. I think, sometimes, it is underevaluated how much Origen draws from Philo. Thus, in an otherwise compelling analysis of Origen's doctrine of the two humans, insisting that it derives from an "overly literal" reading of the doubled creation narrative of Genesis 1 and 2 and is not, therefore, grafted artificially on to the biblical tradition, Edwards seemingly ignores the evident fact that Origen's doctrine and interpretation were drawn from Philo (ibid., 89), which does not, of course, vitiate his point at all. The citation from Origen's *Homilies on Genesis*, offered on p. 104, is practically word for word a quotation from Philo's own *On the Creation*. For discussion, see Daniel Boyarin, "On the History of the Early Phallus," in *Gender and Difference in the Middle Ages*, eds. Sharon Farmer and Carol Pasternack (Minneapolis: University of Minnesota Press, 2003), 3–44.

8. Edwards, *Origen against Plato*, 36–37. In another iteration of this argument I hope to show that it is precisely that which is common to Paul, Clement, Origen that constitutes something that is definitive (by privation) of rabbinic hermeneutics (Daniel Boyarin, "Origenists Aren't the Only Christians," manuscript, 2003). See too Edwards, *Origen against Plato*, 129. In that planned essay, I shall also engage Elizabeth Clark's important critique of my earlier work. I had intended to include this discussion here but reasons of (real) estate prevent me.

Philo, of course, was also an allegorist, so where precisely can the incompletion be, unless we simply say that what was incomplete in Philo was simply that he was not a Christian?—a weak answer in my opinion. What seems to me lacking in Philo's thought is a way of accounting for the fact that he, via interpretation, can accomplish that which Moses himself could not. Christian theories of the Logos Incarnate seem better equipped to address this issue. For Christians, the magic language has appeared on earth and spoken itself, thus answering to both Philo's aporia and Nietzsche's nostalgia. The prologue to the Gospel of John makes this point in its utterance that through the Torah it had proved impossible to communicate Logos to humans and that only through the Incarnation was God made knowable to people.[9] Christian revisions of Philo's theory of the text and of interpretation thus had another answer than Philo's to the question of the source of knowledge of the allegorical meaning.

The Origens of Christian Allegory

In Origen's hermeneutical theory, Logos theology functions in two ways. On the one hand, it provides a philosophical structure. In his *First Principles,* Book IV, we can find one version of his threefold theory of interpretation, whereby the "obvious interpretation" is called the flesh of the scripture, but there are two more levels, the "soul" and the "spiritual law": "For just as man consists of body, soul and spirit, so in the same way does the scripture."[10] In an eloquent passage, Origen "gives us the cosmological-theological key to his exegesis":[11]

All the things in the visible category can be related to the invisible, the corporeal to the incorporeal, and the manifest to those that are hidden: so that the creation of the world itself, fashioned in this wise as it is, can be understood through the divine wisdom, which from actual things and copies teaches us things unseen by means of those that are seen, and carries us over

---

9. For John's Logos as a traditionally Jewish hypostasis, see Daniel Boyarin, "The Gospel of the Memra: Jewish Binitarianism and the Prologue to John," *HTR* 94, (July 2001): 243–84.

10. Origen, *De principiis* 4.2.4 (Origen, *Traité des principes,* ed. and trans. H. Crouzel and M. Simonetti, SC 268 [Paris: Éditions du Cerf, 1980], 313). Translation from *Origen, On First Principles,* trans. G. W. Butterworth, with an introduction by Henri de Lubac (Gloucester, Mass.: Peter Smith, 1973), 276.

11. R. P. Lawson, "Introduction," in *Origen, The Song of Songs: Commentary and Homilies,* trans. R. P. Lawson, ACW 26 (Westminster, Md.: Newman Press, 1957), 9.

from earthly things to heavenly. But this relationship does not obtain only with creatures; the Divine Scripture itself is written with wisdom of a rather similar sort.[12]

The very existence of allegory as a hermeneutical theory is made thus dependent on a Platonic universe, just as it had been in Philo's work as well.[13] There is nothing new in *this* aspect of Origen's theory of interpretation other than the clarity of its articulation.[14] For Origen, as for Philo, the external words of scripture are mere "copies" of words and meanings in the "magic language." I would argue that some version of this ontology of language makes possible all thought of interpretation as translation and not only those methods that we would term allegory proper. Interpretation is always dependent on some articulated or postarticulated Logos. The ultimate figure for the ontotheological structure of scripture is the Incarnation. In the words of R. P. Lawson: "If the Logos in His Incarnation is God-Man, so, too, in the mind of Origen the incarnation of the Pneuma in Holy Scripture is divine-human."[15] There is a virtual doubled Incarnation, then, in Origen's thinking. The Logos is incarnate in Jesus Christ and in scripture as well.[16]

However, Logos theology and in particular the notion of Christ as the Incarnation of the Word does more work for Origen.[17] For one could imagine

---

12. Origen, *Commentarius in Canticum* 3.13.27 (Origen, *Commentaire sur le Cantique des Cantiques*, trans. Luc Brésard and Henri Crouzel, with Marcel Borret, SC 376 [Paris: Éditions du Cerf, 1991], 640). Translation from *Origen, The Song of Songs*, trans. Lawson, 223.

13. For the richest and most developed version of this argument for allegory in general, see Angus John Stewart Fletcher, *Allegory: The Theory of a Symbolic Mode* (Ithaca: Cornell University Press, 1964), a work that has had an enormous, formative impact on my thinking from the moment I read it in the mid-1980s. It should be emphasized, moreover, that in speaking of Origen's Platonism here, I am *not* referring to those aspects of his theology allegedly derived from Plato, as disputed in Edwards, *Origen against Plato*, but rather to a general understanding of the reality as doubled in structure. In this sense I would agree with Edwards (19) that "Paul was as much a Platonist as Clement"—or Origen. The question is surely not, then, whether it is the case that "whatever Origen learned from the Platonists it was not the art of commentary" (Edwards, *Origen against Plato*, 145) but whether the art of commentary itself is subtended by Platonistic structures of understanding of world and Word. I submit that it is, but further discussion will have to remain for another day. Suffice it to say here that I think there is nothing in my intention here contradicted, let alone refuted, by Edwards's excellent book, although such may appear at first glance.

14. As Lamberton shows, the second-century "pagan" philosopher-commentator Numenius also makes his allegorical reading practice dependent on a Platonistic universe. Robert Lamberton, *Homer the Theologian: Neoplatonist Allegorical Reading and the Growth of the Epic Tradition*, TCH (Berkeley and Los Angeles: University of California Press, 1986), 77.

15. Lawson, "Introduction," 9.

16. Rolf Gögler, *Zur Theologie des biblischen Wortes bei Origenes* (Düsseldorf: Patmos-Verlag, 1963), 263.

17. For the transitions between Word theology and later Trinitarian formulae within which the

an ontological structure to both world and Word that would provide theoretically for the presence of a spiritual sense but not guarantee that anyone has access to that sense, as is virtually the case for Philo. However, as Karen Torjesen has written, for Origen "it is the power of the words of the Logos that makes the progression possible. It is the effect of his teaching which causes progress in the soul. If the word of the Logos were not effective, or he were not present teaching, then the steps of the progression would be an empty scaffolding into which the soul could gaze, but not climb."[18] Not only, therefore, does Origen's Logos provide a theological structure and hermeneutical horizon for understanding the nature of scripture and its dual and triple levels of meaning; I wish to suggest that the Logos Incarnate in the actual "person" of Jesus, born in the cradle and on the cross, also provides Origen with a theoretical answer to the question of the source of allegorical knowing:

> This being so, we must outline what seems to us to be the marks of a true understanding of the scriptures. And in the first place we must point out that the aim of the Spirit who, by the providence of God through the Word who was "in the beginning with God," enlightened the servants of the truth, that is, the prophets and apostles, was pre-eminently concerned with the unspeakable mysteries connected with the affairs of men—and by men I mean at the present moment souls that make use of bodies—his purpose being that the man who is capable of being taught might by "searching out" and devoting himself to the "deep things" revealed in the spiritual meaning of the words become partaker of all the doctrines of the Spirit's counsel.[19]

Origen explicitly addresses the implicit problematic of Philo's theory, namely, how may it be possible for a human writer to write in such a way that spiritual truths are, indeed, communicated; how, we might put it, can Origen hope to do better than Moses? Origen exposes this issue when he writes:

> As to the secret meaning which these things contain, however, and the teaching that these strange words labor to express, let us pray the Father of the Almighty Word and Bridegroom, that He Himself will open to us the gates of this mystery, whereby we may be enlightened not only for the understanding of these things, but also for the propagation of them, and may re-

---

Word is primarily figured as Son of God, see Peter Widdicombe, *The Fatherhood of God from Origen to Athanasius*, OTM (Oxford: Clarendon Press, and New York: Oxford University Press, 1994), and see too Virginia Burrus, *Begotten, Not Made: Conceiving Manhood in Late Antiquity*, Figurae (Stanford: Stanford University Press, 2000).

18. Karen Jo Torjesen, *Hermeneutical Procedure and Theological Method in Origen's Exegesis*, PTS 28 (Berlin: Walter de Gruyter, 1986), 137.

19. Origen, *De principiis* 4.2.7 (Origen, *Traité des principes*, SC 268:326–28); translation from *Origen, First Principles*, trans. Butterworth, 282.

ceive also a portion of spiritual eloquence, according to the capacity of those who are to be our readers.[20]

I am taking this, of course, as more than just a pious wish for divine assistance such as any religious writer might invoke, but rather as a specific plea for the Father through the Word to solve a theoretical problem in Origen's hermeneutical theology. In yet another work Origen articulates this clearly: "May you help with your prayers, that the Logos of God may be present with us and deign himself to be the leader of our discourse."[21] This is the way that we need to understand also Origen's talk of interpretation as being via possession of the "Mind of Christ," referring, of course, to Paul's own Wisdom Christology.

As Ronald Heine points out, Clement had identified the mind of Christ with the Holy Spirit.[22] Origen followed his alleged teacher in this identification. The richest text of Origen's for my purpose is also adduced by Heine:

In this way, we can understand the Law correctly, if Jesus reads it to us, so that, as he reads, we may receive his "mind" and understanding. Or is it not to be thought that he understood "mind" from this, who said, "But we have the mind of Christ, that we may know the things which have been given to us by God, which things also we speak"? And [did not] those [have the same understanding] who said, "Was not our heart burning within us when he opened the Scriptures to us in this way?" when he read everything to them, beginning from the Law of Moses up to the prophets, and revealed the things which had been written about himself.[23]

This key passage for Origen's hermeneutical theory needs to be read in the context of its several citations. The first is, of course, from Paul's letter to the Corinthians and the second from the Gospel of Luke. In the second chapter of 1 Corinthians, Paul explains the difference between Christian knowledge and that of Jews previous to himself:

1 When I came to you, brethren, I did not come proclaiming to you the testimony of God in lofty words or wisdom. 2 For I decided to know nothing among you except Jesus Christ and

---

20. Origen, *Commentarius on Canticum* 2.8.13 (Origen, *Commentaire sur le Cantique*, SC 375:414); translation from *Origen, Song of Songs*, trans. Lawson, 151.
21. Origen, *Homiliae in Exodum* 1.1 (Origen, *Homélies sur l'Exode*, ed. and trans. M. Borret, SC 321 [Paris: Éditions du Cerf, 1985], 42). Translation in *Origen: Homilies on Genesis and Exodus*, trans. Ronald E. Heine, FCNT (Washington, D.C.: Catholic University of America Press, 1982), 228.
22. Ronald Heine, "Reading the Bible with Origen," in *The Bible in Greek Christian Antiquity*, ed. Paul M. Blowers (Notre Dame: University of Notre Dame Press, 1997), 141.
23. Origen, *Homiliae in Jesu Nave* 9.8 (Origen, *Homélies sur Josué*, ed. and trans. A. Jaubert, SC 71 [Paris: Éditions du Cerf, 1960], 260); Heine, "Reading the Bible with Origen," 142.

him crucified, and I was with you in weakness and in much fear and trembling; and my speech and my message were not in plausible words of wisdom, but in demonstration of the Spirit and of power, that your faith might not rest in the wisdom of men but in the power of God.

Paul continues a bit further on in the chapter:

10 God has revealed to us through the Spirit. For the Spirit searches everything, even the depths of God. 11 For what person knows a man's thoughts except the spirit of the man which is in him? So also no one comprehends the thoughts of God except the Spirit of God. 12 Now we have received not the spirit of the world, but the Spirit which is from God, that we might understand the gifts bestowed on us by God. 13 And we impart this in words not taught by human wisdom but taught by the Spirit, interpreting spiritual truths to those who possess the Spirit.

And finally Paul completes the argument with the verse crucial for Origen's reading:

16 "For who has known the mind of the Lord so as to instruct him?" But we have the mind of Christ.

It seems to me entirely plausible to read Paul's reference to "gifts" here as an allusion to the Torah, and he is, therefore, producing the earliest version of a Christian hermeneutical theory of allegorical reading, one that insists that scripture can only be interpreted with the direct aid of the Holy Spirit, identified with the mind of Christ who alone knows the mind of the Lord and can, therefore, interpret the Torah as "a secret and hidden wisdom of God, which God decreed before the ages for our glorification."

Even more crucial, however, is the amazing narrative in the last chapter of Luke, in which:

27 And beginning with Moses and all the prophets, he interpreted to them in all the scripture the things concerning himself.... 32 They said to each other, "Did not our hearts burn within us while he talked to us on the road, while he opened to us the scriptures?" ... 36 As they were saying this, Jesus himself stood among them. 37 But they were startled and frightened, and supposed that they saw a spirit. 38 And he said to them, "Why are you troubled, and why do questionings arise in your hearts? 39 See my hands and my feet, that it is I myself; handle me, and see; for a spirit has not flesh and bones as you see that I have." ... 41 And while they still disbelieved for joy, and wondered, he said to them, "Have you anything here to eat?" 42 They gave him a piece of broiled fish, 43 and he took it and ate before them.[24] 44 Then he

---

24. But, of course, we must remember that Origen writes: "Certain people of the simpler sort, not knowing how to distinguish and differentiate between the things ascribed in the Divine Scriptures to

said to them, "These are my words which I spoke to you, while I was still with you, that everything written about me in the law of Moses and the prophets and the psalms must be fulfilled." 45 Then he opened their minds to understand the scriptures.

These two passages together, I suggest, gave Origen everything he needed to "solve" the hermeneutical/epistemological problem that allegorical reading presented. The Spirit of God, identified in Paul's testimony with the mind of Christ, is, for any Christian Logos theologian, necessarily the Logos himself.[25] The passage in Luke provides Origen with an actual correlative for Paul's claim; both the incarnate Logos before the crucifixion and the resurrected but embodied Logos afterward provided the disciples with the only possible and true interpretation of scripture.[26] Torjesen argues for three forms of the mediating activity of the Logos in Origen: the preincarnate activity of revelation to the Old Testament saints and prophets, the Incarnation itself, and the "present activity of the Logos, which is the disclosure of himself to us through the spiritual sense of Scripture."[27] What, I think, she doesn't sufficiently emphasize is the privileged nature of the Incarnation insofar as that is the only moment when the living voice of the Logos is directly present on earth, thus providing through *Jesus'* pedagogy precisely the hermeneutical guide that enables the "present activity of the Logos." In other words, the Incarnation is not only the "paradigm for this pedagogy," as Torjesen would phrase it, but that which

---

the inner and outer man respectively, and being deceived by this identity of nomenclature, have applied themselves to certain absurd fables and silly tales. Thus they even believe that after the resurrection bodily food and drink will be used and taken—food, that is, not only from the True Vine who lives forever, but also from the vines and fruits of the trees about us." Origen, *Commentarius in Canticum*, prologue 2.14 (Origen, *Commentaire sur le Cantique*, SC 375:100); translation from *Origen, Song of Songs*, trans. Lawson, 29.

25. Lest we be tempted to make a distinction here between Christ who incarnates the Logos (second person of the Trinity) and scripture as the incarnation of the spirit (third person), let us not forget that such fully developed Trinitarian doctrine was yet to come. In other passages it is clear that for Origen it is precisely the Logos who is incarnate in scripture as well: "As 'in the Last Days,' the Word of God, which was clothed with the flesh of Mary, proceeded into this world. What was seen in him was one thing; what was understood was something else. For the sight of his flesh was open for all to see, but the knowledge of his divinity was given to the few, even the elect. So also when the Word of God was brought to humans through the Prophets and the Lawgiver, it was not brought without proper clothing. For just as there it was covered with the veil of flesh, so here with the veil of the letter." Origen, *Homiliae in Leviticum* 1.1 (Origen, *Homélies sur le Lévitique*, ed. and trans. M. Borret, SC 286 (Paris: Éditions du Cerf, 1981), 66. Translation in *Origen, Homiliae in Leviticum*, trans. Gary Wayne Barkley, FCNT (Washington, D.C.: Catholic University of America Press, 1990), 29. See discussion in Torjesen, *Origen's Exegesis*, 110.

26. See on this point too the important observations of Edwards, *Origen against Plato*, 134–35.

27. Torjesen, *Origen's Exegesis*, 114.

makes it possible *because he taught how to read scripture*. It is not only that "in the taking on of flesh the Logos makes himself comprehensible to all those who wear flesh," a formulation that sounds almost Athanasian, but that in taking on flesh he could speak the magic language directly to human flesh and thus make himself, for he is the magic language, comprehensible to all those who speak human language.[28] In the Incarnation, the Logos "offered himself to be known,"[29] in a way, I would add, that nothing but a physical body and voice *can* be known.

Let me pursue this point just a bit further, for it is perhaps too subtle a distinction. Torjesen remarks on the duality in which "Scripture is both a mediating activity of the Logos and at the same time has doctrines of the Logos as its content."[30] What I am suggesting is that it is only the presence of the actual living Logos on earth in the incarnate form of the pedagogue Jesus that enables "us" to discover the Logos as the content of scripture. In this way Origen answers the aporia that Philo's work presents.[31] Indeed, "the mediating activity of the Logos in his historical education of the saints provides the source for Scripture as a written document. What they wrote and what they understood originates from their own experience with the pedagogy of the Logos. They wrote by the Spirit what the Logos taught them in order to teach us the same truth. This is true for the New Testament writers as well as for the prophets."[32] I would just add that the teaching of the New Testament writers has a special dispensation and precedence, for it was for them that the Logos directly and without mediation, in his own voice through Jesus' human vocal mechanism, taught them (and thereby us) how to read scripture as referring to him and him alone. "The Logos announces himself, he is the subject matter of his own proclamation,"[33] most fully, however, I would add, when he is present on earth in the body of Jesus.

28. Ibid., 115.
29. Origen, *Commentarius in Canticum* 2.8.21 (Origen, *Commentaire sur le Cantique*, SC 375:418); translation from *Origen, Song of Songs*, trans. Lawson, 153.
30. Torjesen, *Origen's Exegesis*, 119.
31. Cf. "The Logos taught the saints the truths of himself in symbolic form, in the form of law, or of historical events. This pedagogy was designed for all those to whom it was delivered. But it was the saints alone who grasped the spiritual truth presented in this symbolic form. And they reported it again in symbolic form, this time writing in Scripture the symbolic forms of the universal truth, so that the succeeding generations might be able to grasp the spiritual truth through the medium of its symbolic form." Ibid., 140.
32. Ibid., 119.
33. Ibid. See *Commentariis in evangelium Joannis* 13.28 (GCS 10:251–53).

I am not claiming, of course, to have uncovered a new interpretation of Origen different from or even supplemental to Torjesen's but only to be highlighting a particular element in his hermeneutical thought that I find crucial for articulating the way that the particular form of incarnational Christology was to reveal itself as the ma(r)ker of difference between "Judaism" and "Christianity." As Torjesen herself has put it, "In the incarnation the Logos speaks with his own voice. In Scripture he speaks through the mouth of the prophets and saints."[34] Given the universal Platonic understanding that the living voice of the teacher is superior to any "inscription" of that voice, the Incarnation provides, then, for Origen the guarantee of Christian allegorical access to truth and the Incarnation is a hermeneutical moment of full presence of meaning. This is why, again in Torjesen's words, "in the Gospels the Logos is speaking directly to the hearer, not mediated through a history other than his own,"[35] but also equally not mediated through a text other than his own. It seems plausible, then, that for Christian writers, the Incarnation of the Word, or the Holy Spirit that provides direct access to the Logos as well, provides a solution to what must remain a problem for Philo the Jew's theory of allegorical interpretation. The presence on earth of the Word incarnate (or resurrected) in Jesus, the spiritual reader who read scriptures to the Christians and revealed the true interpretation, has made it possible for other Christians to reach the spiritual meaning themselves, thus answering the question that Philo's allegorical theory must needs leave unsolved: "In the incarnation he has created the human conditions of his own perfect intelligibility for all time."[36]

On the other hand, both Origen and his Cappadocian disciple Gregory of Nyssa well understood that given the conditions of human speech, however much Christian speech has been learned from the Logos, it will be imperfect and thus multiple. Martin Irvine has recently made this point well: "The unity of the Logos is fragmented into a multiplicity of temporal discourses which simultaneously attempt and fail to return to its unity; no repetition or multiplication of *logoi* is Logos. The transcendental signified remains beyond the reach of all temporal sign relations yet is immanently manifest in all of them."[37] For midrash, however, in its final development, *there is no transcendental signified.*

---

34. Torjesen, *Origen's Exegesis*, 111.   35. Ibid., 133.
36. Ibid., 115.
37. Martin Irvine, *The Making of Textual Culture: "Grammatica" and Literary Theory, 350–1100* (Cambridge: Cambridge University Press, 1994), 266.

God himself, as we have seen, can only participate, as it were, in the process of unlimited semiosis and thus of limitless interpretation. The result will be not simply a multiplicity of interpretations that we cannot decide between, or even a plethora of interpretations that all stand in the Pleroma of divine meaning, but finally a rabbinic ascesis that virtually eliminates the practice of interpretation entirely. Midrash, in its culminating avatar, eschews not only allegory and a discourse of the true meaning but renounces "interpretation" altogether. It will take, however, some further nuancing and exploration of background before we can arrive at this point. Although Origen's work on the Song has been shown to have close thematic affinities with the interpretations of the midrash,[38] his linguistic strategies are nearly opposite to them. In excess of Philo, for whom the flesh (and fleshly language) are understood as necessary helpers to the spirit (and the allegorical meaning), for Origen the carnal and the spiritual meanings do not parallel each other but are actually opposed to each other, as the body is opposed to the soul. For Origen the very process of allegorical interpretation constitutes *in itself and already* a transcendence of the flesh. Accordingly he understands the divine kiss to refer to the experience of the soul, "when she has begun to discern for herself what was obscure, to unravel what was tangled, to unfold what was involved, to interpret parables and riddles and the sayings of the wise along the lines of her own expert thinking."[39] Since in Origen's Platonism the world of spirit is the world of the intelligible, for him "intellection and loving are one and the same,"[40] and the discovery of the true and pure spiritual meaning behind or trapped in the carnal words constitutes the divine kiss. It enacts that "overcoming carnal desires [which] ultimately enables the soul to return to its original state and become once more a *mens*."[41]

---

38. Ephraim Elimelech Urbach, "The Homiletical Interpretations of the Sages and the Exposition of Origen on Canticles, and the Jewish-Christian Disputation," *ScrHier* 22 (1971): 247–75; Reuven Kimelman, "R. Yoḥanan and Origen on the Song of Songs: A Third-Century Jewish-Christian Disputation," *HTR* 73 (July–October 1980): 567–95.

39. Lawson, "Introduction," 61.

40. Ann W. Astel, *The Song of Songs in the Middle Ages* (Ithaca: Cornell University Press, 1990), 4. See also Gerard E. Caspary, *Politics and Exegesis: Origen and the Two Swords* (Berkeley and Los Angeles: University of California Press, 1979).

41. Astel, *Song of Songs*, 4.

God's Oral Torah: The Kisses of His Mouth

Suggesting that Origen is a Platonist has recently become a matter of some contention, it seems, as it is understood as participating in an anti-Origenist heresiological discourse, a sort of Witch of Endor hunt.[42] Very sophisticated analysis in recent years has shown up the facileness of the usual simplistic accounts of Origen that do in fact draw, even if innocently, on the heresiological tradition.[43] It will be of purpose, therefore, to show what it is that Christian readers from Paul to Origen have in common with each other and with such non-Christians as Philo. One of the best ways that I know of to make that hermeneutical *koine* manifest is to contrast it with another, the seemingly very different tradition of the slightly later Rabbis.[44]

In the midrash on Song of Songs, the kiss is understood quite differently from Origen's reading, albeit still as divine. In Origen, the erotic meanings of the kiss in the first verse of the Song, "Let him kiss me with the kisses of his mouth" are sublimated into intellection, because of his doctrine that the body is a sign of a fall of the soul from God and must be transcended to be reunited with him. In the midrash it is that very body, the actual mouth, that experiences God's kiss:

He will kiss me with the kisses of his mouth: Said Rabbi Yohanan, "An angel would take the Speech from the Holy, Blessed One, each and every word, and court every member of Israel and say to him: Do you accept this Speech? It has such and such many requirements, and such and such many punishments, such and such many matters which are forbidden, and such and such many acts which are mandatory, such and such many easy and difficult actions, and such and such is the reward for fulfilling it. And the Israelite would say to him: Yes! And then he would further say to him: Do you accept the Divinity of the Holy, Blessed One? And he would answer him: Yes and again yes. Immediately, he would kiss him on his mouth, as it

---

42. For my frivolous conceit, see the very unfrivolous and important Patricia Cox Miller, "Origen and the Witch of Endor: Toward an Iconoclastic Typology," in her *The Poetry of Thought in Late Antiquity: Essays in Imagination and Religion* (Burlington, Vt.: Ashgate, 2001), 200–210.

43. Miller, *Poetry of Thought in Late Antiquity;* David Dawson, *Christian Figural Reading and the Fashioning of Identity* (Berkeley and Los Angeles: University of California Press, 2001); Edwards, *Origen against Plato.* I am currently at work on an essay tentatively entitled, "Defending Origen," in which I will treat all of these works at some length, Deo volente.

44. Two important caveats here. One, there is to be taken from here absolutely no implication that the Rabbis are more authentic, purer, less contaminatedly Jewish than Philo or even Origen. Second—a corollary to the first—the rabbinic tradition only itself emerges in time and can be shown to be later, indeed, than the Christian canons of interpretation.

is written, 'You have been made to see in order to know' [Deut. 4:35]—by means of a messenger."

The erotic connotations, overtones, and charges of this description of divine revelation (even the prefiguration of Molly Bloom), as it was experienced by each and every Israelite, are as blunt as could be imagined.[45] Rabbi Yohanan explicitly connects this kiss with the visual experience of seeing God, also a powerful erotic image.[46]

In rabbinic religion there is no invisible God manifested in an Incarnation. God himself is visible (and therefore corporeal).[47] Language also is not divided into a carnal and a spiritual being. Accordingly, there can be no allegory.[48] For rabbinic Judaism, the Song of Songs is the record of an actual, concrete, visible occurrence in the historical life of the people of Israel. When the Rabbis read the Song of Songs, they do not translate its "carnal" meaning into one or more "spiritual" senses; they rather establish a concrete, historical moment in which to contextualize it.[49] It is a love song, a love dialogue to be specific, that was actually (or fictionally, according to some views)[50] uttered by a Lover and a Beloved at a moment of great intimacy, at an actual historical mo-

---

45. Although, to be sure, a very late glossator has added the words, "It didn't really happen so, but he made them hallucinate it." Shimshon Dunsky, ed., *Song of Songs Rabbah* (Tel-Aviv: Dvir, 1980), 13n4.

46. Daniel Boyarin, "The Eye in the Torah: Ocular Desire in Midrashic Hermeneutic," *Critical Inquiry* 16 (spring 1990): 532–50.

47. It is important to emphasize, however, that this does *not* necessarily mean that God has a body of the same substance as a human body. Alon Goshen Gottstein has contributed an excellent discussion of this issue in "The Body as Image of God in Rabbinic Literature," *HTR* 87 (1994): 171–95.

48. I would like to add two clarifications at this point. The first is that the category of "allegory," both as a genre (?) of text production and as a reading practice, is a notoriously slippery one. Therefore, it should be clear that when I say allegoresis in this text I mean allegorical reading of the Philonic-Origenal type, which has a fairly clear structure as well as explicit theoretical underpinnings. It is a hermeneutic structure in which narrative on the physical or worldly level is taken as the sign of invisible and spiritual structures on the level of ideas. It follows, therefore, that literal here is not opposed to metaphorical, for metaphor can belong to the literal pole of such a dichotomy, as was clearly recognized in the Middle Ages. Moreover, such reflections on allegory as de Man's or Benjamin's are not relevant for this issue. Note that I am not claiming here that midrash is absent from Christian reading. The Gospels themselves, Paul, and even much later Christian literature contain much that is midrashic in hermeneutic structure (more, in my opinion, than is currently recognized, e.g., *Piers Plowman*). My claim is, rather, that allegory (in the strict sense) is absent or nearly so in midrash.

49. Daniel Boyarin, *Intertextuality and the Reading of Midrash* (Bloomington: Indiana University Press, 1990), 105–17.

50. See Daniel Boyarin, "Two Introductions to the Midrash on Song of Songs," *Tarbiz* 56 (1987): 479–501.

ment of erotic communion, when God allowed himself to be seen by Israel, either the crossing of the Red Sea or the revelation at Mt. Sinai.

Rabbi Eliezer decoded [*patar*] the verse in the hour that Israel stood at the Sea. *My dove in the cleft of the rock in the hiding place of the steep* [Song 2:14], that they were hidden in the hiding place of the Sea—*Show me your visage;* this is what is written. "Stand forth and see the salvation of the Lord" [Exod. 14:13]—*Let me hear your voice;* this is the singing, as it says, "Then Moses sang" [Exod. 15:1]—*For your voice is lovely;* this is the Song—*And your visage is beautiful;* for Israel were pointing with their fingers and saying "*This* is my God and I will beautify Him" [Exod. 15:2].

Rabbi Akiva decoded the verse in the hour that they stood before Mt. Sinai. *My dove in the cleft of the rock in the hiding place of the steep* (Song 2:14), for they were hidden in the hiding places of Sinai. *Show me your visage,* as it says, "And all of the People saw the voices" [Exod. 20:14]—*Let me hear your voice,* this is the voice from before the Commandments, for it says "All that you say we will do and we will hear" [Exod. 24:7]—*For your voice is pleasant;* this is the voice after the commandments, as it says, "God has heard the voice of your speaking; that which you have said is goodly" [Deut. 5:25].[51]

To be sure, the Lover was a Divine Lover, but the beloveds were actual human beings, and the moment of erotic communion was mystical and visionary. The difference between the midrashic and the allegorical lies not in the thematics of the interpretation but in the language theory underlying the hermeneutic. This is the reverse of what is usually claimed. That is, one typically finds it stated that the method of midrash and of allegory with regard to the Song of Songs is identical, and that only the actual allegorical correspondences have changed, but this is not so in my opinion. In the allegory the metaphors of the language are considered the signs of invisible entities, Platonic ideas of mystical love, while in the midrash they are actually spoken love poetry of an erotic encounter. For many allegorists, the allegorical reading becomes a sublimation of physical love, while for the Rabbis, I would suggest, it is the desublimation of divine love, an understanding of that love through its metaphorical association with literal, human corporeal sexuality. It is not irrelevant to note that the Rabbis all had the experience of carnal love.[52] The Song is

---

51. Dunsky, *Song of Songs Rabbah*, 73.
52. There are ways in which later Christian allegorical readers of the Song seem to be more like the Rabbis *in this respect, at any rate* (Astel, *Song of Songs,* 9–10). It is perhaps no accident that this shift takes place, as Astel notes, when monastic orders are founded who "recruited their members from among adults, all of whom had lived in secular society. Many were drawn from aristocratic circles; a high percentage had been married; most were familiar with secular love literature."

not connected with an invisible meaning but with the text of the Torah, letter with letter, body with body, not body with spirit. This is an entirely different linguistic structure than that of Philo and his followers, even when thematically the readings may turn out to be similar or genetically connected. For the Rabbis, it is the concrete historical experience of the revelation at Sinai that is described by the Song of Songs, while for the allegorists it is the outer manifestation in language of an unchanging inner structure of reality—an abstract ontology, not a concrete history.

The disembodiment of history in allegoresis is most clearly brought out in Origen's brilliant interpretation of the Song of Songs. As the contrast with the midrash helped us to foreground what is distinctive in Origen, the contrast with Origen in turn provides us with an especially effective way of seeing what is different in midrash. In the theoretical justification for allegory in his introduction, Origen remarks:

> So, as we said at the beginning, all the things in the visible category can be related to the invisible, the corporeal to the incorporeal, and the manifest to those that are hidden; so that the creation of the world itself, fashioned in this wise as it is, can be understood through the divine wisdom, which from actual things and copies teaches us things unseen by means of those that are seen, and carries us over from earthly things to heavenly. But this relationship does not obtain only with creatures; the Divine Scripture itself is written with wisdom of a rather similar sort. Because of certain mystical and hidden things the people is visibly led forth from the terrestrial Egypt and journeys through the desert, where there was a biting serpent, and a scorpion, and thirst, and where all the other happenings took place that are recorded. All these events, as we have said, have the aspects and likenesses of certain hidden things. And you will find this correspondence not only in the Old Testament Scriptures, but also in the actions of Our Lord and Saviour that are related in the Gospels.[53]

Origen's text describes a perfect correspondence between the ontology of the world and that of the text. In both there is an outer shell and an inner meaning. The actual historical events described in the biblical narrative are dissolved and resolved into the hidden and invisible spiritual realities that underlie and generate them as material representations.

We can do no better in illustrating the contrast between Origen's hermeneutic understanding and that of midrash than to take his very example. "Because of certain mystical and hidden things the people is visibly led forth from

---

53. Lawson, "Introduction," 223.

the terrestrial Egypt and journeys through the desert, where there was a biting serpent, and a scorpion, and thirst, and where all the other happenings took place that are recorded. All these events, as we have said, have the aspects and likenesses of certain hidden things." When a midrash reads this very text, the scorpion remains a scorpion and the biting serpent a serpent:

And they went out into the Desert of Shur [Exod. 15:2]. This is the Desert of Kub. They have told of the Desert of Kub that it is eight hundred by eight hundred parasangs—all of it full of snakes and scorpions, as it is said, "Who has led us in the great and terrible desert—snake, venomous serpent and scorpion" [Deut. 8:15]. And it says, "Burden of the beasts of the Dry-South, of the land of trial and tribulation, lioness and lion, ... *ef ʿeh*" [Isa. 30:6]. *Ef ʿeh* is the viper. They have told that the viper sees the shadow of a bird flying in the air; he immediately conjoins [to it], and it falls down limb by limb. Even so, "they did not say, 'here is the Lord Who has brought us up from Egypt, Who has led us in the land of Drought and Pits, land of Desolation and the Death-Shadow?'" [Jer. 2:6]. What is Death-Shadow? A place of shadow that death is therewith.

The hermeneutic impulse of this classical midrashic text is to concretize, to make tangible even more strongly than does the biblical text itself the fearsomeness of the physical desert of the physical thirst of the physical fear of snakes and scorpions to which the historical Israel was prey in the desert, and not to translate these into symbols of invisible spiritual truths and entities. For all the similarities and convergences, it seems, midrash and allegory do not yet meet entirely.

Robin Darling Young

CANNIBALISM AND OTHER FAMILY WOES IN LETTER 55 OF EVAGRIUS OF PONTUS

Festschriften constitute, in effect, letters of congratulation in the form of short studies offered to an eminent scholar at the culmination of a career. It may be appropriate, then, to offer as a small part of this Festschrift for an esteemed colleague a study of a letter of Evagrius of Pontus (d. 399) which, small as it is, illuminates the general topic of the work as a whole, namely, the language, literature, and world of early Christian Egypt.

Ironically, the subject of this particular study survives only in languages foreign to that world; and the author of the work under consideration was himself a famous alien to Egypt, although as an ascetic adept he was not unique in that respect. Evagrius's letters, all but one composed during the period of his residence in Nitria and Kellia during the seventeen-year period from 382 to 399, have been lost in their original Greek. Doubtless this accounts for the relative lack of attention accorded them by scholars, as well as the fact that they contain neither the meditative *kephalaia* that characterize his philosophical or exegetical work nor (for the most part) the programmatic theology that characterizes his letter On Faith (63) and his letter To Melania.

Nevertheless, the letters are worth studying because, taken together, they add to the portrait of Evagrius as ascetic guide and teacher. Although a large translation and study of all of them has been the subject of one of the works of Gabriel Bunge, a prominent scholar of Evagrius, they have not been examined with the minute care that will eventually allow them to be linked with other works.¹ And although Bunge translated all the letters from Syriac into German, there is no complete translation into any other foreign language, with the exception of Frankenberg's Greek retroversion, a Herculean effort that nonetheless requires reexamination with the reading of every letter.² Thus the work of understanding and situating Evagrius's letters is just beginning. The work is important not only because it clarifies the thought of Evagrius himself, though; it also provides a significant link between the world of the Greek rhetoric and theology in which Evagrius had been trained, with the literary traditions of epistolary composition, and the world of the more particularly monastic letter as exemplified in the letters of Anthony of Egypt.³

As a way of paying tribute to my good friend and former colleague Fr. David W. Johnson, S.J., this essay supplies some observations about one particular letter of Evagrius in the collection of sixty-four. Letter 55 is an apparently simple example of primary or practical teaching sent to an anonymous monk. Yet it illustrates Evagrius's self-presentation as monastic teacher and physician of souls, his dependence upon scriptural extracts for both diagnosis and cure, and his exegetical program. In addition, it touches upon a topic with which Evagrius himself had had trouble, namely, the way in which the problem of continuing involvement with one's next of kin threatens to derail the monastic life as a daily arrangement and *psychagogia*. How to deal with family members, then, in a monastic setting that also encouraged contact with *kosmikoi* (and, doubtless, their material support) is the overarching concern of the letter. If it does not deal, then, with the theoretical intricacies that make Evagrius a fascinating theologian, it offers some evidence for a problem that has remained current—the stubbornly persistent woes of family life that follow monks into their solitude, while much else of late ancient Egypt has disappeared or is currently evanescing.

---

1. Gabriel Bunge, *Evagrios Pontikos, Briefe aus der Wüste,* Sophia 24 (Trier: Paulinus-Verlag, 1986).
2. W. Frankenberg, *Evagrius Ponticus,* AKGWG, n.s. 13, 2 (Berlin: Weidmannsche Buchhandlung, 1912).
3. See Samuel Rubenson, *The Letters of St. Antony: Monasticism and the Making of a Saint,* SAC (Minneapolis: Fortress Press, 1995). Rubenson, of course, wants to emphasize the connection between Hellenistic schools and rhetorical education and the works of the genuine Anthony; nevertheless, Evagrius still occupies a point midway on a spectrum running from Gregory Nazianzen's elaborate letter writing and that of the Coptic monk.

Translation of Letter 55

In order to have a closer look at the letter, a translation follows. It is made from Frankenberg's Syriac text, although I have also consulted Bunge's German translation and an English translation by Luke Dysinger apparently made from Frankenberg's Greek retroversion.[4]

Not as a wise man, according to the words of the spirit, do I receive admonition as if loving those who reprove me [Prov. 9:8, 9].

But as a man full of passions who labors to be delivered from passions:

For I confess that I am a coward, more than he who feared the serving-girl in the days of Pilate [Matt. 26:69–75].

Then again, because of my fear, I have sought forgiveness, lest I offend the soul that both bears in the flesh and depicts in it the impression of Christ [Eph. 1:13; 4:30]—and receive the punishment of [i.e., due] the trampling bull [Exod. 21:28, 29].

For it is right for someone that admonition be mixed so that he, while he sets forth the matter, will be like clever physicians who conceal the iron [instrument] will cloak the face of fear in the portions of divination.

These things have I said with respect to fear.

Concerning the passions, then, that now lay hold of you, I think that the knowledge is this:

The ideas that molest us: among them there is one kind from the weakness of our will. From nature there are those that are from blood and from our parents; [but] from our will, then, are those that happen to us from anger and from lust.

Those that are from nature molest us over a long time, because it imprints them upon itself through thought and increases in them, so that, as it is said in the scriptures, "pass by swiftly and do not stay in this place" [Prov. 9:18].

Those, then, that are from the will molest the reason if it submits to them, for it is written, "do not will to be with them" [Prov. 24:1]. These ones afflict us, then, over time and by the performance of sin.

Natural intentions are able, then, to awaken anger and lust in scattering the mind in many concerns, unless it is diligent in adding remedies that are suitable: hunger, thirst, keeping watch, withdrawal from the world, and prayer.

And the woman of Samaria who ate her son as a result of her hunger—she will persuade you [2 Kings 6:28, 29].

Those who are full seek everything that comports with their fullness, and scorn the purity of prayer.

And perhaps you will say, "if I am concerned for the lives of those who are my own [family], I am not despising the commandment."

---

4. Luke Dysinger, Letter 55, at www.ldysinger.com/Evagrius/11_Letters.

Recognize the scheme of the evil one, who by means of a good thing accomplishes death in you and through natural thoughts, darkens your mind!

Gaze, instead, on the healer of souls, who by means of helpful battles perfects these thoughts when he says,

"Whoever comes unto me, and does not hate his father and mother and brothers and sisters and also his own soul cannot be my disciple" [Luke 14:26].

In this thing that he thinks, his heart is darkened with these cares.

And do not think it is something great if, on account of the knowledge of God, he will forsake his kindred.

For many who were convinced by idols offered their sons and daughters to demons! [Ps. 105 (106):37–39].

I know many from the brothers in whom these thoughts existed, who fell into danger in that the thoughts were extended in them. And when their parents or siblings joyfully approached [the brothers] in their cells, they did not receive them, for the evil one disguised their intelligence in anger, in the image [here, simulacrum?] of withdrawal.

Remain, then, in the wilderness in stillness, I beg of you, and be constant in prayer that is without anger and without thoughts, and "do not give a place to the evil one" [Eph. 4:27] because the Lord is powerful who calls you, in order that you will lead them to life and give them the inheritance with those being made holy in light [Col. 1:2, and see the entire passage, verse 9–14].

Evagrius's Self-Presentation in Letter 55

That Evagrius was continuously conscious of how his appearance, either by letter or in person, would be received by a potential disciple, can be demonstrated from many of his writings; perhaps the most endearing is his direction to potential monastic teachers to avoid scowling at those who consulted them: "It is necessary that the gnostic not be sullen [σκυθρωπόν—literally, "glaring with the eyes"], nor difficult of access [δυσπρόσιτον] for the reason that it would signify both an ignorance about the inner logic of created things and an unwillingness that all humans be saved and come to a knowledge of the truth" [1 Tim. 2:4].

Evagrius was acutely aware of the importance of image in the encounter between a person seeking knowledge and her or his teacher. Letters, Evagrius believed (along with other ancient authors),[5] mediated the presence of the

---

5. On the topos, see Michaela Zelzer, "Die Briefliteratur," in *Neues Handbuch der Literaturwissenschaft*, vol. 4, *Spätantike mit einem Panorama der byzantinischen Literatur*, ed. Lodewijk J. Engels and

writer through the visual or spoken reading upon their arrival. As Evagrius states in To Melania:

> You know, good Sir, that if those who are far apart from each other, separated by a long distance (something which is apt to happen for many varied reasons), want to know or to make known to each other, their respective intentions and secrets (which should not be learned by everyone, but only by those who have a mind akin to their own), they do this by means of letters. In this way, though they are far apart, they are near each other; though being separated, they see and are seen; though remaining silent, they speak and hear; although they are as it were, asleep, they are awake because their intentions are realized; remaining sick, they are healed; while sitting, they run. Yes, I would even say that although they are dead, they live. (1, 1–12)[6]

Letter 55 is no different; Evagrius writes from a distance to instruct a monk in the necessity of stability in thought against anger, lust, and the unnamed passion that arose upon familial visits—annoyance, frustration, avoidance. In doing so he tries to approach him gently, though not without a reminder of delusion and its consequences.

This may be why Evagrius begins the letter with a sentence signifying his apparent renunciation of his authority but ends it by claiming the very authority that he had previously renounced. Ironically, the initial renunciation is a triple counterclaim: he is not a *sophos,* although, of course, only a sage could have written such a letter or have had one sought from him. In quoting from Proverbs 9, Evagrius renounces any similarity to the author of Proverbs, Solomon the sage—yet he himself had written a set of scholia on Proverbs that authoritatively interpreted the proverbs as sources for monastic practice and contemplation. At the same time, he renounces apostolic status, particularly the status of Paul the sage (i.e., Pharisee and then Christian wise man) as mentioned in Romans 1:22 and 1 Corinthians 1:19. Finally, he renounces any resemblance to "God only wise," as in Romans 16:27 or 1 Corinthians 1:25. Instead, he poses as Peter, triply denying any knowledge of Christ. Evagrius may here be pursuing his typically coy renunciation of his own asserted renunciation, or he may be underlining it; at any rate, he seems to be intent on accom-

---

Heinz Hofmann (Wiesbaden: Aula, 1997), 321–54. See also Martin Parmentier, "Evagrius of Pontus 'Letter to Melania,'" *Bijdragen, tijdschrift voor filosofie en theologie* 46 (1985): 2–38, and Bunge, *Evagrios Pontikos,* 165–200 (a discussion of the entire corpus of Evagrian letters). See also Luther Stirewalt, *Studies in Ancient Greek Epistolography* (Atlanta: Scholars Press, 1993).

6. Parmentier, translation of To Melania 1, 1–12, in "Evagrius of Pontus," 8.

plishing the kind of *synkatabasis* in the first lines of the letter about which he also issues cautions in the *Gnostikos:* "beware lest condescension become a habit for you."[7]

Evagrius, then, presents himself as nonauthoritative and even fearful, perhaps in order to gain the confidence of his addressee, perhaps as part of his own strategy in the monastic combat against thoughts and their prompting demons who, once they saw signs of arrogance instead of humility, engaged in battle to bring down the monastic teacher. No letter writer like Paul, who instructed and straightened the first churches, he is of course, very much like the apostolic letter writer—hardly the first Christian author to feign unlikeness while busily imitating the divine apostle. Thus does he refer to himself as a kind of physician, hiding his instruments under a cloth.[8] The theme of therapeutic dissembling is another frequent reference in Evagrius; to dissemble is to fool the demonic opponent and lure the disciple. Note that the device of pretending to be someone else as part of a teacher-student or physician-patient dialogue is integral to Evagrius's description at the level of the *praktike*—and this is the level at which the entire letter operates.

Unlike the theological letters, 63 and 64, or even other letters that describe the deeper levels of contemplation and thought, Evagrius here deals entirely with the elementary phases of the monastic life: learning to stay in one place and learning to deal with other human beings through whom a monk receives demonic attacks. His instruction, then, is to apply "suitable remedies" of fasting, vigil, withdrawal, and prayer. Against temptations to take care of family members, possibly through monetary donations, Evagrius advises looking away from the "scheme of the evil one" and gazing on the Christ who advises hatred for family when they threaten the status of disciple.

It is at this point, right at the end of the letter, that Evagrius renounces his initial renunciation and presents himself with full apostolic authority by evok-

---

7. "The gnostic [teacher] should be secure in his synkatabasis, lest synkatabasis become for him a habit..." *Gnostikos* 6, in Evagrius of Pontus, *Le gnostique, ou, A celui qui est devenu digne de la science,* ed. and trans. Antoine and Claire Guillaumont, SC 356 (Paris: Éditions du Cerf, 1989), 96–97, with citations of Evagrius's major source, Clement of Alexandria in *Stromateis* 7 in the notes.

8. See *Gnostikos* 33: "That one who heals human beings because of the Lord should take care equally to heal himself, for the gnostikos who applies a medicament to his neighborhood should necessarily heal himself as well." Evagrius, *Gnostique,* SC 356:150–51, with numerous citations of a Christian medical topos that is "banale" already in Evagrius's predecessors Origen and Clement of Alexandria, in notes to the edition by Antoine and Claire Guillaumont.

ing Paul's letters in two quotations: the first, to the Ephesians, calls for the expulsion of the evil one. The second seems to call for a different kind of help for relatives on the part of the monk: responding to the call of Christ, he in some way "lead[s] them to life" and "give[s] them the inheritance with those being made holy in light," i.e., with those becoming angelic—here, surely, with the monastic community, typically self-described as living the *angelikos bios*.

In the course of this one short letter, then, Evagrius has practiced concealment and *synkatabasis* in his initial approach—albeit over the distance traversed by his letter—and also has displayed the pose of humility by renouncing the status of the sage. But as the end of the letter shows, he has drawn near to the recipient in humble and even foolish guise, only to show his true hand at the end—as an authority in the *praktikē*, with strongly hinted-at expertise in the gnostic tradition that can lead to angelic transformation, even for the kinfolk of monks, even if those kinfolk might have preferred actual money to the heavenly inheritance that the monk theoretically mediated to them. Thus the letter practices a kind of epistolary economy dependent upon its actual status as something more than a letter—as an exegetical exercise with therapeutic consequences. The letter, in short, depends upon the scriptures on which Evagrius spent so much time commenting and, if his biographers are right, meditating while trying to stay awake in the confines of his enclosure.

Since it is an exegetical exercise, it is useful to examine the chain of texts that lies under the surface concerns of the letter. Here it can be seen once again that, as for other monastic practitioners of the fourth century, Evagrius understood scripture as a continuous and consistent illustration of the path of the monastic gnostic—one text in different voices, and a medicament just as much as a vessel of hidden meaning or an ethical pattern.

The Exegetical Chain of Letter 55

Although the bulk of the quotations in the exegetical chain of Letter 55 come from Proverbs, it is well here to reverse course and pay attention to the end of the chain first, returning to the narrative texts and then, finally, to the ethical texts that come from Solomon's book. The letter ends with an evocation of exorcism and angelic *psychagogia* into which the maxims of Proverbs and admonitions of the Old Testament and New Testament are telescoped.

The last two texts, as mentioned above, are Pauline. Ephesians 4, having to do with a kind of mental exorcism, bears on the problem, as Evagrius sees it, of anger evoked by parents and siblings: "Do not let the sun go down on your anger, and give no opportunity to the devil." The next text, however, is a reminder of the power of Christ, which itself begins by reminding the Colossians that Paul prays constantly that they be "filled with the knowledge of [God's] will in all wisdom and understanding." Paul wrote, and Evagrius quotes: "May you be strengthened with all power, according to his glorious might, for all endurance and patience with joy, giving thanks to the Father, who has qualified us to share in the heritance of the saints in light. He has delivered us from the dominion of darkness and transferred us to the kingdom of his beloved Son, in whom we have redemption, the forgiveness of sins." This passage itself turns on the cryptic Pauline assertion that Christ is "the image of the invisible God."

For Evagrius, the battle against thoughts, the *logismoi* that were the result of giving opportunity to the devil, was the daily fare of monks and, indeed, of *kosmikoi* too. Allowing anger to last was the passion of *mnesikakia,* the remembrance of evil that became a habit in a mind and could incline it toward a humanly unnatural—i.e., demonic—*katastasis,* or habitual way of being. Thus the expulsion of the demonic was the only way to receive the power of the kingdom of the Son. Evagrius does not mention it in the letter, but for him the kingdom of Christ is the penultimate kingdom, a kind of pre-eschatological state before the true unity in God, which is the restoration of all human beings to their natural *katastasis,* occurs. Here this is consistent with the overall aim of the letter to assist the monk in becoming fixed in the *praktike.*

Expulsion of the devil and reception of power from Christ makes possible the resumption of, and also the mediation of, the angelic life—but the parallel with the baptismal ritual is also unmistakable here, where exorcism precedes reception of the Spirit. This is why, at the letter's beginning, Evagrius portrays himself in the terms of Ephesians 1:13(–14) and 4:30(–31). The first reads: "In [Christ] you also, who have heard the word of truth, the gospel of your salvation, and have believed in him, were sealed with the promised Holy Spirit, which is the guarantee of our inheritance until we acquire possession of it, to the praise of his glory." The second is an admonition: "And do not grieve the Holy Spirit of God, in whom you were sealed for the day of redemption. Let all bitterness and wrath and anger and clamor and slander be put away from you, with all malice, and be kind to one another, tenderhearted, forgiving one another, as God in Christ forgave you." These texts, too, fit into a baptismal context, in which the sealing with the Holy Spirit is an aspect of baptism that instills divine resemblance.

The remainder of the texts fall into the narrative and the gnomic. Evagrius begins by alluding to Proverbs 9:9 and 9:8, respectively: "Give instruction to a sage, and he will be still wiser; Teach a righteous man, and he will increase in learning." And "Do not reprove a scoffer, or he will hate you; reprove a sage, and he will love you."[9] In presenting himself as foolish, Evagrius also poses as the recipient of his letter, who may or may not receive his teaching as a sage, and thus will prove his character.

The next four quotations attest to the violence of animals—i.e., of humans when, in demonic *katastasis,* they resemble animals. Thus Exodus 21:28ff. reads, "When an ox gores a man or a woman to death, the ox shall be stoned"; Proverbs 9:18 refers to a female "animal," a harlot who behaves bestially: "But he does not know that the dead are there [with her], that her guests are in the depths of Sheol." This text has to do with the delusion of lust and the female purveyor of lust. The third text, Proverbs 24:1, refers to male liars—rather than the deluded, the deceivers: "Be not envious of evil men, nor desire to be with them; for their minds devise violence, and their lips talk of mischief." The final text is linked with a fifth, to portray the evil of murder. Chapter 6:28ff of 2 Kings describes a woman tricked into cooking and eating her son first, by a woman who falsely promises that her own son will be next on the menu: "This woman said to me, 'Give your son, that we may eat him today, and we will eat my son tomorrow.' So we boiled my son, and ate him." Psalm 105 (106):37–39 describes the horrors resulting from "mingling with the nations": "They sacrificed their sons and their daughters to the demons; they poured out innocent blood.... Thus they became unclean by their acts, and played the harlot in their doings."

Evagrius had already had practice in the allegorical interpretation of the

---

9. Evagrius's scholion on Proverbs 9:8 survives in Greek: "It is not necessary to 'reprove evil men' who commit sins, but rather to engage in dialogue with them about the fear of God [i.e., the "beginning of wisdom"] who persuades them to stand away from evil." See Evagrius, *Scholia on Proverbs* 108, in *Scholies aux Proverbes,* ed. and trans. Paul Géhin, SC 340 (Paris: Éditions du Cerf, 1988), 206–7, and additional citations in notes.

Psalms and Proverbs, which books, along with Ecclesiastes, constituted the exegetical foundation for his monastic *paideia*. It is plausible to say, then, that his addressee knew, or might soon learn, that the horrors described in the Old Testament texts were, in one sense, historical occurrences of sins requiring both divine anger and divine redemption; in another, more current, sense, they were aspects of the mental life of the monastic aspirant, becoming an animal, or a harlot, or an infanticide, at the urgings of demonic *logismoi*. The only real therapy for this, according to Evagrius's exegetical scheme, is Luke 14:26: "If anyone comes to me and does not hate his own father and mother and wife and children and brothers and sisters, yes, and even his own life, he cannot be my disciple. Whoever does not bear his own cross and come after me, cannot be my disciple."

For Evagrius, the bearing of the cross was the wearing of the monastic garb. What was it, though, to hate the members of one's family? Evagrius really did mean that renunciation, withdrawal, and prayer were the therapy for the attacks of demons through other members of the human community, but there is probably another meaning that the text is adduced to support: parents, spouses, children are also the thoughts that the mind breeds and attaches itself to. Breaking these connections enables the new community of the angels to occupy the mind of the monk.

Conclusion

To a monk still enmeshed in difficult relations with his family, Evagrius wrote a short letter giving advice on how to care properly for his kin—without anger and from a distance. Approaching that monk as a nonsage, Evagrius imitated Paul's pose as a fool and thus legitimately (on his own terms, at any rate) invoked Paul's authority as a sage and an apostolic letter writer. Evagrius, unlike some of Paul's imitators, wrote in his own name, but he transposed Paul's texts by linking them with other evocative texts that displayed the life of the demonic human being by contrast with the life of the human being freed (on the literal level by baptism) from the demonic *katastasis* to both occupy and give as a gift the space and quality of angels. The letter itself was both an instrument and an occasion for mediation by someone who was, of course, also posing as an angel.

Philip Rousseau

THE SUCCESSORS OF PACHOMIUS AND THE NAG HAMMADI CODICES

Exegetical Themes and Literary Structures

I want here to offer reflections on some "post-Pachomian" texts that might clarify possible relations between Pachomius's followers and the creators or collectors or depositors of the "Nag Hammadi Library."[1] That relations were possible has long been acknowledged because of the proximity of the Nag Hammadi site to the Pachomian monasteries of Seneset and Pbow.[2] Among the more stimulating scholars who have tackled the issues recently, Alexandr Khosroyev has shown how ambiguous and shifting a relationship there would have been between Pachomius's successors and *any* other religious group.[3] Similarly, Bernward Büchler has shown not only that Pachomius's principles matched what he regarded as the demands of a Christian vocation, but also that he dedicated himself to ensuring that those demands could

---

1. For comments on an earlier version of this paper, my thanks to David Brakke and Mark Sheridan.
2. I reviewed some aspects of the matter in the introduction to the paperback edition of my *Pachomius: The Making of a Community in Fourth-Century Egypt* (Berkeley and Los Angeles: University of California Press, 1999). One needs to attend also to Manichaean and Melitian communities; see James E. Goehring, "Melitian Monastic Organization: A Challenge to Pachomian Originality," *StPatr* 25 (Louvain: Peeters, 1993): 388–95; reprinted in his *Ascetics, Society, and the Desert: Studies in Early Egyptian Monasticism* (Harrisburg, Pa.: Trinity Press International, 1999), 187–95.
3. What I referred to as "a blurring of the frontier between ascetics and Christians generally" (Rousseau, *Pachomius*, xviii). See Alexandr L. Khosroyev, *Die Bibiothek von Nag Hammadi: Einige Probleme des Christentums in Ägypten während der ersten Jahrhunderte* (Altenberg: Oros Verlag, 1995).

be understood and acted upon by men and women outside the monastery.[4]

Within that context of potential interaction, I want to examine how some well-known Pachomian texts appear to adopt exegetical strategies similar to those represented in some of the Nag Hammadi material. I shall concentrate on the "catecheses" of Theodore and Horsiesios, and on Horsiesios's so-called *Liber* or *Testamentum*. Those texts postdate the death of Pachomius in 346 and correspond roughly in time to the supposed "burial" of the Nag Hammadi codices. Since they reflected situations that Pachomius himself had not faced, they were less constrained by a demand for narrative accuracy. Indeed, even when we bear in mind that Theodore and Horsiesios wished to put their own stamp on Pachomius's legacy,[5] we cannot assume that the surviving catecheses and the *Liber* bring us close to the heart even of their own communities. We do not know how they were created in the first place, whether they were edited by the original speakers, why and where they were preserved, or how much they have been reworked. The *Liber* survives anyway only in a Latin translation by Jerome.[6] We are therefore at several removes from original circumstance.

Nevertheless, what I have called "exegetical strategies" in the post-Pachomian texts may help us to relate them more convincingly to their mid-fourth-century milieu. At a theological level, Theodore and Horsiesios were far from gnostic; but in their methods of presentation, they were, perhaps, typical of their time and setting. I base a possible connection with Nag Hammadi on Michael Williams's work: not solely on his welcome and convincing attempt to "rethink" the notion of "gnosticism," so that it falls apart into its remarkably varied constituents, but also on his belief in a principle of coherence, a habit of analysis, that seems to have governed the compilation of each codex.[7]

---

4. Bernward Büchler, *Die Armut der Armen: Über den ursprünglichen Sinn der Mönchischen Armut* (Munich: Kösel, 1980). For apposite suggestions in a more general context, see Daniel Caner, *Wandering, Begging Monks: Spiritual Authority and the Promotion of Monasticism in Late Antiquity* (Berkeley and Los Angeles: University of California Press, 2002).

5. A point frequently made by James Goehring; see especially "Pachomius' Vision of Heresy: The Development of a Pachomian Tradition," *Muséon* 95 (1982): 241–62, reprinted in his *Ascetics, Society, and the Desert*, 137–61.

6. Where we can check Jerome against Coptic fragments, we find apparent liberties and confusions (evident also in his translations of Pachomius's *Rules*)—an added cause for nervousness. However, at least he bears some sort of witness to fourth-century texts.

7. Michael Allen Williams, *Rethinking "Gnosticism": An Argument for Dismantling a Dubious Category* (Princeton: Princeton University Press, 1996).

Many codices in the Nag Hammadi collection appear to jumble together tractates of widely divergent character. Williams reaches beyond the familiar associations that can be made on the strength of material construction and scribal hands[8] and points to patterns that were, as he puts it, "recycling and repackaging shards from what were, in relative terms, failed religious movements of earlier generations."[9]

Let me pick out two of those patterns, because they suggest a new way of reading Horsiesios in particular. First, there are transitions from ancient to revealed authority, following the canonical structure of the Bible from Genesis to Revelation, from creation to the eschaton. Second, there are sequences based more on instructional or liturgical preoccupations. As we shall see, the two patterns are interrelated.

Of the first pattern, Williams's major example is Codex II. We have a recasting of Genesis (*The Apocryphon of John*),[10] two gospels (the *Gospel of Thomas* and the *Gospel of Philip*), a commentary on passages in Colossians and Ephesians (*The Hypostasis of the Archons*), two eschatological treatises on the soul (*On the Origin of the World* and *The Exegesis on the Soul*), and a concluding dialogue (*The Book of Thomas the Contender*).[11] Williams wants to apply the same argument to Codex III, where we have (as he describes it) another recasting of Genesis (*The Apocryphon of John*), Seth's teaching on the great invisible spirit (*The Gospel of the Egyptians*), further reflections (in the *Eugnōstos*), and Christian fulfillment (in *The Sophia of Jesus Christ* and *The Dialogue of the Savior*).

Turning to the second pattern, the task of spiritual or ascetic formation depends naturally on an interweaving of instructional and liturgical preoccupations. Williams arranges the five tractates of Codex I under the headings invocatory prayer (*The Prayer of the Apostle Paul*), dialogue (*The Apocryphon of James*), homily (*The Gospel of Truth*),[12] eschatology (*The Treatise on the Resur-*

---

8. Although he respects scribal initiative; see his "Interpreting the Nag Hammadi Library as 'Collection(s)' in the History of 'Gnosticism(s),'" in *Les textes de Nag Hammadi et le problème de leur classification*, ed. Louis Painchaud and Anne Pasquier (Louvain: Peeters, 1995), 40.

9. Williams, *Rethinking "Gnosticism,"* 262.

10. Prominent also in codices III, IV, the Berlin codex, and possibly (although it is now missing) XIII. See Williams, "Interpreting the Nag Hammadi Library," 20–32.

11. That final dialogue "serves very nicely as concluding parenesis, hammering home a lesson of ascetic discipline that could easily be seen as the implication of the doctrines and myths in the earlier tractates" (ibid., 30). It is in a different hand.

12. More like a Pauline letter than a gospel (ibid., 14).

rection), and final overview (*The Tripartite Tractate*). He would like to discover kindred patterns in Codex VII: an ancient authority discussing purity and impurity (*The Paraphrase of Shem*), a contrast between true and false fellowship, and between true and false views on the death of Jesus (*The Second Treatise of the Great Seth* and *The Apocalypse of Peter*), a *parainesis* (*The Teachings of Silvanus*), the scribal note on Christ the "wonder extraordinary," a combination of vision and prayer (*The Three Stēlēs of Seth*), and a final scribal blessing.

Williams regards Codices V and XI as more directly concerned with the soul and therefore with spiritual instruction in an even deeper sense. Codex XI is slightly more liturgical in character, creating "a gradual crescendo from the more exoteric homiletic material to the mystical visions at the end."[13] We have a homily on community life (*The Interpretation of Knowledge*), a catechism for initiates (*A Valentinian Exposition*), treatises on anointing, baptism, and the Eucharist, followed by "mystical ascent and vision" (in the *Allogenēs*) and the fragmentary *Hypsiphrōnē*.[14] In Codex V, Williams regards *Eugnōstos* as a prelude to the other four tractates, presenting "the structure of the entire divine realm," followed by *The Apocalypse of Paul* (a picture of the soul ascending to that realm), by *The First* and *Second Apocalypse of James* (particular examples of such an experience—"a paradigm for the ascent of every believer's soul at death"), and then by *The Apocalypse of Adam* (an overview of salvation history).[15]

We should not dismiss these descriptions as too rigid. The point is that the structure *of the codices* need not have been governed by the principles embraced *within individual tractates*. The implied "recycling" could have been inspired by Christian and ascetic principles, and we might expect to find in other contemporary treatises (such as those attributed to Theodore and Horsiesios) similar patterns of construction, and therefore of purpose.

In the catecheses of Theodore and Horsiesios, creation and redemption occupy a central position.[16] By looking at the visible world, at "the great things

---

13. Ibid., 16.

14. Note the passage here from one scribe to another, one theological emphasis to another, and one dialect to another.

15. Williams, "Interpreting the Nag Hammadi Library," 33.

16. L. Th. Lefort, ed. and trans., *Œuvres de s. Pachôme et de ses disciples*, CSCO 159; Scriptores coptici 23 (Coptic texts) and CSCO 160; Scriptores coptici 24 (Latin translations) (Louvain: L. Durbecq, 1956). Theodore's *Catecheses* are presented in the first volume, pp. 37–59; those of Horsiesios, pp. 66–70 (1), 70 (2), 70–71 (3), 72–73 (4), 73–74 (5), 74–75 (6), 75–79 (7). English translation by Armand Veil-

which he has created by his word," one recognizes, according to Horsiesios, how hard it is to say much about God, but one recognizes also a good deal about oneself as a creature: "May you be blessed, Lord, who fashioned me from earth [literally, from soil] when I did not exist."[17] Theodore makes a similar point: "Let us be aware that God is concerned with us, to the end that we may work at that which is needful to the body and that we may become a pure temple for God."[18] Theodore handles with profound tact the notion that the body, like all created things, could reveal the creator:

If the weaknesses of each and every person, which are known to God, were revealed, we should be hard put indeed to answer each other. It is for that reason that we urge you not to think of one another as different from what we see, although in point of fact the full reality of our weakness is not mutually apparent. Indeed, God conceals us from one another in time of weakness.[19]

Horsiesios makes comparable connections: on the one hand, the soul "helps us in the assistance to our body"; on the other, "the miserable soul is all alone when it falls into sin; no one else will offer it a hand in its punishments."[20] He recommends that ascetics should attend to the needs of their souls while they still have bodies—"while we are in the land of tears, our hands and feet free and unfettered, not yet in the tomb and a prey to worms, and while the flesh, an object of concern, is not dissolved and reduced to dust."[21] Hence his lament, "Where is my body [ⲥⲱⲙⲁ], this body that God has afforded me as a field to cultivate, where I might work, and become rich? I have destroyed it, rendered it sterile."[22]

---

leux in his *Pachomian Koinonia*, vol. 3: *Instructions, Letters, and Other Writings of Saint Pachomius and his Disciples*, CSS 47 (Kalamazoo: Cistercian Publications, 1982): Theodore, pp. 91–122; Horsiesios, pp. 135–152. My facility in Coptic is limited; in addition to the translations by Lefort and Veilleux, I have depended on the advice of Janet Timbie.

17. Horsiesios, *Catechesis* 6.2 (Veilleux, *Pachomian Koinonia* 3:144). For "soil," ⲕⲁϩ, see Lefort, *Œuvres de s. Pachôme*, 74.32.

18. Theodore, *Catechesis* 3.41 (Veilleux, *Pachomian Koinonia* 3:116). Compare *Catechesis* 3.33: "Now, Jerusalem is every soul that has become the dwelling place of the Spirit of God.... [The Lord] will grant his bounty to the men who will become his dwelling place" (Veilleux, *Pachomian Koinonia* 3:113).

19. Theodore, *Catechesis* 3.34 (Veilleux, *Pachomian Koinonia* 3:113). He had earlier made the point that "certainly the things of God at times divide us in body but not in heart," *Catechesis* 3.14 (Veilleux, *Pachomian Koinonia* 3:101).

20. Horsiesios, *Catechesis* 1.3, Lefort, *Œuvres de s. Pachôme*, 68.26–29 (Veilleux, *Pachomian Koinonia* 3:137).

21. Horsiesios, *Catechesis* 1.4 (Veilleux, *Pachomian Koinonia* 3:137).

22. Horsiesios, *Catechesis* 1.6 (Veilleux, *Pachomian Koinonia* 3:138). For ⲥⲱⲙⲁ, see Lefort, *Œuvres*

The two Pachomians face up here to questions that afflicted some gnostics; but they do so with a distinct confidence of their own. That does not mean, however, that they adopted their positions in conscious *opposition* to gnostics *specifically*. They could have undertaken their inquiries without rejecting the manner in which others had formulated and resolved the issues. If we are hearing one side in an exegetical discussion, it was a discussion made possible by shared and unthreatening assumptions. As we "dismantle" gnosticism, we can retain what Michael Williams calls "corporeality as a mode of revelation."[23] A number of supposed "gnostics" would have accepted the notion that "precisely in the human body is to be found the best visible trace of the divine in the material world." Some "gnostic" myths "also expressed, ironically, a conviction that the human form in a special way mirrors the divine world."[24]

Now, when Theodore wants his monks to "work at that which is needful to the body," he is attaching value to the visible regime of the monastic life. "Above all," as he puts it, "[God] causes our conscience to burn us at every moment when we do not walk as befits the dignity of the holy vocation of the habit [*schēma*] we wear." His account suggests a public and complex ceremony: "We have all sought to put on the acts of the habit we wear, of the name spoken over us, and of the law that we have promised before God and men faithfully to keep."[25] He speaks also of "the long training [*paideusis*] by which he formed such saints as Joseph."[26] Horsiesios appreciates the same emphases. One's heavenly reward, he says, will be granted "in the measure of each one's toil";[27] and one honors God by "genuine efforts" and "sweat."[28] Such

---

de s. Pachôme, 69.29 (where the Coptic uses a Greek loan-word). Horsiesios called the spiritual adornment of the soul "purity, the pride of the angels [ⲉⲧⲉⲡⲧⲃⲃⲟⲛⲉ ⲡϣⲟⲩϣⲟⲩ ⲛⲛⲁⲅⲅⲉⲗⲟⲥ]." *Catechesis* 4.2 (Lefort, *Œuvres de s. Pachôme,* 72.26–27; Veilleux, *Pachomian Koinonia* 3:142).

23. Williams, *Rethinking "Gnosticism,"* 125.

24. Ibid., 117, 137.

25. Theodore, *Catechesis* 3.1 and 3 (Lefort, *Œuvres de s. Pachôme,* 40; Veilleux, *Pachomian Koinonia* 3:93–94).

26. Theodore, *Catechesis* 3.2 (Lefort, *Œuvres de s. Pachôme,* 40; Veilleux, *Pachomian Koinonia* 3:93). The theme recurs: see especially the opening of 3.6, where *paideuô* (ⲡⲁⲓⲇⲉⲩⲉ) is linked with the vocabulary of the gymnasium (Lefort, *Œuvres de s. Pachôme,* 42.21–22; Veilleux, *Pachomian Koinonia* 3:96).

27. Horsiesios, *Catechesis* 1.3 (Lefort, *Œuvres de s. Pachôme,* 68.2; Veilleux, *Pachomian Koinonia* 3:136), echoing Theodore, *Catechesis* 3.14.

28. Horsiesios, *Catechesis* 3.1 and 2 (Veilleux, *Pachomian Koinonia* 3:139). For Horsiesios's consistent use of the Coptic ⲙ̄ⲛϩⲓⲥⲉ, "toil," in addition to Lefort, *Œuvres de s. Pachôme,* 68.2 (where it gains added force: ⲕⲁⲧⲁ ⲡϥⲓ ⲛ̄ϩⲓⲥⲉ), see 70.30 and 71.1. The generalized nature of the terminology may represent a wish (characteristic also of Shenoute) to reach beyond a monastic audience.

commitment represents, for Theodore, a sharing in the sufferings of Christ. He is thinking not of theological opposition but of "the distress of our bodily needs... as we face the taunts of those who reproach us because of poverty and affliction." He quotes Isaiah: "do not be dismayed because you are disgraced."[29] "With the sole force of your own will," he says, "love the disgrace of the cross."[30] And one is to do so in very concrete circumstances: "If we are sent to work at one of the brothers' occupations, let us toil away at the work to which we have been sent, even if we are struck, insulted, imprisoned, even if we come back to the monastery spattered with blood from the blows."[31]

So, we now have two factors: the attitude of Pachomians to material creation, and their communities' character as visibly segregated and as dedicated to bodily "toil."[32] We should recall at this point Michael Williams's observation that many of the Nag Hammadi speculations on Genesis are combined with *paraineseis,* calculated exhortations to practical virtue. That very similarity should warn us against supposing that Theodore and Horsiesios were relying wholly on an enclosed and defensive position. Theodore refers at one point to "the fragrance of obedience" dispersed through "the holy and true *Koinonia*" (echoing the phraseology of the *Gospel of Truth*),[33] but then suggests almost immediately that the fragrance will reach beyond the monastery limits: it is "a fragrance for those from outside."[34] In the same catechesis, he

---

29. Theodore, *Catechesis* 3.5–7 (Veilleux, *Pachomian Koinonia* 3:96). The appeal to the Old Testament is characteristic, passing over obvious statements made by Jesus about expecting persecution; but see the allusion to Luke 22:28–30 in *Catechesis* 3.14, and to John 15:18 in *Catechesis* 3.32.

30. The element of constraint in ϩⲛ̄ⲡⲉⲩϩⲧⲟⲣ is immediately given liberty by ⲟⲩⲁⲁⲧⲟⲩ, to mean something like feeling the need to make a choice. Theodore, *Catechesis* 3.10 (Lefort, *Œuvres de s. Pachôme,* 45.1–2; Veilleux, *Pachomian Koinonia* 3:99).

31. Theodore, *Catechesis* 3.14 (Lefort, *Œuvres de s. Pachôme,* 46.17–18—and note also ⲛ̄ⲧⲛ̄ϣⲛ̄ϩⲓⲥⲉ, as in n. 28; Veilleux, *Pachomian Koinonia* 3:101). What circumstances are envisaged here?

32. I have suggested elsewhere that the structure of the *Koinōnia* itself was a theological statement, designed to safeguard an orthodox position in regard to the value of the body and its role in self-improvement and redemption: "Orthodoxy and the Coenobite," *StPatr* 30 (1997): 241–58.

33. "The children of the Father are his fragrance"; so in the *Gospel of Truth,* "the Father loves his fragrance and manifests it in every place." (NHC I 3, 34.3–5). A precise parsing of the codices is not necessary to my overall argument, and I have depended substantially on the English translation, James M. Robinson, ed., *The Nag Hammadi Library in English,* 4th rev. ed. (Leiden: Brill, 1996).

34. Theodore, *Catechesis* 3.5 (Lefort, *Œuvres de s. Pachôme,* 41–42; Veilleux, *Pachomian Koinonia* 3: 95). For "those from outside" (ⲛ̄ⲛⲉⲧϩⲓⲃⲟⲗ), see Lefort, *Œuvres de s. Pachôme,* 42.2–3. The Coptic, here (41.27 and 42.2) and in passages discussed below is consistent in its use of ⲥⲧⲟⲓ̈, "fragrance." See also a passage in the "Excerpta" of Theodore (Veilleux's *Fragments* 2; in his *Pachomian Koinonia* 3:133), which mentions "fragrance" (Lefort, *Œuvres de s. Pachôme,* 61a.22) but then praises the guarding of the

warns against giving scandal to those "outside the vocation of the holy *Koinonia*."[35] Horsiesios also describes "the life of our holy fathers" as "perfuming the whole world."[36] The conjunction of self-perfection and engagement with others, including those beyond the community, is highly suggestive. In section 48 of his *Liber,* alluding to Isaiah 61:9, Horsiesios refers to monks as "the seed that God has blessed." He may have remembered Theodore's declaration, "So all who see us will know that we are the seed that God has blessed, as they see our faith, our knowledge [*epistēmē*], our gravity in all things, our humility, and our speech seasoned with salt in the knowledge of the Scriptures and the love of God."[37]

Reflections on the goodness of creation, therefore, on the usefulness of the body, and on the importance of discipline, were combined with an appreciation of a monastery's impact on the surrounding society. To be effective, such a strategy had to focus on biblical texts that were arresting to those who nevertheless reached, on their basis, different theological conclusions. We are brought at this point to Theodore's most complex convictions.

> And he, the Lord of the universe, Jesus Christ, Lord of all, would not so forsake us as to allow to gloat over us those who set up ambushes for Adam's progeny. On the contrary, he has in his kindness made a secret call, Arise, wake up from the sleep of death and from the rottenness of wicked thoughts. And to his angels, mighty forces which carry out what he says, he has given orders to set us free from the shackles of our sins.[38]

That so resounding a summons should be "secret" recalls the "hidden" emphasis in 1 Corinthians 2:7—"the secret and hidden wisdom of God"—and evokes

---

mouth, whether the one so cautious be "a monk or a secular [ⲕⲟⲥⲙⲓⲕⲟⲛ]": "many a man in the world is watchful on this point." *Fragments* 4 has "monks as well as seculars." Lefort, *Œuvres de s. Pachôme,* 62b.3–5; Veilleux, *Pachomian Koinonia* 3:134.

35. Theodore, *Catechesis* 3.43 (Veilleux, *Pachomian Koinonia* 3:117).

36. Horsiesios, *Catechesis* 1.2 (Lefort, *Œuvres de s. Pachôme,* 67.23; Veilleux, *Pachomian Koinonia* 3:136); and see *Catechesis* 3.3. Veilleux notes (*Pachomian Koinonia* 3:120) a phrase in the first Sahidic *Life of Pachomius* 25: "we are the fragrance of the Christ of God." L. Th. Lefort, *S. Pachomii vitae sahidice scriptae,* CSCO 99–100, Scriptores coptici 9–10 (Paris: E Typographeo Reipublicae, 1933), 118.15; English translation in Veilleux, *Pachomian Koinonia,* 1:439. Just immediately prior, Pachomius is likened to Noah, whose sacrifice was fragrant to God (Gen. 8:21). There is, in all this, some reminiscence of 2 Corinthians 2:14; but difference of vocabulary makes dependence difficult to assess.

37. Theodore, *Catechesis* 3.8 (Lefort, *Œuvres de s. Pachôme,* 43–44; Veilleux, *Pachomian Koinonia* 3:97).

38. Theodore, *Catechesis* 3.29 (Lefort, *Œuvres de s. Pachôme,* 53; Veilleux, *Pachomian Koinonia* 3:109–10). The allusion to Ephesians 5:14 includes the point that "secret" things are now exposed.

Matthew 13:35—"what has been hidden since the foundation of the world." Theodore goes on, however, to talk about "the glory that is to be revealed to us" and "the revealing of the sons of God."[39] He then illustrates the complex social setting of that "revealing" (as of "fragrance" in earlier passages):

> Would that we could make known to those who do not know its sweetness the custody of our soul, which is the custody of our lips when there is nothing profitable to say, in order to be a cause of edification for one another and a wholesome example to the novices who have come to us in answer to the Lord's call. We have surrounded ourselves with a saving rampart which is love for God's law and for the vocation of the *Koinonia,* so as to walk on this earth after the manner of heavenly inhabitants and of the life of the august angels, so that all those who see our good works may give glory to God and may know that we are disciples of Christ, so as to love one another without hypocrisy.[40]

At the heart of those allusions—to Ephesians, 1 Corinthians, and Matthew—lies the conviction that a monk's intimate and privileged relation to God is bound up with his capacity to "reveal" his "secret call" to the world. And embedded in the passages just quoted (from *Catechesis* 3) is a clue to the basis of that bond: the notion of rising up and waking from the sleep of death. We see that notion recur in Theodore's use of Matthew 19:27–29.

> Then in reply Peter said to him, "Look, we have left everything and have followed you. So what is there for us?" Jesus said to them, "Amen I say to you, that you who have followed me shall, in the rebirth [ἐν τῇ παλιγγενεσίᾳ], when the son of man is seated on his throne of glory, sit also on twelve thrones, judging the twelve tribes of Israel. And everyone who leaves house or brothers or sisters or father or mother or children or fields for the sake of my name shall receive a hundredfold and shall inherit life unending."

To have "left everything" evokes ascetic dedication; the "rebirth" echoes the rising and waking; and "judging the twelve tribes" means playing a visible, public role.

How does Theodore build up his connections here? The threads to follow are those of rebirth (παλιγγενεσία) and inheritance. In *Catechesis* 2, the *Koinonia* reveals "the life of the Apostles ... to men who desire to follow their model forever." Now here, in *Catechesis* 3, Theodore links that reach across time with the passage from Matthew 19.[41] He also links with the same notion of inheri-

---

39. Theodore, *Catechesis* 3.30—a favorite line of thought; see *Catechesis* 3.5.
40. Theodore, *Catechesis* 3.27 (Veilleux, *Pachomian Koinonia* 3:108–9).
41. Theodore, *Catechesis* 2.1 (Lefort, *Œuvres de s. Pachôme,* 38; Veilleux, *Pachomian Koinonia* 3:91) ("model" is a restoration, at 38a.15–16); *Catechesis* 3.28.

tance the phrase already quoted, "the vocation of the *Koinonia.*"[42] Then comes the revelation, inheritance made visible. Imitation in *Catechesis 2*—if "model" is not misleading—is an imitation in particular of an apostle's hardships; and that makes the monk, in his own way, another "messenger."[43] In *Catechesis 3*, Theodore refers to those "outside," which strikes an apparently exclusive note, until he adds the need to avoid giving scandal to "other men the Lord has edified."[44] Finally, he talks about "the pledge of every good thing he promised to our fathers of the *Koinonia* which he has placed in us beforehand, that we might not be cast away from the holy vocation of rebirth."[45] (The Coptic makes it clear that we are not expected to think of Nicodemus in John 3:3—the Gospel deals there with birth "from above"—but of the "rebirth," the παλιγγενεσία, of Matthew 19.)

So the monastery—or, more precisely, "the vocation of the *Koinonia*"— represents the kingdom, to some extent already come, in which monks, reborn, might share the promised inheritance, as they have shared in suffering. The same line of thought (about the "pledge ... placed in us beforehand") recurs in a slightly different form, when Theodore talks about

> seeing the attitude of the Fathers of the *Koinonia,* and the love which had previously been rooted in them. [That love] has now by Christ's grace *come to light* after we ourselves had shrouded it with the veil of our negligence, while through our lack of fear we had quenched the warmth of the holy Spirit who dwells within us through mercy and not because of our works.[46]

Thus Theodore brings together the notion of qualities rooted within and the notion of the hidden being revealed. Not surprisingly, he promptly repeats the allusion to the awakening (in Ephesians 5):

> On the contrary, in his love he wakens us from the sleep of death, and in his mercy goes on prodding us day by day, saying to our hearts, Wake up, you who sleep, rise from the dead, and Christ will shine on you. Knowing the great grace we have inherited ... let us repent.[47]

---

42. Theodore, *Catechesis* 3.36 (Lefort, *Œuvres de s. Pachôme,* 56.28). See above at nn. 25, 35, and 40.
43. Theodore, *Catechesis* 3.30.
44. Theodore, *Catechesis* 3.43 (Lefort, *Œuvres de s. Pachôme,* 59.16–17; Veilleux, *Pachomian Koinonia* 3:117). The connections with the passages examined above at nn. 34–35 will be obvious.
45. Theodore, *Catechesis* 3.28 (Lefort, *Œuvres de s. Pachôme,* 53, especially at 6; Veilleux, *Pachomian Koinonia* 3:109).
46. Theodore, *Catechesis* 3.36 (Veilleux, *Pachomian Koinonia* 3:114, emphasis added).
47. Theodore, *Catechesis* 3.37 (Veilleux, *Pachomian Koinonia* 3:114–15).

Even in the context of God's promises, therefore, such as those made in Matthew 19, prolonged ascetic discipline is unavoidable: God "in his mercy goes on prodding us *day by day.*" And that extended effort is combined with the concept of rebirth: "Let us know the teaching of Christ the true Doctor; and let us receive with joy the doctrine which flows from his goodness. For during the time we were little ones he fed us with the food of little ones; and *when we began to grow up in the rebirth,* he wanted to nourish us with the food of truth."[48]

One has to accept that the reasoning here is serpentine; but it represents the deepest level of Theodore's philosophy. Let me reiterate the logical sequence. First, we have the secret and the revealed, what is personal and what is shared. Second, the passage from sleep to wakefulness reminds Theodore of the "rebirth" in Matthew. Third, attached to that, comes the notion of inheritance: so the *Koinonia* becomes at once a heritage and a revelation; its discipline, in the richest sense, is a message to the world. And finally, the process of awakening, of being reborn, of bringing hidden things to light, is made possible by the goodness already built into creation. One cannot exaggerate the importance of the phrases we have uncovered: "the pledge...*placed in us* beforehand" (*Catechesis* 3.28), and "the love which had previously been *rooted in them*" (*Catechesis* 3.36).[49] In that conviction lies the principle of the argument's organic unity. An unbroken history reaches from the creation to the present day; and each monk's life is governed by the goodness and destiny of that history. Along another axis, the monk moves from his own fulfillment to his declaration of its meaning for others. At both levels, or in both dimensions, rebirth and revelation represent the force that drives both time in general and the life of the individual.

Gnosticism knew nothing of such conclusions. And yet gnostics would have recognized that the argument itself was an argument about the nature of creation, and about the essential character that creation imparted to the visible world. They were equally eager in their pursuit of that inquiry. Like them,

---

48. Theodore, *Catechesis* 3.43, (Lefort, *Œuvres de s. Pachôme,* 59, with ϩⲛⲡⲉ[ⲭⲡⲟ ⲛ̄ⲕ]ⲉⲥⲟⲡ, "rebirth," at 21–22; Veilleux, *Pachomian Koinonia* 3:118, emphasis added). For a clearer text, see Lefort, *Œuvres de s. Pachôme,* 53.6. There is no rebirth in 1 Corinthians 3:1–3.

49. Emphasis added. See above at nn. 45 and 46. Note the echo in *Ep. Ammon.* 10: "the good which you enjoined for us and *implanted* [ἐνεφύτευσας] *in us,*" ed. and trans. James E. Goehring, *The Letter of Ammon and Pachomian Monasticism,* PTS 27 (Berlin: Walter de Gruyter, 1986), 131.2–3; English translation, 164.

Theodore wanted to grasp as fully as he could the Bible's account of matter and time. And, in ways we shall examine further, he followed a path detectable in the Nag Hammadi material, a path that led from the exegesis of *Genesis* to the defense of a moral program and of the social institutions upon which its success and eventual fulfillment depended.

Horsiesios was less subtle than Theodore, which may explain why he found it hard to compete with his rival, Pachomius's hard-used favorite. Even his *Liber* seems less inspired.[50] I say "even," because it purports to be later than any of the other catecheses. It was his *testamentum*, his last advice. It represents, therefore, the most considered attempt to delineate a "Pachomian tradition" and to bring under its sway every species of variety, omission, and dissent that may in reality have colored the sprawling assortment of communities over which Horsiesios had charge.

Perhaps the most striking feature of the *Liber* is a dependence on the lengthy quotation of scripture.[51] The passages appealed to are not designed to justify opinions but to capture within the present moment of teaching and reflection an economy of salvation that reaches across time. They recount primarily an Old Testament understanding of repentance, of a return to an intimate relation with God.[52] That exegetical habit contributes to a strongly Old Testament image of the monastic community itself. There, too, intimacy with God is both betrayed and regained. Exiled like Israel "in the land of their enemies," "sullied among the dead," monks echo a more ancient refusal to listen to the prophets and to obey the law of Moses.[53] Their salvation lies in learning their "place," which is "the faithful city Sion."[54] Monks will thus be or become "God's special people [*populus Dei peculiaris*]"—a promise that lies close to

---

50. *Liber patris nostri Orsiesii*, re-edited in part, with German translation, by Heinrich Bacht in his *Das Vermächtnis des Ursprungs: Studien zum frühen Mönchtum I*, StTGL 5 (Würzburg: Echter Verlag, 1972), 58–189. Earlier edition by Amand Boon in *Pachomiana latina: Règles et Épitres de s. Pachôme, Épitre de s. Théodore et "Liber" de s. Orsiesios, Texte latin de s. Jérôme*, BRHE 7 (Louvain: Bureaux de la Revue, 1932), 109–47. English translation by Armand Veilleux, in *Pachomian Koinonia*, vol. 3; but the translations here are my own.

51. For the principle, see *Liber* 51, Bacht, *Das Vermächtnis des Ursprungs*, 178; and recall the bald simplicity of *Praecepta* 140: *et omnino nullus erit in monasterio qui non discat litteras et de scripturis aliquid teneat* (Boon, *Pachomiana latina*, 50; there is no surviving Coptic fragment).

52. [*Deus*] *cum sancto sanctus est*, *Liber* 53, Bacht, *Das Vermächtnis des Ursprungs*, 184; evoking Psalm 18 (V. 17).25–26.

53. *Liber* 1 (Bacht, *Das Vermächtnis des Ursprungs*, 60). See also *Liber* 43, with its evocation of the *meretrix civitas fidelis Sion* (Bacht, *Das Vermächtnis des Ursprungs*, 158).

54. As in *Liber* 43. Compare the danger foreseen in *Liber* 2: *amittemus civitatem nostram* (Bacht,

hand within their more immediate tradition: "Let us remember that by the efforts of that man [Pachomius] God has accepted us as his own family."[55]

A bond was established, therefore, between scriptural awareness and the acceptance of monastic order; between the "blessings" of the former and the "discipline" of the latter.[56] The ideal is vividly described: "We have been called to liberty, gathered from different places to become God's single people [*unum Dei populum*]. As it is written, 'I shall take one from this people and two from that family, and I shall lead you into Sion, and I shall give you shepherds after my own heart, who will feed you with discipline [*cum disciplina*].'"[57] Reminiscence of the Old Testament is deeply affected, therefore, by a tension between prophecy and fulfillment. Horsiesios quotes Romans 15:4: "The things written formerly were written for our instruction, so that through endurance and consolation we might have hope."[58] It is on that basis that he sets in motion an easy flow across the centuries. *Liber* 33 provides a good example, stringing beads from Hosea, Psalms, Malachi, Jeremiah, and Ezekiel, passing then to Matthew and Romans, and finally returning to Deuteronomy; a *passeggiata* of which every step rings out the theme of the heart's return to God.[59] Even the New Testament quotations are allowed to retain an Old Testament element of reprimand. Referring to Romans 11:21, for example—"For if God did not spare the natural branches, how much the less will he spare you"—Horsiesios added, "spare us who have failed to fulfill the commands of God."[60] Repentance,

---

Das Vermächtnis des Ursprungs, 60). In regard to the notion of "place," compare *The Gospel of Truth* at *NHC* I 3, 22, 24, and 42–43. The imagery in the *Liber*, however, is more concrete.

55. *Populus peculiaris: Liber* 53 (Bacht, *Das Vermächtnis des Ursprungs*, 184); *in propriam familiam receperit: Liber* 47 (Bacht, *Das Vermächtnis des Ursprungs*, 166). See the observations of Tito Orlandi: "Diversa ancora era la conezione pacomiana di chi voleva recuperare in comunità un 'vero Israele,' cioè un gruppo identificabile immediatamente col popolo di Dio," but then, "Sembra tuttavia che in fondo a tutto ciò ci fosse lo sforzo di recuperare un'innocenza originaria perduta nell'evolversi del processo cosmico." Orlandi, "Giustificazioni dell'encratismo nei testi monastici copti del IV–V secolo," in *La tradizione dell'enkrateia: Motivazione ontologiche e protologiche, atti del Colloquio internazionale, Milano, 20–23 aprile 1982*, ed. Ugo Bianchi (Rome: Edizioni dell'Ateneo, 1985), 362–63.

56. *Liber* 22, where *disciplina* is virtually identified with *beatitudines* (Bacht, *Das Vermächtnis des Ursprungs*, 118).

57. *Liber* 47, quoting Jeremiah 3:14–15 (Bacht, *Das Vermächtnis des Ursprungs*, 168/170).

58. *Liber* 41 (Bacht, *Das Vermächtnis des Ursprungs*, 154). The same point is made in *Liber* 10 (Bacht, *Das Vermächtnis des Ursprungs*, 80).

59. Bacht, *Das Vermächtnis des Ursprungs*, 142/144.

60. *Liber* 2 (Bacht, *Das Vermächtnis des Ursprungs*, 60), echoed at *Liber* 36, followed by another mass of Old Testament quotations (Bacht, *Das Vermächtnis des Ursprungs*, 146).

therefore, gives life to history in the mind of the ascetic. Only that degree of intensity could create the necessary elision between Old Testament events and fourth-century experience. "Accept my words and my ordinances [this is the voice of God in the opening verses of Zechariah], which, through my Spirit, I demanded of my servants the prophets, who were with your fathers." Horsiesios steps straight into the prophet's shoes, while evoking the memory of Pachomius and his companions.[61]

Such continuities are asserted very strongly. The ruin of his city and the ravaging of his vineyard had earned God's condemnation; but, Horsiesios declares, "we shall avoid such [harsh] words." How? By following "the star of Jacob," "the man of Israel" (as in Numbers 24:17–19). Observant monks would heed the words of Jeremiah (31:36): "If that law should pass away before my eyes, then the race of Israel itself could pass away." Horsiesios makes a quick switch to Isaiah (61:8–10), foreshadowing more clearly the monastic future: "I shall surrender their work into the hands of others and make with those an everlasting covenant. Their sons and their grandsons shall be famous among the peoples. All who see them shall know that they are the seed blessed by God and share in the Lord's joy."[62] Pachomius, in his own way "the star of Jacob" and "the man of Israel," occupies a central position in the sweep of time from the prophets to the *Koinonia*. The turning of the heart back to God is identified with the observance of the dead master's precepts; and he is allowed to make his own the words of scripture, "They scorned the law that God bequeathed to them, and they did not listen to the voice of the prophets: so they could not reach their promised rest."[63] Indeed, Pachomius is virtually given the place of Moses himself: "Let us not abandon God's law, which our father bequeathed to us, receiving it from him."[64]

For Horsiesios, therefore, the link between the living and the dead is forged on the basis of biblical prophecy and its fulfillment. That longer story provides the syntax that allows him to describe the status of Pachomius in God's eyes, the lasting value of his heritage, and the dangers inherent in its re-

---

61. *Liber* 49 (Bacht, *Das Vermächtnis des Ursprungs*, 172).
62. *Liber* 48 (Bacht, *Das Vermächtnis des Ursprungs*, 172). On the *semen benedictum a Deo*, see above at n. 37.
63. *Liber* 35 (Bacht, *Das Vermächtnis des Ursprungs*, 146).
64. *Liber* 46 (Bacht, *Das Vermächtnis des Ursprungs*, 162). Horsiesios cast Theodore in the same light, in his third and fourth letters.

jection. At other times, his tone can be less historical: "Let us think on this: the chance that, leaving this world all too soon, we shall, in that time to come, be separated from our fathers and brothers, who have secured the place of victory [*locum victoriae*]."[65] So the line reaching back to the past can also reach upward: "Let us think of [the teachings] handed down by our father as ladders [*scalas*] that lead to the heavenly kingdoms,"[66] where Pachomius stands ready to acknowledge those monks who honor his legacy.[67] To dishonor it was a species of "forgetting [*oblivio*]," by which, "in our wickedness, we abandon the mediator between God and the saints [*mediatoremque Dei atque sanctorum*]."[68] "Forgetting," therefore, or rather not forgetting, was another way in which present intensity could be combined with respect for tradition.

In his assessment of the material world, Horsiesios adopts a balanced view, a view based on his corporate vision of the *Koinonia*. Superiors, at every level of the system, are not to concentrate exclusively either on spiritual or on carnal *alimenta*, "but should offer both spiritual and carnal food in equal proportion [*pariter*]."[69] Spiritual emphases can be made: having alluded to the images of the "locked garden" and "sealed fountain,"[70] Horsiesios continues, referring to ascetics, "The one who is born from God does not sin, for [God's] seed endures in him";[71] he presents the standard contrast between flesh and spirit, not without a sense of superiority ("Know that to the perfect perfect things are given, and that folly is returned to the foolish)";[72] and he implies a great intimacy ("My son, if your heart is wise, you will give joy to my heart, and I shall speak as you speak, so long as you speak rightly").[73] Those spiritual

---

65. Horsiesios, *Liber* 3 (Bacht, *Das Vermächtnis des Ursprungs*, 62). Note the concept of "place" once more, as in n. 54 above.
66. Horsiesios, *Liber* 22 (Bacht, *Das Vermächtnis des Ursprungs*, 112).
67. Horsiesios, *Liber* 12 (Bacht, *Das Vermächtnis des Ursprungs*, 84).
68. Horsiesios, *Liber* 30 (Bacht, *Das Vermächtnis des Ursprungs*, 140). For Pachomius as *mediator*, see pp. 105n81, and 221–24. *Oblivio* occurs also in *Liber* 3 (Bacht, *Das Vermächtnis des Ursprungs*, 62). Compare the use of the concept in the Nag Hammadi documents: *The Teachings of Silvanus*, NHC VII 4, 89 and 98; *The Gospel of Truth*, NHC I 3, 17–18, 20.
69. Horsiesios, *Liber* 7 (Bacht, *Das Vermächtnis des Ursprungs*, 72).
70. Horsiesios, *Liber* 20 (Bacht, *Das Vermächtnis des Ursprungs*, 100). The context suggests baptismal connotations. Compare *Ep. Ammon.* 3 (Goehring, *Letter,* 125.23–25, together with his discussion at 197).
71. Horsiesios, *Liber* 20 (Bacht, *Das Vermächtnis,* 100).
72. Horsiesios, *Liber* 20 (Bacht, *Das Vermächtnis,* 102/104). The appeal is to Matthew 25:29.
73. Proverbs 23:16 (which I have translated freely): *Fili, si sapiens fuerit cor tuum, laetificabis cor meum, et commorabuntur labia mea ad sermones tuos, si tamen recti fuerint*. Horsiesios, *Liber* 20 (Bacht,

qualities are achieved and guaranteed, however, within a system: Horsiesios lays claim to a freedom that consists in choosing renunciation, casting off the *iugum... mundanae servitutis*, in exchange for having every need provided for by caring superiors; and the freedom is achieved, like other qualities, within a dispensation that reaches back to the prophets, passes through the "gospel discipline" and the lives of the apostles, includes "our fathers," and reaches forward to what might be built upon Jesus the cornerstone.[74]

So, even in its more abstract forms, Horsiesios's philosophy was rooted in ascetic practice. "The cross must be the fundamental factor in our life and teaching," he says, "and we have to suffer with Christ."[75] After a long disquisition on truth and light—involving a characteristic *catena* of quotations—he changes tone slightly: "Let us carry out with an eager heart each command of our father and of those who taught us, not only believing in Christ but also suffering for him."[76] There follow more quotations about spirit and light, and then another emphasis of his own (as if to say, this is what spirit and light are about): "Understanding all that, we shall deserve to hear [the words], 'When the just man falls, he shall suffer no harm: for the Lord shall support his hand' (Psalm 37 (V 36):24)."[77] Thus, without becoming infected by complacency, perfect things are given to the perfect.

Let me repeat: I have not attempted here to connect the Pachomian communities with the Nag Hammadi texts by looking in Pachomian material for supposedly gnostic ideas. Rather, prompted to some extent by Michael Williams, I have suggested that the catecheses of Theodore and Horsiesios, and Horsiesios's *Liber*, were, at the level of exegetical method and literary structure, comparable with treatises that we have been accustomed to associate with a "gnostic" tradition. What do I mean here by "method" and "structure"? I have concentrated deliberately on the handling of biblical history, and on the relation it establishes between Old Testament figures or events and fourth-century ascetic experience and discipline. I have also noted how the interpre-

---

Das Vermächtnis des Ursprungs, 104). Bacht points out that Jerome remained close to the LXX here, p. 105n80, even though the Vulgate (*exultabunt renes mei, cum locuta fuerint rectum labia tua*) is "korrekter": καὶ ἐδιατρίψει λόγοις τὰ σὰ χείλη πρὸς τὰ ἐμὰ χείλη, ἐὰν ὀρθὰ ὦσιν. The Coptic version is even more like the LXX.

74. Horsiesios, *Liber* 21 (Bacht, *Das Vermächtnis des Ursprungs*, 106/108/110).
75. Horsiesios, *Liber* 50 (Bacht, *Das Vermächtnis des Ursprungs*, 174/176).
76. Horsiesios, *Liber* 4–5 (Bacht, *Das Vermächtnis des Ursprungs*, 64/66).
77. Horsiesios, *Liber* 5 (Bacht, *Das Vermächtnis des Ursprungs*, 66).

tation of community order raises in its turn questions about the body and the material world, and about the community's relations with the surrounding (human, mortal) society. We are faced with a worldview, not just a spiritual vocabulary: for this handling of history, or relations with the dead, or the understanding of materiality do not exhaust the distinctiveness of the Pachomian sources. The goodness of creation, and therefore of moral effort and the ascetic body, is guaranteed by God's unswerving control of time, manifested in a genuine continuity between the Jewish past and Christian monastic culture. Exegesis, in the hands of Theodore and Horsiesios, is designed to uncover the challenging questions in the biblical text, and to show that the ascetic life, as bequeathed by Pachomius, provides the answers to those questions, and that the very posing and answering of the questions themselves is part of God's providential regard for the monastic community.

But what does even that type of association tell us about the Pachomian world? It would be facile to suppose that Theodore or Horsiesios had before them, or had previously consulted, documents like the Nag Hammadi codices (let alone those codices themselves). If one starts out from that supposition, one becomes instantly entangled in the dissimilarities: for Theodore and Horsiesios clearly did not have a gnostic view of the Bible or the world. However, one might still suggest that they were deliberately countering a gnostic theology uncomfortably close to home, or, alternatively, one might say that they wished to protect themselves against Church authorities, since the codices belonged to their own communities, or to groups within them. Both approaches have been adopted; but it seems to me better to start out from a different premise. Theodore and Horsiesios thought in terms of biblical history; of creation, redemption, and final perfection; of prophecy and fulfillment; of ascetic progress in a material and embodied world; of monastic destiny as an exemplar and instrument of God's historically unfolding plan for humanity. Such emphases gathered, like crystals on a wire, along certain thematic and literary axes, representing especially the sequence of the canonical scriptures and the place of moral development in the extended material and institutional experience of humanity. Several of the Nag Hammadi codices are constructed along those same axes. The conclusions drawn from a reading of the Bible and from observation of the world of experience were different; but the habit of thinking, of exercising curiosity, was closely connected. The identification of ancient figures of wisdom, leading through a sense of New Testament fulfillment, or at least corroboration, and through a series of exhortatory reflections, and culminating in a vision of the future—this describes very closely the flow, if not the content, of Theodore's and Horsiesios's teaching. Within some of the surviving Nag Hammadi codices, there is a similar curve of logic, carrying an ascetic from the warnings and promises of the prophets into the transformation of his own heart and body.

That suggests in turn that people who thought like Theodore and Horsiesios would have found the Nag Hammadi codices useful, once the originally "gnostic" material had been rearranged—"recycled"—according to new patterns. We do not have to believe that Theodore and Horsiesios themselves knew of the codices we now possess (although that remains possible); rather, their comparable habits of exegesis and catechesis make it entirely likely that the Nag Hammadi documents could have taken their surviving form within Christian ascetic society. That could have been the case, *not* because Christian ascetics thought like gnostics, but because they could turn the material to their own use. And that in turn supports the view that Theodore and Horsiesios were neither attacking nor secretly aping contemporary gnostics: rather, gnostics were now so much part of the past that their relics could be taken up in new causes.

Two exciting possibilities are thus created. First, the successors of Pachomius were engaged in a debate with other Christian ascetics, who were drawing different conclusions from similar material. I have no doubt that the chief bones of contention were continuity with the Jewish past and the intrinsic goodness, the moral relevance, of the material world. That may be an argument for suggesting that the surviving codices were *not* products or possessions of the Pachomian communities, but of other ascetic communities living close by. We gain an arresting impression of a populous and varied ascetic milieu and of a readiness among Pachomians to engage in dialogue with other sectors of the contemporary Church. Second, we are able to see how monastic tradition, and more broadly an historical view of material creation, could be used to authenticate what was in practice a sense of novelty, of being possessors of the future. Egyptian monks were studying their Bible in order to reinforce their sense of what other opinions were now passé: they themselves were the masters now of a biblical culture hitherto misused. As is so often the case, the past was evoked in order to define a novelty that might otherwise have remained obscure and ineffective.

James E. Goehring

KEEPING THE MONASTERY CLEAN

A Cleansing Episode from an Excerpt on Abraham of Farshut and Shenoute's Discourse on Purity

An excerpt on the sixth-century Pachomian archimandrite Abraham of Farshut[1] preserved in a fragmentary manuscript from the White Monastery in Upper Egypt records the cleansing of a meeting place in the Pachomian community's central monastery of Pbow following the departure of representatives of the emperor Justinian I.[2] The account represents part of a longer polemic against the emperor for his support of the monastic elements within Egypt that embraced the Chalcedonian ideology. According to the Coptic orthodox story, the presence of the emperor's men had polluted the meeting place. Upon their departure, Abraham instructed his monks to wash the room with water so as to remove the pollution. The brief account of the event, as reported to the emperor, reads in translation as follows:

---

1. For an account of Abraham of Farshut's life, see René-Georges Coquin, "Abraham of Farshut," in *The Coptic Encyclopedia*, ed. Aziz S. Atiya (New York: Macmillan, 1991), 1:11–12, or Paul van Cauwenbergh, *Étude sur les moines d'Égypte depuis le Concile de Chalcédoine (451) jusqu'à l'invasion arabe (640)* (Paris: P. Geuthner, 1914; reprint, Milan: Cisalpino Goliardica, 1973), 154–57.

2. The codex in question, following the sigla developed by Tito Orlandi, is White Monastery codex GB. It contains two texts on Upper Egyptian ascetic figures: a panegyric on Manasseh, and a second text on Moses of Abydos. The excerpt on Abraham of Farshut occupied pages 15–35 of the panegyric on Manasseh. For Orlandi's work, see "Un projet milanais concernant les manuscrits coptes du Monastère Blanc," *Muséon* 85 (1972): 403–13; for up-to-date information of the various White Monastery codices, see http://rmcisadu.let.uniroma1.it/~cmcl/. A brief summary of the manuscript GB's contents can be found in Antonella Campagnano, "Monaci egiziani fra V e VI secolo," *VetChr* 15 (1978): 230–32; see also

And after they [the representatives of the emperor] left, Apa Abraham himself came to the monastery. He went into the meeting place, and everywhere where your men stood and where they sat, he had all the brothers bring water and wash the entire meeting place as though it were polluted by you our lord, the emperor, and all who are under the authority of the Roman Empire.[3]

Unfortunately, the fragmentary nature of the manuscript does not permit a clear understanding of the precise events that led to the cleansing.[4] The first surviving leaf of the excerpt (Coptic pages 15/16) introduces Abraham, reports his appointment as archimandrite of Pbow, and refers to the rise of the "profane emperor Justinian." It goes on to note that four individuals, apparently monks from the Pachomian federation, brought accusations against Abraham.[5] The leaf ends as one of the accusers, a certain Pancharis, prepares to go to the emperor, while Abraham departs to visit Apa Moses, the archimandrite of a neighboring community of monks.

The following three leaves are lost. They may have included an account of the actual events that led Abraham, on his return, to order the cleansing of the meeting room. The next surviving leaf (23/24) picks the story up some time later, when one of the accusers, perhaps Pancharis, is reporting the events to the emperor in Constantinople.[6] The page begins *in medias res* with the accuser's account of Abraham's return to the monastery and the cleansing of the meeting room quoted above. He cites it as evidence of Abraham's opposition to the emperor's religious ideology and calls on the emperor to make an example of Abraham "so that everyone knows what it means to oppose the emperor." He proposes that the leadership of the monastery be handed over to him and his colleagues, who will carry out the emperor's will. "So now," he says,

---

Antonella Campagnano, ed., *Preliminary Editions of Coptic Codices: Monb. GB: Life of Manasses—Encomium of Moses—Encomium of Abraham*, CMCL (Rome: Centro Italiano Microfisches, 1985).

3. From University of Michigan Library, Coptic Ms. 158, 46, column 1, lines 3–27; all translations from the excerpt are my own.

4. Only nine of the original twenty-one pages of the excerpt survive ([15]/[16], [23]/24, [25]/[26], 29/30 and 35). I am currently working on a critical edition of the White Monastery texts, including the excerpt, on Abraham of Farshut.

5. James E. Goehring, "Remembering Abraham of Farshut: History, Hagiography, and the Fate of the Pachomian Tradition," *JECS* 14 (2006): 1–26.

6. The page begins with the end of a sentence that reads, "him until they left and went to them." The antecedents of the pronouns are not clear, though the "they" probably refers to the emperor's representatives.

send for him [Abraham], and bring him here and punish him as a criminal, so that everyone knows what it means to oppose the emperor. Since we will worship with our lord, the emperor, you will give us command of Pbow, and we will carry out every order of our lord the emperor through a command of regal authority.

The emperor follows through on the request. The following surviving pages recount Abraham's summons to Constantinople and preserve portions of the account of his appearance before the emperor. During the audience, the emperor asserts, "Some men here who belong to the Koinonia of Pachomius are faithful men of trust and love the emperor. I will give them the office of archimandrite of Apa Pachomius and allow no one to oppose them." The last two surviving leaves (Coptic pages 29/30 and 35/36) recount the empress's efforts on behalf of Abraham to ensure his return to Egypt and include a letter from Abraham to the monks of the monastery informing them of his banishment by the emperor and calling on the monks to save their souls. The excerpt ends with a reference to Pancharis's entry into the monastery, presumably with the emperor's support as the new Chalcedonian archimandrite.

The content of the excerpt on Abraham of Farshut locates it clearly within the anti-Chalcedonian polemic that defines much of the Coptic literature of the period.[7] The author structures the account so as to draw a sharp distinction between the proponents of Coptic orthodoxy and those of the Chalcedonian heresy. The orthodox archimandrite Apa Abraham is set over against the heretical emperor Justinian I, with a cast of lesser characters aligned with each. Subplots reveal that neither heresy nor orthodoxy is confined within the community controlled by either central figure. Ascetics from Abraham's monastery plot with the emperor against the archimandrite, and the empress herself secretly abets Abraham's escape and return to Egypt. The unfolding of the plot underscores the dangerous nature of the heresy, which destroyed the Coptic orthodox Pachomian community by infiltrating into its very midst, infecting various of its members whose charges against the archimandrite led to his eventual downfall.

In this context, the cleansing episode functions rhetorically to heighten the sense of danger by making the heresy in question more palpable.[8] Just as

---

7. David W. Johnson, "Anti-Chalcedonian Polemics in Coptic Texts, 451–641," in *The Roots of Egyptian Christianity*, ed. Birger A. Pearson and James E. Goehring, SAC (Philadelphia: Fortress Press, 1986), 216–34.

8. Robert Parker, *Miasma: Pollution and Purification in Early Greek Religion* (Oxford: Claren-

the water used in baptism implies the reality of the polluting nature of sin by suggesting that it can be washed away, so the story of the washing of the meeting room imparts a more visible reality to the heresy of Chalcedon by suggesting that its polluting nature, which stains the very room in which the heretics met, can likewise be washed away after they have left. The story frames the entire account in terms of the dualistic rhetorical categories of purity and pollution, orthodoxy and heresy. It works to enact and reinforce the discriminations by which the religious and cultural environment of Coptic orthodoxy exists.[9] I am intrigued here both by the rhetorical power of the cleansing imagery in general, and more specifically by this particular author's use of it in his anti-Chalcedonian polemic. While the power of the image depends ultimately on the deeply rooted nature of the pollution-purification dichotomy in human social, cultural, and religious formation and discourse,[10] it generates its immediate effectiveness within the text by striking a recognizable chord with the particular ascetic tradition of its intended Upper Egyptian audience. The chord in question is the emphasis on purity, which, I will suggest, links the text intertextually with the ascetic discourse of Shenoute of Atripe.

The author of the cleansing episode presents it as part of a report on the latter days of the Coptic orthodox Pachomian movement. The composition of the story, however, occurred at some unknown time and place after the loss of the Pachomian community to the Chalcedonian party, a fact that raises questions both as to the degree of its Pachomian origin and the extent of its later elaboration. The excerpt on Abraham is in fact embedded in a much longer panegyric on the monk Manasseh, a relative of Abraham's, who had likewise joined the Pachomian monastery before departing to found his own community near Farshut.[11] We know also from other sources that Abraham too, after his expulsion from Pbow, eventually established a monastic community in the vicinity of his native Farshut. As both Farshut monasteries were offshoots of the Coptic orthodox Pachomian movement and arose during the period of its

---

don Press, 1983), observes that "purification is one way in which the metaphysical can be made palpable" (19).

9. My language borrows here from Mary Douglas's description of the ritual practices of the Lele people of Central Africa. Mary Douglas, *Purity and Danger: An Analysis of Concepts of Pollution and Taboo* (New York: Praeger, 1966), 170.

10. Ibid.

11. For Manasseh, see René-Georges Coquin, "Manasseh," in Atiya, *Coptic Encyclopedia*, 5:1518; van Cauwenbergh, *Étude sur les moines d'Égypte*, 155–58.

demise,[12] it seems natural to assume that stories about Abraham, the Pachomian movement's last orthodox archimandrite and founder of one of the Farshut communities, would be told and eventually written down within the Farshut monasteries. If such is the case, the stories present the latter days of the Coptic orthodox Pachomian movement as remembered and shaped within the Farshut communities at the time of their composition.

While the origin of the cleansing episode within the Farshut communities makes perfect sense, it is important to consider the possibility that Shenoute's White Monastery, which preserved the story, also played a role in its literary history. The account of Abraham of Farshut found in the Alexandrian Synaxarion reports that following his loss of the Pachomian monastery of Pbow, he proceeded first to the monastery of Shenoute, where he lived and made copies of the rules, before departing to found his own monastery near Farshut.[13] A panegyric on Abraham of Farshut contained in a second White Monastery manuscript further reveals the close connection that had emerged between the Pachomian and Shenoutean systems by the time of its composition.[14] At one point, it appears to conflate the rules of the two communities, advising the monks not to abandon "the laws of the Lord that our fathers gave to us, namely Apa Pachomius and Apa Shenoute."[15] Elsewhere it reports a vision of Apa Abraham in which he "looked and saw our holy fathers of the Koinonia, Apa Pachom and Apa Petronius and Apa Shenoute of the monastery of Atripe," and later aligns Abraham himself with "our ancient fathers and forefathers, that is, Apa Pachom and Apa Shenoute and Apa Petronius and Apa

---

12. James E. Goehring, "Chalcedonian Power Politics and the Demise of Pachomian Monasticism," OP 15 (Claremont, Calif.: Institute for Antiquity and Chriatianity, 1989).

13. The feast day is 24 Tubah, that is, 19 January in the Julian calendar. René Basset, *Le synaxaire arabe jacobite (rédaction copte)*, PO 11, 5 (Paris: Firmin-Didot, 1916; reprint, Tounhout: Brepols, 1973), 684–88; Jacques Forget, *Synaxarium Alexandrinum*, CSCO 48, Scriptores arabici, ser. 3, vol. 18 (Beryti: E Typographeo catholico, 1906), 411–13 (text); CSCO 78, Scriptores arabici, ser. 3, 1 (Rome: Karolus de Luigi, 1921), 401–5 (translation). A passage from a panegyric on Abraham of Farshut preserved in White Monastery codex GC (Vienna, Nationalbibliothek, K 9550ʳ) appears to refer to Abraham's departure from the White Monastery for Farshut.

14. White Monastery codex GC.

15. White Monastery Codex GC 53.i.21–ii.2 (Vienna, Nationalbibliothek, K 9527ʳ). Compare Horsiesios's statement in *Liber Horsiesii* 46. "Let us not abandon the law of God, which our father received from Him and handed down to us," which naturally limits the rule to Pachomius. Translation from Armand Veilleux, *Instructions, Letters, and Other Writings of Saint Pachomius and His Disciples*, vol. 3 of *Pachomian Koinonia* (Kalamazoo: Cistercian Publications, 1982), 204.

Horsiesios."[16] The evidence suggests that by the time of the composition of the accounts of Abraham of Farshut, the characteristics that distinguished the early Pachomian and Shenoutean ascetic ideologies had overlapped to some degree. It is only natural that such an overlap would affect the literary memory of the earlier periods.

This fact is further supported by the likelihood that with the demise of the Coptic orthodox Pachomian community in the sixth century, the White Monastery became the primary repository for, and perhaps to some degree the source of, the various accounts of the Pachomian saints. A wall inscription from the White Monastery, apparently a list of saints' lives possessed by the community, mentions twenty copies of the Life of Pachomius and a Life of Pachomius with Horsiesios and Theodore.[17] That the large majority of the surviving Sahidic lives and works of Pachomius and his successors derive from White Monastery manuscripts confirms the evidence of the inscription.[18] While all of the original copies may have come from the Pachomian communities, the extent of the White Monastery's literary holdings should give one pause. Shenoute's own extensive literary production and his followers' interest

---

16. White Monastery Codex GC 49.1.18–27 (Cairo, Institut français d'archéologie orientale, Coptic ms. 8ʳ) and [84].ii.14–24 (Paris, Bibliothéque Nationale, Copte 129[13] fol. 15ᵛ).

17. Walter Ewing Crum, "Inscription's from Shenoute's Monastery," *JThS* 5 (1904): 566; Tito Orlandi, "The Library of the Monastery of Saint Shenute at Atripe," in *Perspectives on Panopolis: An Egyptian Town from Alexander the Great to the Arab Conquest. Acts from an International Symposium Held in Leiden on 16, 17 and 18 December 1998 (P.L. Bat. 31)*, ed. A. Egberts, Brian Paul Muhs, and Joep van der Vliet (Leiden: Brill, 2002), 213–15. The list includes also a Life of Theodore, which Crum associates with Theodore Startelates or Anatoleus (note 17). If Veilleux's thesis positing an originally independent life of the Pachomian abbot Theodore were correct, then the Theodore in the White Monastery inscription could be the Pachomian Theodore. Armand Veilleux, "Le problème des vies de saint pachôme," *RAM* 42 (1966): 287–305; Armand Veilleux, *La liturgie dans le cénobitisme pachômien au quatrième siècle*, SA 57 (Rome: Herder, 1968), 61–68. In response to criticism of the theory, Veilleux draws back from it some in the introduction to his English edition of the lives (*The Life of Saint Pachomius and His Disciples*, vol. 1 of *Pachomian Koinonia*, 6–8).

18. I am not aware of a study that addresses this fact directly for the Pachomian texts. Lefort lists the manuscripts in his various editions of the works but does not note their origin. See L. Th. Lefort, ed., *S. Pachomii vitae sahidice scriptae*, CSCO 99–100, Scriptores coptici 9–10 (Paris: E Typographeo Reipublicae, 1933), iii–xi; L. Th. Lefort, *Les vies coptes de saint Pachôme et de ses premiers successeurs* (Louvain: Institut Orientaliste, 1943), lxii–xx; L. Th. Lefort, ed. and trans., *Œuvres de s. Pachôme et de ses disciples*, CSCO 159 (Louvain: L. Durbecq, 1956), vi–xxx. Comparison of the manuscripts with those listed in Hyvernat's important article reconstructing the dispersion of the White Monastery's library indicates that most came from that collection. Henri Hyvernat, "Introduction," in E. Porcher, "Analyse de manuscrits coptes 131[1–8] de la Bibliothèque Nationale, avec indication des texts bibliques," *RdE* 1 (1933): 105–16.

in editing and preserving his works indicate the existence of an active scribal culture within the community.[19] The extensive library holdings, only now being fully appreciated, confirm its continuing activity into the twelfth century.[20] Given the evidence, there is every reason to believe that such a culture not only gathered and copied texts but also edited and composed them.[21] The possible influence of the White Monastery's scribal culture on accounts of earlier ascetics must therefore be considered. So, for example, while one cannot know where the original copies of the numerous and varied surviving versions of the Life of Pachomius were produced, given the White Monastery's extensive holdings in this area, one should at least consider the possibility that one or more were produced within the White Monastery itself.[22] The same consideration must be given to the three accounts of Abraham that survive in two White Monastery manuscripts.[23]

The three White Monastery texts, in fact, all of which survive as single witnesses, preserve the most complete accounts of Abraham's life outside of the brief version contained in the synaxarion. This fact alone underscores the community's interest in the figure of Abraham of Farshut. While the composition or editing of the texts within the White Monastery remains an intriguing possibility, there is in the end no certain evidence within the manuscripts to support or deny it. Whether or not they were originally composed in the White Monastery, however, I would contend that by the time of their composition in Upper Egypt, the conflation of the Pachomian and Shenoutean systems necessarily affected their composition. An author who lived in an ascet-

---

19. Stephen L. Emmel, *Shenoute's Literary Corpus*, CSCO 599–600 (Louvain: Peeters, 2004).

20. The surviving dated manuscripts come from the tenth–twelfth centuries. Emmel, *Shenoute's Literary Corpus*, CSCO 599:13; Orlandi, "Library of the Monastery of Saint Shenute," 220.

21. Orlandi ("Library of the Monastery of Saint Shenute," 211–31) offers a good overview of what is known of the library. Orlandi argues that the evidence presupposes a "very cultivated environment" within the monastery that produced "real" Coptic literature as well as translating Greek texts. He notes, however, that witnesses to this cultural activity within the monastery die out after the seventh century (224). He also notes that surviving colophons indicate that codices were both produced in the White Monastery and copied elsewhere and donated to the community. Colophons do not survive, however, for either of the two codices (GB and GC) containing texts on Abraham of Farshut.

22. Orlandi (ibid., 220) notes that "it is possible that scribes, when producing new codices, also reworked some of the texts, creating new texts from pieces of existing ones." It is also possible that they were all originally gathered from the Pachomian communities, where they had been composed, at some point following the loss of their central monastery of Pbow to the Chalcedonian party in the sixth century.

23. These include the excerpt preserved as part of a panegyric on Manasseh contained in Codex GB and the two texts preserved in Codex GC: a panegyric on Abraham of Farshut and a second fragmentary text on Abraham of Farshut. I am currently working on a critical edition of all three.

ic world where Pachomian and Shenoutean history and ideology had joined and grown together to some degree could easily be expected to include elements originally representative of one of the two traditions in a description of the other. The simple inclusion of Shenoute with Pachomius, Petronius, and Horsiesios as the author's ascetic forefathers offers an obvious example of this process.[24] More subtly, I would argue, the cleansing episode contained within the excerpt on Abraham of Farshut represents the influence of the Shenoute's ideology of purity on the literary memory of a Pachomian archimandrite.[25]

Renewed interest in Shenoute, his writings, and his ascetic discourse have begun to shed increasing light on his influential contribution to Upper Egyptian ascetic culture.[26] Recent studies have made clear that his form of coenobitic monasticism can no longer be dismissed as a simple derivative of the earlier Pachomian system. Neither can the rigorous nature of his organization, nor the harshness of his penal system, be written off as products of a ruthless personality. While less appealing to our modern sensitivities than the kinder and gentler monasticism found in the anachronistic Pachomian sources, Shenoute's practices, as a recent Duke University dissertation by Caroline Schroeder has shown, embody a distinctive ascetic ideology centered on the biblical notion of purity.[27] The identification and isolation of this discourse allows for the recognition of its influence in the later tradition.

24. It is possible that this conflation occurred prior to the loss of the Pachomian central monastery of Pbow in the sixth century. It seems more likely, however, that it occurred as a result of the loss. Certainly close relationships existed between the two communities at an earlier stage, but with the loss of the Pachomian Koinonia's central monastery, the White Monastery became the center of Upper Egyptian Coptic orthodox monasticism and the repository of its texts. In the process, the earlier Pachomian history fell into place as part of its history. Shenoute took his place alongside the Pachomian abbots as one of the founding fathers of Upper Egyptian monasticism. Goehring, "Remembering Abraham of Farshut," 1–26.

25. It remains, of course, unclear as to when the ideology of purity affected the Pachomian tradition. It may well have already begun to influence the Pachomian communities prior to Abraham's forced departure from Pbow.

26. Emmel's (*Shenoute's Literary Corpus*) success in reconstructing the Canons and Discourses of Shenoute from the disordered remnants of his writings has given new impetus to the research. The bibliography continues to expand. See especially the longer studies by Rebecca Krawiec, *Shenoute and the Women of the White Monastery: Egyptian Monasticism in Late Antiquity* (Oxford: Oxford University Press, 2002), and Caroline T. Schroeder, "Disciplining the Monastic Body: Asceticism, Ideology, and Gender in the Egyptian Monastery of Shenoute of Atripe" (Ph.D. diss., Duke University, 2002). It is important to remember that Derwas Chitty, in his well-known history of early Christian asceticism, ignored Shenoute. Derwas J. Chitty, *The Desert a City: An Introduction to the Study of Egyptian and Palestinian Monasticism under the Christian Empire* (Oxford: Basil Blackwell, 1966).

27. Schroeder, "Disciplining the Monastic Body." The following discussion of Shenoute's ideology draws heavily from Schroeder's dissertation. I have benefited as well from her responses to my e-mailed

Shenoute's ascetic discourse constructed the monastic community as an integrated body of individuals, the spiritual health and integrity of which depended on the spiritual health of each and every member.[28] Purity of the body, both the individual ascetic body and the corporate monastic body, shaped the understanding of community and informed the ethos of Shenoute's monastic rules.[29] Sin was the polluting agent, ascetic discipline the means of combat. Loss of purity by an individual member of the community affected not only the individual, but through him or her the purity of the community as a whole, threatening in turn the salvation of its other members.[30] The stakes were indeed high. In Schroeder's words,

> Shenoute's ascetic discourse thus foregrounds purity of the body, and he categorizes as defiling not only traditionally polluting activities (such as sex) but disobedience and transgressions more generally. Sin pollutes the body of any monk who violates his or her ascetic vow or the monastic rule, and this sin will spread throughout the monastery, corrupting and defiling the corporate monastic body and thus threatening the salvation of each and every member of the community. Shenoute thus paints a portrait of two monastic bodies whose fates are irrevocably tied together either by the impurities of sin or by the virtues of discipline: the individual monastic body (namely, the monk), and the corporate monastic body. The purity of the corporate monastic body depends upon the purity of every individual monastic body.[31]

The discourse of purity evident in Shenoute's works is decidedly less prevalent in the Pachomian sources.[32] The rules in particular reveal the nature of the distinction. While both communities shared many of the same regulations, different discourses shaped the presentation of individual and communal goals.[33] The Pachomian rules sought to create a peaceful and harmonious community where the individual monk could thrive in the pursuit of his or her spiritual goals. Obedience, individual and communal order, work, efficiency, and productivity shaped the discourse.[34] While the language of purity oc-

---

questions. See also her recent "'A Suitable Abode for Christ': The Church Building as Symbol of Ascetic Renunciation in Early Monasticism," *CH* 73 (2004): 472–521.
  28. Schroeder, "Disciplining the Monastic Body," 4–8.
  29. Ibid., 86–87; cf. Krawiec, *Shenoute and the Women of the White Monastery*, 21.
  30. Schroeder, "Disciplining the Monastic Body," 43.
  31. Ibid., 4–5.   32. Ibid., 7–8.
  33. Ibid., chap. 3, esp. 87, 109–29.
  34. Ibid., 110–13, where she cites Philip Rousseau, *Pachomius: The Making of a Community in Fourth-Century Egypt* (Berkeley and Los Angeles: University of California Press, 1985), 88–104, in support.

curs in the Pachomian texts, it does so rarely, and when it does, it references the actions of an individual monk. The discourse does not read the individual monk's impurity, as Shenoute so often does, in relationship to the purity of the community as a whole.

Shenoute's discourse, on the other hand, situates the rules in the context of a one-body ideology where the sin of the individual body threatens the corporate body. Once allowed entrance into the corporate body, pollution would course through it like a disease. Ascetic discipline served to preserve the purity of the corporate body by preserving the purity of the individual body.[35] Given this discourse, it is not surprising that expulsion became a common form of punishment in Shenoute's monastery.[36] Expulsion removed the diseased member before his or her pollution could spread within the corporate body.

The use of expulsion again underscores the distinction between Shenoute and the early Pachomians. The Pachomian sources indicate that expulsion was employed only rarely. They emphasize, rather, Pachomius's patience in working with sinful monks to ensure their return to spiritual health. In the Pachomian discourse, the sin of the individual monk was not viewed as a dire threat to the purity of the community, but rather as a cause for concern. "If we do good to a bad man," Pachomius asserts in the Bohairic *Life*, "he comes thereby to have a perception of the good. This is God's love, to take pains for each other."[37] In commenting on this text, Philip Rousseau notes that "simply to reject the sinner, therefore, was to repudiate that responsibility: only within the *Koinonia* could the requisite healing, enlightenment, and growth take place."[38] Hope for the sinner's salvation through the efforts of the community underlies the Pachomian discourse. Shenoute's writings, on the other hand, express more often anxiety over the threat posed to the community by the impurity of an individual monk. "The potent anxiety about pollution," Schroeder writes,

is one of the dominant characteristics of the habitas particular to Shenoute's community and writings. Moreover, it marks Deir Anba Shenouda under his tenure as a space filled with a very different ascetic ethos than that which we know about in even its closest neighbors, the Pachomian communities. Purity is the driving engine behind the ritualization process em-

---

35. Ibid., 137–54.
36. Ibid., 129–37.
37. Bohairic Life of Pachomius 42. Translation from Veilleux, *Life of Saint Pachomius*, 66.
38. Rousseau, *Pachomius*, 97, cited by Schroeder, "Disciplining the Monastic Body," 128.

bodied in the rules. Physical and spiritual pollution deny a monk salvation, and then spread like a disease throughout the community, threatening the salvation of all the monks, male or female.[39]

In an additional fascinating chapter, Schroeder maps the influence of Shenoute's discourse of purity on his presentation of the monastery's church.[40] The building becomes a third body, the purity of which depends on the purity of the individual monks within it.[41] Just as the purity of the individual monastic body affects the purity and fate of the corporate monastic body, so the purity of the individual monks within the Church affects the purity and fate of the church. In a sermon celebrating the construction of the new church, for example, Shenoute employs Ezekiel's parable of the wall whitewashed by false prophets and torn down by God to remind his audience of the fate that awaits the church and its monastic congregation should sin or impurity be allowed inside.[42] If it gains entrance, it will spread like a disease through neighboring buildings and communities, eventually corrupting and destroying them. It is important to recognize, however, that in Shenoute's discourse the impurity does not reside in the essential nature of the building. The purity or impurity of the building depends rather on the purity or impurity of those within it.[43] If the impure individuals within it are removed, the building is no longer impure.

It is the distinctive nature of Shenoute's purity discourse over against the discourse evidenced in the early Pachomian sources that suggests that its influence lay behind the inclusion of the cleansing episode in the excerpt on Abraham of Farshut. The borrowing is, of course, not direct. The relationship between the discourse and the text represents a form of intertextuality, understood in the broader sense of textually detectable influences across cultural or discourse boundaries.[44] The purity discourse in the cleansing episode appears to echo the discourse evident in Shenoute's writings. As with any echo,

39. Schroeder, "Disciplining the Monastic Body," 153.
40. Ibid., chap. 4, 155–241; Schroeder, "'Suitable Abode.'"
41. Schroeder, "Disciplining the Monastic Body," 157; Schroeder, "'Suitable Abode,'" 494–96.
42. Ezekiel 13:10–11; Schroeder, "Disciplining the Monastic Body," 195; Schroeder, "'Suitable Abode,'" 506.
43. Schroeder, "Disciplining the Monastic Body," 185; Schroeder, "'Suitable Abode,'" 497.
44. The relationship is not one between specific texts, but rather between the discourses that lie behind the texts. See Richard Valantasis, "The Nuptial Chamber Revisited: The *Acts of Thomas* and Cultural Intertextuality," *Semeia* 80 (1997): 261–76.

what one "hears" is affected both by the distance of the echo from its original source and the intervening space through which it has passed. By listening carefully, one can hear various patterns, recognizing within them similarities with and differences from the original. Beyond the obvious shared interest in purity, for example, the cleansing episode, by focusing on the purity of the meeting room, seems to echo Shenoute's mapping of the purity discourse onto the monastery's church. The purity of the meeting room, like the purity of the church, becomes a symbol for the purity of the community. Polluted by the presence of corrupt individuals, in this case the representatives of the emperor, it requires cleansing so as to rid the community of the threat inherent in the pollution. If the Coptic term ⲥⲱⲟⲩϩ, translated above as meeting place or room, should be understood more specifically as a "meeting-place for service" or church (ⲉⲕⲕⲗⲏⲥⲓⲁ),[45] then the meeting room in question could well be the great basilica at Pbow, in which case the echo would seem to be even more pronounced.

At the same time, unique aspects of the author's application of the purity theme to the meeting room are readily apparent. Shenoute's use, for example, focuses on pollution that arises from within the community, while the author of the cleansing episode applies it to an external threat. It is not errant monks from within the monastery who form the basis of the threat in the cleansing episode, but rather the emperor's representatives, who come into the monastery from without.[46] In the story they symbolize not only the power of the emperor but, more important, the non-Egyptian heresy of Chalcedon that he supports. It is the stain of heresy that must be washed away.

Shenoute's use of the purity and pollution imagery remains more metaphorical than that of the author of the cleansing episode. While both assert that the presence of polluted individuals within the building pollute the building, Shenoute does not claim that the pollution transfers to the material structure of the building, where it remains after the polluted individuals have been expelled, threatening to pollute others. In Shenoute's discourse, the church functions simply as a potent symbol for the monastic congregation as

---

45. Walter Ewing Crum, *A Coptic Dictionary* (Oxford: Clarendon Press, 1939), 373b.

46. One should note that there are Chalcedonian elements within the monastery as well, namely, those monks who accuse Abraham to the emperor. But in the cleansing episode, the polluting figures come from outside the community.

a whole. It is polluted by virtue of the presence of polluted individuals within it. For the author of the cleansing episode, on the other hand, the pollution of the meeting room has to do with the actual spread of the pollution from the polluted individuals to the material structure of the building, where it presumably continues to threaten those who enter the building even after the polluted individuals have left.

The author appears here to draw more literally on the biblical notion that physical contact with an unclean person, place, or thing renders a person, place, or thing unclean.[47] In the Levitical tradition, leprosy and bodily discharges both appear as polluting agents. Contact with either not only renders a person, place, or thing unclean but establishes the person, place, or thing in turn as a new source in a chain of pollution. Cleansing of the person, place, or thing is required in order to break the chain. Leprosy, for example, understood as uncleanness, infected not only the individual, rendering him unclean, but potentially through him his garments and house, which then had to be cleansed or destroyed lest the disease spread further through the community (Lev. 13:47–59; 14:33–48). While the effectiveness of this practice in the case of a communicable disease like leprosy is clear, the biblical tradition extends the same rules to cover a wide range of bodily discharges. According to Leviticus 15:4–7, "Every bed on which he who has the discharge lies shall be unclean; and everything on which he sits shall be unclean. And anyone who touches his bed shall wash his clothes and bathe himself in water, and be unclean until the evening. And anyone who sits on anything on which the one who has the discharge has sat shall wash his clothes and bathe himself in water, and be unclean until the evening."[48] In the same way, the author of the cleansing episode asserts that the places where the emperor's men stood and sat are polluted and must be washed clean with water.[49]

---

47. The basic notion is, of course, widespread in the ancient Mediterranean world, and influence from outside the biblical realm cannot be discounted. The extension of the contagious nature of the pollution beyond its initial source, however, appears most pronounced in the biblical text. Parker (*Miasma*, 53–54) notes little evidence for such a view in the Greek sources. The reliance of Egyptian monasticism in general on the bible supports it as the primary source (see, for example, Douglas Burton-Christie, *The Word in the Desert: Scripture and the Quest for Holiness in Early Christian Monasticism* [Oxford: Oxford University Press, 1993]), albeit filtered through the early Christian tradition.

48. Revised Standard Version.

49. The closest example of which I am aware of the cleansing of a building polluted by ideological opponents is that of the Donatists' washing of the walls of the sanctuaries used by their opponents in Optatus, *Adversus Parmenianum Donastistam* 6.6; see *Optatus: Against the Donatists*, trans. Mark J.

Shenoute does, on occasion, draw on the same Levitical traditions to make a case for the cleansing of the monastic community.[50] He does not, however, apply the Levitical notion of the pollution's spread to and through inanimate objects literally to the sins and ascetic transgressions he is confronting. The contagious nature of the polluting agent in Leviticus serves simply as a metaphor for the threat that sin poses to the monastic congregation. In *This Great House,* for example, a work celebrating the construction of the monastery's church, he turns to the example of leprosy to support his case that impurity, like a contagious disease, must be removed lest it spread throughout the monastic congregation.[51] It is the contagious nature of leprosy in general that parallels the nature of sin, not the specific patterns through which it spreads. So too in a series of letters in Canon 8, Shenoute uses the image of a garment polluted by disease or destroyed by moths as a metaphor for the community.[52] In *So Listen,* his own garment, contaminated by illness, functions as the metaphor.[53] The monastery, polluted by transgressions, could, like the contaminat-

---

Edwards, TTH 27 (Liverpool: Liverpool University Press, 1997), 123. Maureen Tilley and Peter Brown both called my attention to this reference.

50. It is interesting to note here again the difference between Shenoute and the early Pachomians as evidenced in their sources. In the Pachomian sources, only a single brief reference to the Levitical sections dealing with this type of pollution occurs, and it is not used as part of an argument about purity of the community. Pachomius's third letter includes a passage in which he calls on the monks to "remember that, concerning the menstruating woman, a commandment was given to expel her because her 'ways are strewn with thorns.'" While the reference to the menstruating woman reflects Leviticus 15:19–30, its connection to Proverbs 15:19, "her ways are strewn with thorns," shifts it away from its original emphasis on purity to become part of an extended call for proper ascetic behavior. The menstruating woman is expelled because "her ways are strewn with thorns" (Prov. 15:19), not because she threatens to pollute the community by corrupting those who come into contact with her. Six additional ascetic proverbs, three of which derive from Proverbs ("Poverty humbles man"), Ecclesiastes ("The house groans under the idleness of the hands"), and Lamentations ("Do not 'collapse under blows from sticks'"), follow immediately on the above passage and reinforce the point. In the Pachomian world, the ascetic discourse made little use of the biblical discourse of pollution. Veilleux, *Instructions, Letters, and Other Writings,* 240–41 for the scripture citation index, 54 for the citation from Pachomius's letter. The translation given above is Veilleux's.

51. Canon 7, White Monastery Codex XU, 410–11. For a published version, see Émile Amélineau, *Oeuvres de Schenoudi: Texte copte et tranduction française,* 2 vols. (Paris: Ernest Leroux, 1907–14), 203. Cited in Schroeder, "Disciplining the Monastic Body," 2:26.

52. Rebecca Krawiec communicated with me concerning the texts in Canon 8 and supplied me with a copy of her article "Clothes Make the Monk: The Rhetoric of Clothing in Late Antique Monasticism," which was originally delivered at the "Living for Eternity: Monasticism in Egypt" symposium held at the University of Minnesota, 6–9 March 2003, and scheduled for publication in its proceedings.

53. Krawiec, "Clothes Make the Monk," 9–10; Dwight W. Young, "Additional Fragments of Shenute's *Eighth Canon,*" *APF* 44 (1998): 47–68.

ed garment, be improved through "washing." While the contamination of the garment corresponds literally to the description of the leper's garment in Leviticus, Shenoute shifts to metaphor when he applies the image of the garment to the monastery. The pollution of the individual monastic body affects the corporate monastic body as the disease affects the garment. Shenoute does not equate the garment with the physical structures of the monastery.

In a second letter, *Who But God Is the Witness,* he uses the example of a garment destroyed by moths to represent the destructive spread of sin and ascetic transgressions within the community.[54] He includes in the letter two extended passages from Leviticus, one from chapter 13 dealing with the treatment of a leper's garments and the second from chapter 14 dealing with the treatment of his house.[55] In both cases, contact with the leper has polluted the inanimate objects, the garment and the house, necessitating their cleansing or destruction. While the full letter in question remains to be edited, it appears again that Shenoute uses the texts metaphorically. Transgressions threaten to spread through the monastic congregation as leprosy, polluting bodily discharges, or destructive moths spread on a garment. They pollute it or devour it and eventually destroy it. The survival of the congregation, like the survival of the garment, depends on the effective treating of the cause of its pollution or destruction. The washing of the garment, which removes the pollution, corresponds to the cleansing of the congregation, which for Shenoute included the expulsion of the offending members.

While Shenoute accepts the Levitical notion that disease (leprosy) and bodily discharges can pollute an inanimate object (garment or house), he does not transfer the notion literally to the ascetic transgressions and sins that concern him. Sin does not spread from the sinner to his garment. It does not move through the community by infecting inanimate objects (garments, chairs, beds, etc.) that in turn infect others who come into contact with them. The biblical imagery of pollution serves Shenoute rather as a metaphor for the spiritual corruption effected in the person and his community through sin.

---

54. Krawiec, "Clothes Make the Monk," 12–13; Dwight W. Young, "Pages from a Copy of Shenute's *Eighth Canon,*" *Orientalia* 67 (1998): 64–84.

55. The Leviticus references were brought to my attention by Rebecca Krawiec and Andrew Crislip. The references appear as marginal notes, probably in Hyvernat's writing, on photographs of the pages housed at the Catholic University of America (e-mail from Janet Timbie, who noted also that Shenoute uses Lev. 19 in his *Righteous Art Thou*).

The author of the cleansing episode in the excerpt on Abraham of Farshut, by contrast, applied the biblical accounts literally to the pollution of heresy. The internal logic of the account assumes that the meeting room must be washed because the pollution of the emperor's representatives remained in the room after they had left, adhering like a disease to the places where they had stood and sat. Those locations now threaten, like the bed and chair of the person with a discharge in Leviticus, to pollute all who come into contact with them. They, like the bed and chair, must be cleansed to stem the spread of the pollution and return the community to its proper state of purity. The literal translation of the Levitical codes to the case of heresy within the monastery moves beyond their metaphorical use in Shenoute. While the shared use of the tradition locates the author literally within the trajectory of Shenoute's purity discourse, his unique use of the discourse offers evidence of a continuing creativity within the monastic tradition.

Given the evidence of Shenoute's role in the development of the purity discourse in Upper Egyptian asceticism, it seems likely that its influence lay behind the inclusion of the cleansing episode in a late Pachomian tradition. While it is impossible to know with assurance where and when the purity discourse affected the memory of Abraham of Farshut, it seems apparent that it did. Its appearance as an intertexual echo in a later hagiographic text points to the continuing influence of Shenoute and his community in the history of Egyptian monasticism and the production of its collective memory. At the same time, the unique aspects of the echo and its effective use within the excerpt illustrate the creative abilities of the later Egyptian monastic authors. The author of the cleansing episode does not simply borrow from Shenoute's discourse, but rather, the discourse has so influenced his tradition that it naturally becomes part of his own creative endeavor.[56] He moves beyond Shenoute in his emphasis on the cleansing of surfaces touched by polluted persons, thereby making even more palpable the dangers inherent in the heresy of Chalcedon. The story rhetorically increases the threat of heresy by equating it with a contagious disease caught not only through direct contact with a heretic or his

---

56. The specific content of the cleansing episode, for example, is not paralleled in Shenoute's writings to the best of my knowledge. It may well have derived from other sources (see note 50 above). My point is not that the influence was so direct, but rather that it occurred at a deeper level, creating an environment in which such borrowing would seem only natural.

writings but even by sitting or standing where he has stood or sat. Like the early AIDS rumors that one could contract the disease by touching an object previously touched by an infected person, the episode fosters fear of contagion and strengthens the desire for separation. It uses the notions of purity and impurity to define and confirm the boundaries of Coptic orthodoxy.

As Mary Douglas has shown, "rituals of purity and impurity create unity in experience. So far from being aberrations from the central project of religion, they are positive contributions to atonement. By their means, symbolic patterns are worked out and publicly displayed. Within these patterns disparate elements are related and disparate experience is given meaning."[57] Douglas contends that the particular rituals and rules governing purity and impurity participate broadly in the creation and maintenance of the very boundaries that define community. Together with the myths and stories that support them, they exert social pressure toward good citizenship by encouraging behaviors identified as pure while discouraging others characterized as polluting or impure. Through the repetitious discriminations practiced through rituals, rules, and stories, individual cultures continually confirm their own particular social and spiritual cosmos. As Douglas observes with respect to the Lele of Central Africa, "Endlessly they enact the discriminations by which their society and its cultural environment exist, and methodically they punish or attribute misfortune to breaches of avoidance rules." In their practices, they "visibly enact the central discriminations of their cosmos."[58]

In a literate society, the text functions likewise continually to enact the central discriminations of the community's cosmos. So the cleansing episode in the excerpt on Abraham of Farshut functions within the excerpt to enact visibly a central discrimination of the Coptic orthodox cosmos by distinguishing the proper and pure behavior of Coptic orthodoxy from the improper, contagious pollution of the Chalcedonian heresy. While the impact of the ideological conflict on Abraham's community is evident in the account of his clash with the emperor, it is the cleansing episode that most visibly discriminates between the orthodoxy and heresy of the two theologies by aligning the former with purity and the latter with pollution. To allow the Chalcedonian pollution into the community is to undo the discriminations through which

---

57. Douglas, *Purity and Danger*, 2–3.
58. Ibid., 170.

the orthodox Coptic community and its religious environment exist. In literary terms, the inclusion of the cleansing episode, which allows that Abraham purified the meeting room and hence the monastery for a time, creates a framework whereby the ultimate loss of Pbow to the Chalcedonian party corresponds to the spread of the pollution throughout the institution. Polluted to its core, the orthodox have no choice but to leave, and the Coptic orthodox monastic tradition has no choice but to quarantine the Pachomian institution, effectively removing it from its future history.[59] By remembering the loss of the Pachomian community in this way, the later community behind the text continually reaffirms the dangers of Chalcedon, reinforcing in the process the boundaries of its own orthodoxy.

59. Goehring, "Chalcedonian Power Politics."

David Frankfurter

ILLUMINATING THE CULT OF KOTHOS

The Panegyric on Macarius and Local Religion in Fifth-Century Egypt

The *Panegyric on Macarius of Tkow*, which David Johnson has bequeathed to generations of historians of late antiquity through his expert CSCO edition, is certainly as deceptive a document of early Christianity as it is rich in peculiar details. Consumed as it is with anti-Chalcedonian polemic and the promotion of an obscure Monophysite holy man, the *Panegyric*'s depiction of traditional Egyptian temple religion as something still abiding in the region of Tkow (chapter 5) would seem to be mere window dressing for the construction of Macarius's heroic sainthood.[1] "Not only did the man vehemently oppose Chalcedonian officials," the text seems to proclaim, "he even purified his

---

1. On anti-Chalcedonian polemic in the *Panegyric*, see David W. Johnson, "Anti-Chalcedonian Polemics in Coptic Texts, 451–641," in *The Roots of Egyptian Christianity*, ed. Birger A. Pearson and James E. Goehring (Philadelphia: Fortress Press, 1986), 216–34; and Stephen Emmel, "Immer erst das Kleingedruckte lesen: 'Die Pointe verstehen' in dem koptischen Panegyrikos auf Makarios von Tkōou," in *Ägypten—Münster: Kulturwissenschaftliche Studien zu Ägypten, dem Vorderen Orient und verwandten Gebieten*, ed. Anke Ilona Blöbaum, Jochem Kahl, and Simon D. Schweitzer (Wiesbaden: Harrassowitz, 2003), 91–104. For more on the construction of Macarius's sainthood, see David Frankfurter, "Urban Shrine and Rural Saint in Fifth-Century Alexandria," in *Pilgrimage in Graeco-Roman and Early Christian Antiquity: Seeing the Gods*, ed. Jas Elsner and Ian Rutherford (Oxford: Oxford University Press, 2006), 435–49.

region of heathens and their nefarious child-sacrifice cults!" That the story of his crusade on a temple of "Kothos" culminates in Macarius's successful invocation of fire from heaven only makes this story more dubious, since this detail simply expands the *Panegyric*'s larger claim that Macarius is a new Elijah.[2]

Is the *Panegyric*, then, worth anything more than an example of how antiheathen conflict could still make a good read in the seventh and eighth centuries? I have long taken the position that the story of Macarius's crusade on the temple of Kothos preserves much authentic reminiscence of how some Egyptian cults maintained themselves well past the general decline of temples in the third century *at the same time as* it cleaves to hagiographical caricatures and conventions of heroization. In the sections that follow, I will outline my position that, while the story is prima facie legend, it recalls many authentic aspects and dynamics of local cults in Egypt—indeed, that cults *like* that of Kothos managed to persevere much the way Pseudo-Dioscorus imagined this one.

Résumé of Macarius and the Cult of Kothos (*Panegyric* 5)

Chapter 5 of the *Panegyric* describes an Egyptian temple cult "on the west bank of the Nile" that perseveres in Macarius's time despite a growing population of Christians. Its god is named "Kothos" (or "Gothos" in Ms. Pierpont Morgan Coptic 609), and its local devotees keep domestic shrines to him as well as gather by his temple for specific occasions. The drama of the chapter, however, revolves around a rumor among the local Christians that the priests of Kothos steal Christian children, sacrifice them on the temple's inner altar, and extract their intestines to use as harp strings, from whose sounds they can find buried treasure. The Christians complain to Macarius, who forces himself inside the temple with several monks despite armed opposition by the local community of Kothos devotees. Just as the monks enter, however, they are jumped by a group of priests, who bind them for sacrifice to Kothos. Macarius prays to Christ for help, and just in the nick of time Besa—Shenoute's successor as abbot of the Atripe monastery—arrives and releases the monks with a

---

2. Cf. 1 Kings 18:37–38. On Macarius and other Egyptian Christian holy men as new Elijahs, see David Frankfurter, *Elijah in Upper Egypt: The Coptic Apocalypse of Elijah and Early Egyptian Christianity* (Minneapolis: Fortress Press, 1993), 65–74.

magical prayer. In the end, Macarius leads all the monks in invoking fire from heaven to burn the temple to the ground. Then they storm the village, burning sacred images (and Kothos's high priest), baptizing some heathens, and chasing off the resistant devotees of Kothos. Thus Christianity triumphs in the village.

The audience is meant to understand that these things took place (a) shortly after the death of Shenoute—hence, the later fifth century—and (b) somewhere in the region of Tkow (Qaw el-Kebir) and not too distant from Shenoute's monastery in Atripe (such that Besa could reach the bound Macarius); hence, the countryside above Panopolis. It was in this area, coincidentally, that Shenoute himself had tried to invade a town similarly aloof from Christianization, Plewit.[3]

"A village where they worship an idol called Kothos"

Coptic authors like Shenoute customarily caricatured the dwindling Egyptian deities by Greek names like Kronos or Pan, only occasionally allowing to their audiences that Egyptian names such as Min or Bes persevered in local nomenclature.[4] Thus it is dubious that the *Panegyric* should use an unidentifiable or made-up name to describe such a typical example of local temple cult. From what god, then, would *Kothos* derive? I am grateful to Robert Ritner of the Oriental Institute of the University of Chicago for proposing a connection between ⲕⲟⲑⲟⲥ—or, more significantly in the Pierpont Morgan manuscript, ⲅⲟⲑⲟⲥ—and *Agathos Daimon,* the deity of civic fortune associated most closely with the city of Alexandria but well known in Upper Egypt too as an *interpretatio graeca* of the Egyptian god *Shai.* This proposal, as we will see, makes sense historically and geographically.

Shai, as Jan Quaegebeur showed in his monograph on the subject, was

---

3. Besa, *Life of Shenoute,* 83–84, with Serge Sauneron, *Villes et légendes d'Égypte,* 2d ed. (Cairo: IFAO, 1983), 104–7.

4. See in general Jacques Van der Vliet, "Spätantikes Heidentum in Ägypten im Spiegel der koptischen Literatur," in *Begegnung von Heidentum und Christentum im spätantiken Ägypten,* ed. Dietrich Willers, RB 1 (Riggisberg: Abegg-Stiftung, 1993), 99–130, esp. 110–18. On Pan/Min, see Stephen L. Emmel, "Ithyphallic Gods and Undetected Ligatures: Pan is Not 'Ours,' He is Min," *GM* 141 (1994): 43–46. On Bes, see Walter Till, "Life of Moses of Abydos," in *Koptische Heiligen- und Martyrerlegenden,* ed. Walter Till (Rome: Pontifical Institute for Oriental Studies, 1936), 46–81; Émile Amélineau, *Monuments pour servir à l'histoire de l'Égypte chrétienne aux IVᵉ et Vᵉ siècles,* MMAF 4 (Paris: Ernest Leroux, 1888–95), fasc. 2, 679–706; and Mark Moussa, *Abba Moses of Abydos* (master's thesis, Catholic University of America, 1998).

principally associated in popular Egyptian religion with local protection and civic fortune and yet, by the time of the Greek and Demotic "magical" papyri, had become the object of priestly "pantheization"—association with the highest cosmic powers.[5] Much as Isis, Bes, and Mandulis had been variously abstracted into cosmic deities, so priests in the third century CE might invoke Shai as

> You from the four winds, god, ruler of all, who have breathed spirits into men for life, master of the good things in the world, . . . lord, whose hidden name is ineffable. The daimons, hearing it, are terrified. . . . Heaven is your head; ether, body; earth, feet; and the water around you, Ocean, Agathos Daimon. You are lord, the begetter and nourisher and increaser of all.[6]

And yet the god retained his local associations and value well into the fifth century, for Shenoute of Atripe, in his sermon "The Lord Thundered," lambastes his audience:

> Woe to any man or woman who gives thanks to demons, saying that "Today is the worship of ϣⲁⲓ, or ϣⲁⲓ of the village or ϣⲁⲓ of the home," while burning lamps for empty things and offering incense in the name of phantoms.[7]

Shenoute refers to a domestic cult here, not necessarily rooted in a particular temple; but this complaint offers clear evidence that devotion to *Shai/Agathos Daimon* continued in the region of Panopolis into the fifth century.[8] Nor does Shenoute's witness seem to be a fluke. Mummy labels from Achmim (I/II CE) show that Shai was often celebrated in theophoric names—e.g., Old Coptic ⲧϣⲉⲛϣⲁⲓⲥ, "daughter of Shai"—while a ἱερὸν' Ἀγαθοῦ Δαίμονος is attested in an inventory of buildings in III CE Panopolis. Shai, as Quaegebeur observes, had a particular popularity in the region of Panopolis.[9]

---

5. Jan Quaegebeur, *Le dieu égyptien Shaï dans la religion et l'onomastique*, OLA 2 (Louvain: Leuven University Press, 1975), 160–70. See *PDM* xiv.33, 49, 60, 565; *PGM* IV.1607; XIII.772.

6. *PGM* XII.238–44, trans. Morton Smith, in Hans Dieter Betz, ed., *The Greek Magical Papyri in Translation, Including the Demotic Spells* 1 (Chicago: University of Chicago Press, 1986), 162; cf. re-edited text in Robert W. Daniel, *Two Greek Magical Papyri in the National Museum of Antiquities in Leiden: A Photographic Edition of J384 and J395* (*PGM* XII and XIII), P. Col. 19 (Opladen: Westdeutscher Verlag, 1991), 14.

7. Shenoute, Discourses 4: The Lord Thundered (codex DU), p. 45, Émile Amélineau, ed., *Oeuvres de Schenoudi: Texte copte et tranduction française* (Paris: Leroux, 1907–14), 1:379. Cf. Stephen L. Emmel, *Shenoute's Literary Corpus*, CSCO 600 (Louvain: Peeters, 2004), 613–15, 925–26.

8. Cf. David Frankfurter, *Religion in Roman Egypt: Assimilation and Resistance* (Princeton: Princeton University Press, 1998), 63–64, 136–38.

9. Mummy labels: Georg Steindorff, "Zwei altkoptische Mumienetiketten," *ZÄS* 28 (1890): 49–53;

There are no other details to the *Panegyric*'s cult of Kothos that distinguish it specifically as a *Shai*-cult. The high priest's invocation of Kothos as "commander of the air, brother of Apollo" (5.11) could as easily be a caricature of heathen prayer as an authentic reflection of the pantheistic *Agathos Daimon*. Details of human sacrifice, as I will discuss below, derive from polemical and literary *topoi* of subhuman religion, while the broader outlines of the cult, its priesthood, and its devotional practices all reflect typical Egyptian temple religion. Probably the safest inference form the preservation of the name *Agathos Daimon* in the *Panegyric* and its correspondence to the well-attested *Shai*-cult would be that this god was remembered (by its Greek name) as genuinely popular in the region of Panopolis.

"An idol ... mounted in the niches [ⲉⲭⲚⲚⲉⲩⲱⲟⲩⲱⲧ] *of their houses"*

The *Panegyric* describes with some element of curiosity how Kothos devotees "bow down their heads and worship him [ϣⲁⲩⲟⲃⲃⲓⲟⲭⲱⲟⲩ ⲉⲡⲉⲥⲏⲧ Ⲛⲥⲉⲟⲩⲱϣⲧ ⲛⲁϥ]" whenever they enter their homes. Like Shenoute's reference to *Shai* celebrations and their domestic expressions, like lighting lamps, the *Panegyric*'s glimpse of devotion before domestic altars more likely reflects authentic local practice than hagiographical caricature, even if it is a reminiscence drawn from more general lore than the single cult. It parallels other hagiographical depictions of traditional shrines in domestic spaces. While the image inevitably functions as a prelude to Christian triumph—the Kothos images are ultimately burned in the village center—there is reason to believe memories of such shrines continued in relationship to dwellings or even to Christian domestic altars.[10]

The notion that a main temple image might in some way be preserved in miniature in a domestic wall niche is supported by evidence both archeological and comparative. Wall niches, both in central rooms and door areas, are

---

on dating, cf. Mark Smith, "Dating Anthropoid Mummy Cases from Akhmim: The Evidence of the Demotic Inscriptions," in *Portraits and Masks: Burial Customs in Roman Egypt*, ed. M. L. Bierbrier (London: British Museum, 1997), 66–71. Panopolite shrine: P. Gen. Inv. 108, A/II/5, Victor Martin, "Réléve topographique des immeubles d'une metropole," in *RPap* 2 (Paris: Presses Universitaires de France, 1962): 37–73, esp. 65. In general, see Quaegebeur, *Le dieu égyptien Shaï*, 163–65.

10. Cf. Besa, *Life of Shenoute*, 126; Pseudo-Cyril, "Miracles of the Three Youths," fol. 181ʳ, ed. Henri de Vis, *Homélies coptes de la Vaticane* 2, CBibCopte 6 (Louvain: Peeters, 1990), 187. See discussion of domestic shrines in Frankfurter, *Religion in Roman Egypt*, 131–42.

a standard feature of Egyptian homes through the Roman period; and many of the terra-cotta and wood figurines of Egyptian deities can be linked to such niches.[11] But we can best understand the nature of such domestic shrines by comparison with those in other, modern cultures. Domestic shrines corresponding to regional or national shrines are typical orientation points in homes throughout European and Latin American Christianity and Asian cultures. Images and their various accoutrements (flowers, candles, vessels, tokens) bring together the owner's experience of the principal local temple and its festivals with her sense of other shrines and spirits in the world—perhaps ancestral, perhaps of distant pilgrimage centers. The domestic shrine is revitalized on a regular basis, with domestic celebrations shared among many homes (as Shenoute describes above) or from temple processions, which often involve the scattering or dispensing of beneficent materials. The domestic shrine serves as the locus of personal or family-based invocations—for health or fortune or, most likely in late antique Egypt, safety from divisive or afflicting forces. Hence the form of the god (or the supplementary gods) on the domestic altar will represent a particularly helpful or gracious aspect of the complex deity portrayed in the temple: Horus armed with a sword or carrying a cornucopia, for example, or Isis radiating maternal fruitfulness from her exposed vulva.[12] An especially pertinent example would be a small faience image of a squatting Bes, the popular protective and fertility god, in the collection of Eton College. The image is embedded in a block of wood, quite likely a doorpost, where the image would guard the interior from the vantage of the threshold (not unlike the Jewish *mezuzah*).[13]

If one were to take the domestic images described in the *Panegyric* strictly in terms of the *Agathos Daimon/Shai* designation, then the image in the nich-

---

11. Françoise Dunand, *Religion populaire en Égypte romaine*, EPRO 77 (Leiden: Brill, 1979); Marguerite Rassart-Debergh, "De l'icône païenne à l'icône chrétienne," *MCopte* 18 (1990): 39–70, esp. 48–49. In Coptic literature, ϣⲟⲩϣⲧ might contain either heathen images on the wall or Christian objects: s.v., Walter Ewing Crum, *A Coptic Dictionary* (Oxford: Clarendon Press, 1939), 608b. See in general David G. Orr, "Roman Domestic Religion: The Evidence of the Household Shrines," *ANRW* II.16 (1978), 1557–91, and Anna Stevens, "The Material Evidence for Domestic Religion at Amarna and Preliminary Remarks on Its Interpretation," *JEA* 89 (2003): 143–68.

12. Cf. Dunand, *Religion populaire en Égypte romaine*, 60–92, 134–61.

13. ECM 1508, in Hans D. Schneider et al., *The Small Masterpieces of Egyptian Art: Selections from the Myers Museum at Eton College* (Leiden: Rijksmuseum van Oudheden, 2003), #97. I am grateful to Curator Nicholas Reeves for consultation on this piece.

es would probably be in the form of a looped serpent, perhaps with the face of an associated god, as *Agathos Daimon/Shai* was popularly represented in terra-cotta during the Roman era.[14] But there is no archeological evidence that domestic shrines were so strictly imitative. The *Panegyric*'s picture of a monolithic Kothos devotion may well serve the dramatic narrative and mask a more complex relationship between the deities predominating on domestic altars (like Bes, Toutou, Harpocrates, and Isis) and those who lived in the principal temples. That is to say, the "memory" of traditional Egyptian domestic cult that the *Panegyric* preserves may have been altered for narrative effect or been simplified over time. What remains valuable in the narrative for the historian of late antique Egypt is the general picture of the importance of domestic cult and its potential correspondence to temple activities.

The Kothos devotees "came out with rakes in their hands"

In hagiographical convention, monks and bishops are pitted most dramatically against demons of heathen cult sites, then sorcerers (often a caricatured type of priest), and then temple priests—although the last quite often made especially good converts in stories of Christianization.[15] Local peasantry, however, made a more problematic literary antagonist, since the Christian crusaders meant ultimately to win their hearts and minds (even by destroying their images). Even as etiology—where the hagiography is read aloud to describe how "our" region embraced Christ through "that" saint's efforts—the text had to show some continuity between "us" now and our heathen ancestors then, and the saint's warfare against those ancestors, or vice versa, might disrupt this intrinsic continuity. Even in the story of Elijah battling the priests of Baal that offered such an inspiring model to monks and their hagiographers, the Baal-seduced audience of Israelites does not oppose the prophet but watches carefully the rival endeavors of the ritual experts.[16]

I would argue, then, that the opposition of local communities *to* the incursions of Christian holy men represents not hagiographical *topos* but in fact

---

14. *Égypte romaine: L'autre Égypte* (Marseille: Musées de Marseille, 1997), 216–17.

15. On monks versus demons, see Sidney Aufrère, "L'Égypte traditionnelle, ses démons vus par les premiers chrétiens," *Études Coptes* V, ed. M. Rassart-Debergh, CBibCopte 10 (Paris: Peeters, 1998), 63–92, and David Brakke, *Demons and the Making of the Monk* (Cambridge: Harvard University Press, 2006); on monks versus sorcerers and priests, see David Frankfurter, "The Perils of Love: Magic and Countermagic in Coptic Egypt," *JHSex* 10 (2001): 480–500, esp. 497–98.

16. 1 Kings 18:20–24, 30, 36–40.

authentic recollection of people in active defense of their sacred places and religious traditions against figures understood (quite accurately) as dangerous. In Egypt one finds such scenarios in Besa's account of Abbot Shenoute's crusade on Plewit (early fifth century) and in Zachariah of Mytilene's account of the *philoponoi* and monks' attack on the Isis temple of Menouthis (489 CE).[17] Elsewhere, in Gaza, townspeople rise up against Bishop Porphyry, while throughout the Levant, Sozomen reports credibly, local people take up arms against crusading bishops.[18] The *Panegyric*, to be sure, elaborates popular resistance with dramatic details: "they came out with rods, swords, spears, and axes in their hands," the Cairo manuscript expands; they proudly address Macarius, challenging him to depart; they even momentarily allow him to enter the temple before the priests take over. The details are basically fictionalized to build up Macarius's dramatic obstacles. Yet the story reflects accurately on historical villagers' readiness to defend their religious sites against Christian incursion.

Religious regionalism and localism in Egypt often led to violent defense, according to both papyri and outsiders' (often amused) reports.[19] Crossculturally, villagers will inevitably perceive an iconoclastic assault like that posed by Christian bishops and monks in late antiquity (and Catholic and Protestant missionaries in modern times) as a threat to social and moral wellbeing, to cosmic stability and beneficence, and to relations with ancestors. When there is an opportunity and effective leadership, like a god's oracle as the *Panegyric* imagines, people will often fight aggressively to maintain tradition. The *Panegyric*'s scenario of village mobilization to defend the local cult offers an instructive example of one of the dynamics in religious continuity in late antiquity: not just villages in geographical isolation or the creative amalgamations of local superstition and Christian saints that Shenoute laments, but full-scale resistance.[20]

17. Plewit: see note 3 above, with Van der Vliet, "Spätantikes Heidentum in Ägypten," 107–8. Menouthis: Zachariah, *Vita Severi*, in M.-A. Kugener, ed., *Zacharie le scholiastique: Vie de Sévère*, PO 2.1 (Paris: Firmin-Didot, 1904), 16–35.
18. Mark the Deacon, *Vita Porphyrii* 17–24; Sozomen, *HE* 7.15. Cf. Raymond Van Dam, "From Paganism to Christianity in Late Antique Gaza," *Viator* 16 (1985): 1–20, esp. 10–13.
19. E.g., Plutarch, *De Iside et Osiride* 72; Juvenal, *Satire* 15. Cf. K. A. D. Smelik and E. A. Hemelrijk, "'Who knows not what monsters demented Egypt worships?' Opinions on Egyptian Animal Worship in Antiquity as Part of the Ancient Conception of Egypt," *ANRW* II.17.4 (1984): 1852–2357, and David Frankfurter, "Lest Egypt's City Be Deserted: Religion and Ideology in the Egyptian Response to the Jewish Revolt," *JJS* 43 (1992): 203–20.
20. See in general Frankfurter, *Religion in Roman Egypt*, 66–70.

"slaying the little children [of the Christians] and pouring (out) their blood upon the altar of their god.... [and] removing their intestines...for harp [strings]"

This is an artful and entirely fictional caricature of traditional Egyptian cult that belongs to the wider Greco-Roman (and certainly cross-cultural) folklore of the Savage Other and his ritual atrocities. One notes in this case a deliberate parody of Hellenic tradition: rather than eaten or disemboweled simply for magical ingredients, the little Christian children's bodies are harvested for harp strings. This last feature partially evokes the Egyptian *bnt*-harp, once of some ritual importance in temple cult; but the use of the Greek ⲕⲓⲑⲁⲣⲁ clearly carries classical associations.[21] Evoking no doubt both classical and Egyptian musical practices, the harp here encapsulates heathenism and its ritual accoutrements. The mellifluous strumming of temple harps now amounts to nothing more than insidious *epoidai*—incantation-songs—serving heathen greed and exploiting children's bodies.[22]

The preparation of these harps is also associated with the spectacle of blood sacrifice, an activity more central to Christian caricatures of a persecuting *Hellenismos* than to actual Egyptian temple cult. By late antiquity the specter of blood sacrifice formed the basis of a Christian "atrocity" folklore, wherein offering rites served as both the context for horrific martyrdoms and a symbol of Julianic polytheism. Indeed, H. A. Drake has argued that by the late fourth century sacrifice's associations with persecution and atrocity in Christian legend directly fuelled Christian aggression against local temple cults.[23] The *Pan-*

---

21. Cf. Jaroslav Černý, *Coptic Etymological Dictionary* (Oxford: Clarendon Press, 1976), 24, s.v., ⲃⲟⲓⲛⲉ; Lise Manniche, *Ancient Egyptian Musical Instruments* (Munich: Deutscher Kunstverlag, 1975), 36–46; Sibylle Emerit, "À propos de l'origine des interdits musicaux dans l'Égypte ancienne," *BIFAO* 102 (2002): 196–98.

22. On such images of sorcery, see Richard Gordon, "Lucan's Erictho," in *Homo Viator,* ed. Michael Whitby, Philip Hardie, and Mary Whitby (Bristol: Bristol Classical Press, 1987), 231–41. On chanted *epoidai* as the basis of Greek "magic" (actual rituals and literary representations), see W. D. Furley, "Besprechung und Behandlung: Zur Form und Funktion von *Epôidai* in der griechischen Zaubermedizin," in *Philanthropia dai Eusebeia: Festschrift für A. Dihle zum 70. Geburtstag,* ed. Glenn W. Most, H. Petersmann, and A. M. Ritter (Göttingen: Vandenhoeck und Ruprecht, 1993), 80–104. On the perceived dangers of ritual music and sounds, see Sarah Iles Johnston, "The Song of the *Iunx:* Magic and Rhetoric in Pythian 4," *TAPA* 125 (1995): 177–206.

23. H. A. Drake, "Lambs into Lions: Explaining Early Christian Intolerance," *P&P* 153 (1996): 33–36.

egyric, of course, reflects precisely this pattern of atrocity recitation leading to violent repression of heathen cult. The pattern may have been particularly relevant in Egypt, where martyrology was especially celebrated—even before the establishment of martyr shrines—and the imagery of blood sacrifice and the torments of Christian heroes were alive in many Christians' minds.[24]

We can understand the *Panegyric*'s particular evocation of this atrocity folklore in two contexts: the ancient literary tradition of imputing "ritual" atrocities to a distant or subversive Other, and the historical possibility that legends like this one actually were circulating orally around some of the remaining native cults in the fifth century. We may take the literary tradition first. Analogues to the secret Kothos child sacrifices appear in ancient geography (e.g., Scythians) and with voyeuristic detail in novels of the Greco-Roman world (Lollianos, Achilles Tatius). Barbarian cultures just on the periphery of the empire are portrayed as practicing human sacrifice and the disemboweling of victims; and it is usually the chaste hero who observes the rites secretly while his comely betrothed lies bound on the savages' altar.[25] But already in the second century CE these titillating scenarios had a parallel life as subversion myths: Bacchantes and Christians with their nefarious cannibalistic and incestuous rites, followed by heretics—Satanic devotees within Christendom, as in Epiphanius's pornographic depiction of Gnostics.[26] J. Rives has effectively shown the utility of these allegations for relegating the subject—Christians, heretics, or in this case heathens—to the realm of the savage and subhuman,

---

24. Along with Eusebius, *HE* 6.5, and Palladius, *Historia Lausiaca* 3, see evidence for Egyptian martyrological preoccupations discussed in Frankfurter, *Elijah in Upper Egypt*, chap. 6, and David Frankfurter, "The Cult of the Martyrs in Egypt before Constantine: The Evidence of the Coptic *Apocalypse of Elijah*," *VC* 48 (1994): 25–47; L.-Th Lefort, "La chasse aux reliques des martyrs en Égypte au IVe siècle," *NClio* 6 (1954): 225–30; Jürgen Horn, *Studien zu den Märtyrern des nördlichen Oberägypten*, Göttinger Orientforschungen 15 (Wiesbaden: Harrassowitz, 1986); and A. Piankoff, "The Osireion of Seti I at Abydos during the Greco-Roman Period and the Christian Occupation," *BSAC* 15 (1958–60): 134–37.

25. Ancient geography: François Hartog, *Memories of Odysseus: Frontier Tales from Ancient Greece*, trans. Janet Lloyd (Chicago: University of Chicago Press, 2001), 133–40; Wilfried Nippel, "The Construction of the 'Other,'" in *Greeks and Barbarians*, ed. Thomas Harrison (New York: Routledge, 2002), 278–310. Ancient novels: Arthur Darby Nock, "Greek Novels and Egyptian Religion," in *Essays on Religion and the Ancient World*, ed. Zeph Stewart (Oxford: Clarendon Press, 1972), 1:170–71; Jack J. Winkler, "Lollianos and the Desperadoes," *JHS* 100 (1980): 155–81. In general, J. B. Rives, "Human Sacrifice among Pagans and Christians," *JRS* 85 (1995): 65–85, and for Coptic literature, Van der Vliet, "Spätantikes Heidentum in Ägypten," 108n45.

26. Livy, *Ab urbe condita* 39.8–14; Minucius Felix, *Octavius* 9.5–7; Athenagoras, *Legatio* 3.1, 31.1; Tertullian, *Ad Uxorem* 2.4–5. "Gnostics": Epiphanius of Salamis, *Panarion* 26.3.3–5.7.

while Norman Cohn and others have shown the continuity of these atrocity legends into the Middle Ages, promulgated by monks and bishops, applied often to Jewish religion, and eventually incorporated in the fifteenth century as the witches' Sabbat.[27] In the case of the cult of Kothos, the revelation (or even suspicion) that ostensibly neighborly traditionalists are actually stealing Christian children to sacrifice and disembowel for sorcery signifies that they are really inhuman predators—monsters—to be destroyed.

But the pervasiveness of these atrocity legends in oral as well as literary—and popular as well as official—contexts begs the question: Could such stories have actually circulated among fifth-century Egyptian Christian villagers about the temple cult still maintained in their vicinity? Might the *Panegyric* actually recall a historical conspiracy panic focused on traditionalists in which Macarius himself served as mobilizer? The possibility can be raised only through a series of historical and ethnographic parallels. We do know from papyri and literary sources that during the second century CE in Egypt such rumor panics swirled around Jews, who were imagined as cannibals.[28] So this kind of social phenomenon, attested in Rome and North Africa regarding Christians, was not unknown in Egypt also. From a comparative perspective, we might consider the polarizing discourse of devil worship that leaders like Shenoute wielded liberally against traditionalists (although not explicit in the description of Kothos), magnifying fears of demons with the legendary horrors of heathen sacrifice. This polarizing discourse might well exacerbate latent hostilities between Christian and traditional villagers in such a way as to feed such a rumor panic. Ethnographic studies of mixed (Christian/traditional) towns in Africa suggest that relations remain quite tense, as each side views the other in extreme caricature and as directly contributing to moral and supernatural disorder. (This is especially the case when Christian missionaries from outside play a role in defining local Christian identity.) The quotidian practicality and ancestral cycles with which villagers had always associated the traditional cult and its shrines become quickly overshadowed in Christian villagers' minds by ideologically borne caricatures of heathendom and devil worship. Tolerant coexistence gives way to anxiety and hostility.[29]

27. Rives, "Human Sacrifice"; Norman Cohn, *Europe's Inner Demons*, rev. ed. (Chicago: University of Chicago Press, 1993), chaps. 1–4; and David Frankfurter, *Evil Incarnate: Rumors of Demonic Conspiracy and Satanic Abuse in History* (Princeton: Princeton University Press, 2006).

28. Apion *apud* Josephus, *Against Apion* 2.91–96; Cassius Dio 68.32; *CPJ* 437.

29. Cf. Birgit Meyer, "Beyond Syncretism: Translation and Diabolization in the Appropriation of

It is hard to imagine this situation *not* taking shape in the period of the historical Macarius. Indeed, I have proposed that a like situation actually *did* precipitate a village riot to which Besa, Shenoute's successor, referred in a fifth-century sermon delivered somewhere in Panopolis. In this case, the abbot's chastisement of Christian villagers for "fighting over a piece of wood" seems to point to their assault against an Egyptian divine image and its devotees.[30] In the *Panegyric* too, at the triumphant conclusion to the Kothos episode, Macarius incites local Christians to purge the village of heathen images. Those Kothos devotees who do not submit to baptism "fled with only their idols to the desert," and "the Christians dwelt in their houses" (5.11).

We can do no more than raise the possibility of such a rumor panic about traditional Egyptian cult, although the comparative evidence, both from the Roman Empire and cross-culturally, lends this historical reconstruction some credibility. At the very least, the *Panegyric*'s scenario of heathen infanticidal cult atrocities offers an important variant of a widespread myth of the Other in antiquity, here neatly woven into immediate cultural images of sacrifice and religious practice.

Conclusions

In her exhaustive analysis of the modes of Christianization in late antique Egypt, Ewa Wipszycka used the *Panegyric* as another example—alongside Shenoute's escapades and stories of Moses of Abydos, John the Little, and others—of the strongly local character of indigenous religion, such that it could be maintained well through the fifth century in many places. Christianization, she argued, was not a steady wave drawing over the countryside but a village-by-village phenomenon; nor was it (as Johannes Leipoldt once argued) a cultural revitalization movement through which Egyptian peasants opposed themselves to elite "Hellenes." Rather, hagiographical texts like the *Panegyric* recall

---

Protestantism in Africa," in *Syncretism/Anti-Syncretism: The Politics of Religious Synthesis,* ed. Charles Stewart and Rosalind Shaw (London: Routledge, 1994), 45–68; Birgit Meyer, *Translating the Devil: Religion and Modernity among the Ewe in Ghana* (Trenton: Africa World Press, 1999); and Andrew Walsh, "Preserving Bodies, Saving Souls: Religious Incongruity in a Northern Malagasy Mining Town," *JRAfr* 32 (2002): 366–92.

30. Besa, frg. 41: "To the Dignitaries and People of the Village," in K. H. Kuhn, ed. and trans., *Letters and Sermons of Besa,* CSCO 157–58, Scriptores coptici 21–22 (Louvain: Durbecq, 1956), 21:129–30 (text), 22:123–24 (translation). See David Frankfurter, "'Things Unbefitting Christians': Violence and Christianization in Fifth-Century Panopolis," *JECS* 8 (2000): 273–95.

over and over that rural Christianization involved monks and bishops moving on isolated communities with self-sustained religious traditions.[31] By the fifth century, as so many of the texts show, such communities might also include a small population of Christians, converts of another age. Did they join for the charisma of some holy man, or simply for Christianity's imperial caché? These individual Christians would share local sensibilities and annual festivals with the traditional cult devotees, as seems to have been common throughout late antique Christendom, or else they might segregate themselves as a persecuted minority, as the *Panegyric* imagines.[32]

Despite our inability to fix the cult of Kothos and its destruction to a specific time in the fifth century and a particular site in the Panopolite region, the *Panegyric* provides a priceless picture, authentic in many details, of persisting Egyptian religion and perhaps even of the historical cult of Shai. We can acknowledge a great degree of hagiographical convention in the images of secret cult atrocity and of pitched battle against heathendom; but ultimately these conventions simply augment a story with multiple points of authenticity. "History," such as it emerges in this scenario, lies not in the specific acts of the holy man Macarius or the specific narrative of destruction of the temple, but rather in the evolution of the religious landscape: the disruptions in cult that it involved and the persisting features—niches, ruins, even spirits—that had to be negotiated.[33]

---

31. Ewa Wipszycka, "La christianisation de l'Égypte aux IVe–VIe siècles. Aspects sociaux et ethniques," *Aegyptus* 68 (1988): 117–65, esp. 142–58.

32. On the continuation of local religious traditions and perspectives among Christians, see C. Guignebert, "Les demi-chrétiens et leur place dans l'église antique," *RHR* 88 (1923): 65–102; Valerie I. J. Flint, *The Rise of Magic in Early Medieval Europe* (Princeton: Princeton University Press, 1991); Ramsay MacMullen, *Christianity and Paganism in the Fourth to Eighth Centuries* (New Haven: Yale University Press, 1997), chap. 4; and on Egypt, Frankfurter, *Religion in Roman Egypt*, 193–95, 265–72, and David Frankfurter, "Syncretism and the Holy Man in Late Antique Egypt," *JECS* 11 (2003): 339–85.

33. Cf. David Frankfurter, "Hagiography and the Reconstruction of Local Religion in Late Antique Egypt: Memories, Inventions, and Landscapes," *Church History and Religious Culture* 86 (2006, forthcoming).

BIBLIOGRAPHY

Aarsleff, Hans. *From Locke to Saussure: Essays on the Study of Language and Intellectual History*. Minneapolis: University of Minnesota Press, 1982.
Alcock, Anthony. "Two Notes on Egyptian Monasticism." *Aegyptus* 67 (1987): 189–90.
Allberry, C. R. C., ed. and trans. *A Manichaean Psalm-Book Part II*. Manichaean Manuscripts in the Chester Beatty Collection, vol. 2. Stuttgart: W. Kohlhammer, 1938.
Amélineau, Émile. "Voyage d'un moine égyptien dans le désert." *Recueil des travaux relatifs à la philologie et à l'archéologie égyptiennes et assyriennes* 6 (1885): 166–94.
———. *Monuments pour servir à l'histoire de l'Égypte chrétienne aux IVe, Ve, VIe, et VIIe siècles. Texte copte publié et traduit*. MMAF 4. Paris: Ernest Leroux, 1888–95.
———, ed. and trans. *Oeuvres de Schenoudi: Texte copte et traduction française*. 2 vols. Paris: Ernest Leroux, 1907–14.
Astel, Ann W. *The Song of Songs in the Middle Ages*. Ithaca: Cornell University Press, 1990.
Aufrère, Sidney. "L'Égypte traditionnelle, ses démons vus par les premiers chrétiens." In *Études Coptes V*, ed. M. Rassart-Debergh, 63–92. CBibCopte 10. Paris: Peeters, 1998.
Bacht, Heinrich. *Das Vermächtnis des Ursprungs: Studien zum frühen Mönchtum I*. StTGL 5. Würzburg: Echter Verlag, 1972.
Barnes, T. D. "The Edition of Eusebius' Ecclesiastical History." *GRBS* 21 (1980): 191–201.
Basset, René. *Le synaxaire arabe jacobite (rédaction copte)*. PO 11, 5. Paris: Firmin-Didot, 1916. Reprint, Tounhout: Brepols, 1973.
Bauer, Walter. *Orthodoxy and Heresy in Earliest Christianity*. Trans. and ed. Robert A. Kraft et al. Philadelphia: Fortress Press, 1971.
Baumeister, Theofried. "Koptische Kirchengeschichte: Zum Stand der Forschung." In *Actes du IVe Congrès Copte, Louvain-la-Neuve, 5–10 septembre 1988*, ed. M. Rassart-Debergh and J. Ries, 2:115–24. Louvain-la-Neuve: Université Catholique de Louvain, Institut Orientaliste, 1992.
Behlmer, Heike. *Schenute von Atripe: De iudicio (Torino, Museo Egizio, Cat. 63000, Cod. IV)*. Catalogo del Museo Egizio di Torino, Serie Prima—Monumenti e Testi 8. Turin: Ministero per i Beni Culturale e Ambientali, 1996.
Berkey, Jonathan. *The Transmission of Knowledge in Medieval Cairo: A Social History of Islamic Education*. Princeton: Princeton University Press, 1992.

Bernardin, J. B. "A Coptic Sermon Attributed to St. Athanasius." *JTS* 38 (1937): 113–29.
———. "The Resurrection of Lazarus." *AJSL* 57 (1940): 262–90.
Berschin, Walter. *Medioevo greco-latino: Da Gerolamo Niccoló Cusano.* Naples: Liguori, 1989.
Besa. *Life of Shenoute.* Ed. and trans. David N. Bell. CSS 73. Kalamazoo: Cistercian Publications, 1983.
Betz, Hans Dieter, ed. *The Greek Magical Papyri in Translation, Including the Demotic Spells.* Chicago: University of Chicago Press, 1986.
Blasberg, C. "Anapher." In *Historisches Wörterbuch der Rhetorik,* ed. Gert Ueding. 6 vols. 1:542–45. Darmstadt: Wissenschaftliche Buchgesellschaft, 1992.
Bolman, Elizabeth S., ed. *Monastic Visions: Wall Paintings in the Monastery of St. Antony at the Red Sea.* New Haven: Yale University Press, 2002.
Boole, George. *The Mathematical Analysis of Logic, Being an Essay towards a Calculus of Deductive Reasoning.* Cambridge: Philosophical Library, 1847. Reprint, Oxford: Oxford University Press, 1948.
———. *An Investigation of the Laws of Thought, on Which Are Founded the Mathematical Theories of Logic and Probabilities.* London: Walton and Maberly, 1854. Reprint, New York: Dover, 1951 and 1958.
———. *George Boole's Collected Logical Works.* 2 vols. Chicago: Open Court, 1916.
Boon, Amand. *Pachomiana latina: Règles et épitres de s. Pachôme, épitre de s. Théodore et "Liber" de s. Orsiesios, Texte latin de s. Jérôme.* BRHE 7. Louvain: Bureaux de la Revue, 1932.
Boyarin, Daniel. "Two Introductions to the Midrash on Song of Songs." *Tarbiz* 56 (1987): 479–501.
———. "The Eye in the Torah: Ocular Desire in Midrashic Hermeneutic." *Critical Inquiry* 16 (spring 1990): 532–50.
———. *Intertextuality and the Reading of Midrash.* Bloomington: Indiana University Press, 1990.
———. "The Gospel of the Memra: Jewish Binitarianism and the Prologue to John." *HTR* 94 (July 2001): 243–84.
———. "On the History of the Early Phallus." In *Gender and Difference in the Middle Ages,* ed. Sharon Farmer and Carol Pasternack, 3–44. Minneapolis: University of Minnesota Press, 2003.
———. "Origenists Aren't the Only Christians." Manuscript. 2003.
Brakke, David. *Demons and the Making of the Monk.* Cambridge: Harvard University Press, 2006.
Brakmann, Heinzgerd. "Eine oder zwei koptische Kirchengeschichte?" *Muséon* 87 (1974): 129–42.
Broadbent, T. A. A. "Boole, George." In *Dictionary of Scientific Biography,* ed. Charles Coulston Gillispie. 14 vols. 2:293–98. New York: Charles Scribner's Sons, 1970.
Bsciai, Agapio. "Novum Auctarium Lexici Sahidico-Coptici. II (n, o, p, q)." *ZÄS* 25 (1887): 57–73.

Büchler, Bernward. *Die Armut der Armen: Über den ursprünglichen Sinn der Mönchischen Armut*. Munich: Kösel, 1980.
Budge, E. A. W., ed. *Coptic Martyrdoms etc. in the Dialect of Upper Egypt, Edited, with English Translations*. London: British Museum, 1914.
Bunge, Gabriel. *Evagrios Pontikos: Briefe aus der Wüste*. Sophia 24. Trier: Paulinus-Verlag, 1986.
Burrus, Virginia. *Begotten, Not Made: Conceiving Manhood in Late Antiquity*. Stanford: Stanford University Press, 2000.
Burton-Christie, Douglas. *The Word in the Desert: Scripture and the Quest for Holiness in Early Christian Monasticism*. Oxford: Oxford University Press, 1993.
Buzi, Paola. *Titoli e autori nella letteratura copta. Studio storico e tipologico*. BSEP 2. Pisa: Giardini, 2005.
Cameron, Ron. *The Other Gospels: Non-Canonical Gospel Texts*. Philadelphia: Westminster Press, 1982.
Campagnano, Antonella. "Monaci egiziani fra V e VI secolo." *VetChr* 15 (1978): 223–46.
———, ed. *Preliminary Editions of Coptic Codices: Monb. GB: Life of Manasses—Encomium of Moses—Encomium of Abraham*. CMCL. Rome: Centro Italiano Microfiches, 1985.
Camplani, Alberto. "Un Episodio della recezione de ΠΕΡΙ ΕΥΧΗΣ in Egitto." SEAug 57 (1997): 159–72.
Caner, Daniel. *Wandering, Begging Monks: Spiritual Authority and the Promotion of Monasticism in Late Antiquity*. TCH 33. Berkeley and Los Angeles: University of California Press, 2002.
Cannuyer, Christian. "L'identité des sarabaïtes, ces moines d'Égypte que méprisait Jean Cassien." *Mélanges de science religieuse* 58 (April–June 2001): 7–19.
Caspary, Gerard E. *Politics and Exegesis: Origen and the Two Swords*. Berkeley and Los Angeles: University of California Press, 1979.
Cassian, John. *Conlationes patrum XXIV*. Ed. Michael Petschenig. CSEL 13.2. Vindobonae: C. Geroldi Filium Bibliopolam Academiae, 1886.
———. *Conférences*. Ed. and trans. E. Pichery. SC 42, 54, 64. Paris: Éditions du Cerf, 1955, 1958, 1959.
Černý, Jaroslav. *Coptic Etymological Dictionary*. Cambridge: Cambridge University Press, 1976.
Chadwick, Henry. *The Sentences of Sextus: A Contribution to the History of Early Christian Ethics*. TS, n.s. 5. Cambridge: Cambridge University Press, 1959.
Chaine, Marius. "Le Triadon: Son auteur, la date de sa composition." *Bulletin de l'Association des Amis de l'Art Copte* 2 (1936): 9–24.
Chapman, P. "'Homily on the Passion and the Resurrection' Attributed to Euodius of Rome." In *Homiletica from the Pierpont Morgan Library: Seven Coptic Homilies Attributed to Basil the Great, John Chrysostom, and Euodius of Rome*, ed. Leo Depuydt et al. CSCO 524.79–106 (text), 525.83–114 (translation). Scriptores coptici 43–44. Louvain: Peeters, 1991.

Chitty, Derwas J. *The Desert a City: An Introduction to the Study of Egyptian and Palestinian Monasticism under the Christian Empire.* Oxford: Basil Blackwell, 1966.

Choat, Malcolm. "Philological and Historical Approaches to the 'Third Type' of Egyptian Monk." In *Coptic Studies on the Threshold of a New Millennium: Proceedings of the Seventh International Congress of Coptic Studies,* ed. Mat Immerzeel and Jacques Van der Vliet. OLA 132–33. 133.857–65. Louvain: Peeters, 2004.

———. "Thomas the 'Wanderer' in a Coptic List of Apostles." *Orientalia* 74 (2005): 83–85.

Church, Alonzo. "A Bibliography of Symbolic Logic." *JSL* 1, no. 4 (1936): 121–218.

Clark, Elizabeth. *The Origenist Controversy.* Princeton: Princeton University Press, 1992.

Cohn, Norman. *Europe's Inner Demons.* Rev. ed. Chicago: University of Chicago Press, 1993.

Collins, J. J. "Sibylline Oracles." In *The Old Testament Apocrypha,* ed. James H. Charlesworth. 2 vols. 1:317–472. Garden City, N.Y.: Doubleday, 1983.

Coquin, René-Georges. "Abraham of Farshut." In *The Coptic Encyclopedia,* ed. Aziz S. Atiya. 8 vols. 1:11–12. New York: Macmillan, 1991.

———. "Barsum the Naked, Saint." In *The Coptic Encyclopedia,* ed. Aziz S. Atiya. 8 vols. 2:348–9. New York: Macmillan, 1991.

———. "Manasseh." In *The Coptic Encyclopedia,* ed. Aziz S. Atiya. 8 vols. 5:1518. New York: Macmillan, 1991.

———. "Discours attribué au Patriarche Cyrille, sur la dédicace de l'église de S. Raphaël, rapportant les propos de son oncle Théophile." *BSAC* 33 (1994): 25–56.

Crum, Walter Ewing. "Eusebius and Coptic Church Histories." *PSBA* 24 (1902): 68–84.

———. "Inscription's from Shenoute's Monastery." *JThS* 5 (1904): 566.

———. *Der Papyruscodex Saec. VI–VII der Phillipps-Bibliothek in Cheltenham: Koptische theologische Schriften Strassburg.* SWGS 18. Strassburg: K. J. Trübner, 1915.

———. *A Coptic Dictionary.* Oxford: Clarendon Press, 1939.

Daniel, Robert W. *Two Greek Magical Papyri in the National Museum of Antiquities in Leiden: A Photographic Edition of J384 and J395. PGM XII and XIII.* Opladen: Westdeutscher Verlag, 1991.

Davis, Stephen J. *The Cult of Saint Thecla: A Tradition of Women's Piety in Late Antiquity.* Oxford: Oxford University Press, 2001.

Dawson, David. *Allegorical Readers and Cultural Revision in Ancient Alexandria.* Berkeley and Los Angeles: University of California Press, 1992.

———. *Christian Figural Reading and the Fashioning of Identity.* Berkeley and Los Angeles: University of California Press, 2001.

Den Heijer, Johannes. *Mawhub Ibn Mansur et l'historiographie copto-arabe. Étude sur la composition de l'Histoire des Patriarches d'Alexandrie.* CSCO 513, Subsidia 83. Louvain: Peeters, 1989.

———. "À propos de la traduction copte de l'Histoire ecclésiastique d'Eusèbe de Césarée: nouvelle remarques sur les parties perdues." In *Actes du IVe Congrès Copte, Louvain-la-Neuve, 5–10 septembre 1988,* ed. M. Rassart-Debergh and J. Ries. 2 vols. 2:185–93. Louvain-la-Neuve: Université Catholique de Louvain, Institut Orientaliste, 1992.

Depuydt, Leo. *Catalogue of Coptic Manuscripts in the Pierpont Morgan Library*. Corpus of Illuminated Manuscripts 4–5. Louvain: Peeters, 1993.
———. "Champollion's Ideogram and Saussure's *signe linguistique*." *Orientalia* 64 (1995): 1–11.
———. "Sentence Pattern and Verb Form: Egyptian Grammar since Polotsky." *Muséon* 108 (1995): 39–48.
———. "Condition and Premise in Egyptian and Elsewhere and the Laws of Thought in Expanded Boolean Algebra." *ZÄS* 126 (1999): 97–111.
———. "Contrast in Egyptian and in General and the Laws of Thought in Boolean Algebra." *GBS* 2 (1999): 37–60.
———. "The Meaning of the Coptic Particle ⲡⲱ and Related Constructions in Semitic and Other Languages." *JCS* 3 (2001): 113–28.
Diekamp, Franz. *Doctrina patrum de incarnatione verbi*. Münster: Aschendorff, 1907.
Dorival, Gilles. "Les débuts du christianisme à Alexandrie." In *Alexandrie: Une mégapole cosmopolite. Actes du 9ème colloque de la Villa Kérylos à Beaulieu-sur-Mer les 2 & 3 Octobre 1998*, 157–74. Paris: Académie des Inscriptions et Belles-Lettres, 1999.
Douglas, Mary. *Purity and Danger: An Analysis of Concepts of Pollution and Taboo*. New York: Praeger, 1966.
Drake, H. A. "Lambs into Lions: Explaining Early Christian Intolerance." *P&P* 153 (1996): 3–36.
Duensing, H. "Epistula Apostolorum." In *New Testament Apocrypha*, ed. Edgar Hennecke and Wilhelm Schneemelcher, trans. Robert McLachlan Wilson. 2 vols. 1:189–227. Philadelphia: Westminster Press, 1963.
Dunand, Françoise. *Religion populaire en Égypte romaine*. EPRO 77. Leiden: Brill, 1979.
Dunsky, Shimshon, ed. *Song of Songs Rabbah*. Tel-Aviv: Dvir, 1980.
Edwards, Mark J. *Origen against Plato*. ASPTLA. Burlington, Vt.: Ashgate, 2002.
Égypte romaine: L'autre Égypte. Marseille: Musées de Marseille, 1997.
Elm, Susanna. *"Virgins of God": The Making of Asceticism in Late Antiquity*. Oxford: Clarendon Press, 1994.
Emerit, Sibylle. "À propos de l'origine des interdits musicaux dans l'Égypte ancienne." *BIFAO* 102 (2002): 196–98.
Emmel, Stephen L. "Ithyphallic Gods and Undetected Ligatures: Pan Is Not 'Ours,' He Is Min." *GM* 141 (1994): 43–46.
———. "Theophilus's Festal Letter of 401 as Quoted by Shenute." In *Divitiae Aegypti*, ed. Cäcilia Fluck et al., 93–98. Wiesbaden: Reichert, 1995.
———. "Immer erst das Kleingedruckte lesen: 'Die Pointe verstehen' in dem koptischen Panegyrikos auf Makarios von Tkōou." In *Ägypten—Münster: Kulturwissenschaftliche Studien zu Ägypten, dem Vorderen Orient und verwandten Gebieten*, ed. Anke Ilona Blöbaum, Jochem Kahl, and Simon D. Schweitzer, 91–104. Wiesbaden: Harrassowitz, 2003.
———. *Shenoute's Literary Corpus*. CSCO 599–600, Subsidia 111–12. Louvain: Peeters, 2004.

Engberg-Pedersen, Troels. "Philo's *De Vita Contemplativa* as a Philosopher's Dream." *JSJ* 30 (1999): 40–64.
Eusebius of Caesarea. *Eusèbe de Césarée: Histoire ecclésiastique*. 3d ed. Ed. and trans. G. Bardy. SC 31. Paris: Éditions du Cerf, 1986.
Evagrius of Pontus. *Scholies aux Proverbes*. Ed. and trans. Paul Géhin. SC 340. Paris: Éditions du Cerf, 1988.
———. *Le gnostique, ou, A celui qui est devenu digne de la science*. Ed. and trans. Antoine and Claire Guillaumont. SC 356. Paris: Éditions du Cerf, 1989.
Evelyn-White, Hugh G. *The Monasteries of the Wadi 'n Natrûn*. 3 vols. New York: Metropolitan Museum of Art, 1926–33.
Evetts, B. *History of the Patriarchs of the Coptic Church of Alexandria*. PO 1, 2, 4 (101–214, 381–518); 5, 1 (1–215); 10, 5 (357–551). Paris: Firmin-Didot, 1904–15.
Festugière, A. J. *Ephèse et Chalcédoine: Actes des Conciles*. Paris: Beauchesne, 1982.
Fletcher, Angus John Stewart. *Allegory: The Theory of a Symbolic Mode*. Ithaca: Cornell University Press, 1964.
Flint, Valerie I. J. *The Rise of Magic in Early Medieval Europe*. Princeton: Princeton University Press, 1991.
Forget, Jacques. *Synaxarium Alexandrinum*. CSCO 47–49, 67, 78, 90. Beirut: E Typographeo Catholico, 1905–26. Reprint, Louvain: L. Durbecq, 1953–54.
Frankenberg, W. *Evagrius Ponticus*. AKGWG, n.s. 13, 2. Berlin: Weidmannsche Buchhandlung, 1912.
Frankfurter, David. "Lest Egypt's City Be Deserted: Religion and Ideology in the Egyptian Response to the Jewish Revolt." *JJS* 43 (1992): 203–20.
———. *Elijah in Upper Egypt: The Apocalypse of Elijah and Early Egyptian Christianity*. SAC. Minneapolis: Fortress Press, 1993.
———. "The Cult of the Martyrs in Egypt before Constantine: The Evidence of the Coptic *Apocalypse of Elijah*." *VC* 48 (1994): 25–47.
———. *Religion in Roman Egypt: Assimilation and Resistance*. Princeton: Princeton University Press, 1998.
———. "'Things Unbefitting Christians': Violence and Christianization in Fifth-Century Panopolis." *JECS* 8 (2000): 273–95.
———. "The Perils of Love: Magic and Countermagic in Coptic Egypt." *JHSex* 10 (2001): 480–500.
———. "Syncretism and the Holy Man in Late Antique Egypt." *JECS* 11 (2003): 339–85.
———. "Urban Shrine and Rural Saint in Fifth-Century Alexandria." In *Pilgrimage in Graeco-Roman and Early Christian Antiquity: Seeing the Gods,* ed. Jas Elsner and Ian Rutherford, 435–49. Oxford: Oxford University Press, 2006.
———. *Evil Incarnate: Rumors of Demonic Conspiracy and Satanic Abuse*. Princeton: Princeton University Press, 2006.
———. "Hagiography and the Reconstruction of Local Religion in Late Antique Egypt: Memories, Inventions, and Landscapes." *Church History and Religious Culture* 86 (forthcoming).

Friedman, Florence D. *Beyond the Pharaohs: Egypt and the Copts in the 2nd to 7th Centuries A.D.* [Providence:] Rhode Island School of Design, Museum of Art, 1989.

Furley, W. D. "Besprechung und Behandlung: Zur Form und Funktion von *Epôidai* in der griechischen Zaubermedizin." In *Philanthropia kai Eusebeia: Festschrift für A. Dihle zum 70. Geburtstag,* ed. Glenn W. Most, H. Petersmann, and A. M. Ritter, 80–104. Göttingen: Vandenhoeck and Ruprecht, 1993.

Gaddis, Michael. "Nestorius." In *Late Antiquity: A Guide to the Postclassical World,* ed. G. W. Bowersock, Peter Brown, and Oleg Grabar, 603–4. Cambridge: Belknap Press, 1999.

Gardner, Iain. *The Kephalaia of the Teacher: The Edited Coptic Manichaean Texts in Translation with Commentary.* Leiden: Brill, 1995.

Gignac, Francis Thomas. *A Grammar of the Greek Papyri of the Roman and Byzantine Periods.* 2 vols. to date. TDSA LV-1/2. Milan: Istituto Editoriale Cisalpino–La Goliardica, 1976, 1981.

Girard, Louis Saint-Paul. "Un fragment sahidique de la vie de Saint Arsène le grand precepteur des enfants de Théodose, anachorète a Scété et a Toura (vers 410)." *BIFAO* 30 (1931): 195–99.

Gögler, Rolf. *Zur Theologie des biblischen Wortes bei Origenes.* Düsseldorf: Patmos-Verlag, 1963.

Goehring, James E. "Pachomius' Vision of Heresy: The Development of a Pachomian Tradition." *Muséon* 95 (1982): 241–62. Reprinted in Goehring, *Ascetics, Society, and the Desert: Studies in Early Egyptian Monasticism* (Harrisburg, Pa.: Trinity Press International, 1999), 137–61.

———. *The Letter of Ammon and Pachomian Monasticism.* PTS 27. Berlin: Walter de Gruyter, 1986.

———. "Chalcedonian Power Politics and the Demise of Pachomian Monasticism." OP 15. Claremont, Calif.: Institute for Antiquity and Christianity, 1989. Reprinted in Goehring, *Ascetics, Society, and the Desert: Studies in Early Egyptian Monasticism* (Harrisburg, Pa.: Trinity Press International, 1999), 241–61.

———. "The World Engaged: The Social and Economic World of Early Egyptian Monasticism." In *Gnosticism and the Early Christian World: In Honor of James M. Robinson,* ed. James E. Goehring, Charles W. Hedrick, and Jack T. Sanders, 134–44. Sonoma, Calif.: Polebridge Press, 1990. Reprinted in Goehring, *Ascetics, Society, and the Desert: Studies in Early Egyptian Monasticism* (Harrisburg, Pa.: Trinity Press International, 1999), 39–52.

———. "The Origins of Monasticism." In *Eusebius, Christianity, and Judaism,* ed. Harold W. Attridge and Gohei Hata, 235–55. Detroit: Wayne State University Press, 1992. Reprinted in Goehring, *Ascetics, Society, and the Desert: Studies in Early Egyptian Monasticism* (Harrisburg, Pa.: Trinity Press International, 1999), 13–35.

———. "Through a Glass Darkly: Diverse Images of the Ἀποτακτικοί(αί) in Early Egyptian Monasticism." In *Discursive Formations, Ascetic Piety, and the Interpretation of Early Christian Literature, Part 2,* ed. Vincent L. Wimbush. Atlanta: Scholars Press, 1992. = *Semeia* 58 (1992): 25–45. Reprinted in Goehring, *Ascetics, Society, and the Des-*

ert: Studies in Early Egyptian Monasticism (Harrisburg, Pa.: Trinity Press International, 1999), 53–72.

———. "The Encroaching Desert: Literary Production and Ascetic Space in Early Christian Egypt." *JECS* 1 (1993): 281–96. Reprinted in Goehring, *Ascetics, Society, and the Desert: Studies in Early Egyptian Monasticism* (Harrisburg, Pa.: Trinity Press International, 1999), 73–88.

———. "Melitian Monastic Organization: A Challenge to Pachomian Originality." *StPatr* 25 (1993): 388–95. Reprinted in Goehring, *Ascetics, Society, and the Desert: Studies in Early Egyptian Monasticism* (Harrisburg, Pa.: Trinity Press International, 1999), 187–95.

———. "Withdrawing from the Desert: Pachomius and the Development of Village Monasticism in Upper Egypt." *HTR* 89 (1996): 267–85. Reprinted in Goehring, *Ascetics, Society, and the Desert: Studies in Early Egyptian Monasticism* (Harrisburg, Pa.: Trinity Press International, 1999), 89–109.

———. "Monastic Diversity and Ideological Boundaries in Fourth-Century Christian Egypt." *JECS* 5 (1997): 61–84. Reprinted in Goehring, *Ascetics, Society, and the Desert: Studies in Early Egyptian Monasticism* (Harrisburg, Pa.: Trinity Press International, 1999), 196–218.

———. *Ascetics, Society, and the Desert: Studies in Early Egyptian Monasticism.* SAC. Harrisburg, Pa.: Trinity Press International, 1999.

———. "Remembering Abraham of Farshut: History, Hagiography, and the Fate of the Pachomian Tradition." *JECS* 14 (2006): 1–26.

Gordon, Richard. "Lucan's Erictho." In *Homo Viator,* ed. Michael Whitby, Philip Hardie, and Mary Whitby, 231–41. Bristol: Bristol Classical Press, 1987.

Gottstein, Alon Goshen. "The Body as Image of God in Rabbinic Literature." *HTR* 87 (1994): 171–95.

Grant, Robert. *Eusebius as Church Historian.* Oxford: Clarendon Press, 1980.

Gribomont, Jean. "L'historiographie du trone d'Alexandrie avec quelques remarques sur S. Mercure, S. Basile et S. Eusèbe de Samosate." *RSLR* 7 (1971): 478–90.

Griffith, Sidney H. "'Singles' in God's Service: Thoughts on the Ihidaye from the Works of Aphrahat and Ephraem the Syrian." *The Harp* 4 (1991): 145–59.

———. "'Monks,' 'Singles,' and the 'Sons of the Covenant': Reflections on Syriac Ascetic Terminology." In *Eulogēma: Studies in Honor of Robert Taft, S.J.,* ed. E. Carr, S. Parenti, A. A. Thiermeyer, and E. Velkovska, 141–60. StAns 110. Rome: [Centro Studi S. Anselmo,] 1993.

———. "Asceticism in the Church of Syria: The Hermeneutics of Early Syrian Monasticism." In *Asceticism,* ed. Vincent L. Wimbush and Richard Valantasis, 220–45. New York: Oxford University Press, 1995.

Grillmeier, Aloys. *Christ in Christian Tradition.* Trans. O. C. Dean. London: Mowbray, 1995.

Guerrier, Louis, with Sylvain Grébaut. *Le Testament en Galilée de Notre Seigneur Jésus Christ.* PO 9.3. Paris: Firmin-Didot, 1913.

Guignebert, C. "Les demi-chrétiens et leur place dans l'église antique." *RHR* 88 (1923): 65–102.

Guillaumont, Antoine. "Les 'Remnuoth' de saint Jérôme." In *Christianisme d'Égypte: Hommages à René-Georges Coquin.* CBibCopte 9. Paris: Peeters, 1995, 87–92.

Guillaumont, Antoine, Henri-Charles Puech, Gilles Quispel, Walter Till, and Yassah 'Abd Al Masîh. *The Gospel According to Thomas: Coptic Text Established and Translated.* Leiden: Brill, and New York: Harper & Row, 1959.

Gunther, J. J. "Syrian Christian Dualism." *VC* 25 (1971): 81–93.

Haase, Felix. *Die koptischen Quellen zum Konzil um Nicäa.* Paderborn: Ferdinand Schöningh, 1920.

Halsall, A. W. "Apostrophe." In *Historisches Wörterbuch der Rhetorik,* ed. Gert Ueding. 6 vols. 1:830–36. Darmstadt: Wissenschaftliche Buchgesellschaft, 1992.

Hartog, François. *Memories of Odysseus: Frontier Tales from Ancient Greece.* Trans. Janet Lloyd. Chicago: University of Chicago Press, 2001.

Hebbelynck, Adolphe, and Arnold van Lantschoot. *Codices Coptici Vaticani, Barberiniani, Borgiani, Rossiani.* Vatican City: Bibliotheca Vaticana, 1937.

Heine, Ronald E. "Reading the Bible with Origen." In *The Bible in Greek Christian Antiquity,* ed. Paul M. Blowers, 131–48. Notre Dame: University of Notre Dame Press, 1997.

Helderman, J. "Jablonski en Te Water. Twee Koptologen uit de tijd van de 'Verlichtung.'" *Phoenix* 30 (1984): 54–62.

Hengel, Martin. "Messianische Hoffnung und politischer 'Radikalismus' in der jüdisch-hellenistischen Diaspora." In *Apocalypticism in the Mediterranean World and the Near East: Proceedings of the International Colloquium on Apocalypticism, Uppsala, August 12–17, 1979,* ed. David Hellholm, 655–86. Tübingen: Mohr Siebeck, 1983.

Hill, Charles E. "The Epistula Apostolorum: An Asian Tract from the Time of Polycarp." *JECS* 7 (1999): 1–53.

Hills, Julian. *Tradition and Composition in the Epistula Apostolorum.* HDR 24. Minneapolis: Fortress Press, 1990.

Horn, Jürgen. *Studien zu den Märtyrern des nordlichen Oberägypten.* Göttinger Orientforschungen 15. Wiesbaden: Harrassowitz, 1986.

———. "Tria sunt in Aegypto genera monachorum: Die ägyptischen Bezeichnungen für die 'dritte Art' des Mönchtums bei Hieronymus und Johannes Cassianus." In *Quaerentes Scientiam: Festgabe für Wolfhart Westendorf zu seinem 70 Geburtstag,* ed. Heike Behlmer, 63–76. Göttingen: Seminar für Ägyptologie und Koptologie, 1994.

Horner, George William. *The Coptic Version of the New Testament in the Northern Dialect Otherwise Called Memphitic and Bohairic with Introduction, Critical Apparatus, and Literal English Translation. Vol. II. The Gospels of S. Luke and S. John Edited from MS. Huntington 17 in the Bodleian Library.* Oxford: Clarendon Press, 1898.

Hornschuh, Manfred. *Studien zur Epistula Apostolorum.* PTS 5. Berlin: Walter de Gruyter, 1965.

Horsley, G. H. R. *New Documents Illustrating Early Christianity: A Review of the Greek Inscriptions and Papyri Published in 1976.* North Ride, N.S.W.: Macquarie University, Ancient History Documentary Research Centre, 1981.

Hsia, R. Po-chia. *The Myth of Ritual Murder: Jews and Magic in Reformation Germany.* New Haven: Yale University Press, 1988.

Hyvernat, Henri. "Introduction." In E. Porcher, "Analyse de manuscripts coptes 131$^{1-8}$ de la Bibliothèque Nationale, avec indication des texts bibliques." *RdE* 1 (1933): 105–16.

———. Unpublished catalogue of the Coptic Manuscripts in the Pierpont Morgan Library—New York City, 1933. Washington, D.C.: Catholic University of America, Institute of Christian Oriental Research.

———, ed. *Les Actes des Martyrs de l'Égypte tires des manuscrits coptes de la Bibliothèque Vaticane et du Musee Borgia.* Paris: Ernest Leroux, 1886–87.

Irvine, Martin. *The Making of Textual Culture: "Grammatica" and Literary Theory, 350–1100.* Cambridge: Cambridge University Press, 1994.

Jablonski, Paul Ernst. *Pauli Ernesti Iablonskii Opuscula.* Ed. Iona Guilielmus te Water. 4 vols. Lugduni Batavorum: Luchtmans, 1804–13.

Jacoby, Adolf. "Der Name der Sarabaiten." *Recueil de travaux relatifs à la philologie et à l'archéologie égyptiennes et assyriennes* 34 [i.e., n.s. 2] (1912): 15–16.

Jakab, Attila. *Ecclesia alexandrina: Evolution sociale et institutionnelle du christianisme alexandrin (IIe et IIIe siècles).* Bern: Peter Lang, 2001.

Jerome. *Epistulae.* Ed. I. Hilberg. CSEL 54–56. Vienna: F. Tempsky, 1910–18.

Johnson, David W. "Coptic Sources of the History of the Patriarchs of Alexandria." Ph.D. diss., Catholic University of America, 1973.

———. "Further Fragments of a Coptic History of the Church: Cambridge Or.1699R." *Enchoria* 6 (1976): 7–17.

———. "Further Remarks on the Arabic History of the Patriarchs of Alexandria." *OrChr* 61 (1977): 103–16.

———. *A Panegyric on Macarius Bishop of Tkôw Attributed to Dioscorus of Alexandria.* CSCO 415–16. Louvain: Secrétariat du CorpusSCO, 1980.

———. "Anti-Chalcedonian Polemics in Coptic Texts, 451–641." In *The Roots of Egyptian Christianity,* ed. Birger A. Pearson and James E. Goehring, 216–34. SAC. Philadelphia: Fortress Press, 1986.

Johnson, George. "Obituary of Claude E. Shannon." *New York Times,* 27 February 2001, B7.

Johnston, Sarah Iles. "The Song of the *Iunx:* Magic and Rhetoric in *Pythian* 4." *TAPA* 125 (1995): 177–206.

Judge, E. A. "The Earliest Use of Monachos for 'Monk' (P. Coll. Youtie 77) and the Origins of Monasticism." *JAC* 20 (1977): 72–89.

Judge, E. A., and S. R. Pickering. "Papyrus Documentation of Church and Community in Egypt." *JAC* 20 (1977): 47–71.

Kemp, Eric W. "Bishops and Presbyters at Alexandria." *JEH* 6 (1955): 125–42.

Kennedy, George A. *Classical Rhetoric and Its Christian and Secular Tradition from Ancient to Modern Times.* 2d ed. Chapel Hill: University of North Carolina Press, 1999.

———, trans., with introduction and notes. *Progymnasmata: Greek Textbooks of Prose Composition and Rhetoric.* Atlanta: Society of Biblical Literature, 2003.

Khosroyev, Alexandr L. *Die Bibiothek von Nag Hammadi: Einige Probleme des Christentums in Ägypten während der ersten Jahrhunderte.* Altenberg: Oros Verlag, 1995.
Kimelman, Reuven. "R. Yohanan and Origen on the Song of Songs: A Third-Century Jewish-Christian Disputation." *HTR* 73 (July–October 1980): 567–95.
Klenk, Virginia. *Understanding Symbolic Logic.* Englewood Cliffs, N.J.: Prentice-Hall, 1983.
Klijn, A. F. J. "The 'Single One' in the Gospel of Thomas." *JBL* 81 (1962): 271–78.
———. "Jewish Christianity in Egypt." In *The Roots of Egyptian Christianity,* ed. Birger A. Pearson and James E. Goehring, 161–75. SAC. Philadelphia: Fortress Press, 1986.
Koester, Helmut. *Introduction to the New Testament.* Vol. 2, *History and Literature of Early Christianity.* 2d ed. New York: Walter de Gruyter, 2000.
Kraft, Robert A. *Barnabas and the Didache.* Vol. 3 of *The Apostolic Fathers: A New Translation and Commentary,* ed. Robert M. Grant. Toronto: Thomas Nelson and Sons, 1965.
Kramer, Bärbel, and John C. Shelton. *Das Archiv des Nepheros und verwandte Texte.* Aegyptiaca Treverensia 4. Mainz am Rhein: Philipp von Zabern, 1987.
Kramer, Johannes. *Glossaria bilinguia in papyris et membranis reperta.* Bonn: R. Habelt, 1983.
Krause, Martin. "Ein Vorschlagsschreiben für einen Priester." In *Lingua Restituta Orientalis: Festgabe für Julius Assfalg,* ed. Regine Schulz and Manfred Görg, 195–202. Ägypten und Altes Testament 20. Wiesbaden: In Kommission bei Otto Harrassowitz, 1990.
———. "Report on Research in Coptic Papyrology and Epigraphy." In *Acts of the Fifth International Congress of Coptic Studies, Washington, 12–15 August 1992,* ed. Tito Orlandi and David W. Johnson. 3 vols. 1:77–95. Rome: C.I.M., 1993.
Krawiec, Rebecca. *Shenoute and the Women of the White Monastery: Egyptian Monasticism in Late Antiquity.* Oxford: Oxford University Press, 2002.
———. "Clothes Make the Monk: The Rhetoric of Clothing in Late Antique Monasticism." Paper delivered at the "Living for Eternity: Monasticism in Egypt" symposium held at the University of Minnesota, 6–9 March 2003.
Kugener, M.-A., ed. *Zacharie le scholastique: Vie de Sévère.* PO 2.1. Paris: Firmin-Didot, 1904.
Kuhn, K. H., ed. and trans. *Letters and Sermons of Besa.* CSCO 157–58. Scriptores coptici 21–22. Louvain: Durbecq, 1956.
Lake, Kirsopp. *The Apostolic Fathers.* 2 vols. LCL. Cambridge: Harvard University Press, 1912.
Lamberton, Robert. *Homer the Theologian: Neoplatonist Allegorical Reading and the Growth of the Epic Tradition.* TCH. Berkeley and Los Angeles: University of California Press, 1986.
Lausberg, H. *Handbuch der literarischen Rhetorik.* 3d ed. Stuttgart: Franz Steiner, 1990.
Lawson, R. P. "Introduction." In *Origen, the Song of Songs: Commentary and Homilies.* Trans. R. P. Lawson. ACW 26. Westminster, Md.: Newman Press, 1957.
Layton, Bentley. *Catalogue of Coptic Literary Manuscripts in the British Library Acquired since the Year 1906.* London: British Library, 1987.
———. "Social Structure and Food Consumption in an Early Christian Monastery: The Evi-

dence of Shenoute's *Canons* and the White Monastery Federation A.D. 385–465." *Muséon* 115 (2002): 25–55.

———. *A Coptic Grammar with Chrestomathy and Glossary: Sahidic Dialect.* 2d ed. Porta linguarum orientalium, n.s. 20. Wiesbaden: Harrassowitz Verlag, 2004.

Lefort, L. Th. "Littérature bohaïrique." *Muséon* 44 (1931): 115–35.

———. *Les vies coptes de saint Pachôme et de ses premiers successeurs.* Louvain: Institut Orientaliste, 1943.

———. "La chasse aux reliques des martyrs en Égypte au IVᵉ siècle." *Nclio* 6 (1954): 225–30.

———, ed. and trans. *Œuvres de s. Pachôme et de ses disciples.* CSCO 159–60. Scriptores coptici 23–24. Louvain: L. Durbecq, 1956.

———. *S. Pachomii vitae sahidice scriptae.* CSCO 99–100. Scriptores coptici 9–10. Paris: E Typographeo Reipublicae, 1933.

Lemm, Oscar von, ed.. "Koptische Fragmente zur Patriarchengeschichte Alexandriens." *MASP, VIIe série* 36 (1888): 1–45.

———. *Das Triadon: Ein sahidisches Gedicht mit arabischer Übersetzung.* St. Petersburg: Académie Impériale des Sciences, 1903.

Llewelyn, S. R. *New Documents Illustrating Early Christianity.* Vol. 9, *A Review of the Greek Inscriptions and Papyri Published in 1986–87.* Grand Rapids: Eerdmans, 2002.

Löhr, Winfred. *Basilides und seine Schule: Eine Studie zur Theologie- und Kirchengeschichte des zweitzen Jahrhunderts.* WUNT 83. Tübingen: Mohr Siebeck, 1996.

Loofs, Friedrich. *Nestoriana.* Halle: Max Niemeyer, 1905.

Luft, Ulrich, ed. *Das Archiv von Illahun: Briefe 1.* HPSMB 1. Berlin: Akademie-Verlag, 1992.

MacCoull, Leslie S. B. "A Coptic Marriage Contract in the Pierpont Morgan Library." In *Actes du XVe congrès international de papyrologie,* ed. Jean Bingen and Georges Nachtergaell. 4 vols. 2:116–23. Brussels: Fondation Égyptologique Reine Élisabeth, 1978–79.

MacMullen, Ramsay. *Christianity and Paganism in the Fourth to Eighth Centuries.* New Haven: Yale University Press, 1997.

Mallon, André. "Catalogue des *Scalae* coptes de la Bibliothèque Nationale de Paris." *Mélanges de l'Université Saint Joseph, Beyrouth* 4 (1910): 57–90.

Manniche, Lise. *Ancient Egyptian Musical Instruments.* Munich: Deutscher Kunstverlag, 1975.

Markschies, Christoph. *Valentinus Gnosticus? Untersuchungen zur valentinianischen Gnosis mit einem Kommentar zu den Fragmenten Valentins.* WUNT 65. Tübingen: Mohr Siebeck, 1992.

Martin, Annick, and Micheline Albert. *Histoire "acephale" et index syriaque des "Lettres festales" d'Athanase d'Alexandrie.* SC 317. Paris: Éditions du Cerf, 1985.

Martin, Josef. *Antike Rhetorik, Technik und Methode.* HA 2.3. Munich: Beck, 1974.

Martin, Victor. "Rélève topographique des immeubles d'une metropole." *RPap* 2 (1962): 37–73.

Méhat, André. "'Vraie' et 'fausse' gnose d'après Clément d'Alexandrie." In *The Rediscovery of Gnosticism: Proceedings of the Conference at Yale March 1978.* Vol. 1, *The School of Valentinus,* ed. Bentley Layton, 426–33. SHR 41. Leiden: Brill, 1980.

Meyer, Birgit. "Beyond Syncretism: Translation and Diabolization in the Appropriation of

Protestantism in Africa." In *Syncretism/Anti-Syncretism: The Politics of Religious Synthesis*, ed. Charles Stewart and Rosalind Shaw, 45–68. London: Routledge, 1994.

———. *Translating the Devil: Religion and Modernity among the Ewe in Ghana.* Trenton: Africa World Press, 1999.

Miller, Patricia Cox. "Origen and the Witch of Endor: Toward an Iconoclastic Typology." In Patricia Cox Miller, *The Poetry of Thought in Late Antiquity: Essays in Imagination and Religion*, 200–210. Burlington, Vt.: Ashgate, 2001.

Modrzejewski, Joseph M. *The Jews of Egypt from Ramses II to Emperor Hadrian.* Trans. Robert Cornman. Princeton: Princeton University Press, 1997.

Morard, Françoise E. "Monachos, moine. Histoire du terme grec jusqu'au 4e siècle: Influences bibliques et gnostiques." *FZPhTh* 20 (1973): 332–411.

———. "Encore quelques réflexions sur monachos." *VC* 34 (1980): 395–401.

Moussa, Mark. "Abba Moses of Abydos." Master's thesis, Catholic University of America, 1998.

Müller, C. Detlef G. *Die alte koptische Predigt (Versuch eines Ueberblicks).* Ph.D. diss., Heidelberg 1953; Darmstadt 1954.

———. "Einige Bemerkungen zur 'ars praedicandi' der alten koptischen Kirche." *Muséon* 67 (1954): 231–70.

———. "Koptische Redekunst und Griechische Rhetorik." *Muséon* 69 (1956): 53–72.

———. "Koptische Homiletik." In *Kindlers Literatur Lexikon*, ed. Wolfgang von Einsiedel and Gert Woerner. 7 vols. 6:5339–42. Zürich: Kindler Verlag, 1970.

Munier, Henri. *Manuscrits coptes.* CGC 74. Cairo: IFAO, 1916.

———. *La Scala copte 44 de la Bibliothèque Nationale de Paris. Tome Premier: Transcription.* Bibliothèque d'études coptes 2. Cairo: Institut Français d'Archéologie Orientale, 1930.

Nagel, Peter. "Die Psalmoi Sarakoton des manichäischen psalmbuches." *OLZ* 62 (1967): 123–30.

———, trans. *Das Triadon: Ein sahidisches Lehrgedicht des 14. Jahrhunderts.* Wissenschaftliche Beiträge/Martin-Luther-Universität Halle-Wittenberg, 1983/23 (K7). Halle (Saale): Abt. Wissenschaftspublizistik der Martin-Luther-Universität Halle-Wittenberg, 1983.

Netton, I. R. "Riḥla." *EI²* 7, fasc. 139–40 (1994): 528.

Nippel, Wilfried. "The Construction of the 'Other.'" In *Greeks and Barbarians*, ed. Thomas Harrison, 278–310. New York: Routledge, 2002.

Nock, Arthur Darby. "Greek Novels and Egyptian Religion." In *Essays on Religion and the Ancient World*, ed. Zeph Stewart. 2 vols. 1:170–71. Oxford: Clarendon Press, 1972.

Norden, Eduard. *Die antike Kunstprosa vom VI. Jahrhundert v. Chr. bis in die Zeit der Renaissance.* 2 vols. Leipzig: Teubner, 1923.

Old, Hughes Oliphant. *The Reading and Preaching of the Scriptures in the Worship of the Christian Church.* Vol. 2, *The Patristic Age.* Grand Rapids: Eerdmans, 1998.

O'Leary, De Lacy. *The Saints of Egypt.* London: SPCK, and New York: Macmillan, 1939.

Olivar, Alexandre. *La predicación cristiana antigua.* BH 189. Barcelona: Editorial Herder, 1991.

Optatus. *Optatus: Against the Donatists.* Trans. Mark J. Edwards. TTH 27. Liverpool: Liverpool University Press, 1997.

Origen. *Origen: The Song of Songs: Commentary and Homilies.* Trans. R. P. Lawson. ACW 26. Westminster, Md.: Newman Press, 1957.

———. *Homélies sur Josué.* Ed. and trans. A. Jaubert. SC 71. Paris: Éditions du Cerf, 1960.

———. *Origen: Contra Celsum.* Trans. and ed. Henry Chadwick. Cambridge: Cambridge University Press, 1965.

———. *Origen: On First Principles.* Trans. G. W. Butterworth, with an introduction by Henri de Lubac. Gloucester, Mass.: Peter Smith, 1973.

———. *Traité des principes.* Ed. and trans. H. Crouzel and M. Simonetti. SC 268. Paris: Éditions du Cerf, 1980.

———. *Homélies sur le Lévitique.* Ed. and trans. M. Borret. SC 286. Paris: Éditions du Cerf, 1981.

———. *Origen: Homilies on Genesis and Exodus.* Trans. Ronald E. Heine. FCNT. Washington, D.C.: Catholic University of America Press, 1982.

———. *Homélies sur l'Exode.* Ed. and trans. M. Borret. SC 321. Paris: Éditions du Cerf, 1985.

———. *Origen: Homiliae in Leviticum.* Trans. Gary Wayne Barkley. FCNT. Washington, D.C.: Catholic University of America Press, 1990.

———. *Commentaire sur le Cantique des Cantiques.* Ed. and trans. Luc Brésard and Henri Crouzel, with Marcel Borret. SC 375–76. Paris: Éditions du Cerf, 1991.

Orlandi, Tito. "Uno scritto di Teofilo alessandrino sulla distruzione del Serapeum?" *Par* 121 (1968): 295–304.

———. *Storia della Chiesa di Alessandria.* TDSA 17 and 31. Milan: Cisalpino, 1968 and 1970.

———. *Studi Copti: 1) Un encomio di Marco evangelista; 2) Le fonti copte della storia dei patriarchi di Alessandra; 3) La leggenda di S. Mercurio.* TDSA 22. Milan: Cisalpino, 1968.

———. *Testi Copti: 1) Encomio di Atanasio; 2) Vita di Atanasio.* TDSA 21. Milan: Cisalpino, 1968.

———. "Un frammento copto di Teofilo di Alessandria." *RivSO* 44 (1969): 23–26.

———. "La versione copta (saidica) dell'Encomio di Pietro Alessandrino." *RivSO* 45 (1970): 151–75.

———. "Un projet milanais concernant les manuscripts coptes du Monastère Blanc." *Muséon* 85 (1972): 403–13.

———. "Ricerche su una storia ecclesiastica alessandrina del IV secolo." *VetChr* 11 (1974): 269–312.

———. "Gregorio di Nissa nella letteratura copta." *VetChr* 18 (1981): 333–39.

———. "A Catechesis against Apocryphal Texts by Shenute and the Gnostic Texts of Nag Hammadi." *HTR* 75 (1982): 85–95.

———. "Giustificazioni dell'encratismo nei testi monastici copti del IV–V secolo." In *La tradizione dell'enkrateia: Motivazione ontologiche e protologiche, atti del Colloquio internazionale, Milano, 20–23 aprile 1982,* ed. Ugo Bianchi, 341–68. Rome: Edizioni dell'Ateneo, 1985.

———. "Nuovi frammenti della Historia Ecclesiastica copta." In *Studi in onore di Edda Bresciani*, ed. S. F. Bondì, 363–84. Pisa: Giardini, 1985.
———. "Coptic Literature." In *The Roots of Egyptian Christianity*, ed. Birger A. Pearson and James E. Goehring, 51–81. SAC. Philadelphia: Fortress Press, 1986.
———. "Due fogli papiracei da Medinet Madi (Fayum): L'historia Horsiesi." *EVO* 13 (1990): 109–26.
———. "Cycles." In *The Coptic Encyclopedia*, ed. Aziz S. Atiya. 8 vols. 3:666–68. New York: Macmillan, 1991.
———. "La traduzione copta di Eusebio di Cesarea, HE." *AttiLin*, 9th ser., 5 (1994): 399–456.
———. "Claudio Martire e Anatolio di Laodicea: Un problema letterario fra III e VI secolo." In *Divitiae Aegypti: Koptologische und verwandte Studien zu Ehren von Martin Krause*, ed. Cäcilia Fluck, 237–45. Wiesbaden: L. Reichert, 1995.
———. "The Library of the Monastery of Saint Shenute at Atripe." In *Perspectives on Panopolis: An Egyptian Town from Alexander the Great to the Arab Conquest. Acts from an International Symposium Held in Leiden on 16, 17 and 18 December 1998 (P.L. Bat. 31)*, ed. A. Egberts, Brian Paul Muhs, and Joep van der Vliet, 211–31. Leiden: Brill, 2002.
———, ed. and trans. *Shenute contra Origenistas: Testo con introduzione e traduzione*. Rome: Centro Italiano Microfiches, 1985.
Orlandi, Tito, and Sara Di Giuseppe Camaioni. *Passione e miracoli di S. Mercurio*. TDSA 54. Milan: Cisalpino-Goliardica, 1976.
Orr, David G. "Roman Domestic Religion: The Evidence of the Household Shrines." *ANRW* 2 (1978): 1557–91.
Paget, James C. *The Epistle of Barnabas: Outlook and Background*. WUNT 64. Tübingen: Mohr Siebeck, 1994.
Parker, Robert. *Miasma: Pollution and Purification in Early Greek Religion*. Oxford: Clarendon Press, 1983.
Parmentier, Martin. "Evagrius of Pontus 'Letter to Melania.'" *Bijdragen, tijdschrift voor filosofie en theologie* 46 (1985): 2–38.
Pearson, Birger A. "The Pierpont Morgan Fragments of a Coptic Enoch Apocryphon." In *Studies on the Testament of Abraham*, ed. G. W. E. Nickelsburg, 227–83. SBLSCS 6. Missoula: Scholars Press, 1976.
———. "Philo, Gnosis, and the New Testament." In *The New Testament and Gnosis: Essays in Honour of Robert McL. Wilson*, ed. A. H. B. Logan and A. J. M. Wedderburn, 73–89. Edinburgh: T. and T. Clark, 1983. Reprinted in *Gnosticism, Judaism, and Egyptian Christianity*, ed. Birger A. Pearson (Minneapolis: Fortress Press, 1990), 165–82.
———. "Earliest Christianity in Egypt: Some Observations." In *The Roots of Egyptian Christianity*, ed. Birger A. Pearson and James E. Goehring, 132–60. SAC. Philadelphia: Fortress Press, 1986.
———. "Gnosticism in Early Egyptian Christianity." In *Gnosticism, Judaism, and Egyptian Christianity*, ed. Birger A. Pearson, 194–213. SAC. Minneapolis: Fortress Press, 1990.

———. "Pre-Valentinian Gnosticism in Alexandria." In *The Future of Early Christianity: Essays in Honor of Helmut Koester*, ed. Birger A. Pearson, 455–66. Minneapolis: Fortress Press, 1991.

———. "Christianity in Egypt." In *ABD*, ed. David Noel Freedman, 1:954–60. New York: Doubleday, 1992.

———. "The *Acts of Mark* and the Topography of Ancient Alexandria." In *Alexandrian Studies in Memoriam Daoud Abdu Daoud*, ed. Nabil Swelim, 239–46. SAA 45 (1993). Alexandria: Archeological Society of Alexandria, 1994. Reprinted in SBLSP (Atlanta: Scholars Press, 1997), 273–84.

———. "The Coptic Inscriptions in the Church of St. Antony." In *Monastic Visions: Wall Paintings in the Monastery of St. Antony at the Red Sea*, ed. Elizabeth S. Bolman, 217–39. New Haven: Yale University Press, 2002.

———. "Cracking a Conundrum: Christian Origins in Egypt." *StTh* 57 (2003): 1–15.

———. *Gnosticism and Christianity in Roman and Coptic Egypt*. SAC. New York: T. & T. Clark International, 2004.

———. "Basilides the Gnostic." In *A Companion to Second-Century Christian "Heretics,"* ed. Antti Marjanen and Petri Luomanen, 1–31. VCSupp 76. Leiden: Brill, 2005.

———, ed. *Gnosticism, Judaism, and Egyptian Christianity*. SAC. Minneapolis: Fortress Press, 1990.

Pearson, Birger A., and James E. Goehring, eds. *The Roots of Egyptian Christianity*. SAC. Philadelphia: Fortress Press, 1986.

Pedersen, Nils Arne. *Studies in the Sermon on the Great War: Investigations of a Manichaean-Coptic Text from the Fourth Century*. Aarhus: Aarhus University Press, 1996.

Peirce, Charles Sanders. "On an Improvement in Boole's Calculus of Logic (Presented 12 March 1867)." *PAAAS* 7 (1865–68): 250–61.

Perrin, Nicholas. *Thomas and Tatian*. Academica Biblica 5. Atlanta: Society of Biblical Literature, 2002.

Petersen, Theodore C. Unpublished notebook. Coptic Documentary Papyri in the Pierpont Morgan Collection, document 12. Washington, D.C.: Catholic University of America, Institute of Christian Oriental Research, n.d.

Philo of Alexandria. *Philo of Alexandria: The Contemplative Life, the Giants, and Selections*. Ed. and trans. David Winston. CWS. New York: Paulist Press, 1981.

Piankoff, A. "The Osireion of Seti I at Abydos during the Greco-Roman Period and the Christian Occupation." *BSAC* 15 (1958–60): 134–37.

Poirier, Paul-Hubert. "L'Évangile selon Thomas (*log.* 16 et 23) et Aphraate (*Dém.* XVIII, 10–11)." In *Mélanges Antoine Guillaumont: Contributions à l'étude des christianismes orientaux*, 15–18. Cahiers d'Orientalisme 20. Genève: Patrick Cramer, 1988.

Polotsky, H. J. "Deux verbes auxiliaries méconnus du copte." *GLECS* 3 (1937): 1–3. Reprinted in Polotsky, *Collected Papers* (Jerusalem: Magnes Press, 1971), 99–101.

———. "Une règle concernant l'emploi des formes verbales dans la phrase interrogative en néo-égyptien." *ASAE* 40 (1940): 241–45. Reprinted in Polotsky, *Collected Papers* (Jerusalem: Magnes Press, 1971), 33–37.

———. *Études de syntaxe copte.* Cairo: Société d'Archéologie Copte, 1944. Reprinted in Polotsky, *Collected Papers* (Jerusalem: Magnes Press, 1971), 102–207.

———. *Collected Papers.* Jerusalem: Magnes Press, 1971.

Quaegebeur, Jan. *Le dieu égyptien Shaï dans la religion et l'onomastique.* OLA 2. Louvain: Leuven University Press, 1975.

Quatremère, Étienne Marc. *Recherches critiques et historiques sur la langue et la littérature de l'Égypte.* Paris: Imprimerie Impériale, 1808.

———. *Memoires geographiques et historiques sur l'Égypte, et sur quelques voisines.* 2 vols. Paris: F. Schoell, 1811.

Quecke, Hans. *Das Lukasevangelium Saïdisch: Text der Handschrift PPalau Rib. Inv.-Nr. 181 mit den Varianten der Handschrift M 569.* Barcelona: Papyrologica Castroctaviana, 1977.

———. *Das Johannesevangelium Saïdisch: Text der Handschrift PPaulau Rib. Inv.-Nr. 183 mit den Varianten der Handschriften 813 und 814 der Chester Beatty Library und der Handschrift M 569.* Rome: Papyrologica Castroctaviana, 1984.

Rassart-Debergh, Marguerite. "De l'icône païenne à l'icône chrétienne." *MCopte* 18 (1990): 39–70.

Rassart-Debergh, Marguerite, and J. Ries, eds. *Actes du IVe Congrès Copte, Louvain-la-Neuve, 5–10 septembre 1988.* 2 vols. Louvain-la-Neuve: Université Catholique de Louvain, Institut Orientaliste, 1992.

Rénaudot, Eusèbe. *Historia Patriarcharum Alexandrinorum Jacobitarum a D. Marco usque ad finem saeculi XIII.* Paris: Franciscum Fournier, 1713.

Revillout, Eugène. "Le Concile de Nicée." *JA* 7 (1875): 209–66.

Riedel, Wilhelm. *Die Kirchenrechtsquellen des Patriarchats Alexandrien. Zusammengestellt und zum Teil übersetzt.* Leipzig: A. Deichert'sche Verlagsbuchhandlung, 1900.

Riedel, Wilhelm, and Walter E. Crum. *The Canons of Athanasius of Alexandria: The Arabic and Coptic Versions Edited and Translated with Introductions, Notes, and Appendices.* London: Williams and Norgate, 1904.

Ritter, Adolf M. "De Polycarp à Clément: Aux origins d'Alexandrie chrétienne." In *ΑΛΕΞΑΝΔPINA: Hellénisme, judaïsme et christianisme à Alexandrie. Mélanges offerts au P. Claude Mondésert,* 151–72. Paris: Éditions du Cerf, 1987.

Rives, J. B. "Human Sacrifice among Pagans and Christians." *JRS* 85 (1995): 65–85.

Roberts, Colin H. *Manuscript, Society, and Belief in Early Christian Egypt.* The Schweich Lectures of the British Academy, 1977. London: Oxford University Press, 1979.

Robinson, James M., ed. *The Nag Hammadi Library in English.* 4th rev. ed. Leiden: Brill, 1996.

Roncaglia, Martiniano P. "Dioscorus I." In *The Coptic Encyclopedia,* ed. Aziz S. Atiya. 8 vols. 3:912–15. New York: Macmillan, 1991.

Rousseau, Philip. "Orthodoxy and the Coenobite." *StPatr* 30 (1997): 241–58.

———. *Pachomius: The Making of a Community in Fourth-Century Egypt.* TCH 6. Berkeley and Los Angeles: University of California Press, 1985. Updated version with new preface, 1999.

Rubenson, Samuel. *The Letters of St. Antony: Origenist Theology, Monastic Tradition, and the Making of a Saint.* Bibliotheca historico-ecclesiastica Lundensis 24. Lund: Lund University Press, 1990. Reprinted with an English translation of the Letters of Antony as *The Letters of St. Antony: Monasticism and the Making of a Saint* (Minneapolis: Fortress Press, 1995).

Runia, David T. *Philo in Early Christian Literature: A Survey.* CRINT 3.3. Assen: Van Gorcum, and Minneapolis: Fortress Press, 1993.

Sachot, M. "Homilie." *RAC* 16:148–75.

Sauneron, Serge. *Villes et légendes d'Égypte.* 2d ed. Cairo: IFAO, 1983.

Saussure, Ferdinand de. *Cours de linguistique générale.* Paris: Payot, 1972.

Schmidt, Carl, Pierre Lacau, and Isaak Wajnberg. *Gespräche Jesu mit seinem Jüngern nach der Auferstehung: Ein katholisch-apostolisches Sendschreiben des 2. Jahrhunderts.* TU 43. Leipzig: J. C. Hinrichs, 1919.

Schneemelcher, Wilhelm, ed. *New Testament Apocrypha.* 2 vols. Rev. ed. Trans. Robert McLachlan Wilson. Cambridge: James Clarke and Co., and Louisville, Ky.: Westminster/John Knox Press, 1991, 1992.

Schneider, Hans D. *The Small Masterpieces of Egyptian Art: Selections from the Myers Museum at Eton College.* Leiden: Rijksmuseum von Oudheden, 2003.

Schöpsdau, K. "Exordium." In *Historisches Wörterbuch der Rhetorik,* ed. Gert Ueding. 6 vols. 3:136–40. Darmstadt: Wissenschaftliche Buchgesellschaft, 1996.

Schroeder, Caroline T. "Disciplining the Monastic Body: Asceticism, Ideology, and Gender in the Egyptian Monastery of Shenoute of Atripe." Ph.D. diss., Duke University, 2002.

———. "'A Suitable Abode for Christ': The Church Building as Symbol of Ascetic Renunciation in Early Monasticism." *CH* 73 (2004): 472–521.

Sethe, Kurt. "Untersuchungen über die ägyptischen Zahlwörter." *ZÄS* 47 (1910): 1–41.

Shannon, Claude E. "A Symbolic Analysis of Relay and Switching Circuits." *TAIE* 57 (1938): 713–23. Reprinted in *Claude Elwood Shannon: Collected Papers,* ed. N. J. A. Sloane and Aaron D. Wyner (New York: Institute of Electrical and Electronics Engineers, 1993), 471–95.

———. *The Mathematical Theory of Communication. Bell System Technical Journal* (July 1948): 379–423, and (October 1948): 623–56. Reprinted with minor corrections and additions in Claude E. Shannon and Warren Weaver, *The Mathematical Theory of Communication* (Urbana: University of Illinois Press, 1963).

———. "The Bandwagon." *Institute of Radio Engineers: Transactions on Information Theory* (became *IEEE*) 2 (1956): 3. Reprinted in *Claude Elwood Shannon: Collected Papers,* ed. N. J. A. Sloane and Aaron D. Wyner (New York: Institute of Electrical and Electronics Engineers, 1993), 462.

———. *Claude Elwood Shannon: Collected Papers.* Ed. N. J. A. Sloane and Aaron D. Wyner. New York: Institute of Electrical and Electronics Engineers, 1993.

Shannon, Claude E., and Warren Weaver. *The Mathematical Theory of Communication.* Urbana: University of Illinois Press, 1963.

Sheridan, J. Mark. *Rufus of Shotep: Homilies on the Gospels of Matthew and Luke; Introduction, Text, Translation, Commentary.* Unione Accademica Nazionale. CMCL. Rome: C.I.M., 1998.

———. "A Homily on the Death of the Virgin Mary Attributed to Evodius of Rome." In *Coptic Studies on the Threshold of a New Millennium: Proceedings of the Seventh International Congress of Coptic Studies, Leiden 2000,* ed. Mat Immerzeel and Jacques Van der Vliet, OLA 132–33, 132.393–405. Louvain: Peeters, 2004.

Shisha-Halevy, Ariel. "Bohairic." In *The Coptic Encyclopedia,* ed. Aziz S. Atiya. 8 vols. 8:53–60. New York: Macmillan, 1991.

Shoemaker, Stephen J. "The Sahidic Coptic Homily on the Dormition of the Virgin Attributed to Evodius of Rome: An Edition from Morgan MSS 596 & 598 with Translation." *AB* 14 (1999): 241–83.

———. *Ancient Traditions of the Virgin Mary's Dormition and Assumption.* OECS. Oxford: Oxford University Press, 2002.

Smelik, K. A. D., and E. A. Hemelrijk. "'Who knows not what monsters demented Egypt worships?' Opinions on Egyptian Animal Worship in Antiquity as Part of the Ancient Conception of Egypt." *ANRW* 2 (1984): 1852–2357.

Smith, Mark. "Dating Anthropoid Mummy Cases from Akhmim: The Evidence of the Demotic Inscriptions." In *Portraits and Masks: Burial Customs in Roman Egypt,* ed. M. L. Bierbrier, 66–71. London: British Museum, 1997.

Smith, Morton. *Clement of Alexandria and a Secret Gospel of Mark.* Cambridge: Harvard University Press, 1973.

Speyer, Wolfgang. *Die literarische Fälschung im heidnischen und christlichen Altertum: Ein Versuch ihrer Deutung.* Munich: C. H. Beck, 1971.

———. "Fälschung, pseudoepigraphische freie Erfindung und 'echte' religiöse Pseudepigraphie." In *Pseudepigraha I,* ed. Kurt von Fritz, 331–66. Vandouevres-Geneve: Fondation Hardt, 1972.

Spiegelberg, Wilhelm. *Koptisches Handwörterbuch.* Heidelberg: Carl Winters Universitätsbuchhandlung, 1921.

Stander, Hendrik. "Stylistic Devices and Homiletic Techniques in Ps.-Epiphanius' Festal Sermons." In *Nova et Vetera: Patristic Studies in Honor of Thomas Patrick Halton,* ed. John Petruccione, 96–114. Washington, D.C.: Catholic University of America Press, 1998.

Steiger, T. "Homilie." In *Historisches Wörterbuch der Rhetorik,* ed. Gert Ueding. 6 vols. 3:1510–21. Darmstadt: Wissenschaftliche Buchgesellschaft, 1996.

Steindorff, Georg. "Zwei altkoptische Mumienetiketten." *ZÄS* 28 (1890): 49–53.

Stern, Ludwig. *Koptische Grammatik.* Leipzig: T. O. Weigel, 1880. Reprint, Osnabrück: Biblio Verlag, 1971.

Stevens, Anna. "The Material Evidence for Domestic Religion at Amarna and Preliminary Remarks on Its Interpretation." *JEA* 89 (2003): 143–68.

Stewart-Sykes, Alistair. "The Asian Context for the New Prophecy and of *Epistula Apostolorum.*" *VC* 51 (1997): 416–38.

———. *The Lamb's High Feast: Melito, Peri Pascha, and the Quartodeciman Paschal Liturgy of Sardis*. VCSupp 42. Leiden: Brill, 1998.

Stirewalt, Luther. *Studies in Ancient Greek Epistolography*. Atlanta: Scholars Press, 1993.

Struik, Dirk J. *A Concise History of Mathematics*. 4th rev. ed. New York: Dover Publications, 1987.

Taylor, Joan E. *Jewish Women Philosophers of First-Century Alexandria: Philo's "Therapeutae" Reconsidered*. Oxford: Oxford University Press, 2003.

Telfer, W. "Episcopal Succession in Egypt." *JEH* 3 (1952): 1–13.

Thompson, Herbert. "Dioscorus and Shenoute." In *Recueil d'études égyptologiques dédiées à la mémoire de Jean-François Champollion à l'occasion du centenaire de la lettre à M. Dacier relative à l'alphabet des hiéroglyphes phonétiques lue à l'Académie des inscriptions et belles-lettres le 27 septembre 1822*, 367–76. BEHE 234. Paris: Librairie Ancienne Honoré Champion, Édouard Champion, 1922.

———. *The Gospel of St. John According to the Earliest Coptic Manuscript: Edited with a Translation*. London: British School of Archaeology in Egypt, 1923.

Till, Walter, ed. "Life of Moses of Abydos." In *Koptische Heiligen- und Martyrerlegenden*, ed. Walter Till, 46–81. Rome: Pontifical Institute for Oriental Studies, 1936.

Torjesen, Karen Jo. *Hermeneutical Procedure and Theological Method in Origen's Exegesis*. PTS 28. Berlin: Walter de Gruyter, 1986.

Urbach, Ephraim Elimelech. "The Homiletical Interpretations of the Sages and the Exposition of Origen on Canticles, and the Jewish-Christian Disputation." *ScrHier* 22 (1971): 247–75.

Valantasis, Richard. "The Nuptial Chamber Revisited: The *Acts of Thomas* and Cultural Intertextuality." *Semeia* 80 (1997): 261–76.

Van Cauwenbergh, Paul. *Étude sur les moines d'Égypte depuis le Concile de Chalcédoine (451) jusqu'à l'invasion arabe (640)*. Paris: P. Geuthner, 1914. Reprint, Milan: Cisalpino Goliardica, 1973.

Van Dam, Raymond. "From Paganism to Christianity in Late Antique Gaza." *Viator* 16 (1985): 1–20.

Van den Broek, Rouel. "Jewish and Platonic Speculations in Early Alexandrian Theology: Eugnostus, Philo, Valentinus, and Origen." In *The Roots of Egyptian Christianity*, ed. Birger A. Pearson and James E. Goehring, 190–203. SAC. Philadelphia: Fortress Press, 1986.

———. "The Authentikos Logos: A New Document of Christian Platonism." In *Studies in Gnosticism and Alexandrian Christianity*, ed. Rouel van den Broek, 206–34. NHMS 39. Leiden: Brill, 1996.

———. "Der Bericht des koptischen Kyrillos von Jerusalem über das Hebräerevangelium." In *Studies in Gnosticism and Alexandrian Christianity*, ed. Rouel van den Broek, 142–56. NHMS 39. Leiden: Brill, 1996.

———. "Juden und Christen in Alexandrien im 2. und 3. Jahrhundert." In *Studies in Gnosticism and Alexandrian Christianity*, ed. Rouel van den Broek, 181–96. NHMS 39. Leiden: Brill, 1996.

Van den Hoek, Annewies. *Clement of Alexandria and His Use of Philo in the Stromateis: An Early Christian Reshaping of a Jewish Model.* VCSupp 3. Leiden: Brill, 1988.

———. "How Alexandrian Was Clement of Alexandria? Reflections on Clement and His Alexandrian Background." *HeyJ* 31 (1990): 179–94.

Van der Vliet, Jacques. "Spätantikes Heidentum in Ägypten im Spiegel der koptischen Literatur." In *Begegnung von Heidentum und Christentum im spätantiken Ägypten,* ed. Dietrich Willers, 99–130. RB 1. Riggisberg: Abegg-Stiftung, 1993.

Van Lantschoot, Arnold. *Recueil des colophons des manuscrits chrétiens d'Égypte.* BiM 1. Louvain: J.-B. Istas, 1929.

Veilleux, Armand. "Le problème des Vies de Saint Pachôme." *RAM* 42 (1966): 287–305.

———. *La liturgie dans le cénobitisme pachômien au quatrième siècle.* SA 57. Rome: Herder, 1968.

———. *Pachomian Koinonia.* 3 vols. CSS 45–47. Kalamazoo: Cistercian Publications, 1980–82.

Vis, Henri de. *Homélies coptes de la Vaticane 2.* CBC 6. Louvain: Peeters, 1990.

Vivian, Tim. *St. Peter of Alexandria: Bishop and Martyr.* SAC. Philadelphia: Fortress Press, 1988.

Volkmann, R. *Rhetorik der Griechen und Römer.* HKA 2, 3. 3d ed. Ed. Caspar Hammer. Munich: Beck, 1901.

Vycichl, Werner. *Dictionnaire étymologique de la langue copte.* Louvain: Peeters, 1983.

Walsh, Andrew. "Preserving Bodies, Saving Souls: Religious Incongruity in a Northern Malagasy Mining Town." *JRAfr* 32 (2002): 366–92.

Wansleben, Johann Michael. *Histoire de l'Église d'Alexandrie, fondée par S. Marc, que nous appelons celle des Jacobites-Coptes.* Paris: Chez la Veuve Clousier et Pierre Promé, 1677.

Wessely, Carl. *Griechische und koptische Texte theologischen Inhalts.* 5 vols. StPal 9, 11 12, 15, 18. Leipzig: E. Avenarius, 1909–17.

Westendorf, Wolfhart. *Koptisches Handwörterbuch.* Heidelberg: Carl Winter Universitätsverlag, 1965, 1977.

Wheeler, Samuel. *Deconstruction as Analytic Philosophy.* CMP. Stanford: Stanford University Press, 2000.

White, Caroline. *Early Christian Lives.* London: Penguin Books, 1998.

Widdicombe, Peter. *The Fatherhood of God from Origen to Athanasius.* OTM. Oxford: Clarendon Press, and New York: Oxford University Press, 1994.

Williams, Michael Allen. "Interpreting the Nag Hammadi Library as 'Collection(s)' in the History of 'Gnosticism(s).'" In *Les textes de Nag Hammadi et le problème de leur classification,* ed. Louis Painchaud and Anne Pasquier, 3–50. Louvain: Peeters, 1995.

———. *Rethinking "Gnosticism:" An Argument for Dismantling a Dubious Category.* Princeton: Princeton University Press, 1996.

Winkelmann, Friedhelm. "Die handschriftliche Überlieferung der Vita Metrophanis et Alexandri." *StPatr* 7 = TU 92 (1966): 106–14.

———. *Untersuchungen zur Kirchengeschichte des Gelasios von Kaisareia.* SDAW, 1965, no. 3. Berlin: Akademie-Verlag, 1966.

Winkler, Jack J. "Lollianos and the Desperadoes." *JHS* 100 (1980): 155–81.
Winlock, H. *The Monastery of Epiphanius at Thebes.* 2 vols. New York: [Metropolitan Museum of Art,] 1926.
Winston, David. "Philo and the Contemplative Life." In *Jewish Spirituality from the Bible through the Middle Ages,* ed. Arthur Green, 198–231. WS 13. New York: Crossroad, 1988.
Wipszycka, Ewa. "La christianisation de l'Égypte aux IVe–VIe siècles. Aspects sociaux et ethniques." *Aegyptus* 68 (1988): 117–65. Reprinted in Ewa Wipszycka, *Études sur le christianisme dans l'Égypte de l'antiquité tardive* (Rome: Institutum Patristicum Augustinianum, 1996), 63–105.
———. "Fonctionnement de l'Église égyptienne aux IVe–VIIIe siècles (sur quelques aspects)." In *Itinéraires d'Égypte: Mélanges offerts au père Maurice Martin s.j.,* ed. Christian Décobert, 115–45. Bibliothèque d'étude 107. Cairo: IFAO, 1992. Reprinted in Ewa Wipszycka, *Études sur la christianisme dans l'Égypte de l'antiquité tardive* (Rome: Institutum Patristicum Augustinianum, 1996), 195–224.
———. "Les ordres mineurs dans l'eglise d'Égypte du IVe au VIIIe siècle." *JJP* 23 (1993): 181–215. Reprinted in Ewa Wipszycka, *Études sur la chistianisme dans l'Égypte de l'antiquité tardive* (Rome: Institutum Patristicum Augustinianum, 1996), 225–55.
———. "Le monachisme égyptien et les villes." *Trauvaux et mémoires* 12 (1994): 1–44. Reprinted in Ewa Wipszycka, *Études sur le christianisme dans l'Égypte de l'antiquité tardive* (Rome: Institutum Patristicum Augustinianum, 1996), 281–336.
———. *Études sur le christianisme dans l'Égypte de l'antiquité tardive.* SEAug 52. Rome: Institutum Patristicum Augustinianum, 1996.
———. "Les communautés monastiques dans l'Égypte Byzantine." In *Valeur et distance: Identités et sociétés en Égypte,* ed. Christian Décobert, 71–82. Collection l'atelier méditerranéen. Paris: Maisonneuve et Larose, 2000.
———. "Ἀναχωρητής, ἐρημίτης, ἔγκλειστος, ἀποτακτικός. Sur la terminologie monastique en Égypte." *JJP* 31 (2001): 147–68.
Young, Dwight W. "Additional Fragments of Shenute's *Eighth Canon*." *APF* 44 (1998): 47–68.
———. "Pages from a Copy of Shenute's *Eighth Canon*." *Orientalia* 67 (1998): 64–84.
Zanetti, Ugo. "La vie de saint Jean higoumène de Scété au VIIe siècle." *AB* 114 (1996): 273–405.
———. "Arabe serākūdā = copte sarakote = 'gyrovagues' dans la vie de s. Jean de Scété." *AB* 115 (1997): 280.
Zelzer, Michaela. "Die Briefliteratur." In *Neues Handbuch der Literaturwissenschaft.* Vol. 4, *Spätantike mit einem Panorama der byzantinischen Literatur,* ed. Lodewijk J. Engels and Heinz Hofmann, 321–54. Wiesbaden: Aula, 1997.
Zoega, Georg. *Catalogus Codicum Copticorum Manuscriptorum qui in Museo Borgiano Velitris Adservantur.* Rome: Sacrae Congregationis de Propaganda Fide, 1810.

CONTRIBUTORS

Monica J. Blanchard
CURATOR, SEMITICS/ICOR LIBRARIES
The Catholic University of America
Washington, D.C.

Daniel Boyarin
HERMANN P. AND SOPHIA TAUBMAN PROFESSOR
OF TALMUDIC CULTURE
University of California
Berkeley, California

Leo Depuydt
ASSOCIATE PROFESSOR OF EGYPTOLOGY
Brown University
Providence, Rhode Island

David Frankfurter
PROFESSOR OF HISTORY AND RELIGIOUS STUDIES
University of New Hampshire
Durham, New Hampshire

James E. Goehring
PROFESSOR OF RELIGION
University of Mary Washington
Fredericksburg, Virginia

CONTRIBUTORS

Tito Orlandi
PROFESSOR OF COPTIC STUDIES
University of Rome
Rome, Italy

Birger A. Pearson
PROFESSOR EMERITUS OF RELIGIOUS STUDIES
University of California
Santa Barbara, California

Philip Rousseau
ANDREW W. MELLON PROFESSOR OF EARLY CHRISTIAN STUDIES
The Catholic University of America
Washington, D.C.

Mark Sheridan
VICE RECTOR AND DEAN OF THE FACULTY
Pontificio Ateneo S. Anselmo
Rome, Italy

Janet A. Timbie
ADJUNCT ASSOCIATE PROFESSOR
The Catholic University of America
Washington, D.C.

Robin Darling Young
ASSOCIATE PROFESSOR OF THEOLOGY
University of Notre Dame
South Bend, Indiana

GENERAL INDEX

Abel, killing of, 38
Abilius, 106n40
Abraham of Farshut, xi, 158–75
abstraction, faculty of, 87n27
abuse, terms of, 60
Acacius of Caesarea, 5, 11
Achillas, 16
actions. *See* works
Acts of Mark, 98
Adam, 114; burial of, 38, 39
Africa: atrocity folklore in, 186
Agathos Daimon, 178–82
Agrippinus, 14
Akiva, Rabbi, 127
Alarichus, 17t
Alcock, Anthony, 53–54
Alexander, 16, 17t
Alexandria (Egypt): bishops of, 4, 15–16, 17t, 19–20, 105–6; Christianity in, 4–24, 56, 97–111; Church in, 4–24; gods of, 178; Judaism in, 98–105, 114; man of, 51n111; patriarchate in, 4, 15, 23. *See also History of the Patriarchs of Alexandria*
Allberry, C. R. C., 54–55
allegory: Christian, 116–24; as interpretation, xi, 113, 115–18, 139; lack of in Judaism, 126–29
Allogenes, 143
altars, household, 180–82
Amélineau, Émile, 49n3, 62, 69, 70
anaphora, 31–39, 41–42, 48
Anatolius, 17t, 163n17
anchorites, 49–50, 107–8
angelikos bios, 136
angels, 125, 147–48; community of, 136, 139; grieving of, 39; homilies on, 26; transformation into, 136–37

anger: deliverance from, 132, 133, 134, 137–38; divine, 139
animals: violence of, 138–39
Annianus, 14, 106n40
annoyance: etymology of, 55
anointing, 34, 143
Anthony of Egypt, 107–10; letters from, 131
Antioch: sources from, 20
antitheses, 34, 38, 48
apocalypse, 104–5; Coptic, 102n21
Apocalypse of Adam, 143
Apocalypse of Elijah, 102n20
Apocalypse of Paul, 143
Apocalypse of Peter, 143
apocrypha: books of, 63, 64; traditions of, 47
Apocryphon of James, 142
Apocryphon of John, 142
Apollinaris of Laodicea, 68
Apollos, 101
apostles, 41, 104, 134; Coptic list of, 60; Jesus' appearances to, 43–44; Jesus' call to, 32, 35, 133, 136, 139, 147–48; lives of, 148–49, 155. *See also* disciples; *and individuals by name*
apostrophe, 34–36, 41–42, 48
apotaktikai, 108–9. *See also* renunciation
Arab Conquest, 28, 97
Arabic language: church histories in, 5–7, 9, 13–15; translations from, 55–59
Arcadius, 17t, 21
Arianism/Arius, 17t, 19, 21, 23, 63
Aristotle: logic of, 74; rhetorical theory of, 27n7
Arsenius, 17t, 21
ascetics: adepts among, 130; Christian, 102, 103, 140n3, 157; discipline of, 148, 150, 153, 154–57, 165–67; Jewish, 110; lifestyles of, 60, 142, 144;

213

ascetics: *(cont.)*
  transgressions by, 171–72; Upper Egyptian, 161, 163–65, 173; village, 51n11, 108–9
Athanasius, 17t, 40; *De Lazaro e mortuis reuocato*, 30; exiles of, 20, 23; festal letters of, 4, 19; life of, 5, 13, 16; *Resurrection of Lazarus*, 30–39; sermons by, 26, 30–39, 47; writings of, 15, 21, 58, 122
atonement, 174. *See also* cleansing; forgiveness
Atripe. *See* White Monastery
atrocity folklore, 184–88
attention, faculty of, 87n27
attribution, false, 28
Authoritative Teaching, 104–5
authorship, fictive, 28, 40
Avilius, 14

Baal: priests of, 182
Bacchantes, 185
baptism, 137–38, 139, 143, 161
barbarians: medical practice among, 114
Bardesanes, 17t
Barnes, Timothy, 13
Barsûm, 56n35
Basil: Julian and, 20; sermons of, 31; stewardship of, 8–9
Basilides, 17t, 100n13, 102, 105
Bauer, Walter, 98, 99, 100n13
Baumeister, Theofried, 7
Bes, 178, 179, 181–82
Besa, 177–78, 183, 187
Bible, 10, 68; canonical structure of, 142; concepts of purity in, 165–74; creation story in, 151; gnostic view of, 156–57; history in, 155; homilies on, 26, 37; traditions in, 115n7; use of, 147. *See also* New Testament; Old Testament; prophecy/prophets. *For citations, see* Index to Scripture
binary digits, 75–76
bishops: Alexandrian, 4, 15–16, 17t, 19–20, 105–6; episcopacies, 13; heathens opposed by, 182–83, 186, 188. *See also History of the Patriarchs of Alexandria*
Blanchard, Monica J., x, 49
blessings, monastic, 152
body: care of, 144–47; death of, 66–67, 69–70; divine resident in, 145; pollution of, 166, 170–72; questions about, 156; resurrection of, 63, 121n24; soul vs., 124, 125, 154; transformation of, 157

Book of Nestorius, 70–71
Book of Thomas the Contender, 142
Boole, George, x; *Investigation of the Laws of Thought*, 73–74, 76; laws of, 72–94
Boolean algebra, 75–76, 79–81, 86, 87
Boolean logic, x, 73–74, 77, 83–87
Borgia codex, 6–7
Boyarin, Daniel, x, xi, 113
brain: computer compared to, 76, 83; science of, 80
Brakmann, Heinzgerd, 7
Broadbent, T. A. A., 81
Büchler, Bernward, 140
Bunge, Gabriel, 130–31, 132
Bush, Vannevar, 75
Byzantine chronicles, 21, 22

Caesarea: painting of Mercurius in, 5
cannibalism, 132, 138–39, 185–86
Cannuyer, Christian, 52
Canons of Athanasius of Alexandria, 58
Canopus (Egypt), 17t; temple at, 20
Carpocrates, 100n13, 102
Cassian, John: on monastic congregations, x, 49–50, 52–53, 60
catecheses. *See* Horsiesios; Theodore of Mopsuestia
Catholic Church, 58n41, 59; Egyptian, 112; missionaries of, 183, 186
causality: chains of, 85
Celadios, 14
cenobites. *See* coenobites
Cerdo, 14, 106
Cerinthus, 111
Černý, Jaroslav, 51n11
Chalcedonian heresy, 17t, 158, 160–61, 164n22, 169; aftermath of, 5, 23; opposition to, 4, 71, 173–76; terminology of, 28
chaos theory, 85
children: sacrifice of, 132, 138–39, 177, 184–87
chiliasm, 102, 106
Choat, Malcolm, 52, 59–60
choice, 85–86
chora: churches of, 106
Christianity/Christians: Alexandrian, 4–24, 97–112; ascetic, 102, 103, 140n3, 157; Asian, 111–12; cannibalism of, 185; doctrines of, 5; Egyptian, ix–xi, 3–24, 26, 97–112, 130, 187–88; first-century, xi; Judaism's connections with, xi, 98–

105, 110, 112, 123, 156–57; knowledge in, 119–20; life of, 115; literature of, 59, 126n48; Near Eastern, ix; orthodox, 99, 158–62, 174–75; proto-orthodox, 105, 111; traditions of, 5, 60; triumphs of, 178, 180, 182–83, 187–88; universal, 5, 18, 21. *See also* Coptic Church

Christology: Arian, 63; incarnational, 123; Nestorian, 61, 63; Shenoutean, 69, 71; Wisdom, 119. *See also* Jesus Christ

Clark, Elizabeth, 61, 115n8

classes. *See* indefinite classes; supplementary classes

Claudius: consulate of, 44–45

cleansing, 32, 158–77

cleft sentences, 80, 91–92

Clement of Alexandria, x, 101, 102, 104; Platonism of, xi, 114n3, 117n13; writings of, 106, 115, 135n8

clerics, Egyptian, 4. *See also* bishops; priests

codex: definition of, 8. *See also* Nag Hammadi codices; White Monastery

coenobites, 49–50, 107–9, 165

Cohn, Norman, 186

Collatio Ioviani et Luci ariani, 20

collection: etymology of, 49n3

commandments. *See* laws

commentaries: in homilies, 47

communication theory, 75–76

community: etymology of, 53–54

community life: homily on, 143. *See also* monasteries; monks

composition: Coptic methods of, 30; fictive, 44–45; pseudepigraphical, 39–47; techniques of, 46–47. *See also* language

computer: compared to brain, 76, 83; computer age, 75–76; design of, ix

conception, faculty of, 87n27

condescension, deliverance from, 135

condition: premise and, 72–73, 78–79, 83, 85–87

congregations: Christian, 105; monastic, 49n3, 50

conscience, 145

Constantine (emperor), 12

Constantine of Sioüt, 5

contemplation, 115, 134

converts, Christian, 106, 182–83, 188

Coptic Church, 3–24, 26, 56–57, 70; orthodoxy in, 160–61, 174–75. *See also* Egypt, Christianity in

Coptic language: Bohairic literature in, 15, 26, 27–28, 49n3, 58, 167; church histories in, 5–7, 10–15, 18, 20, 22–24, 60; compositional methods of, 30; grammar of, 72–74, 80, 87–89, 92–94; inscriptions in, 107; literature in, 61, 102n20, 158, 164n21; Sahidic literature in, 15, 28, 49n3, 55–56, 59, 163; sermons in, 25–48; sixth century, 48, 102n21; texts in, 51, 53–56, 59, 111–12; translations of, x, 4, 18, 53, 71, 110

Coptic studies, ix–xi, 3, 6

Corinth: Christianity in, 101

corroboration: questions for, 89–93

Council of Chalcedon, 20. *See also* Chalcedonian heresy

Council of Ephesus, 22, 23, 63, 64; documents from, x, 70–71

covenant, 153

creation: goodness of, 150–51, 156–57; material, 143–47, 150–51; stories of, 38, 115n7, 116, 128, 151

cross: bearing of, 139, 155; disgrace of, 146; of light, 20. *See also* Jesus Christ

Crum, Walter Ewing, 7, 8–9, 11–12, 163n17; on monastic congregations, 49n3, 50–51, 53–54

crusaders, Christian, 182–83

cybernetics, 76n6

Cyril of Alexandria, 22, 23; *Contra Iulianum*, 17t; homilies of, 16, 26; life of, 16

Cyril of Jerusalem, 17t

Damian, homilies by, 29

darkness: etymology of, 55

David, 41, 58

Dawson, David, 114–15

death, 40, 143, 156; fear of, 35; Jesus' triumph over, 32, 36, 68; power of, 104, 133; sleep of, 148–49

Decius, 12

deductive thinking, 84

definition, final, 79, 88–89, 91

delusion: deliverance from, 134, 138

Demetrius, 14–15, 106–7, 111

Den Heijer, Johannes, 7, 14, 15

Depuydt, Leo, x, 57–58, 72

derivations, 83–84, 86, 90

description: in sermons, 31, 48n48

development: Boole's theorem of, 81

devil, 64, 133, 139; expulsion of, 135–37; worship of, 185–86

Dialogue of the Savior, 142

Didymus the Jew, 44–45

Diocletian: persecutions by, 10, 12

Dionysius of Alexandria, 15, 18, 102n20, 106

Dioscorus, 17t, 22; episcopate of, 16, 23, 63; letter from, 63
disciples: Jesus' call to, 35; requirements for, 133, 135, 139, 148; seventy/seventy-two, 40, 41. *See also* Apostles
discipline, monastic, 147, 150, 152, 155, 166
discourse: types of, 27
diseases, contagious, 170–74
disobedience, 166. *See also* obedience
Donatists: cleansing by, 170n49
Dorival, Gilles, 109
double sheet: definition of, 8
Douglas, Mary, 161n9, 174
Drake, H. A., 184
Dysinger, Luke, 132

ecphrasis (description), 31, 48n48
Edwards, Mark J., 115
Egypt: Christianity in, ix–xi, 3–24, 26, 97–112, 130, 187–88; gods of, 176–88; local religion in, 176–88; monasticism in, 49–60, 102, 107–10, 140–75; paganism in, x, 100; theological controversies in, 61
Egyptian language. *See* Coptic language
Eliezer, Rabbi, 127
Elijah, 102n20, 177, 182
Emmel, Stephen L., 62, 165n26
emperors, 17t. *See also individuals by name*
emphasis: definition of, 80–81; question and, 87–89
emphasis, contrastive, 72, 78–81, 83, 85; propositions and, 92–93; questions and, 73, 87–89, 91–92, 94
encomium, 27, 47
Encomium in Demetrium et Petrum, 15
Encomium in Marcarium, 22
Encomium in Mercurium (Acacius), 5, 11
Encomium in Petrum ep. Alexandriae, 14–15
end times, 102n21, 104–5
endurance, 137
English language: translations in, 132
Ephesus, 17t; Christianity in, 101. *See also* Council of Ephesus
epideictic rhetoric, 27
Epiphanius: depiction of Gnostics by, 185
epistēmē, 147
Epistle of Barnabas, 100–103, 110
Epistula Apostolorum, 111–12
epoidai, 184. *See also* songs, heathen

eremitic monasticism, 109
Erête, 49n3
Ermahnungen, 26. *See also* exhortations
erotic communion, 126–27
Erzählungen (stories), 26
Ethiopic language: translations from, 111–12
Eucharist, 143; nature of, 63
Eugnōstos the Blessed, 102, 143
Euler, Leonhard, 82
Eumenes, 14
Eusebius of Caesarea: *Ecclesiastical History*, 4, 7, 9–13, 15–20, 45; list of bishops by, 106
Evagrius of Pontus, exegesis of, x, 130–39; *Kephalaia*, 130; Letter 55, x, 130–39; Letter 63, 130, 135; Letter 64, 135; *On Faith*, 130, 135; *To Melania*, 130, 134
Evelyn-White, Hugh G., 51n11
evil one. *See* devil
Evodius of Rome: homilies by, 28, 39–47
Excerpt, the (manuscript), 10
exegesis, x, 26, 130–39; exegetical homilies, 25n1
Exegesis on the Soul, 142
exhortations, 26–27, 30, 38
exorcism, 136–37
exordium, 31, 37–41, 48
expulsion: of devils, 135–37; of monks, 167
Ezekiel, 41, 168

facts: relations among, 89–91
faith, monastic, 147
falsehood, 90; commitment to, 91–93
families: forsaking of, 148; monks' relations to, 130–39
Farshut communities, 161–62
fasting, 132, 135
fear: of God, 132, 138n9; lack of, 149
fellowship, 143
festschriften, 130
fifth century: Coptic works from, 102; Greek works from, x, 48; local religions during, 176–88; sermons from, 26; theological controversies during, 61
First and Second Apocalypse of James, 143
first century: Christianity during, xi, 98–99, 101, 111; Judaism during, 100–101
flesh: of Jesus, 132; language of, 122, 124; of scripture, 116–17; spirit and, 154. *See also* body
flood story (Genesis), 38
focalization, 78, 80

"Fonte A," 15–16
forensic rhetoric, 27, 46, 47
forgetting: avoidance of, 154
forgiveness, 132, 137–38
fourth century: asceticism during, 155; atrocity folklore from, 184–85; Greek works from, x, 48; monasticism during, 109, 136, 141, 153; theological controversies during, 61
Fragesatz, 88. *See also* questions
fragment: definition of, 8
fragrances, 146, 147n36, 148
Frankenberg, W., 131, 132
Frankfurter, David, x, 176
freedom, monastic, 155
freeloader: etymology of, 59
French language, 77, 94

Gaza (Egypt), 183
German language, 92–93, 94; translations in, 132
Girard, Louis Saint-Paul, 7
gloom: etymology of, 55
Glyph transliteration font, 73
gnomic texts, 138
gnosis, 102
Gnosticism, 102–3, 150–51; depictions of, 185; in early Egyptian Christianity, 98–99, 100n13, 101n15, 105; texts of, 61, 111–12
gnostics, 133, 136, 141, 145, 155. *See also* teachers/teaching
Gnostikos (Evagrius), 135
God: anger of, 58n41; authority of, 47; children of, 146n33; commandments of, 38; fear of, 132, 138n9; forgiveness by, 138; gifts from, 120; grieving by, 38–39; honoring of, 145, 148; intimacy with, 151–54; Jesus' relation with, 68, 137; knowledge of, 133; love from, 147, 167; nourishment from, 44; people of, 152; plan of, 156; promises of, 150; revelation from, 116, 120, 123–24, 153; seeing, 126–27; sons of, 148; thanksgiving to, 137; unity of, 104; will of, 137; wisdom of, 120, 134, 147–48; Word of, 119, 121n25, 144. *See also* Trinity
gods. *See* Egypt; *and individual gods by name*
Goehring, James, x, xi, 97, 107, 158
Goldstine, H. H., 75
goodness, 150, 156–57
Gospel of Philip, 142
Gospel of the Egyptians, 103–4, 142
Gospel of the Hebrews, 103

Gospel of Thomas, 50–51, 109–10, 142
Gospel of Truth, 142, 146, 152n54
Gospels: discipline of, 155; embellishment of, 46–47; Jesus' actions in, 123, 126n48, 128
grace, 149
grammar, 72–73, 78–79, 82, 85–94. *See also* language
Greece: early Christianity in, 99–100; folklore of, 184–85; medical sects in, 114; paganism in, 100; theology in, 131
Greek language: church histories in, 5–7, 9, 11–15, 18, 20, 22; Egyptians speaking, 103; grammar of, 93, 94; rhetoric in, x, 27, 30, 48, 131; texts in, 4, 51, 54–55, 59, 71, 130–31; translations from, 110, 111, 164n21
Gregory of Nyssa, 123; sermons of, 31
Gregory Nazianzen: letter of, 131n3; sermons of, 31
Gribomont, Jean, 7, 14
Grillmeier, Aloys, 61, 69, 70, 71
Guarimpotus, 16
Guillaumont, Antoine, 52, 135n8
gymnasium: vocabulary of, 145n26

habits (dress), 145
hadith, 57. *See also* traditions
hagiographical texts, 16, 19–21, 23, 177, 180, 182–83, 187–88
Hamartolos, George, 21
harlots, 138, 139
Harpocrates, 182
harp strings, children sacrificed for, 184
healing, 135n8; by Jesus, 32–33; of sinners, 167–68. *See also* cleansing
health, spiritual, 166–67
hearts: transformation of, 153–55, 157
heathens: atrocity folklore regarding, 184–86; Christian opposition to, 176–78, 182–83, 186–88; prayers of, 180; songs of, 58, 184–85; worship by, 39
heaven, 137, 143, 154
Heine, Ronald E., 119
Hellenismos, 184–85, 187
Heracles, 15, 106
heresies, 17t, 58n41, 61, 102, 105. *See also specific heresies*
hermeneutics: of depth, 113; Origen's, 117–23, 128–29; rabbinic, 115n8, 125, 126n48, 127
hermits, 107. *See also* withdrawal

heroization, 176–77
high priests: polemics against, 37, 44–45
Hill, Charles E., 112
Historia acephala (anonymous), 4
Historia Horsiesi (Horsiesios), 16
Histories of the Church. See (Twelve) Histories of the Church
historiography, Christian, 21
History of the Patriarchs of Alexandria (HPA), 3–4, 6–7, 9, 13–17, 22, 45n44
Holy Spirit: counsel of, 118, 132; defilement of, 58n41; descent of, 38, 68; dwelling place of, 144n18, 149; reception of, 137–38; revelation through, 58, 119, 120–24. *See also* Trinity
homilies: Coptic, 14–16, 25–48; definitions of, 25n1, 29n13; fictive elements in, 40n38, 44–45. *See also* sermons
Homilies on Genesis (Origen), 115n7
Honorius, 17t, 21
Horn, Jürgen, 52
Hornschuh, Manfred, 112
Horsiesios: catecheses of, x–xi, 141–57, 162n15, 163, 165; history by, 16; *Liber/Testamentum*, 141, 147, 151n54, 155, 162n15
Horus, 181
humility, 135, 136, 147
Hypostasis of the Archons, 142
Hypsiphrōnē, 143
Hyvernat, Henri, 163n18

ideas, 86n27. *See also* thoughts
idols: worship of, 39, 103, 133
image: of teachers, 133–36
imagination, faculty of, 87n27
impurity, 143, 168, 171, 174. *See also* pollution; purity
incarnation, 67, 116–19, 121–23, 126
incipient thought, 73, 83–94
indefinite classes, 86n25
infanticide, 132, 138–39, 177, 184–87
information theory, ix, x, 73–82
inheritance, 137, 148–50
Institute of Christian Oriental Research, 62
intellect, 73, 90–91, 124
intentions, natural, 132–33
International Association of Coptic Studies, 3
interpretation, xi, 113–29; allegorical, xi, 113, 116–24, 139; Christian, 125n44; rabbinic, xi, 125–29
Interpretation of Knowledge, 143

intonation, 91, 94
Irenaeus of Lyon, 107; *Against Heresies*, 107n44
Irvine, Martin, 123
Isaac of Karanis, 108–9
Isaiah, 41
Isis, 179, 181–82; temple of, 183
Islam, 57
Israel: God seen by, 126–27; history of, 128–29, 153; twelve tribes of, 148; worship of idols by, 182. *See also* Jews; Judaism
Iustus, 14

Jablonski, Paul Ernst, 50–51
Jacob, star of, 153
Jakab, Attila, 104
Jerome: *De viris illustribus*, 21; *Life of Paul of Thebes*, 108; on monastic congregations, x, 49–50, 52–53, 57n40, 60, 108; translations by, 71n49, 141, 154n73; writings of, 21, 105
Jerusalem: Christianity's origins in, 98, 100, 104; cross of light over, 20; symbolism of, 144n18; temple at, 20
Jesus Christ: actions of, 123, 126n48, 128; appearances of, 43–44; body of, 31–33, 35–36, 65–71; call from, 32, 35, 111, 133, 136, 139, 147–48; commandments of, 38; crucifixion of, 38–39, 44–47, 64–71; defilement of, 58n41; divinity of, 35, 64–71; God's relation with, 68, 137; grace of, 149; grieving by, 39; humanity of, 41–42, 68, 114n3, 132; kingdom of, 137; knowledge of, 134; life from, 32–33, 35–36; as Logos, 117–19; as Messiah, 100; mind of, 68n33, 119–21; miracles of, 31–33, 37; power of, 137; preexistence of, 64–71; prophecies regarding, 104; Resurrection of, 35–36, 39, 44–47, 114n3, 120–21; soul of, 67–70; sufferings of, 37–39, 66, 146, 149, 155; teachings of, 121–23, 146n29, 150; trial of, 45–47. *See also* Christology; Trinity; Word, incarnation of
Jewish Christians, 102–3, 105, 112. *See also* Judaism
Jews: polemics against, 38–39, 42–43, 45–46. *See also* Judaism
John (apostle), 111
John (hegoumen of Scetis), 59
John Chrysostom, 17t, 21
Johnson, David W., ix, x, xi, xix, 3, 7, 14, 82, 98, 111, 113, 131, 176
John the Little, 187
Joseph, 145

Jovian, 17t, 20
joy, 137, 150, 154
Judaism, 186; Christianity's connections with, xi, 98–105, 110, 112, 123, 156–57; knowledge in, 119–20; laws of, 83; revolt of, 99–102; sects in, 113–14; traditions of, 60. *See also* Jews
Judge, E. A., 108–9
judgment, final, 37, 38–39
Julian (bishop), 14, 106
Julian (emperor), 17t, 20; *Adversus Galilaeos*, 22, 23; killing of, 5, 20; martyrs of, 23; polytheism of, 184
Justinian I, 158–60, 174; representatives of, 169, 173
Juvenal, 17t

Karanis: papyrus from, 108
katastasis, 137, 138, 139
Kellia, x
Kerygma Petri, 99n8, 104
Khosroyev, Alexandr L., 140
Kiss: in Song of Songs, xi, 124, 125–29
Klijn, A. F. J., 111–12
knowledge: acquisition of, 90; allegorical, 118; differences in, 119–20; of Jesus, 134; of monks, 147
Koester, Helmut, 112
koine, 125
Koinonia, 146–50, 153–54, 167; fathers of, 162; monastery of, 165n24
kosmikoi, 137
Kothos: cult of, x, 176–88
Kramer, Bärbel, 57n40
Kronos, 178

Lagrange, Joseph-Louis, 82
language: as expression of thought, 86; fleshly, 124; human, 122; ontology of, 113, 117, 128; rabbinic, 126, 128; study of, ix–x, 73–82, 85–94, 130; theological, 29; theory of, 127. *See also* magic language; Nicene language; *and specific languages*
Late Antique Studies, xi
Latin language: church histories in, 15–16; grammar of, 94; rhetoric in, 27; texts in, 51, 71; translations from, 141
laws: of God, 148, 153, 162; Jewish, 83; Mosaic, 119; obedience to, 132; spiritual, 116–17
Lawson, R. P., 117

Lazarus: resurrection of, 30–39
learning, 138. *See also* teachers/teaching; wisdom
Leipoldt, Johannes, 187
Lele people, 161n9, 174
leprosy, 170–72; Jesus' cleansing of, 32
Levant (Egypt), 183
Life of Apa Onophrios, 49n3
Life of Athanasius, 16
Life of Cyril, 16
Life of Pachomius, 164
Life of Pamin, 59
Life of St. John, 59
Life of Theodore, 163n17
linguistics, 76. *See also* language
literature: information theory and, 78; monastic, 27; sermons as, 27–29; structures of, 140–57. *See also* Coptic language
liturgical writings, 29, 142–43
logia (sayings), 50–51
logic, x, 81, 83–87, 89. *See also* Boolean logic
logismoi, 137, 139. *See also* thoughts
Logos: Christology of, 104; Incarnation of, 116–19; Philo's doctrine of, 100; teaching by, 121–23; theology of, 100, 113–14, 116–19
love: from God, 147, 167; monastic, 149–50; Platonic, 124, 127
Luke: homilies on, 29n13
lust: deliverance from, 132, 134, 138

Macarius (monk): library of, 26n4; text in library of, 58
Macarius of Tkow, 22; panegyric on, 176–88. *See also* Chalcedonian heresy
MacLaurin's theorem, 81–82
magic language, 114, 116–17, 122, 178
man: creation of, 38; spirit of, 120
Manasseh: panegyric on, 158n3, 161, 164n23
Mandulis, 179
Mani: heresies of, 63; life of, 13
Manichaeism, 61; literature of, 54–55, 59; monks, 140n2
manuscripts: definition of, 8; studies of, ix. *See also specific manuscripts*
Marcionites, 105
Mark: in Alexandria, 46n44; legend of, 98; life of, 14; successors of, 106
marriage feast, analogy to, 38, 40–41
Martha (sister of Lazarus), 34
martyrdoms, 184–85; Julian and, 23; year of, 55

Mary (mother of Jesus). *See* Virgin Mary
Mary (sister of Lazarus), 34
mathematics, 76, 81–82, 84, 90; of *n*-dimensional spaces, 79; numbers, 74
Matthew: homilies on, 29n13
Mawhub, 14
Maximus, 15
meaning, levels of, 118, 123–24
Melitian monks, 57–58, 59, 140n2
Melitius, 17t, 19, 58
Melito of Sardis, 112
Menander, 17t
Menouthis (Egypt), 183
mercantilism: words from, 53
Mercurius, 5, 9, 20
messianism, Jewish, 100, 101–2
metaphors, 126n48, 127
Middle Egyptian language, 73
midrash, 123–25, 126n48, 127–29
millennium, 102n20. *See also* end times
Min, 178
mind: impulses affecting, 83–87; of Jesus, 68n33, 119–21; laws of, 74, 79n14, 80–81; operations of, 83, 93; scattering of, 132; structure of, 84–85
miracle stories, 5, 27, 31–33, 37
missionaries, Christian, 183, 186
mnesikakia, 137. *See also* anger
Modrzejewski, Joseph M., 99–100
monachos, 109–10. *See also* ascetics
monasteries: cleanliness of, 158–75; congregations in, 49n3; discipline in, 147, 150, 152, 155, 166; Egyptian, 49–60, 102, 107–10, 140–75; founding of, 127n52; Jewish roots of, 110; life in, 135, 145–46; literature of, 27, 59–60; relationship with society, 156; sermons in, 26
Monastery of Shenoute at Atripe, 162, 178; library of, 6. *See also* White Monastery
Monastery of St. Antony, 107
monks: advice to, x, 130–39; discipline of, 145, 147, 150, 152, 155, 166; Egyptian, 49–60, 102, 107–10, 140–75; families of, 130–39; heathens opposed by, 182–83, 186, 188; Pachomian, 23, 107–10, 140–75; relationship to God, 148; requirements for, 140–41, 143; sins by, 166–69
Monophysite holy man. *See* Macarius of Tkow
moon worship, 39
moral qualities: development of, 26, 156; words for, 53
Moses, 116, 118, 120, 153; covenant of, 103; laws of, 119, 121, 151; song of, 127; teachings of, 45; writings of, 114–15
Moses of Abydos, 158n3, 159, 187
Müller, C. D. G., x, 25–30
multitudes, feeding of, 32
Munier, Henri, 7
murder, 138
myths: subversion of, 185

Nagel, Peter, 51n11, 55
Nag Hammadi codices, xi, 61, 104–5, 140–57, 141
narrative, 126n48, 138
nature, 81, 132
Near East: Christianity in, ix, 23
negative theology, 104
neighborhood: etymology of, 53–54
Nepos of Arsinoe, 106
Nero, 45
Nestorius, 17t; death of, 63; heresy of, 61, 63; Shenoute's commentary on, 64–71
New Testament, 26; admonitions in, 136, 152; fulfillment of, 122, 156–57. *See also* Gospels
Nicene language, 68
Nicodemus, 149
Nietzsche, Friedrich, 116
Noah: sacrifice of, 147n36
Norden, Eduard, 27

obedience, 146, 166
observations, 80–81, 90
Old Testament, 151–53, 155; admonitions in, 136, 139, 146n29; fulfillment of, 153; revelation in, 121, 128. *See also* Torah
On the Origin of the World, 142
Optatus, 170n49
Origen, x, xi, 101, 113–29; exegesis of, 63, 116–17; *First Principles*, 116; homilies of, 47, 115n7; Platonism of, 117n13, 123–25; Shenoute's commentary on, 61, 70; writings of, 106, 115, 135n8
Orlandi, Tito, ix–x, 3, 61–63, 64, 67, 69, 158n2
orthodoxy, Christian, 99, 158–62, 174–75

Pachomian community, xi, 22, 23, 140–75
Pachomius, 107–10, 162; death of, 141; life of, 163–64; successors to, 140–57
paganism, 39, 100; transition from, x. *See also* heathens; religion
paideia/paideusis (training), 139, 145. *See also* discipline, monastic

GENERAL INDEX 221

Pan, 178
Pancharis, 159
Panegyric on Macarius, x, 176–88
panegyrics, 27
Panopolis (Egypt): local religions of, 178–79, 188
paraineseis, 146. See also exhortations
Paraphrase of Shem, 143
parasite: etymology of, 59
parsimony, scientific, 72
particles, enclitic, 93
Pascal, Blaise, 74
Paschal Homily (Melito), 112
passeggiata, 152
Passio Metrophanis et Alexandri, 4; Metaphrastic version of, 14
Passion of Jesus: sermons on, 39, 44–47
passions: deliverance from, 132, 134, 137
Passio Petri alexandrini, 4, 5, 15–16, 19
patience, 137
patriarchate, Alexandrian, 4, 15, 23. See also bishops; *History of the Patriarchs of Alexandria*
Paul: allegory used by, 115; Christology of, 119–21; death of, 45; painting of, 108; Platonism of, 117n13, 125; writings of, 101, 126n48, 134–37, 139
Pbow (monastery), 140, 158–75
Pearson, Birger A., x, xi, 97
peasants: local religions defended by, 182–83, 187
Peirce, Charles Sanders, 74n1, 75
perfection, 147, 155, 156
perorations: in homilies, 37, 39
persecutions, 10, 12, 146n29
Persia: war with Rome, 5
Peter, 104, 148; career of, 15; death of, 45; denials by, 134; episcopacy of, 10, 17t, 18, 19; Evodius as successor to, 40n38, 44–45
Peter II, 16
Petronius, 162, 165
Pharisees: polemics against, 37
Philip of Anatolia, 16, 17t, 20–21
Philo Judaeus, xi, 100–101, 110, 113–29; *On Rewards and Punishments*, 100; *On the Contemplative Life*, 115; *On the Creation*, 115n7
philology, 82
philoponoi: temples attacked by, 183
philosophy, 74, 114
Philotheos. *See* Pirothe
physicians, 132, 135
Pierpont Morgan Library manuscripts: M609, 177–78; M634, 57–58

pilgrimage, Islamic, 57
Pirothe, 8
place, notion of, 152n54
Platonism: Christian, 104–5, 114n3; love in, 127; of Origen, 117, 123–25; of Philo, 101
Plerophories/plerophory, 16, 18, 22, 23
Plewit (Egypt), 178, 183
Pneuma: incarnation of, 117
polemics, 37, 38–39
politeuma, Jewish, 98–99
pollution: biblical accounts of, 170–73; from heresy, 174–75; from sin, 161, 166–69
Polotsky, H. J., 82, 87–88
Pontius Pilate, 45, 47
Porphyry, 183
praktike, 135–37
prayer, 132–33, 135, 139; heathen, 39, 180; invocatory, 142; magical, 178; vision and, 143
Prayer of the Apostle Paul, 142
preaching: forms of, 25n1, 27; Greek, 26; text-based, 25n1, 29n13, 30–39, 47. See also homilies; sermons
predicates, 77n10
predigt, 25, 27–29
premise: condition and, 72–73, 78–79, 83, 85–87
presbyterate, 105–6
pretending, 135. See also therapeutic dissembling
priests: ordination of, 57; Origenist, 63; temple, 182–83. See also bishops; high priests
primary propositions, 89–93
Primus/Sabinus, 14, 106n40
probability theory, 74
Proclus of Constantinople: sermons of, 31
proemium, 31. See also exordium
progymnasmata: study of, 48n48. See also composition
pronouns: indefinite, 94; interrogative, 92, 94
prophecy/prophets: biblical, 104, 153; fulfillment of, 156–57; laws of, 119, 121; revelation through, 120–23, 155; sayings of, 114
propositions: affirmative, 78n.10, 93; formation of, 73, 77, 83–94; types of, 89–93
Proterius, 17t
Protestant Church: missionaries from, 183
proto-orthodox theology, 105, 111
"Psalms of the Pilgrims," 55
pseudepigraphical compositions, 39–47
Pseudo-Dioscorus, 177
Pseudo-Epiphanius: sermons of, 31

psogos, 37. *See also* polemics
psychagogia, monastic, 131, 136
purity, 143, 144, 161; biblical concepts of, 165–74; of prayer, 132; rituals of, 174; Shenoutean ideas about, xi, 161, 165–74

Qaw el-Kebir (Egypt). *See* Tkow
Quaegebeur, Jan, 179
Quartodeciman Easter praxis, 111
Quatremère, Étienne, 6
questions, 83; Boolean definition of, 88–89; contrastive emphasis and, 73, 87–89, 91–92, 94; types of, 72–73, 88–91. *See also* pronouns; rhetorical questions
quire: definition of, 8

rabbis, 124, 125–29
rahhâlin, 56–57, 59. *See also* wanderer
Rakotis (Egypt), 103. *See also* Alexandria
reading: of letters, 134; of sermons, 28
reality, 84, 87; inner, 128
reasoning, 90. *See also* logic
rebirth, 148–50, 154. *See also* transformation
redactions/redactors, 18, 20–22; Alexandrian, 13–14; scribes as, 10; Timothean, 16
redemption, 137–39, 143–44, 146n32, 151, 156, 166–68
Relatio Theophili, 16
religion: local, 176–88; rabbinic, 126; temple, 176, 180–82
remnuoth (monks), x, 49–60, 108–9. *See also* Christianity/Christians; Islam; Judaism
Rénaudot, Eusèbe, 6–7
renunciation, 108, 136, 139, 155
repentance, 149, 152–53
resurrection: of the body, 63, 121n24; of Jesus, 35–36, 39, 44–47, 114n3, 120–21
revelation: authority of, 142; dialogues of, 111; divine, 126, 148–50; modes of, 145
rewards, heavenly, 145
rhetoric: Coptic, 25–48; criticism of, x; epideictic, 27; forensic, 27, 46, 47; Greek, x, 27, 30, 48, 131; Latin, 27
rhetorical questions, x, 72–73, 89, 93
Riedlinger, Albert, 76n7
Ritner, Robert, 178
Rives, J., 185
Roberts, Colin H., 98
rogue: etymology of, 51n11

Rome: atrocity folklore in, 184–87; Christian Church in, 13; laws of, 45–46; war with Persia, 5
Rousseau, Philip, x–xi, 140, 167
Rubenson, Samuel, 131n3
Rufinus of Aquileia, 18, 19
Rufus of Shotep, 29
Russell, Bertrand, 74

sacrifices: of children, 132, 138–39, 177, 184–87; human, 180, 184–87; impure, 58n41
saints: Christian, 183; homilies on, 26; inheritance of, 137; Pachomian, 163; relationship to God, 154; revelation to, 121–23
salvation. *See* redemption
Samaria: woman from, 132, 138–39
as-Sammanûdî, Yûhannâ, 55
sarabaitae, x, 49–60, 109
Sarakote monks, 57–58. *See also* Melitian monks
Sarapis, temple at, 20
saubes (monks), 49. *See also* coenobites
Saussure, Ferdinand de, 76
Savage Other, 184–85, 187
scalae manuscripts, 55–57, 59
schêma (habits), 145
Schmidt, Carl, 111
scholastic logic, 74, 78n10
Schröder, Friedrich Wilhelm Karl Ernst, 74n1
Schroeder, Caroline T., 165–68
scribes: errors by, 14; redactions by, 10; work of, 142, 164
scriptures: canonical, 156; interpretation of, 115–18, 120–23, 128; use of, x, 131, 136, 147, 151–52. *See also* Bible; *and specific works*
secondary propositions, 89–93
second century: atrocity folklore from, 185; Christianity during, xi, 4, 99–101, 104–5, 111; monasticism during, 110
Second Treatise of the Great Seth, 143
secrets: of God, 147–48, 150
sects, 113–14
self-perfection, 147. *See also* perfection
Seneset (monastery), 140
sentences: Boole's interpretations of, 77; cleft, 80, 91–92
Sentences of Sextus, 104–5
Septuagint, 100
serākûdâ, 58–59
Serapeum, 17t

sermons: Coptic, x, 25–48; definitions of, 25n1; Greek, 25–27; ninth century, 26; public reading of, 28; translations of, 30–31. *See also* homilies
Seth: teachings of, 142
Sethe, Kurt, 94n39
Severus of Ashmunein, 14
sexual transgressions, 166. *See also* sin/sinners
Shai, 178–82, 188
Shannon, Claude E., x, 75–76, 78, 87
sheet: definition of, 8
Shelton, John C., 57n40
Shenoute of Atripe, 17t; Christology of, 69, 71; crusades by, 183, 186–87; death of, 178; Discourse on Purity, 161, 165–74; discourses of, x, xi, 27; *I Am Amazed*, 61–70; ideology of, 164–65; *Lord Thundered*, 179; sermons of, 179–81; *So Listen*, 171; successor to, 177, 187; *This Great House*, 171; *Who but God Is the Witness*, 172; writings of, 10, 22, 162–63
shrines, household, 180–82
Sibylline writings, 103–4
signs, 113, 123–24, 127; arbitrariness of, 76n7, 77; Boole's definition of, 76–77; fixedness of, 76n7, 77
Simon Magus, 111
simple apprehension, faculty of, 87n27
simpliciores, 102
Sinai, Mount: revelation on, 127–28
sin/sinners, 132, 139, 144; cleansing of, 39, 58n41, 161; forgiveness of, 137–38, 147; individual, 166–69; nature of, 171–72
Sion, 151–52
Socrates Scholasticus, 19
solitaries, 108–10
Solomon, 41, 134, 136
Sophia of Jesus Christ, 142
Sophia/*sophos*, 113, 134. *See also* wisdom
sorcerers, 111, 182–83, 186
soul: body versus, 124, 125, 154; doctrine of, 105, 142–44; immortality of, 66–69; of Jesus, 67–70; of Lazarus, 35; preexistence of, 63; progress of, 118; of scripture, 116–17; virtues in, 100, 148
sounds: patterns of, 77. *See also* intonation
Sozomen, 4, 19, 183
specification, 89–92
speculation, 26
speech: Christian, 123–24; divine, 113–29; human, 123–24, 127; monastic, 147–48, 154

spirit, 68, 154, 155. *See also* Holy Spirit
star worship, 39
Stern, Ludwig, 72, 73, 87
stewardship, 8–9
stories, 26, 27
Struik, Dirk J., 82
subjects, grammatical, 77n10
sun worship, 39
supplementary classes, 80–81, 83–84, 92
Sibylline writings, 103
symbolic logic, 74n1, 75n5, 76n7
synagogues, 105
synkatabasis, 135–36
synkrisis, 48n48
Syria, 110n59
Syriac language: texts in, 51; translations from, 132

Tatian, 17t; *Diatessaron*, 110n59
Taylor's theorem, 81–82
teachers/teaching, 105–6, 121–23, 130–39, 142–43, 150–51, 154
Teachings of Silvanus, 100–101, 104, 143
temples: attacks on, 182–83, 188; religion of, 176–82
tenses, second, 80, 87–88, 91–92
text-based preaching, 25n1, 29n13, 30–39, 47
texts: criticism of, x; ontology of, 128
thematic homilies, 25n1
Theodore (monk): catecheses of, x–xi, 141–57
Theodore of Mopsuestia, 163
Theodore Stratelates, 163n17
Theodoret of Cyrrus, 19, 20; homilies of, 26
Theodosius, 21
theology. *See* Egypt; Greece; Logos
Theonas, 15
Theophanes, 21, 22
Theophilus of Alexandria, 16, 17t; actions against temples by, 20, 23; festal letter of, 62–63, 70–71; works of, 21
theorems, mathematical, 76
Theotokos. *See* Virgin Mary
Therapeutae, 110
therapeutic dissembling, 135, 136, 139
thesis, 48n48
things: relations among, 89–92
third century: monasticism during, 109
Thomas, 34–36, 60. *See also Gospel of Thomas*
thoughts: battle against, 132–35, 137, 139; deductive, 84; expression of, 86–87; formation of,

thoughts: *(cont.)*
  83–94; history of, 73; human, 120; laws of, 72, 73–82, 88–90, 93; natural, 132; nature of, 72, 79–81, 84; structure of, 84, 87; subjects of, 92–93; universe of, 80. *See also* mind
Three Stēlēs of Seth, 143
Timbie, Janet, x, 61
Timothy Aelurus: Church history by, 3–7, 9–24
Tkow (Egypt), 176, 178
topos, 182. *See also* hagiographical texts
Torah, 116, 120, 125–29
Torjesen, Karen Jo, 118, 121–23
Toutou, 182
traditions: biblical, 115n7; hagiographic, 19–21; Judeo-Christian, 60; literary, 131; respect for, 154
Trajan: Jewish revolt against, 99–102
transformation, 136–37, 153–55, 157. *See also* rebirth
transgressions. *See* sin/sinners
translation: errors in, 11, 14; interpretation as, 117; methods of, ix, 12; of sermons, 30–31. *See also specific languages*
traveler: etymology of, 57, 59
Treatise on the Resurrection, 142–43
Triadon, 56, 59
Trinity: defilement of, 58n41; doctrine of, 121n25. *See also* God; Holy Spirit; Jesus Christ
Tripartite Tractate, 143
truth, 90, 123, 155; absolute, 83, 113; commitment to, 91–93; food of, 150; knowledge of, 133, 137; spiritual, 122n31; universal, 122n31
Tukey, John W., 76
Turing, Alan M., 75
Twelve, the. *See* apostles
(Twelve) Histories of the Church (Timothy Aelurus), 3–7, 9–24

vagrant: etymology of, 54
Valens, 21
Valentinian Exposition, A, 143
Valentinian I, 21
Valentinus, 100n13, 102, 105
Van den Broek, Rouel, 103, 105
Van Lantschoot, Arnold, 9
Veilleux, Armand, 163n17, 171n50
verbs, Egyptian, 72
vices: catalogues of, 30. *See also* sin/sinners
Victor, 22
Vienna fragment, 9–10

vigils, monastic, 132, 135
Virgin Mary: death of, 43–44, 47; defilement of, 58n41; homilies on, 26, 39–44, 47; life of, 57; role of, 65, 67–68
virtues, 100, 146
visions, 126–27, 143
Vita Metrophanis et Alexandri, 19
vocations, Christian, 140–41, 145, 148–49
Volkmann, R., 27
Von Lemm, Oscar, 6–7
Vycichl, Werner, 50n7, 51n11

wall niches, 180–82, 188
wanderer: etymology of, 54–55, 57, 59–60
Wansleben, Johann Michael, 6
weaknesses, human, 144. *See also* sin/sinners
Weaver, Warren, 75n6
Wessely, Carl, 7
Wheeler, Samuel, 114n3
White Monastery, 158, 162, 165n24; manuscripts from, xi, 6–11, 13, 16, 18, 21, 158n2, 163–64; WM Codex GB, 158-60, 164n21, 23; WM Codex GC, 162-63, 164n21, 23; WM Codex XU, 171n51
Wiener, Norbert, 76n6
will: of God, 137; human, 83, 85–86, 132, 146
Williams, Michael Allen, x–xi, 141, 142–43, 145, 146, 155
Wipszycka, Ewa, 109, 187
wisdom: divine, 116, 120, 128; human, 132, 134, 138, 154, 156–57
wisdom theology, 101, 104, 119
witches' Sabbat, 186
withdrawal, 132, 135, 139
woman: creation of, 38; menstruating, 171n50
Word: incarnation of, 67, 116–19, 123
words, interrogative, 92
works: of Jesus, 123, 126n48, 128; of man, 145, 148
worlds, multiple, 63
worship: heathen, 39; heretical, 105n38; impure, 58n41

Yohanan, Rabbi, 125, 126
Young, Robin Darling, x, 130

Zachariah of Mytilene, 183
Zanetti, Ugo, 52, 58–59
Zoega, Georg, 6
Zonaras, John, 21, 22

INDEX TO SCRIPTURE

OLD TESTAMENT

Genesis, 47, 142, 146, 152
  1–2, 115n7
  1:26, 38
  8:21, 147n36

Exodus
  14:13, 127
  15:1, 127
  15:2, 127, 129
  20:14, 127
  21:28, 138
  21:28–29, 127, 132
  24:7, 127

Leviticus, 173
  13, 172
  13:47–59, 170
  14, 172
  14:33–48, 170
  15:4–7, 170–71
  15:19–30, 171n50

Numbers
  24:17–19, 153

Deuteronomy, 152
  5:25, 127
  8:15, 129

2 Kings
  6:28–29, 132
  6:28–39, 138

Psalms, 54–55, 121, 139, 152
  37:24, 155
  105(106):37–39, 133, 138

Proverbs, x, 136, 139
  9, 134
  9:8–9, 132, 138
  9:18, 132, 138
  15:19, 171n50
  23:26, 154n73
  24:1, 132, 138

Ecclesiastes, 139

Song of Songs, 124, 125–28
  1.2, xi
  2:14, 127

Isaiah, 146
  1:3, 44
  19:1, 41
  30:6, 129
  61:8–10, 153
  61:9, 147

Lamentations, 171n50

Ezekiel, 152

Hosea, 152

Zechariah, 153

Malachi, 152

NEW TESTAMENT

Matthew, 148, 152
  1:18, 67, 68
  1:23, 65
  2:13, 65
  5:13, 41
  8:23–27, 33
  9:1–8, 33
  9:18–26, 33

  9:20–22, 32
  12:10, 33
  13:35, 148
  14:15–21, 32
  14:22–36, 33
  16:9, 32
  19:27–29, 148–50
  20:29–34, 32

  26:69–75, 132
  27:46, 65, 66

Mark
  1:23–26, 33
  2:1–12, 33
  3:5, 33
  4:25–41, 33

5:1–13, 33
5:22–43, 33
5:25–34, 32
6:35–44, 32
6:45–52, 33
7:32–35, 33
8:19, 32
11:13, 33
11:20, 33

Luke, 40, 119, 120–21, 121
1:35, 67, 68
1:56, 65
1:79, 32
2:7, 44
2:52, 42n41
5:12, 32
5:17–26, 33
6:9–11, 42
8:22–25, 33
8:41–56, 33
8:43–48, 32
9:12–17, 32
10:1, 41
14:26, 133, 139
14:33, 108
15:6, 32
17:11–17, 32
17:11–19, 32
17:12–14, 32
22:18–30, 146n29
24:39, 64–65

John, 33, 38, 111
prologue, 116
1:14, 67
2:2–11, 33
3:3, 149

6:5–13, 32
6:16–21, 33
6:32, 44
9:6, 32
10:16, 32
11, 36, 47
11:1–3, 34
11:14–16, 34
11:35, 39
11:46–50, 37
15:18, 146n29
18:25, 93
19:9, 47
19:10, 47
19:11, 47
19:37, 65
21:25, 33, 46
38, 39

Acts, 22
2:23, 42
2:36, 42
3:15, 42
4:10, 42
5:30, 42
10:39, 42
18:24, 101
19:1, 101

Romans, 152
1:22, 134
11:21, 152
15:4, 152
16:27, 134

1 Corinthians, 119, 148
1–4, 101
1:12, 101

1:19, 134
1:25, 134
2:7, 147–48
2:8, 65
2:14, 147n36
3:4–22, 101
4:6, 101
16:12, 101
16:19, 49n3

Ephesians, 136, 142, 148
1:13–14, 132, 137
4, 137
4:27, 133
4:30, 132
4:30–31, 137
5, 149
5:14, 147n38

Colossians, 137, 142
1:2, 133
1:9–14, 133

1 Timothy
2:4, 133
6:20, 102

Hebrews
2:14, 67, 70
9:4, 41

1 Peter
4:1, 66

1 John
1:1–10, 65

The World of Early Egyptian Christianity: Language, Literature, and Social Context
was designed and typeset in Garamond by Kachergis Book Design of Pittsboro,
North Carolina. It was printed by Lightning Source, Inc., La Vergne, Tennessee.

www.ingramcontent.com/pod-product-compliance
Lightning Source LLC
Chambersburg PA
CBHW031413290426
44110CB00011B/359